Love You Bunches
Happy Birthday ♡ Lara, Zoe + Lucy Lou

MW00784349

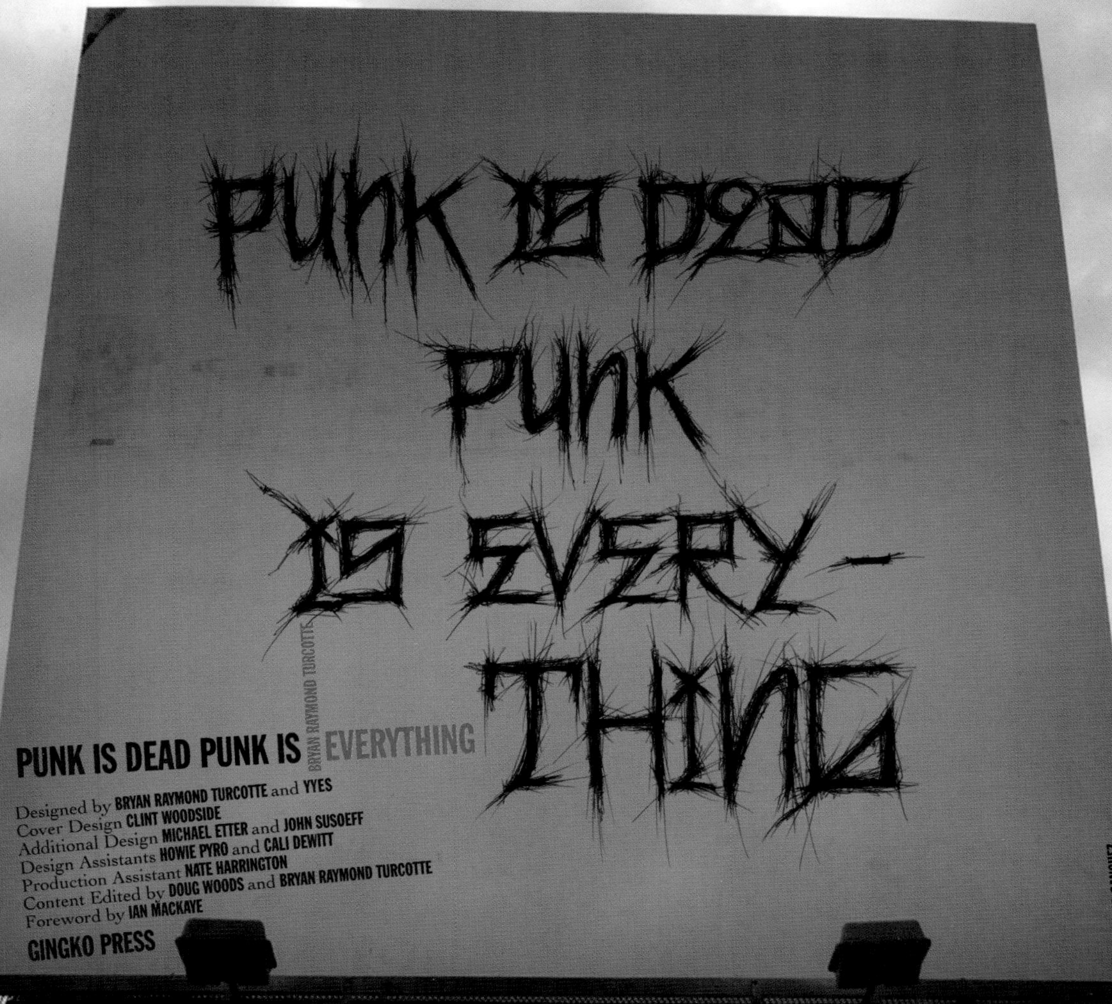
PUNK IS DEAD
PUNK
IS EVERY-
THING
PUNK IS DEAD PUNK IS EVERYTHING
BRYAN RAYMOND TURCOTTE
Designed by BRYAN RAYMOND TURCOTTE and YYES
Cover Design CLINT WOODSIDE
Additional Design MICHAEL ETTER and JOHN SUSOEFF
Design Assistants HOWIE PYRO and CALI DEWITT
Production Assistant NATE HARRINGTON
Content Edited by DOUG WOODS and BRYAN RAYMOND TURCOTTE
Foreword by IAN MACKAYE
GINGKO PRESS
TYPE: RICHARD SANCHEZ
REGENCY

FROM THE COLLECTIONS OF:

Ian Mackaye
Bryan Ray Turcotte
Cali DeWitt
Doug Woods

Bruce Kalberg
Randall J. 'Biscuit' Turner
Lisa Deanne Smith
Bev. Davies

Matt Borruso
Robert Dapello
Michelle Marini
Patrick Miller
Jeff Nelson
Mattias Gephart
Hikaru Iwanaga
Sam McPheeters
Ed Colver
Jeff Gold

Howie Pyro

Dave Sardy
Marina Zurkow
Jeff Newton
Jim Jocoy

Tim Tanooka
Arturo Vega
Aaron White
Craig Ibarra
Alice Bag
Margaret Saadi Kramer

James Stark
Randy Kaye
Cundo Si Murad
Pleasant Gehman
Carl Swanberg

Wayne Kramer
Heather Conley

Jim Kenney
Andy Franzle
Andrea Zollo

Nathan Gates
Jason Honea
Tony Alva
Richard Sanchez
Matt Neth
Eileen Polk
Jeremy Benson
Don Bolles
David Yow

Mike Watt
Tim Biskup
Andy Rosen
Joe Sib
Franz Stahl
Dave Markey
Mariko Jones

Justin Pearson
John John Jesse

Jessie Tappis
Jordan Tappis
Della Chaffee
Bayliss Glasscock
Ambrose Dubeck

First Published in the USA as a hardcover in 2007

Revised paperback edition published in September 2022 by

Gingko Press in Association with Kill Your Idols

First paperback edition

Gingko Press Inc.
2332 4th St., Suite E
Berkeley, CA 94710
www.gingkopress.com

ISBN: 978-3-943330-62-5

Printed in Malaysia

Kill Your Idols

CHRIS GATES 'BIG BOYS' AT LIBERTY LUNCH, 1984

Christopher T. Miller
Mark Mothersbaugh
Gary Panter
Eric Rife
Winston Smith
Chris D.
Gira/Jarboe
Frank Kozik
Mike Piscitelli
Chris Leister
Chris Gates
Nikki Sudden
Paul Stottler

Carl Schneider
Rojer Trilling
Steve Shayer
Shari Bricker
Mike Davis

Gavin O'Brien
John Holmstrom
Jesse Malin
Matt Arluck
Murray Bowles

Nathan Harrington
Mark McCoy
Jeroen Vrijhoef
Marcel Palijama
Andy Coronado

Vincent Gallo
Andrea Blaine
Corey O'Brien
Dr. Strange

Chris Shary
Bryan Knox

Mike Crescione
John Evicci
Niki Syxx
Dusty Watson
John Blair

Jay Diola
Dean Spunt
Randy Randall
Cara Green
Dave Burks
Robbie Conal
Michael Etter

Pat Fear
Bill Bartell
Iris Berry
Luis Farfan
Michael Belfer

Pat Toves
Cynthia Connolly
Susan Winsberg
Connie Winsberg

Trudie
Mike Ott
Chris Thompson
Jill Ash
Leslie Walters

PLEASE NOTE

We are very sorry but

POGO DANCING

OR SIMILAR

IS NOT ALLOWED DUE TO
ACCIDENTS & INJURIES
DURING RECENT WEEKS

CONTRIBUTING WRITERS:

Cali DeWitt
Doug Woods
Sam McPheeters

Mad Marc Rude

Arturo Vega
Wayne Kramer
Margaret Saadi Kramer
Malcolm McLaren
Jason Honea
Tony Alva

Richard Sanchez
Eileen Polk

Miriam Linna
Steve McDonald
Don Bolles
Kid Congo Powers
David Yow
Johnny Thunders

Randall J 'Biscuit' Turner

Justin Pearson
Nathan Harrington

Rodney Bingenheimer
Gexa X

Annie Anxiety
John John Jesse
Andy Rosen
Joe Sib

John Susoeff
Franz Stahl
Dave Markey
Howie Pyro
Jesse Malin
Mark McCoy
Jeroen Vrijhoef
Andy Coronado
Jay Diola

Dave Burks
Duane Peters
Robbie Conal
Pat DiPuccio
Michael Etter
Azazel Jacobs

Pat Fear
Bill Bartell
Iris Berry
Luis Farfan

Jack Rabid
Michael Belfer
Pat Toves

Trudie

Mike Ott
Chris Thompson
Dean Spunt
Randy Randall
Aaron White

Sean Reveron
Spencer Eells Moody
Marina Zurkow

Jill Ash

FLYER 'WALLPAPER' BY DAVE MARKEY

EVERY
THING
BRYAN RAYMOND TURCOTTE
WHEN THE FRINGE MEETS THE FAMOUS
THE MYTH TAKES ON THE LEGEND THE
BEAUTIFUL, THE UGLY, THE ESSENTIAL,
AND THE NEVER WAS BECOME EVERYTHING
THAT MATTERS THE MOST. THE CONTRAST
AS WELL AS THE STITCHED TOGETHER
MADE PUNK TRUE. THE BOOKENDS,
THE OPPOSITES THE OUTER EDGES,
WHEN THE SMALLEST OF THINGS
EVOLVES INTO THE MOST SIGNIFICANT
OF THINGS. SOMETHING DIES AND
ANOTHER IS BORN. PUNK IS DEAD,
PUNK IS EVERYTHING!
KILL
YOUR
IDOLS
HÜSKER DÜ
FEAR
ALBUM
VICTIM OF
ADOLESCENTS
DESCENDENTS
BLACK

DOUG WOODS

Today Punk is everywhere. It wasn't always that way. As a kid, it was so encouraging to see someone else with a screwed-up haircut on the street who I knew I could relate to. Eventually kids like us met and formed small networks within our communities. This is how the Punk

scene spread. Soon, small and big towns all over had a Punk problem. The twisted roots of this problem were angry, bored and disenfranchised youth and the music, philosophy and look that personified them. In 1981 I bought a Black Flag single at a music store. It was not a record store. They sold guitars and amps. There weren't any record stores that would sell a Black Flag single back then, at least not in this small Northern California town. The lady behind the counter didn't really know what it was. She said that some kid had asked her to order it for him, which she did, but he hadn't picked it up. She was glad I bought it because she didn't sell records and didn't want to be stuck with it. Her clientele consisted of middle aged Rock musicians, most of whom were in bands that were still playing Doobie Brothers or Allman Brothers covers. That was our community. My Mom was not glad I bought the record because she didn't think "Nervous

Breakdown" was very positive music. It wasn't, but at

twelve years of age, I discovered that those songs would keep me sane through some trying times to come. Not long after, my Mom decided that I should go live with my Dad and I found my way back to Los Angeles. My Dad didn't think much of "Nervous Breakdown" either. I found satisfaction in knowing that I'd discovered something that freaked out even my open minded parents. By then I looked weird, acted weird, sang weird songs and even wanted my own weird band. It was clear to me that the mainstream sucked and I knew punk messed with mainstream society. This was a real challenge to the yuppy-used-to-be-free-thinking-hippy-types who were now a lot of our parents, teachers and a lot of peoples bosses. Punk also got me beat up. No one really liked us.

For a while it seemed that this was a movement that was going to take society to a more potent cultural level. Punk was stronger, more diverse and angrier than the Flower Power movement. It was also more accepting, forgiving and forward thinking than our Sixties predecessors were.

We lacked the noble cause of a Vietnam war to protest but we had a culture war of our own to instigate. Punk reminded people that things had not changed much for our parents since Nixon, and that

the kids were not alright. We wanted to kick the asses of those who had made America boring. We challenged those who said things were cool. Things were not cool, and we knew. It was the Cold War. In the mean time, all anyone on the outside seemed to know about Punk was the propaganda they saw on television. Even my Mom bought that crap she saw the infamous CHIPS episode where a fake Punk band played to a rowdy crowd singing "I dig pain. . .", and then went on to get busted by Eric Estrada for slashing tires. Ponche saved them

in the end by introducing them to Bell Bottoms and mellow rock. There was also the QUINCY episode involving a wayward punker who kills his girl

friend. Our televised revenge came when John Belushi convinced producer Lorne Michaels to let FEAR play on Saturday Night Live on October 31st, 1981. Belushi made a cameo appearance that night, his last on SNL ever. FEAR also got to bring along an appreciative audience. The studio was almost destroyed on live television. Punk had overwhelemed what was then the most subversive show on television. It has never aired again. Even SNL couldn't handle that much reality.This was the time when America was really beginning to feel the ripples of a heavy stone that had been cast accross the Atlantic a few years earlier. The Sex Pistols, brought to us through the brilliant media manipulation of Malcolm McLaren, and

the famous swindle they pulled. The 'Pistols career was always on the line and couldn't have lasted, but that didn't stop thousands of garage bands all over the world from wanting to be like them. The successful

failures that McLaren brought us, inspired many to try do things on their own terms, dispite airplay or club support or any particular talent. That was the punk ideal, Do It Yourself, Think Different. Anyway, some former-yuppy-used-to-be-free-thinker-

hippy-type got the brilliant idea of his own and co-opted the quintessential trappings of the Punk definition and turned it toward marketing. Today we have joe Strummer singing "London's Calling" to a Jaguar commercial. Is that any different than Bob Dylan singing for Mercedes Benz? It's kind of ironic really. It's as if they stole McLaren's idea.

Punk meant think different, now that is a sales pitch. It's comforting that there are still independently minded people out there today doing disservice to the grandly consolidated, well branded corporations who really do have too much control over what we see and think. Magazines like Adbusters and artists like Robbie Conal, Shepard Fairey and Banksy are challenging us to continue questioning authority. Writers like William Gibson, who's latest book tells the tale of a man who is allergic to logos,

illustrated the growing pains of the post-punk generation coming of age in the era computer. Artists like Vincent Gallo make films whose success is measured not by what is said about them in the pages of

Variety, but by being uncomprimising in their often uncomfortable subject matter and tone. Entrepreneurs like Ian McKay are showing us that one can be a long term success without selling out in ways that sacrifice ideals. There are still a lot of garage bands. There are still a lot of punks. We just don't all have mowhawks anymore. That doesn't shock people, it just sells 7-UP. Basquiat was Punk on canvas.

He was hardcore. It's been said that he was known to throw-up in his paint, mix it in, put it all onto canvas and laugh that it might hang in a museum one day. Now it does. Something we can'tblame Malcolm Mclaren for is

rehashing anything. He used the media to reach out and shock people with the Sex Pistols. When the shock wore off, he moved on to Hip Hop. Meanwhile, the media caught on to the value in what he had done. Punk became an accepted marketing commodity. It is now a vehicle to market to the next aging generation of consumers. Today

the Sex Pistols reunite for a Levis sposored

tour instead of a Sex Shop sponsored tour. Malcolm Mclaren has, however, remained distant from this practice and has become an articulate critic of how counter culture has been co-opted to promote pop culture.

MURRAY BOWLES

JOHN SUSOEFF

So What's Punk? Two hundred something pages later, are we any closer to an aswer? I mean, really, ask a hundred punks, get a hundred answers. Ask a hundred pundits, sociologists, scenemakers, hangers-on, groupies... get another hundred answers. A musical revolution? Sure. A fashion statement? For some. An art scene? Yes. A

highly effective way to piss off your parents? The best. It's probably pointless to try and put a finger on the exact meaning of punk, the experience being such a distinctly personal thing. Without real radio airplay or tv time,

it's always been necessary for you to venture out to the right clubs, the right record and book stores in order to find punk. That makes it a participatory sport, and not one you can follow from a safe distance. Even then, everyone standing shoulder to shoulder at the same gig or store is sure to give you a different take. Some of that is simply sociological: of course the music was going to mean something altogether different to a suburban upper middle class teenager, than it would to a gutter punk. Different again for a small-town kid steeped in boredom and isolation, and something else entirely to a writer or an academic. Whatever your link to the scene, the punk

adventure requires some real effort, attracts more than its share of characters onstage and off, everyone of whom is

armed with an opinion on what's punk. This was never more obvious than the music's 25th anniversary. Punk's Silver Jubilee is long gone, and not a moment too soon. With every rock mag scurrying around to put together their obligatory Special Punk Commemorative Issue, no stone went unturned and every dustbin emptied in music journalism's quest for old-schoolers to share their brand of revisionist history (i.e. what you missed out on a quarter of a century ago).1977, as few of you will remember, was a musical year dominated by Debby Boone's "You Light Up My Life," (number one for ten saccharine-coated weeks) "Saturday Night Fever,"(2) Elvis' bloated corpse

pants-down on the floor of his bathroom, and 500,000

suburbanite teens locking themselves into their basements and garages with Fenders in a frenzied attempt to learn "Eruption." Meanwhile, Punk was a series of small but powerful explosions going off in

New York, then the UK, California, and eventually all parts between. For all its heart and fury, Punk was not going to be the entity to rise up and slay Pop and AOR.(3) Punk burned brightly, spawned some fascinating (and some not-so fascinating) musical variations, and went into it's death spiral around 1982. In Punk Is Dead!Punk Is Everything! we tried to

follow punk's legacy beyond it's short life span. You have to look past what is sold to you as alternative music and pop punk these days to have any meaningful conversation about punk.(4) You'll obviously find punk's stamp on current versions of hardcore, grindcore, death metal, etc., but it was also a big part of new wave and college rock in the '80s, modern rock and grunge in the '90s and so-called Garage

Rock today. Punk has filtered into commercial pop music several times over the years, with current examples Avril

Lavigne, Dashboard Confessional and Good Charlotte adapting the style and attitude of punk without playing one lick of the music. Punk's influences on

pop culture range from the utterly ridiculous to the not-so-sublime. In Massachusetts and New York you can stay in shape by taking a punk rock aerobics class (go to punkaerobics.com, I couldn't make this shit up.) You may have seen Greil Marcus' great book, Lipstick Traces, searching for punk's roots

in the Dada movement and the Situationists, rewritten into a remarkably interesting piece of theater. Take a look in any good bookstore, and you'll find shelves full of writing on the subject of punk rock. Punk's heavyweights in

the art world are obviously Raymond Pettibon and Gary Panter, but close examination of art galleries, magazines and street art yields a whole generation of new artists influenced by the art and graphics of punk rock, like Victor Gastelum and Emek, and an artist who may not listen to the music but could be the most punk rock of them all, Robbie Conal. The fashion world jumped onto punk's bandwagon from the get-go (as

it does with every trend) and never let go, stealing and re-stealing, recycling punk's look constantly in high fashion's neverending battle to stay fresh and profitable. And the truth of it is, it's all there for the stealing. Punk was amazing, but it was just another loud and outrageous link in the pop culture chain. There are obvious ripoffs and cliches to be found in the various translations this many generations later, and my socialist-leaning friends

are going to have to forgive me, but flipping channels and hearing the Ramones selling me cellular phone service, or the Clash or the Buzzcocks pimp me a set of wheels somehow just doesn't offend me.(5) More important than artistic, musical or fashion influences, the

greater victory would be ours if punk's call to activism was revived. After a too-long period of time when irony and emotional detachment were the hallmarks of cool, it would be great to see more people join the crowds protesting the meetings of the International Monetary Fund, The G8, The World Health Organization, Genetically Modified Food, and War (Not In Our Name, if not entirely successful in it's mission, was pretty punk rock).6 Fat Mike of NOFX stirs it up with Punkvoter.com in heroic fashion, and all the bands participating on the compilation CDs Bands Against Bush is heartening. Log on and check out the links. The spirit of punk is alive in those who try and push out from beyond the security of their television set and six-pack. It's about moving forward and shouting when something is worth shouting about. Punks who haven't learned anything since '77, sitting still and grinding their teeth, listening to the same ten records over and over, chanting that back in the day mantra are just as tired as that pony-tailed guy in the Saab you see on the freeway next to you rocking out to a Kansas record. Punk has changed, and change is not just a good thing, it's the best thing. What's punk? Like the cover says, Punk is everything. Deal.

(1) Somehow, it emerged that Sid Vicious had been crowned punk's poster boy by the musical press. A third rate bass player who wasn't even the most interesting person in his band, Sid's sneer was on the cover of most of the aforementioned punk special editions, confirming for me that very few rock rag

editors think very hard about punk rock. (2) Scoff if you want: Disco, along with punk, was the last form of music that broke without the record companies having a clue of its existence. (3) Hip-Hop would do that some years later. Oh, and the industry acronym AOR stood for Album-Oriented Rock, the droning cloud of flatulent excess from which

punk emerged (think The Eagles, Boston, Foreigner...you get the picture.) (4) Slagging off the Blink 182s and Offspings became the punk national pasttime for awhile, but it does no good to debate the authenticity of commercial pop: better to use that

energy searching for something better. (5) After all, I'm under no obligation to buy any of the shit– the commercials have a good beat and I can dance to it. (6) Having a nest of vipers in the

White House might help people get worked up - by the time the Bush administration is done lying to you, raping the environment and eroding your civil rights, I HOPE you're good and pissed.

IAN MACKAYE SPEAKS TO BRYAN RAYMOND TURCOTTE

BRT: We've tried to read as many of your interviews from the past as we could find in order to come up with some questions that would be, you know, original and not like constantly repeating the same old stuff.

IAN: (Laughs) But repetition is where it's at! People always say to me "Aw, I've been searching trying to find a question you haven't been asked" and I'm like but why not ask the same question because then you get to judge where I stand on the same issue.

BRT: Totally. Well for this we decided to focus on one larger issue or question. The title of the book is 'Punk is Dead – Punk is Everything' we feel not that punk is in fact dead, but more that it is an idea that is being reinvented over and over. Thus it dies and is reborn. It becomes everything. Can we talk about that? The arc of punk rock from your experience?

IAN: First of all, I would agree with you about the idea that punk is everything. Punk rock, really, if you ask me what it meant, it just means human. It's just human beings, just life, it's just about being alive. It's an attempt to be declarative; it's humans who are on the margins. Punk rock is something on the outside of what the mainstream is and because of that it's a free space. Because when you're a deviant, you share your zone with other deviants, like others who are deviating from society. And so my first experience with punk rock, of course, was first arguing the idea of it being just a look, right? Thinking oh it was just a look. Thinking, to myself, "Oh those guys look so stupid." Or they look so weird. Or they kind of scare me and they're weird looking because they have pink hair. So punk was a look, like a fashion thing. And then punk became a musical thing cause I heard the records for the first time. My first experience with hearing the music was in 1978. After arguing with a friend of mine about who rocked harder, Ted Nugent or The Ramones, he just said "Well, here, you should listen to records before you just talk about them." I had never heard them before so I listened. I got Generation X, The Damned maybe, and The Jam, and The Clash, definitely The Clash. And what happened was, it scared me at first. It didn't scare me like that I was scared to listen to it, it scared me because it revealed sort of a world I had no idea existed. When something has an effect on me like that, when something is sort of beyond my comprehension at first, I run towards it because I want to understand, I'm so curious about it. And when I first heard this music, it baffled me. I understood that it was music but it didn't sound like anything that I'd ever heard before. My first impression was "This is not music!" It just didn't make any sense to me. But, one record that did connect with me was the first Sex Pistols album. It was the most kind of rock and roll'ish sounding record to me. That was the bridge for me; that was my, what do you call it?

Gateway. That was my gateway into punk. No doubt it was still fierce. It blew my mind. But, it was a turning point for me. Suddenly when the penny dropped, suddenly things came into view. I started to understand it. Then I was like wow! So my second interaction with punk I started to understand it as a musical form and as an idea. Don't get me wrong, these bands did not sound like each other to me. What they sounded like was that they were all on the margins. They were all presenting new ideas and new approaches without being caught up in the kind of strictures of what the rock industry wanted to present as rock and roll. They were not bothered with all that and that really impressed me. I grew up in a family where I was really taught to question authority. I was taught that the government is probably lying if not definitely so. That's the environment I grew up in. I was born in 1962. I lived in Washington DC. My family, my parents, were liberals, and still are liberals. Growing up during the civil rights era and the anti-Vietnam war era and women's lib and all the sort of liberation stuff that was happening, I was just surrounded by that stuff. So, for me it was completely, absolutely normal to do that. By the late 70's I was so baffled by the people in my high school, largely my world then, I was so baffled by their disinterest in questioning authority, or if they did question, it was merely to get high which seemed like basically just worshipping a different authority, if you know what I mean. So first it was a fashion thing, then it was a music thing. And then I went to go see my first show, which was The Cramps. What I saw there was a room full of people who were challenging conventional thinking on every front and I realized that, whoa there's no limit to this! It's not a lifestyle, it's just a way of being. Ideas, thinking, life. "Lifestyle" suggests that it's something you can check in or check out of. I remember seeing shows where people were playing entire sets on kitchen equipment. I was NOT thinking "Hey, this work out too great but it was cool that you tried. Go and do it again. Come up with something else. For me,

when I realized I can do this and I got into the idea of ...g music. I realized this is not royalty, these are human ...s and I'm a human being. And the punk audience in ...ind, you basically had people who were just interested ...at you got, and so come on! What you got? **BRT:** The ...ragement to just sort of lay it on the table. **IAN:** In my

..., if you're a punk, then you think about it. Because so ... things in this world, in this life, in this society, they exist ...use people don't think about it. So many negative destruc-...hings...foolish...things like war, they only exist because people ... think about them. They've been hoodwinked into not thinking ... them. So for me, the third thing that happened to me was

that punk was really an idea that you re

ally thought about. I understand that that doesn't square up with what a lot of people consider to be punk which is that super nihilistic thing. But I never saw punk as nihilistic. **BRT:** So then you start a band. **IAN:** I first played the bass, which was largely because the people I was playing with already had a guitar player and a singer and Jeff who played timpani in our school said "I'll play drums." I'd already learned how to play Smoke on the Water on one string so I figured I could

handle bass. So when we started to play, obviously the first thing we did, we were listening to the Sex Pistols and other bands like that and we tried to sound just like them, that's what you do. You try to play music like other bands you like. This is what I love the most looking back on this, this is what I'm most interested in: when you have

young people or people who are young with their instruments, who are new to their instruments, when they are playing their instruments... they are listening and they are heavily influenced by something and they're trying to

sound like that thing they are listening to, what's ...happening is that their relationship to their instrument ...s so rudimentary they think they sound like that. But ...nobody else thinks they sound like that. What we were ...rying to do, we were trying to play like the Sex Pistols ...or The

...Ramones and then, or course, we saw the Bad Brains. It ...blew our minds! They were right there in DC, they were ...people we knew, we got to know them, they were our ...riends, they hung out with us. They were also the most ...celestial band in the world. And you thought, good God, ...hese people are right here! They took it to such a higher ...evel for us: now we wanna sound like them! But

...ve never sounded like the Bad Brains. **BRT:** In fact you ...ound totally like yourselves. **IAN:** We sounded like the ...Teen Idles. That's innovation. And that's what fucking ...ascinates me forever. And that's why, when I think about ...punk I always think about either young kids who are just ...starting to play or people who are new to their in

...struments and that's punk to me. People who will respect ...hat first transition, those are punks. Those people who ...are open to the reinterpretation. That's punk rock.

BRT: And then you guys influenced a whole gener-...ation of kids who were listening to Teen Idles and Minor ...Threat and then Fugazi. **IAN:** And that's the point. I've ...said this a million times: music kicked my ass and I just

intend to return the favor. That's the genesis for me in terms of punk; that was how I was inspired by music. Now that I've gotten older, I listen to all music. It's crazy how much music I listen to. I'm so

interested in it. I'm so interested in it. And what I've realized is, it's never genre specific. There is some music I like better than others but ultimately what I'm looking for, is music that sounds like it's being made by people who don't have a choice in the matter. **IAN:** And that threat carries through all genres. It all has the same punk vibe even though the music sounds so different. It's all there. Right now I'm in

my room, I'm looking at a Deadbeats single on Dangerhouse and that music blew my mind. What's compelling to me about that music was that if they were referencing anything in

the past, I have no idea what it was. **BRT:** If bands are out there cutting their teeth on stuff that you can't even imagine, and you're digging the bands as you are and that sort of becomes the counter culture and thus punk rock. But the bands that are just hanging onto a certain sound and you can see all their references and see all their influences becomes not as interesting or not as counter culture, it's just regurgitation. **IAN:** If you become predictable, you're just not doing the job.

BRT: You're not giving it back. **IAN:** I remember someone once said to me,

like, "So where are all the hippies now? They were going to change the world so where are they?" And that was a way of trying to dismiss hippies. I understand

why people had a problem with hippies because hippies had been co-opted by the industry, by society so in a lot of ways it was kind of embarrassing and I could

see why people thought hippies were so lame-o. The fact of the matter is, when you get down to it, the hippie generation, or whatever you want to call it, they were some ass kickers! And they went against a society that was so rigid and so hardcore that what they did was incredible. So when people say to me where are they hippies

now? They're all around us, man. Either they're people who just don't identify as such or they're just out there living, living their lives, doing good, doing the best they can. **BRT:** I think it translated into counterculture in a different way. We certainly wouldn't have had that or even punk ... without them. **IAN:** And punk will

for me, punk is hippie, is beat, is whatever. It goes way back. Check this out. Part of the problem that punk ran into in terms of that is that it largely has manifested as a musical form, considered by many a pop-music form. Around the turn of the century, somebody created a way to record music and then sell those recordings. Prior to that, you couldn't sell music. You sell sheet music and you could charge for performances. But you couldn't sell music. It was like selling air. It would be like selling water because water was just in the river.

It would be like you're walking down the street and someone says "Hey I'll charge you ten bucks for a breath of air." And you're like, okay, but I'm breathing, why would I pay for it? And water was the same way, and that's why when they started to bottle water it was so shocking. But there are aspects of bottled water which are very convenient. If you happen to be in a car driving, you have a bottle of water. And in the same way, if you happen to be in a car and you want to listen to music you can put on your plastic thing and listen to music. So there are certainly positive

aspects of that. But music itself... see, you can sell records and CDs and you can sell tapes. And you can sell MP3s or digital downloads. But you can't sell music, cause music is free. It's just free. But the industry which formed around the ability to reproduce sound on pieces of plastic or

whatever, what happened was they kind of became the gatekeepers, they owned music all of a sudden, the idea of music. They had a product and they were selling that product. As with all things, the longer they had the monopoly on that, the more time they had to fine tune their ability to sell it. And if you have something that's

really precious but you want to sell a lot of them, the way you do that is to make them less precious. What you do with something like music, for instance, is you make it into entertainment. But music is not merely entertainment. Music is sacred.

Music is a form of communication that predates language. And music has attended almost every important event in the history of the world. So music is sacred. There may be music that is entertainment,

but music is sacred.

Go Naztic!

with

the Nazti Skinz

and

25 Suaves

&

Zeek Sheck

@ Nov. 24th

the Smell 247 S Main St Los Angeles

Myths
vs
Legends

nein

Ron Delsener Presents
ONE OF THE NICE THINGS ABOUT NEW YORK!
The
New York Dolls
Beacon Theatre
New Year's Eve
Dec. 31
1 A.M.
All Seats
Gen'l Admission
$6.50
In Advance
$7.50
Day of Show
DAVID JOHANSEN
New York Dolls
JERRY NOLAN
New York Dolls
JOHNNY THUNDERS
New York Dolls
ARTHUR KANE
New York Dolls
SYLVAIN SYLVAIN
New York Dolls

LY NEW YORK APPEARANCE

they return to Europe!

E

AGE

RS-SAT.

13-

New York Dolls

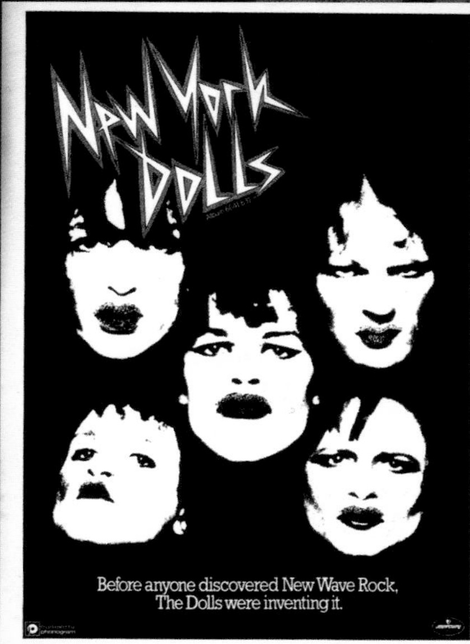
New York Dolls
Before anyone discovered New Wave Rock,
The Dolls were inventing it.

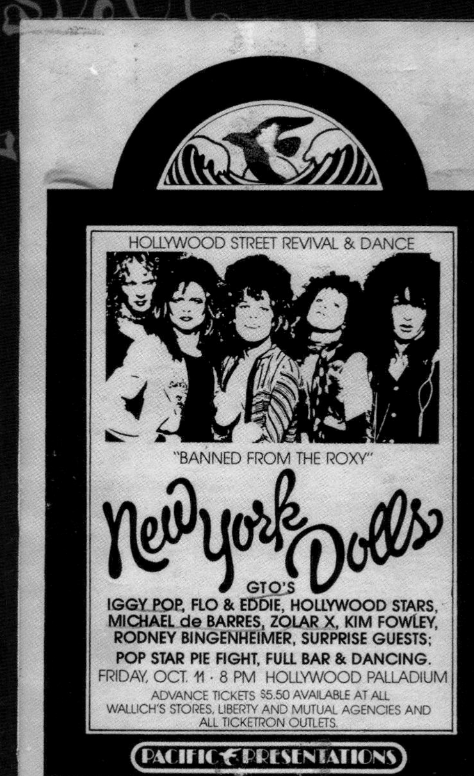
HOLLYWOOD STREET REVIVAL & DANCE
"BANNED FROM THE ROXY"
New York Dolls
GTO'S
IGGY POP, FLO & EDDIE, HOLLYWOOD STARS,
MICHAEL de BARRES, ZOLAR X, KIM FOWLEY,
RODNEY BINGENHEIMER, SURPRISE GUESTS;
POP STAR PIE FIGHT, FULL BAR & DANCING.
FRIDAY, OCT. 11 · 8 PM HOLLYWOOD PALLADIUM
ADVANCE TICKETS $5.50 AVAILABLE AT ALL
WALLICH'S STORES, LIBERTY AND MUTUAL AGENCIES AND
ALL TICKETRON OUTLETS.
PACIFIC PRESENTATIONS

New York Dolls
Tomorrow
Youngstown, Ohio
N.Y. Dolls

BACKSTAGE PASS STOLEN BY HOWIE PYRO OFF THE CASH REGISTER AT BLEEKER BOBS IN 1977.

I was fresh out of prison in 1979 when I met Johnny Thunders. Of course, I knew about him and his first band The New York Dolls back in '73, or maybe it was '74. Anyway, a mutual friend told me that Johnny wanted to meet me and requested that I come down to Bookies Club

in Detroit where he was playing with his new band The Heartbreakers. I was back on the streets after a couple of years of forced retirement courtesy of the federal government and itching to get back into the world of music. I got to the club and got word they wanted me to join them on the encore. Cool by me. I settled in to check them out. See what had been going on while I was gone.

They were a fun band in a loosey-goosey way. All short tunes and sloppy guitars. Johnny had a great snarley attitude, and I soon realized that Jerry Nolan was the real secret weapon of the band and clearly the best all-around musician of the bunch. His tempos were solid and he

rocked with an authentic rock & roll feel on the drums. Their show featured a steady stream of between song bickering from Johnny and Walter Lure. They were the punk rock Lucy and Ricky playing the dozens. They all showed a sense of style in their clothes with Johnny having the most flair and the others affecting a lower east side "trash and vaudeville" look. The audience reacted to them with great enthusiasm and they were having a ball. I sat in with them on their encore song, "Do You Love Me?" by the Contours. The band seemed impressed that I knew the correct notes on the mandolin-sounding guitar intro, "You broke my heart...." After the show, I went to the dressing

RUSS GIBB PRESENTS IN DETROIT
MC5
WICKED RELIGION · THE MAXX
FRI APRIL 4·5 SAT
SUN APRIL 6 · P.G.&E. · JAMES GANG
GRANDE BALLROOM

room to meet Johnny and the fellows and stepped into a black hole. Johnny and Jerry were in a bathroom stall shooting up. This was disconcerting to me because this was the same scene that I had lived through years earlier

in the MC5. I had starred in this movie myself, and now, just out of the penitentiary for activities related to this kind of behavior, this didn't bode well. Déjà vu all over again. Johnny emerged from the stall high as a kite, blood dripping from his abscessed arm and in a great mood. Mr. Charming. He invited me to join him and his drug dealer/ manager to a party with "ounces of cocaine." I passed,

for now. Rock & roll or, if you prefer, punk rock, is only the surface of the story, the tip of this iceberg. The real story is deeper and, at its core, it's a story of addiction. Addiction to the myth of fame. Addiction to the myth of power. And mostly, addiction to drugs. There is no other way to talk about what happened without framing it in these terms. As much as I'd like to tell a glorious punk rock tale replete with romantic heroes and brave individuals fighting for their art, that ain't the deal here. So if

WAYNE KRAMER

you're looking for electric guitars, leather jackets and groupie sex, then forget it. Back in the dressing room, I was reeling. With hindsight, I know

now, the whole dynamic of our relationship was summarized right there. I was confronted with a version of myself in Johnny and I was invited to dive head first, straight into the deep end of Hell, and I did. Not that I made an actual choice to do

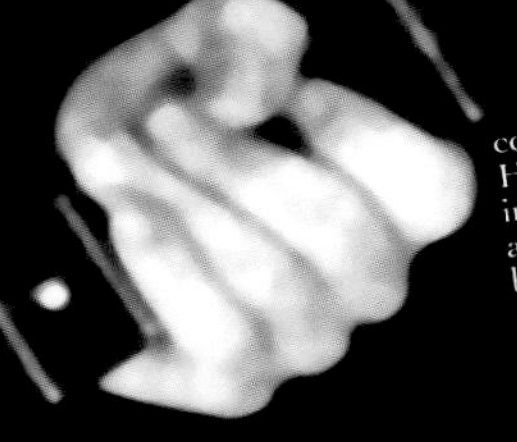
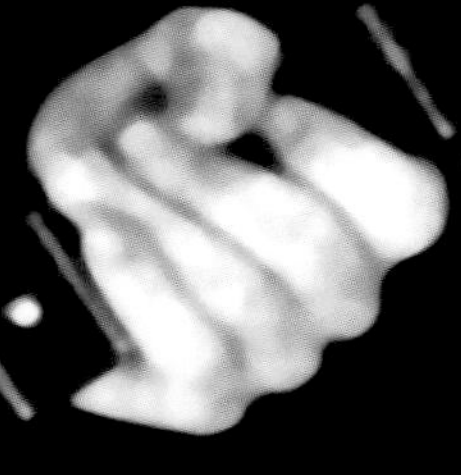

that, because I had no choice. I thought I had the power to say no, but I didn't. I sat in the Federal Correctional Institution at Lexington Kentucky for a long time thinking about how I was going to straighten up. I was going to get my career back on track. I was gonna get my shit together. Get serious. Yea right. I believed I actually had the power to change Johnny Thunders. And this was the subtext for Gang War and a great deal of my own life. I really believed back then

that success in the music business was more powerful than drug addiction or alcoholism. I also believed that there was something in this for me. I was going to return back to the world of music a conquering hero. Yea, Johnny Thunders and me. Well, at least it looked good on paper. It had a nice ring to it. Both of us bringing a little cache to the

table. Next stop: The Big Time. But the reality of the situation was way different. It was such a disaster, trying to compete with the disease that plagued us both that neither one of us knew we even

had. I completely disregarded everything I knew to be the truth and swallowed the lie completely. I really thought I was wiser, smarter and knew all the tricks. I was going to be the one to beat the odds.

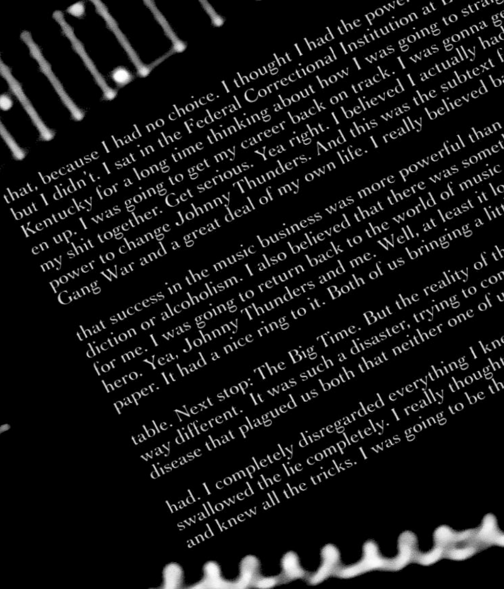

RUSS · GIBB · PRESENTS AT THE GRANDE · BALLROOM
MC5
FRI. JAN. 24 ~ TRAIN · MARCH BROS.
SAT. JAN. 25 ~ MARCH BROS. · PIERS
SUN. JAN. 26 · TAJ MAHAL · ASIAN FLU
DESIGN · ROBIN SOMMERS

ROBIN SOMMERS

Our misadventures were, naturally, mind-numbingly predictable and about as glamorous as sticking a needle into

the ball of your eye. While Johnny lived in Detroit we would drink and take pills, cocaine, whatever was around. We played shows around the Midwest for a while then we relocated to New York City and tried to work up and down the East Coast. Of course, right away, every gig we attempted to play degenerated into a dope-fiend hustle. Living on the

Lower East Side in the early '80s was like living in a heroin supermarket 24-7.

I knew the heroin boys and was trying to stay away from them. But when we both moved back to NYC — Johnny's neighborhood — it was all over. Johnny reverted into a true street rat junkie and

I was right there with him. We never had a chance. Because of that, the band never had a chance either. We changed bass players and drummers all the time. Sensible cats just wouldn't put up with the shenanigans. Any thoughts of actually working on music were absurd. After a few months he tried to pull a

scam on me and I cut him loose. It ended that quickly. I would see him around town sometimes or run into him copping down on Avenue D. By the mid '80s

I entered the Beth Israel Methadone treatment program and began my long road to recovery. Johnny found new

00180 190 4 25 7
FCI LEX

00180 190 4 25 7
FCI LEX

collaborators and continued to get sicker and sicker. He didn't die young, nor did he leave a good-looking corpse. He died slowly, getting worse and worse as his body lost its fight against the disease, bit-by-bit, day by day. In the end, it just killed him, as it must. He was resilient; he lived longer

than I thought he would. He died curled up in a fetal position, under the sink in a hotel room in New Orleans. It wasn't a good death; it's not sexy or heroic. I tell the tale not because I'm smart or tough or a survivor or any of that clichéd crap. There wa

a time when Johnny and I were the same guy, jus like all alkies and junkies are the same. I was as si as Johnny, but I changed. Only difference was, at a certain point, I asked for help and found it. Simple as that. Not easy, but simple. I do know t Johnny brought joy into this world with his mus I know every life has value. But contributing to the mythology can be dangerous. Just take a loo

around at the attrition rate in this game. In the first century B.C., the Roman Statesman Cicer remarked, "Although physicians frequently kn their patients will die of a given disease, they r tell them so. To warn of an evil is justified only along with the warning, there is a way of esca

If there is a crime in all this it's that it didn't h be this way. Bye-bye Johnny.

GANG WAR
Featuring: Johnny Thunders, Wayne Kramer
March 18
GANG WARS
featuring Johnny Thunder
& Wayne Kramer
BAR
7690109
BORED

HEARTBREAKERS with JOHNNY THUNDER
TRACK RECORD
A DIRKSEN-MILLER PRODUCTION
and THE LIARS WITH DV 8
and Imposters WITH Seizure
Tuesday SEPTEMBER 19
MABUHAY GARDENS
443 Broadway San Francisco
956-3315
11pm
Wednesday SEPTEMBER 20
DESIGN: Roger I Reyes
ROGER I. REYES
HEARTBREAKERS
Get off the FUCKING PHONE
L.A.M.F.
THE HEARTBREAKERS
C.B.G.B.'s
Fri., Sat., Sun.
August 15, 16, 17
315 Bowery at Bleecker 982-4052
Two shows nightly plus BLONDIE and THE TALKING HEADS.
New York to interv
programm
terview Th
docume
NIKKI SUDDEN
1 4

Johnny Thunders had a charming way of getting nice stuff from his fans. He'd say; "Gimmie dat!!" and just start grabbing. It was amazing how many women gladly removed their shirts at his insistence. Once he got a monkey fur coat off a girl that way, it matched his hair beautifully. Johnny was also

great at distracting the bartender and stealing booze. He'd throw something and as soon as the bartender looked to see what the noise was, he would vault over the bar in a flash and grab any full bottle. Unfortunately he couldn't read the labels in the dark so anyone on one of these adventures with him could get stuck with drinking Schnapps or Pernod and

ursing a wicked hangover. One night after I'd ormed my way into Max's third floor – the inner anctum of backstage – a joint was being passed round before the Heartbreakers set. I must have

ooked like Bogart because Thunders came over and said "Gimmie dat" and grabbed the joint from my hand. I thought it was funny, but my friend Debette, a groupie and porn star and one of Johnny's "other"

girlfriends, besides his wife Julie, used the incident to cause a scene. As I sat there giggling, Debette screamed "Don't take that from her like that!" and swiped the crumbling roach from Johnny's hand. This was definitely a breech of backstage etiquette.

Julie, a small tyke compared to the rest of us, pounced on Debette immediately and began pummeling her and shoving her out into the stairwell. Everyone in the room jumped up to follow the action since the excitement of a fight was even more thrilling than being backstage. Like a ball of scrapping

kittens, Julie and Debette began tumbling down the stairs with arms and legs flailing. At the bottom of the long black stairwell, a lone security guard was trying to hold back the crowd waiting outside to get into the club. Julie shoved Debette out the front entrance between the two glass doors, and the security

guard, who sussed out the situation immediately, grabbed Debette and pinned her arms behind her back while Julie kicked her in the stomach several times. No one would dare do that to Julie because she was always pregnant. I was enraged by the injustice, so I grabbed the 300 pound bouncer by his trendy punk dog collar and began to twist. By this time everyone from backstage was standing behind Julie in the stairwell laughing at us.

We must have been quite a sight! The guard almost had Debette subdued when like a harpy from hell I had him by the throat. He couldn't let go of Debette in order to extricate my grip from his neck accessory, so

he began yelling; "Get her off of me,.. Get Her Off of Me!" meanwhile the paying audience, which had been kept waiting outside for too long, began pushing its way into the club. So Julie, thinking fast, quickly shut the glass doors and locked all of us

outside. Finally, Billy Thompson, the guitarist from the Senders, grabbed me by the waist and wrenched my hands from the dog collar and carried me away

to the Greek diner around the corner

to cool off. The next night I returned to the scene of the crime, because the Heartbreakers were playing at Max's again. I apologized to the bouncer who rolled his eyes

as he held the door for me. I didn't go backstage that night, but when I saw Johnny he said "Hey Babe" and winked.

EILEEN POLK

THUNDERS AND DEE DEE'S LEGS AT MAX'S BY EILEEN POLK

THE HEARTBREAKERS
at MAX'S KANSAS CITY
JULY 23 & 24

SPOT NEWS AND PICTURES OF
THE HEARTBRAKERS
SHUT UP! NO MATTER WHAT HE IS— WHAT HE'S DONE— DON'T YOU DARE TALK ABOUT HIM LIKE THAT!
ROXY CLUB
+ Siouxsie and the Banshees
OKAY, TIGRESS! HE'S ALL YOURS!
WED. 2nd MAR.
8:30-1 AM, adm. £1.50
41-43 Neal Street London W.C.2. Tel: 836 8811
I... JUST CAN'T... HELP IT!

NOTE: MISSPELLED HEARTBRAKERS

DD

DALA-DEMOKRATEN

Måndagen den 20 juni 1983

STJÄRNAN DROGAD

när han framträdde tre timmar försenad

"EN TRAGEDI"

hela Dalarnas lokaltidnin

In Loving Memory of

Johnny Genzale Thunders

July 15, 1952 - April 23, 1991

Prayer to St. Jude
To be said in cases despaired of
St. Jude, glorious Apostle, faithful
Servant and friend of Jesus,
the name of the traitor
has caused you to be forgotten
by many, but the true Church
invokes you universally as the
Patron of things despaired of:
pray for me, who am so miserable:
pray for me, that finally I may
receive the consolations and
the succor of Heaven in all my
necessities, tribulations
and sufferings, particularly Johnny,
and that I may bless God with the
Elect throughout Eternity.
Amen

HARDEN FUNERAL HOME

(718) 229-3055

OHNN

CBGB
and
OMFUG
5 BOWERY
(at Bleecker)
2) 982-4052
hows 9:30
d Midnight
& Thurs. Jan. 28 & 29
UARDIAN
STORM
CATS
RI & SAT & SUN
Jan 30 31 Feb 1
ARTBREAKERS
RAMONES
RAMONES
ARTBREAKERS
ARTBREAKERS
RAMONES
Mon. & Tues.
TION SHOWCASE
Sat Sun Feb 6, 7, 8
NK VILLE
CITY LIGHTS
Fri Only
EAT MISTAQUE
Sat only
IONEY DAVIS
Sun only
SHADOW
VALENTINES WEEKEND
E MIAMIS
LONDIE
HEARTBREAKERS
ON THE ROCKS
BLEECKER & BROADWAY
THURS.-SAT., NOV. 11-13
HEARTBREAKERS
ON THE ROCKS
BLEECKER & BROADWAY
THURS.-SAT., NOV. 11-13
HEARTBREAKERS
ON THE ROCKS
BLEECKER & BROADWAY
THURS.-SAT., NOV. 11-13
HEARTBREAKERS
ON THE ROCKS
BLEECKER & BROADWAY
THURS.-SAT., NOV. 11-13

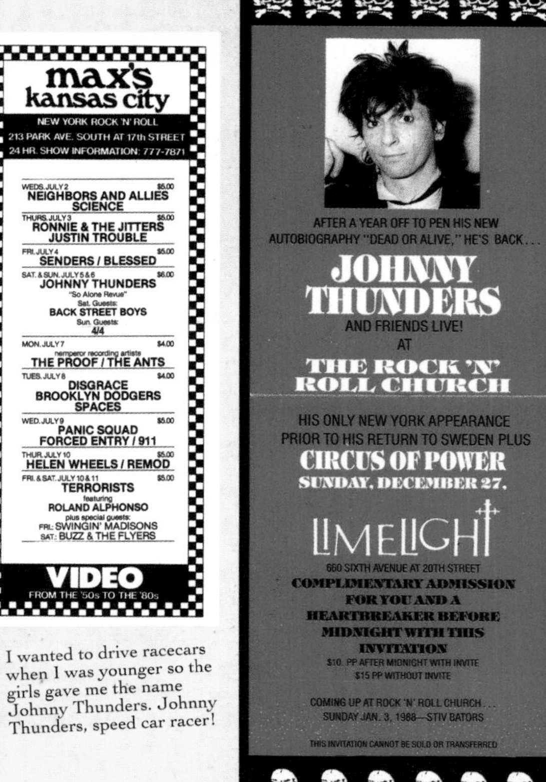
max's kansas city
NEW YORK ROCK 'N' ROLL
213 PARK AVE. SOUTH AT 17th STREET
24 HR. SHOW INFORMATION: 777-7871
WEDS. JULY 2 $5.00
NEIGHBORS AND ALLIES
SCIENCE
THURS. JULY 3 $5.00
RONNIE & THE JITTERS
JUSTIN TROUBLE
FRI. JULY 4 $5.00
SENDERS / BLESSED
SAT. & SUN. JULY 5 & 6 $6.00
JOHNNY THUNDERS
"So Alone Revue"
Sat. Guests:
BACK STREET BOYS
Sun. Guests:
4/4
MON. JULY 7 $4.00
nemperor recording artists
THE PROOF / THE ANTS
TUES. JULY 8 $4.00
DISGRACE
BROOKLYN DODGERS
SPACES
WED. JULY 9 $5.00
PANIC SQUAD
FORCED ENTRY / 911
THUR. JULY 10 $5.00
HELEN WHEELS / REMOD
FRI. & SAT. JULY 10 & 11 $5.00
TERRORISTS
featuring
ROLAND ALPHONSO
plus special guests:
FRI.: SWINGIN' MADISONS
SAT.: BUZZ & THE FLYERS
VIDEO
FROM THE '50s TO THE '80s
AFTER A YEAR OFF TO PEN HIS NEW AUTOBIOGRAPHY "DEAD OR ALIVE," HE'S BACK...
JOHNNY THUNDERS
AND FRIENDS LIVE!
AT
THE ROCK 'N' ROLL CHURCH
HIS ONLY NEW YORK APPEARANCE
PRIOR TO HIS RETURN TO SWEDEN PLUS
CIRCUS OF POWER
SUNDAY, DECEMBER 27,
LIMELIGHT
660 SIXTH AVENUE AT 20TH STREET
COMPLIMENTARY ADMISSION FOR YOU AND A HEARTBREAKER BEFORE MIDNIGHT WITH THIS INVITATION
$10. PP AFTER MIDNIGHT WITH INVITE
$15 PP WITHOUT INVITE
COMING UP AT ROCK 'N' ROLL CHURCH...
SUNDAY JAN. 3, 1988—STIV BATORS
THIS INVITATION CANNOT BE SOLD OR TRANSFERRED

I wanted to drive racecars when I was younger so the girls gave me the name Johnny Thunders. Johnny Thunders, speed car racer!

JOHNNY THUNDERS

L.A.M.F. L.A.M.F.
L.A.M.F. L.A.M.F.

EN CONCIERTO
JOHNNY THUNDERS
+ DISTRITO 14
FIESTA 2º ANIVERSARIO
Bruto

IN MEMORY OF
Johnny Thunders
1952 1991

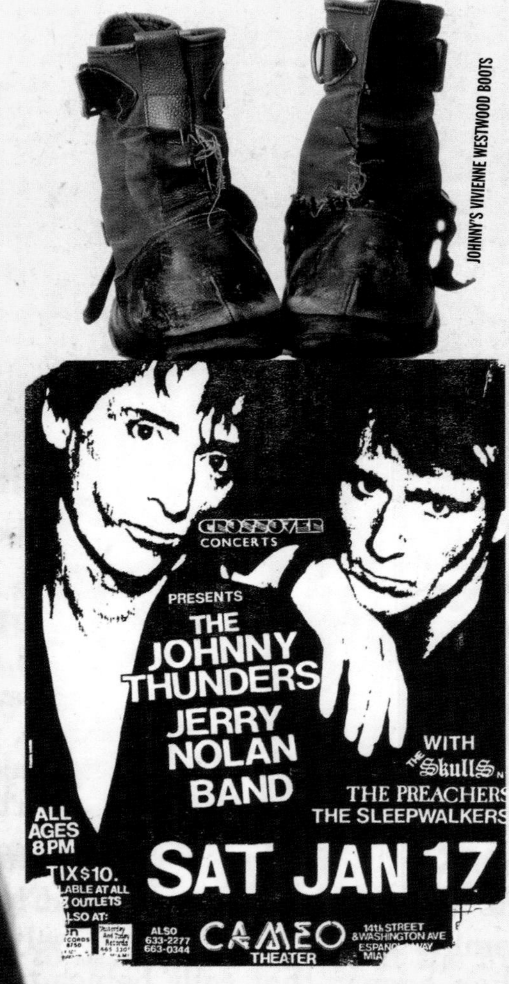
CROSSOVER CONCERTS
PRESENTS
THE JOHNNY THUNDERS
JERRY NOLAN BAND
WITH
THE SKULLS
THE PREACHERS
THE SLEEPWALKERS
ALL AGES
8PM
TIX $10.
SAT JAN 17
CAMEO THEATER
14th STREET & WASHINGTON AVE

JOHNNY'S VIVIENNE WESTWOOD BOOTS

"DOUBLE TROUBLE"
LEE BLACK CHILDERS and NEAL PETERS

MICK ROCK
DEAD BOYS
Special Guests
Weirdos
WEIRDOS
Friday Jan 29
9pm
STIV BATORS · JOHNNY BLITZ · CHEETAH CHROME · JEFF MAGNUM
VARIETY ARTS CENTER
LIVE MUSIC • THEATRE • FILM • DANCING • DINING
Variety Arts Center
GOLDENVOICE
BY A ROUTE OBSCURE AND LONELY,
HAUNTED BY ILL ANGELS ONLY,
WHERE AN EIDOLON, NAMED NIGHT,
ON A BLACK THRONE REIGNS UPRIGHT,
I HAVE WANDERED HOME BUT NEWLY
FROM THIS ULTIMATE DIM THULE.
FROM DREAM-LAND BY EDGARD ALLAN POE
1990
STIV BATOR
NO COMPROMISE NO REGRETS
LOVE TO DEATH S. TO C. C. TO S.
1949
The family of
Stiv BATOR
acknowledges with
grateful appreciation
your kind expression
of sympathy.
In Loving Memory of
Stephen (Stiv) Bator
Born October 22,1949
Died June 3,1990
RESURRECTION PRAYER
MOST merciful Father, we commend our departed into your hands. We are filled with the sure hope that our departed will rise again on the Last Day with all who have died in Christ. We thank you for all the good things you have given during our departed's earthly life.
O Father, in your great mercy, accept our prayer that the Gates of Paradise may be opened for your servant. In our turn, may we too be comforted by the words of faith until we greet Christ in glory and are united with you and our departed.
Through Christ our Lord,
Amen.
McCLURKIN FUNERAL HOME
GIRARD, OHIO 44420
PIETÀ No. 2

ALL THIS

DEAD BOYS FAN CLUB, 3412 NEW UTRECHT AVE, BKLYN N.Y. 11219

DEAD BOYS

THE WIZARD OF LOVE
YOUNG LOUD AND SNOTTY
TOTAL CONTROL
1977
CONFIDENTIAL
SONIC REDUCER
deadboys
BUZZCOCKS
LOVE
PROBLEMS
SIN
Dedicated to all music lovers
THE CLASH
YOUNG
LOUD
AND SNOTTY
ROCKABILLIES FOR BRITAIN

UK INVASION TOUR 1977

WITH THE DAMNED

18th Nov - CORN EXCHANGE, CAMBRIDGE	30th Nov - DEMONT, LEICESTER
19th Nov - HULL UNIVERSITY	2nd Dec - KINGS HALL, DERBY
20th Nov - ELIZABETHAN, MANCHESTER	3rd Dec - PIER PAVILLION, HASTINGS
21st Nov - BIRMINGHAM, TOP RANK	5th Dec - SOUTHAMPTON, TOP RANK
22nd Nov - LOCARNO, COVENTRY	6th Dec - CARDIFF, TOP RANK
23rd Nov - TOP RANK, SHEFFIELD	7th Dec - LIVERPOOL UNIVERSITY
25th Nov - ROUNDHOUSE, LONDON	8th Dec - HUDDERSFIELD POLYTECHNIC
26th Nov - ROUNDHOUSE, LONDON	9th Dec - CLOUDS BALLROOM, EDINBURGH
27th Nov - ROUNDHOUSE, LONDON	10th Dec - STRATHCLYDE, GLASGOW
28th Nov - DEMONT, LEICESTER	11th Dec - NEWCASTLE CITY HALL

THE ALBUM: 'YOUNG LOUD AND SNOTTY' 9103 321

THE SINGLE: 'SONIC REDUCER' 6078 604

DEAD BOYS

AND MORE

FRIDAY * * * * JAN. *11
DEAD BOYS!!
plus
JOHN CADILLAC'S / THE TESTORS
BOB-A-LOOS
hot club
21 & SOUTH
545-5051

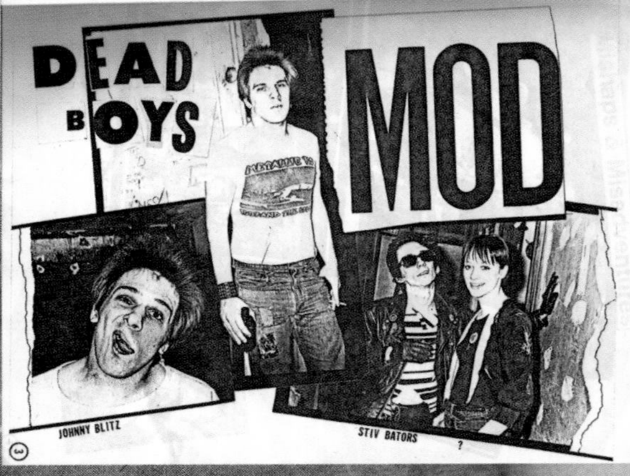
DEAD BOYS
MOD
JOHNNY BLITZ
STIV BATORS
?

Dead Boys,

MICHAEL ALAGO

dead boys
Join
NOW
DEAD BOYS FAN CLUB
5412 NEW UTRECHT AVE
BROOKLYN, NY 11219
$4.00 membership (USA
$5.00 membership (OUT OF USA
ALL THIS AND MORE

MARGARET SAADI KRAMER

I was 18 when I arrived in the middle of the Dead Boys' story. There was no life experience that could have prepared me for the next 10 years I spent in their world. I'm now more than twice the age I was when I first stepped into their rehearsal room in down

town Youngstown in the Fall of 1986. They were all so many years older than I was and they were all crazy in a post-traumatic-stress-disorder kind of way. Stiv and Jimmy were incredibly funny guys. Stiv had a low-pitched staccato and his pronunciation was affected

by an odd malformation on his upper lip. It made the words come out with a little clip at the end. Complicated by the fact that he was physically weasel-y, he didn't elicit trust in people. Cheetah ran around on his tip toes, pointing and shouting non sequiturs. The others teased him. They smoked and drank a lot. They had created their own language and were resuscitating their favorite phrases to try to confuse me and amuse one another. It worked. We all

laughed our asses off. The reunion in New York City a few weeks later on Halloween night was my first time traveling to NYC alone. My taxi was egged between the airport and the hotel. (How did

that punk get an egg through such a tiny opening while we rolled by? Incredible.) I met Joey Ramone and Johnny Thunders for the first time in the dressing room. Johnny was a weird pirate parody of himself. Joey was charming. It was great, but a definitely registers in my memory banks as surreal. I was a budding

writer and they welcomed me into their secret society. I recorded our first meeting. It was the first of many that would follow. It's uncomfortable for me listening to them again now. Our Ohio accents are endearing, but it's actually the sound of my own voice on the ta that's disconcerting. I wondered if hearing Stiv mig be too sad, but it's nice. He was my friend for almo five years. They were consequential years for me.

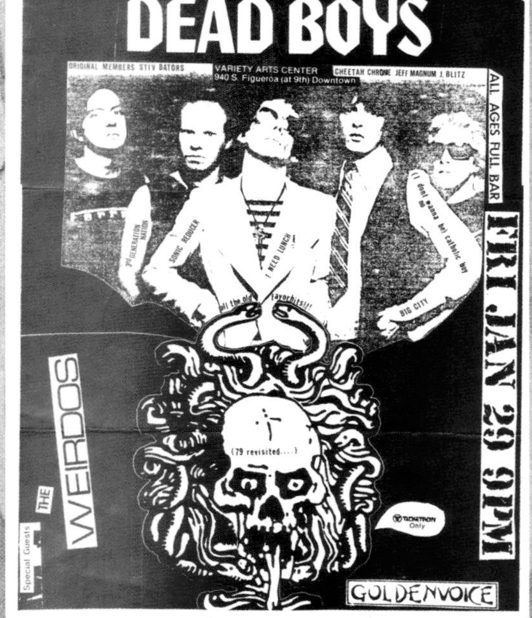
DEAD BOYS
ORIGINAL MEMBERS STIV BATORS
VARIETY ARTS CENTER
940 S. Figueroa (at 9th) Downtown
CHEETAH CHROME JEFF MAGNUM J. BLITZ
ALL AGES FULL BAR
FRI JAN 29 9PM
Special Guests
THE
WEIRDOS
GOLDENVOICE

BOOKIES
Destroy all Monsters
Johnny 3s
from Chicago
MAY 25 → 26
PUNK
HARROW COLLEGE of HIGHER EDUCATION
presents
a select date on a 5 day tour
DESTROY ALL MONSTERS
FROM DETROIT, USA
featuring iggy pop stooges + mc5 bass guitarist and starring niagra sings
+ support
7o clock till 10.30
FRIDAY 12 OCTOBER in the anscombe hall
BAR DISCO Tickets £1 in adv. £1·20 at door
DESTROY
ALL MONSTERS!
DESTROY ALL MONSTERS IS DISTORTO, PSYCHEDELIC, CHAOTIC, HIGH ENERGY LEVEL MUSIC.
THE RETURN OF
Destroy all Monsters
NOV. 13
"AND YOU GO TO A CLUB ... ON A TUESDAY NIGHT..."
IN CONCERT WITH
MOTOR CITY SHOWCASE
ALL FLYERS THIS PAGE: MIKE DAVIS

LEFT TO RIGHT: RON ASHETON, MIKE DAVIS, ROB KING, AND NIAGARA

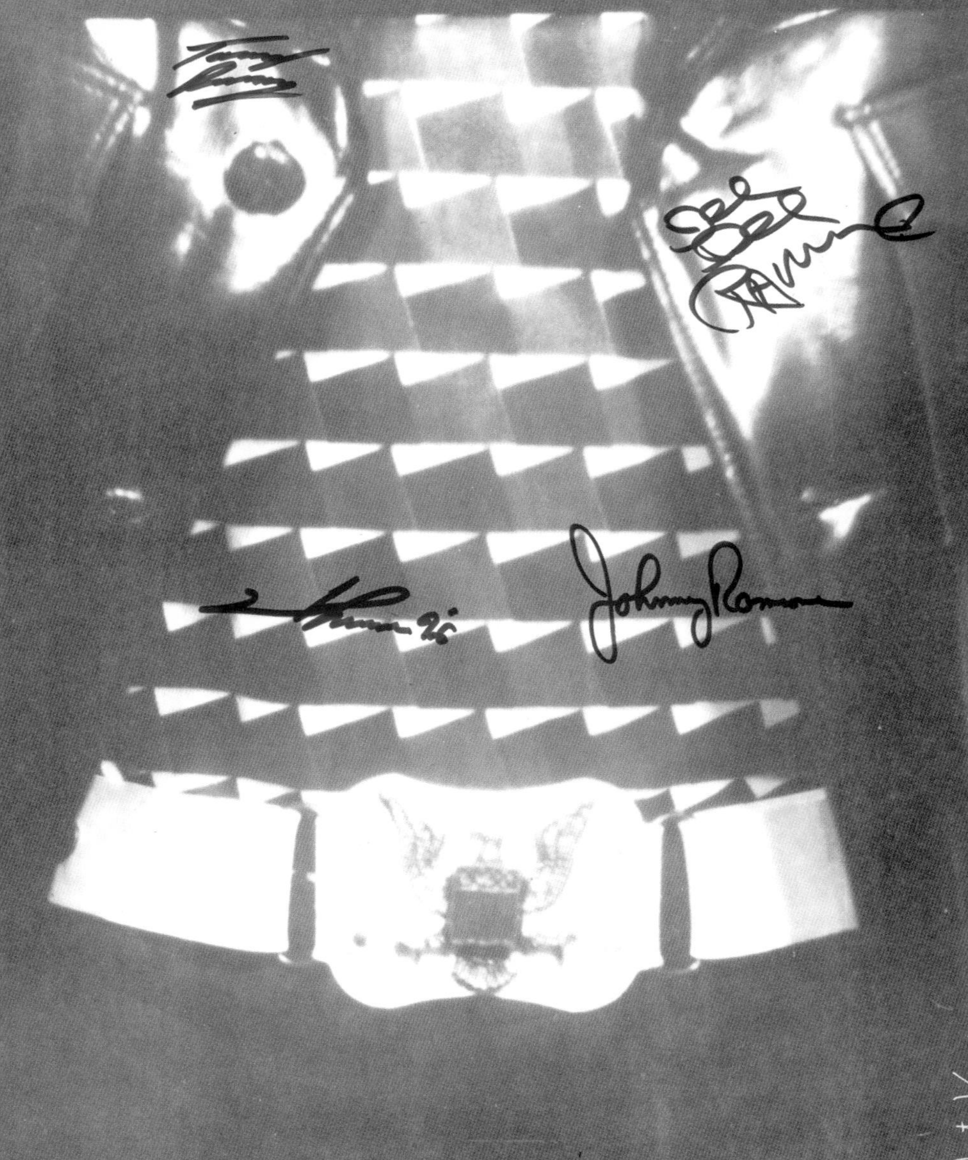
RAMONES

JOHNNY
JOEY
DEEDEE
TOMMY

ARTURO VEGA

In the summer of 1973 I was working at an Orange Julius on 42nd. Street. On the same block there used to be a photo booth. That's where I took the photos that became the first Ramones poster ever which was used to promote the band at the 1975 CBGB Unsigned Band

Festival. These images were also used to create the back cover and inner sleeve of the band's first album. The "First Eagle" was a belt buckle from a Navy Music Band uniform, which I bought at a surplus store also on 42nd. Street. I

also took color Polaroid's at Playland Arcade right on Times Square including one where I am wearing the arrow head T-shirt that inspired the pattern for the eagle's center shield in

the Ramones logo, which I designed for the second album Leave Home in 1977.

Savage Voodoo Nuns
a Halloween Sin-Sa-Shun
featuring
Tomatá du Plenty
Fayette
John Flowers
Arturo
Kate Parker
Montana
John Heys
lights by Lou Sozzi
showtime 10:00
Oct 31 - Nov 3
thurs - sun nights
at CBGB Bowery at Bleecker
also with Blondie and ~ The Ramones

RAMONES

BAYOU CITY THEATRE
MARCH 21, 1994
HOUSTON, TEXAS
TICKETS AVAILABLE AT ALL TICKET MASTER OUTLETS OR CHARGE BY PHONE (713)629-3700

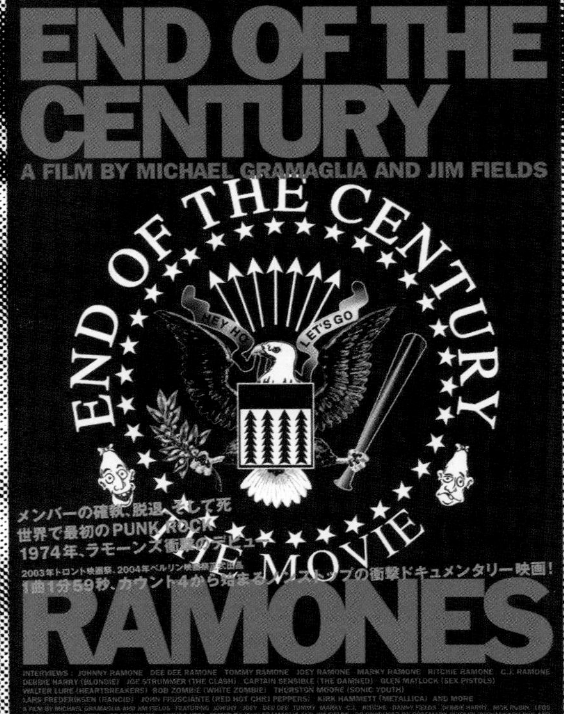
END OF THE CENTURY
A FILM BY MICHAEL GRAMAGLIA AND JIM FIELDS
END OF THE CENTURY
HEY HO
LET'S GO
THE MOVIE
世界で最初のPUNK ROCK
RAMONES
INTERVIEWS : JOHNNY RAMONE DEE DEE RAMONE TOMMY RAMONE JOEY RAMONE MARKY RAMONE RITCHIE RAMONE C.J. RAMONE
DEBBIE HARRY (BLONDIE) JOE STRUMMER (THE CLASH) CAPTAIN SENSIBLE (THE DAMNED) GLEN MATLOCK (SEX PISTOLS)
WALTER LURE (HEARTBREAKERS) ROB ZOMBIE (WHITE ZOMBIE) THURSTON MOORE (SONIC YOUTH)
LARS FREDERIKSEN (RANCID) JOHN FRUSCIANTE (RED HOT CHILI PEPPERS) KIRK HAMMETT (METALLICA) AND MORE

RAMONES
RAMONES
JOHNNY
JOEY
DEE DEE
TOMMY
PUNK ROCK

PUNK ROCK BALL-ROOM BLITZ!
GOLDEN WEST BALL ROOM
The RAMONES
With
THE DOGS
PLUS
KEZY & KROQ
SPECIAL GUEST
VAN HALEN
SUN MARCH 13
$5.
8:30 PM
GOLDEN WEST BALLROOM
12400 Studebaker Rd. Norwalk, Ca.
Tickets at the Box Office & TICKETRON
info: (213) 868-4761

HALL PASS
Johnny Ramone
Principal
Joey Ramone
Custodian
ROCK 'N' ROLL HIGH SCHOOL
Dee Dee Ramone
Guidance Counselor
Marky Ramone
Study-Hall Monitor
©1979 Sire Records Company Printed In U.S.A.

THE FRONT BIT
THOUGHT YOU MIGHT LIKE TO SEE THE ORIGINAL IDEA FOR THE SLEEVE OF "ROAD TO RUIN". GUS MOORHEAD OF GLASGOW IS THE ARTIST - THE RAMONES TOOK IT BACK TO NYC AND GOT 'PUNK' MAG'S JOHN HARSTROM TO REDO IT (WITH THE NEW DRUMMER)

GUS MOORHEAD

Jubilee: official
Ramones drop 'sniff' track
RAMONES
THE RAMONES
FRIDAY 20th MAY
TALKING HEADS
COMING...
PUNK ROCK!
HEARTBREAKERS
JUNE 3rd
A BONE-CHILLING, NERVE-FRYING EPIC... WILL KEEP YOU SCREAMING FOR DAYS!
GOD SAVE THE QUEEN
CLASH
SNIFFIN GLUE...

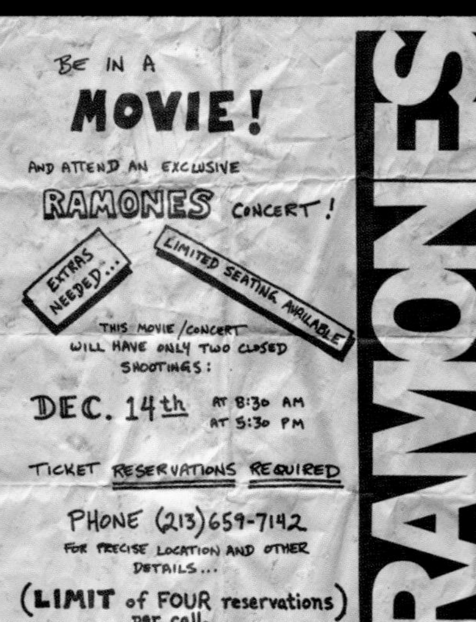
BE IN A
MOVIE!
AND ATTEND AN EXCLUSIVE
RAMONES CONCERT!
EXTRAS NEEDED...
LIMITED SEATING AVAILABLE
THIS MOVIE/CONCERT WILL HAVE ONLY TWO CLOSED SHOOTINGS:
DEC. 14th AT 8:30 AM AT 5:30 PM
TICKET RESERVATIONS REQUIRED
PHONE (213) 659-7142
FOR PRECISE LOCATION AND OTHER DETAILS...
(LIMIT of FOUR reservations) per call.
RAMONES

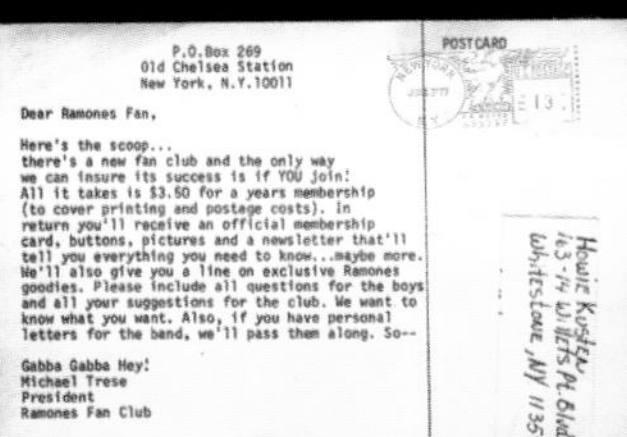

P.O.Box 269
Old Chelsea Station
New York, N.Y.10011

Dear Ramones Fan,

Here's the scoop...
there's a new fan club and the only way we can insure its success is if YOU join! All it takes is $3.50 for a years membership (to cover printing and postage costs). In return you'll receive an official membership card, buttons, pictures and a newsletter that'll tell you everything you need to know...maybe more. We'll also give you a line on exclusive Ramones goodies. Please include all questions for the boys and all your suggestions for the club. We want to know what you want. Also, if you have personal letters for the band, we'll pass them along. So--

Gabba Gabba Hey!
Michael Trese
President
Ramones Fan Club

POSTCARD

Howie Kusten
163-14 Willets Pt. Blvd
Whitestone, NY 11357

LOST BOYS announces:
RAMONES • DICTATORS • CRAMPS
FEB.6 8:30PM
WOLSEY HALL, New Haven
tickets: $3.00 R-T Bus $5.50
TICKETRON on sale 1/14
info: (212) 262-7290

THE FLAMIN GROOVIES/RAMONES
ROXY

HEY HO! LET'S GO!
RAMONES FAN CLUB
YEAH, babes, you heard right —
RAMONES FAN CLUB!
& WE heard you wanted one —
SO, here it is!
RAMONES FAN CLUB
Box 269
Old Chelsea Station
New York, N.Y. 10011

EILEEN POLK

In a city like New York with 8 million people, there are very few outlets for stress if you cannot afford to escape. You can get in fights, become inebriated, go to horror movies or carnival rides at Coney Island to screech your head off. If you can't afford that – you can stick your head in a bucket and scream. Thirty years ago it was even worse. Crime, noise and garbage was everywhere. Driving through

the east Village the cops would roll their windows up & barrel through, heading to nicer crime ridden areas they could actually do something about. Dollar movies in run down theaters were a staple of East Village life. Most of us were more familiar with icons of silent films, Buster Keaton, Clara Bow, and Jean Cocteau than whatever crappy bands with Farrah Fawcett hairdos were playing Madison

Square Garden. After the New York Dolls broke up, the music scene sucked so

we made up our own scene and didn't expect anyone to care. Early Punk was kind of an archaic revival, inspired by Vaudeville, B movies, bikers, girl gangs and trash subculture, anything but the mediocre mass consumer culture you could see on TV. For a movie date with Dee Dee, I heard that Todd Browning's "Freaks" was playing at the theater on 2nd avenue and asked him to go with me to see it. He said Joey had already seen "Freaks" and recommended that film too so we went and

he was blown away. "Freaks" is about a group of Circus oddities that take revenge on their oppressors. In one of the most chilling and memorable scenes, the Freaks dance around the evil ones singing "We accept you one of us, one

of us!" and then plan to kill and maim them. This became the Ramones song "Pinhead". Dee Dee and I liked going to horror movies. A dark theater was the best place to scream. We saw "Food of the Gods" and every time a giant rat or chicken would attack someone, Dee Dee would suddenly jump in his seat and grab me, which would make us both scream. Since we both had PTSD and an unusually sensitive startle

response this was an endless source of fun. Dee Dee was frustrated that the band did not always appreciate his

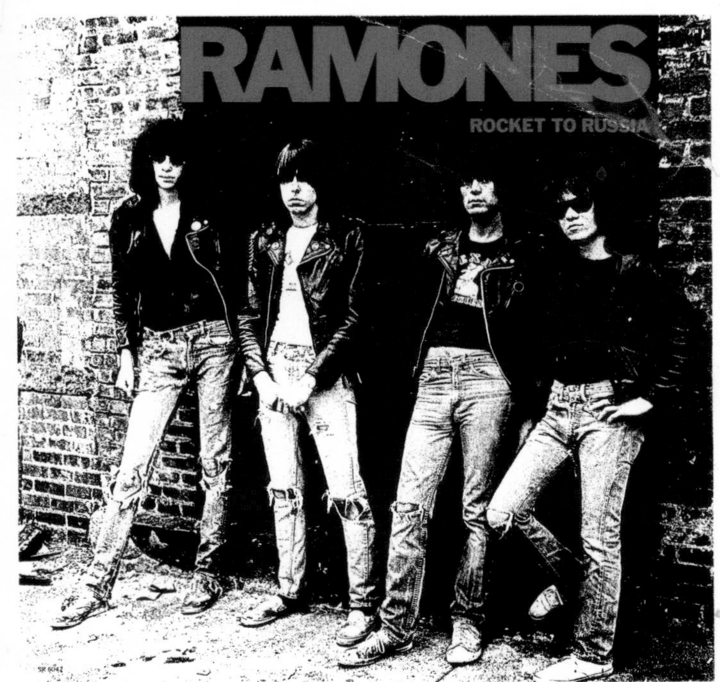
RAMONES
ROCKET TO RUSSIA
IN CONCERT

JANUARY 27, 1978
SANTA MONICA CIVIC
AUDITORIUM
8:00 P.M.

songs. He had a wonderful sardonic sense of humor and was more of an autistic savant, then a dumb boy toy that the press made him out to be. One morning Dee Dee said that Richard Hell was coming over to work on a song that Tommy and Johnny didn't want the Ramones to do. Richard showed up with his acoustic guitar and they wrote "Chinese Rocks". After the Ramones went to California Dee Dee showed up at my mother's house

unexpectedly after the tour and he had all his stuff with him. He told me that we couldn't sleep together because he had the crabs "from borrowing Arturo's bathing suit". I said "Oh that's a good one!" My mom's place was right across from St. Vincent's Hospital free clinic and I had seen every band in New York line up with their girlfriends outside the VD clinic after every tour – so I had no illusions. Since I didn't want my poor mother to be shocked into heart failure by Dee Dee's return -I grabbed a sheet of paper from the pile of assorted shopping bags that was his luggage and wrote a sign "Do Not Wake Me Up"

and tacked it to the attic door where we slept. The next morning I realized I'd taken some of his writing to make the sign. I apologized and Dee Dee said: "That's really funny because I wrote the song for you". It was "Locket Love". I finally had to admit to myself that Dee Dee was too much trouble even for me to cope with so I gave up. When the next Ramones' album came out "Locket Love" was on it but he changed the last line from "Hang on I'm getting stronger" to "Hang on you're a goner". I still think it's sweet.

THE
FAN CLUB
PO BOX
310
VERNON N.J.
07462

WOLFS
BLOOD

SAMHAIN

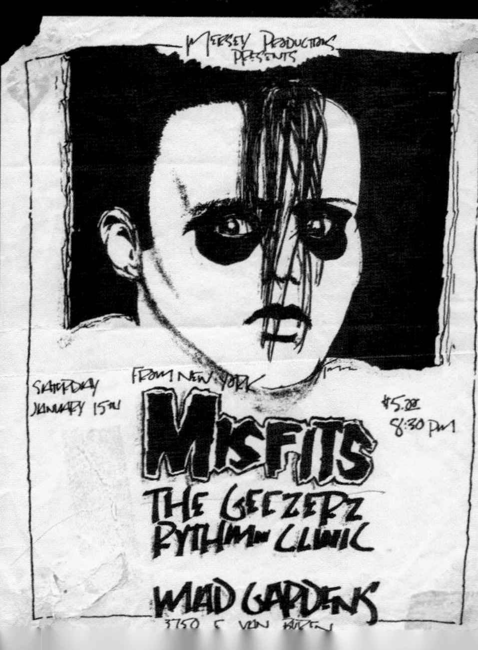
MERSEY PRODUCTIONS
PRESENTS
FROM NEW YORK
SATURDAY
JANUARY 15TH
$5.00
8:30 PM
MISFITS
THE GEEZERZ
RYTHMN CLINIC
MAD GARDENS

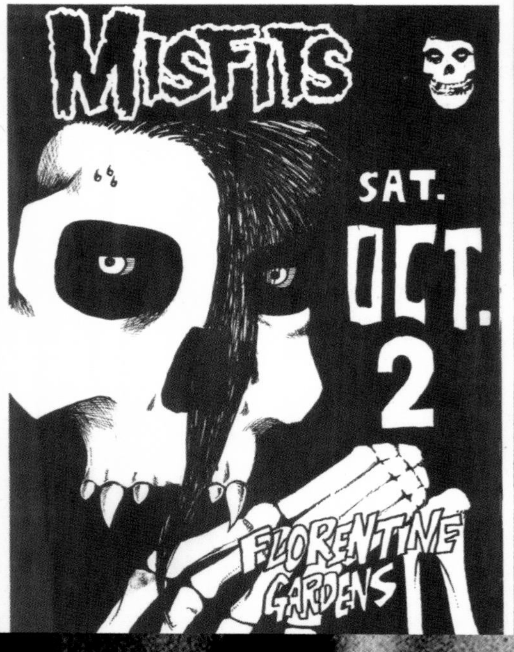
MISFITS
SAT.
OCT.
2
FLORENTINE GARDENS

MISFITS
THE EXPLOITED
7 SECONDS
Fenders
521 EAST FIRST ST.
(LONG BEACH)
C.T. 2
PRODUCTIONS
FRI. OCT 31

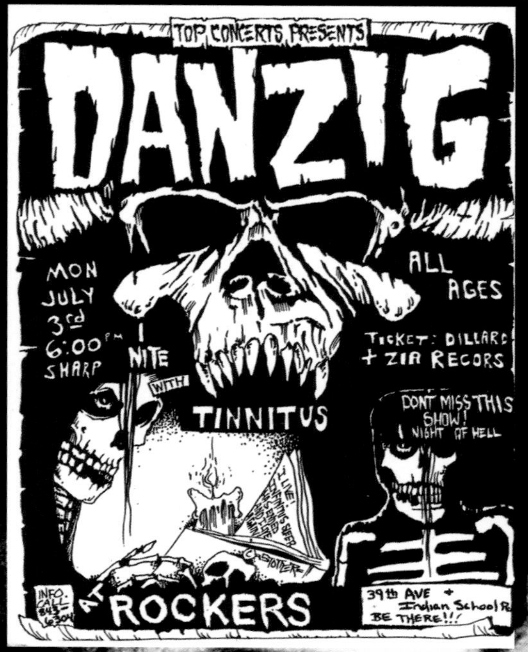
TOP CONCERTS PRESENTS
DANZIG
MON
JULY
3rd
6:00 PM
SHARP
NITE
ALL
AGES
Ticket: DILLARD
+ ZIA RECORS
WITH
TINNITUS
DONT MISS THIS SHOW!
NIGHT OF HELL
AT ROCKERS
39th AVE + Indian School Rd
BE THERE!!!

PAUL STOTTLER

9:00
THE MISFITS
NECROS
FRI.OCT30
UKRANIAN HALL: between St Marks & 9th on 2nd Ave

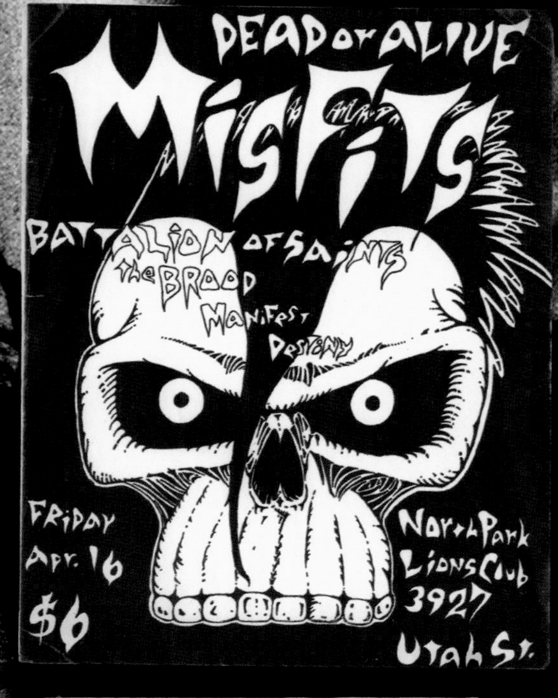
DEAD or ALIVE
MISFITS
BATTALION OF SAINTS
the BROOD
MANIFEST DESTINY
Friday
Apr. 16
$6
North Park
Lions Club
3927
Utah St.

Celebrate
TIM SOMMER'S
And
JACK RABID'S
Twentieth
Birthday Bash
SATURDAY
MARCH 27
WITH
THE MISFITS
DJ
Tim
Sommer
KRAUT
EVEN
WORSE
I'll be there!
IRVING PLAZA

EASTER HORROR SHOW
MISFITS
FLESHEATERS
UNDEAD
MEAT PUPPETS
JODY FOSTER'S ARMY
DEADLY REIGN
SATURDAY, APRIL 10. 9 TO 2AM
ELITE CLUB
1805 GEARY ST.

TIM MAZE PRESENTS
SAMHAIN
8:00 PM
THE FURY OF
SAMHAIN
THIS TIME.
WHITE
FLAG
+
Poison 13
MAY 2ND
WABASH HALL
WHERE UNIVERSITY MEETS 805
PLAN 9

BILLY STARK
BLESSED
AT CBGB TUES OCT 9
CBGB
SCREW
AT MAXS SAT NOV 3
LET THE BLESSED
take your measure
MOTHERS DAY MAY 14TH AT MAX'S KANSAS CITY
CAN YOU FIND THE 4 MISTAKES?
THE Blessed
MAXS KANSAS CITY
THE BLESSED
THE
HOWIE PYRO
I don't know why, but I have always had a passion for printed paper. From a very early age with comics, monster magazines & bubblegum cards to movie posters, record covers & many fly-ers & posters in this book. I have a deep need to save everything. When I saw these primitive posters they described exactly what I felt & what I heard. I would fill shopping bag after shopping bag with them knowing I'd need them for
something some day, and their day has come. I still save every scrap of paper that catches my eye and I'm glad this true youth art form is being recognized the world over for what it is. You can call it whatever you want...

THE POSSESSION OF
max's
kansas city
MON.
APR/L 16, 1979
THE
BLESSED

East Village Eye Summer 1980
25
NEW YORK NEW WAVE ROCKNROLL RADIO
THE BLESSED
WHBI
COSMOPOLITAN BROADCASTING CORPORATION
20,000 WATTS
STEREO
105.9
WEDNESDAY, THURSDAY, FRIDAY
MORNINGS
SUNDAY NIGHTS 2-4 AM:
IRVING PLAZA ROCK 'N ROLL SHOW
BARRY PUBLICATIONS

HOWIE PYRO
BLESSED
MAX'S SAT. JUN. 30
HOWIE PYRO

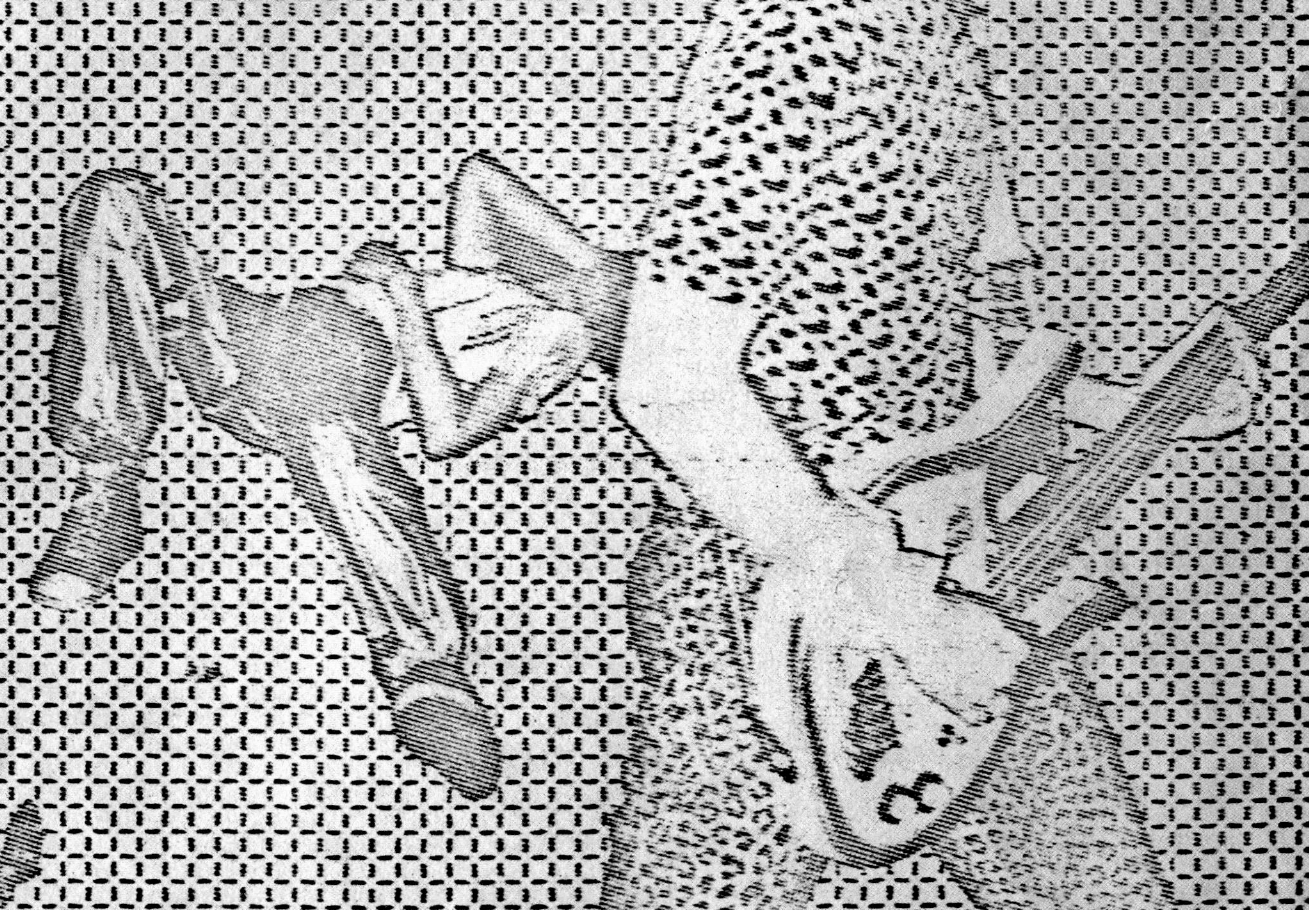

MIDNITE
MAY 28
Cycle Slut
THURSDAYS
ONLY $5.00!
PRESENTS
BASEMENT OF
THE LISMAR
LOUNGE...
41 FIRST AVE.
FREAKS
WITH
THE SKULLS

HOWIE PYRO

HOWIE PYRO
BLESSED
MAX'S
WED. AUG. 29

FREAKS
EARLY SHOW
9:30 PM
NEW MUSIC SEMINAR
FRI. JULY 14TH
CBGB
315 BOWERY
WITH:
PRONG 10:30 PM
RAGING SLAB 11:30 PM
WHITE ZOMBIE 12:30 AM
DEADON 1:30 AM

FREAKS
HEAVY ORANGE
TUES.
JULY 26TH
WITH THE CHEEPSKATES
ROCK
622 BROADWAY (AT HOUSTON)
AT: BIG KAHUNA

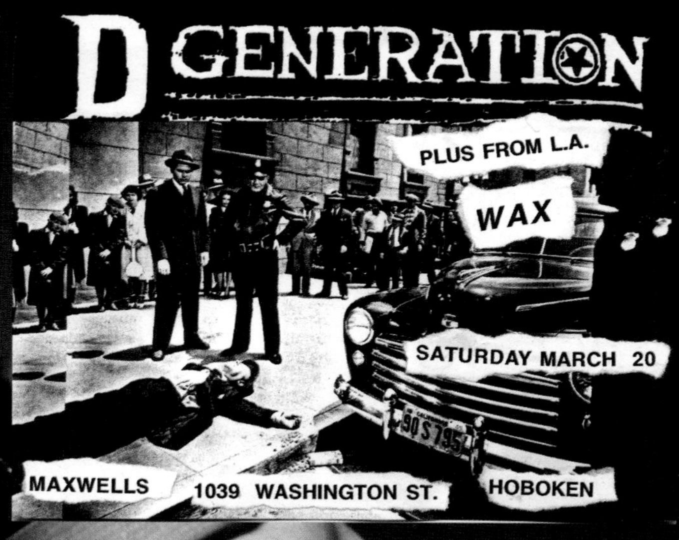
D GENERATION
PLUS FROM L.A.
WAX
SATURDAY MARCH 20
90 S 795
MAXWELLS
1039 WASHINGTON ST.
HOBOKEN

D GENERATION

D GENERATION
Murphy's Law
7:30 PM
All Ages
Coney Island High
15 St. Marks Place bet. 2nd & 3rd Aves.
212-674-7959
Advance Tickets Available!
Costume Contest with cash prizes and special guests judges!
HALLOWEEN BASH!
Friday, October 31, 1997
with Backseat Driver
The Shooting Party
Electric Monster
Heal!
Under The Gun
Electric Frankenstein

NEW YEAR'S EVE !
D GENERATION
TUES. 31 DECEMBER 1991
UNACHICKS
KAREN BLACK
OODOO DOLLS
MAJYK PYRATE
FUR
TABASCO ROAD
CBGB
OMFUG
315 Bowery NYC • (212) 982-4052

D GENERATION

MORE STARS THAN

HOWIE PYRO

When I was a kid, before punk rock, I was obsessed with rock & roll. I was rabidly listening to the Velvets/Lou Reed, Alice Cooper, Sweet, Slade, Bowie, Roxy Music, mott plus 50's & 60's stuff. I was avidly pouring over Rock Scene & Creem magazines...my bibles! Both of these mags leaned heavily towards the underground, so around

1975/76 when punk was brewing I was quite aware of it, though unable to hear it. When punk really started to take shape & records started to be released, I became obsessed. I'd go to the Palladium on

14th street (now an NYU dorm like CBGB will be soon) an all ages concert hall, and walk up to 17th street & Park Ave. south & peek into the window of Max's Kansas City. I was too young to get into what seemed to be this mythological magic wonderland I had been reading about for years. Sometime in 1976 the first punk store in the USA opened on St. marks place in the Lower East Side of Manhat-tan: Manic Panic. I was their first employee. The minute I entered a was accepted into this new world, this fantasy underground, I neve

looked back. I never went home again (I'd sleep in the store or in park), and no one came looking for me. When I finally got to wal into the upstairs of Max's Kansas City, I knew...this is it! /somew I belong! It was unbelievably exciting. I think I saw Blondie, Su

& the Cramps that night. My mind was blown.These people we stars. If Richard Hell or Stiv Bators came walking down St. Ma

Place or dropped into Manic Panic (a regular occurrence) I wa

HOWIE PYRO & KID CONGO - PHOTOBOOTH, HOLLYWOOD 1978

k! Soon after going to Max's that first time I
d getting to know people and was let into CBGB's
gh I was way too young to go near a bar) and saw
amones, Dead Boys, Damned and all the rest.
ted meeting a few kids my age or younger that
d weird and roamed the streets like myself. We

ed a band called The Blessed. Named partly in
of the damned, partly from a line in the Bowie
"Hang On To Yourself", & partly from an
ground comic we loved called "Binky Brown
The Holy Virgin Mary". This was when we
l to know people & get into the clubs for free. I
nber going to see the Heartbreakers at the Village

n NYC when they came back from the Anarchy
vith the Sex Pistols. I had a camera and was
ly taking pictures of the show, but I was taking
es of people in the audience like Richard Hell or
e County. They must have thought I was crazy,
these years later I know what I felt was true.
hose people/bands & that time was a very special
lot of these people became life long friends And
e lost a lot of them along the way (R.I.P.).

vill always hold a special place in my heart.
ever I see any of these people today I get a
ip my spine seeing them through my teenage
ecalling those early days when I first disco-
his special world, which I have never left.

ERE ARE IN HEAVEN!
upstairs at max's kansas city
Wed. Sept. 16, $5: Snatch 22, Hibiscus & the Screaming Violets, Pleazer
Thur. Sept. 17, $5: Afraid of the Dark, The Breakfast Club, The Worst
Fri. Sept. 18, $6: Stimulators, Nekron 99
Sat. Sept. 19, $6: The Rattlers, The Workers
Sun & Mon. — Closed
Tue. Sept. 22, $5: Sarah Steele Television Show
Wed. Sept. 23, $5: Arthur Monroe Zone, The Decoys, Malcolm Tent
Thur. Sept. 24, $5: Zainegrea, Autonomy, Headlines
Fri. Sept. 25, $6: Sic F*cks, Sally Dick & Jane
Sat. Sept. 26, $6: Lenny Kaye Connection, Ex-Husbands
212 777-7871

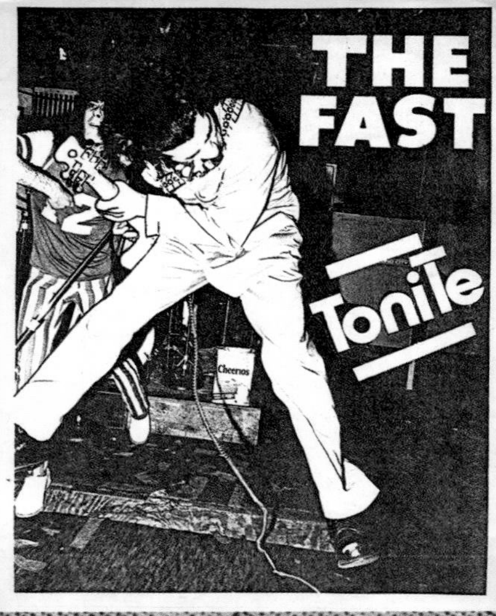
THE
FAST
Tonite

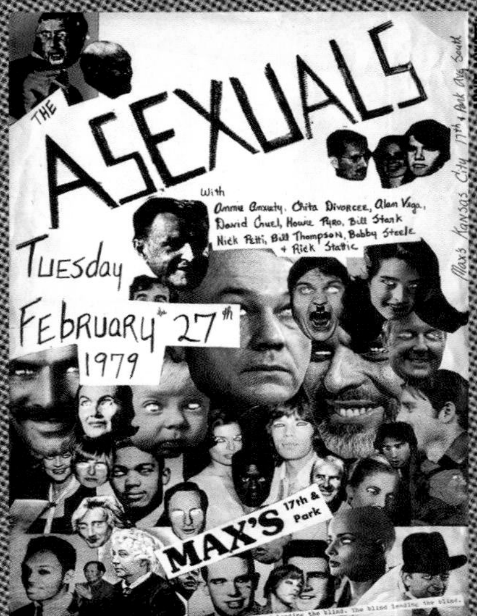
THE
ASEXUALS
with
Annie Anxiety, Chita Divorcee, Alan Vega,
David Cruel, Howie Pyro, Bill Stank
Nick Petti, Bill Thompson, Bobby Steele
+ Rick Static
Tuesday
February 27th
1979
MAX'S 17th & Park

LIVE AT MAX'S OCTOBER 15 & 16
RAM RECORDING ARTISTS
WAYNE COUNTY AND THE BACK STREET BOYS
CHERRY VANILLA AND HER STATEN ISLAND BAND
THE FAST

THURSDAY
JUNE 14th
COME
TO
THE
Puberty
Ball
SEE LIVE!
THE
BLESSED
MUDD CLUB 77 WHITE ST.

EILEEN POLK

CONCERT BILL

CBGB & OMFUG
315 BOWERY
NYC10003

ALEXANDER HAMMER
-Presents-
SUN. APRIL 24
Reagan Youth
Beastie Boys
The Blessed
Artless
You Suck
SUN. MAY 1
Circle Jerks
The MISGUIDED
The ABUSED

Doors Open 7pm Show Starts 8pm
Over 18 Only
at GILDERSLEEVES
331 Bowery (212) 533-3940

max's kansas city
Wayne County & The Backstreet Boys
LIMITED EDITION
COLLECTOR'S SINGLE
ON SALE
HERE

THE
DEMONS
CBGB'S
315BOWERY(AT BLEECKER)
TUESDAY JANUARY 4th

STEELTIPS
CBGB
AUG. 10
315
BOWERY
(AT BLEECKER)
NYC

OCT 31
HALLOWEEN
THE MONSTER MOSH
CRO-MAGS
NEVER MORE
MAMMOTH
CAUSE FOR ALARM
ULTRA VIOLENCE
REAGAN YOUTH
PSYCHOS
MURPHY'S LAW
CBGBS

WE GOT FIFI MEET US
WITH THE CASH AT
7th STREET AND AVE A
DEC 15th AT MIDNIGHT OR
THE POOCH DIES!

THIEVES IN THE NIGHT

THE YET ANOTHER RAG POSTER CHILDREN

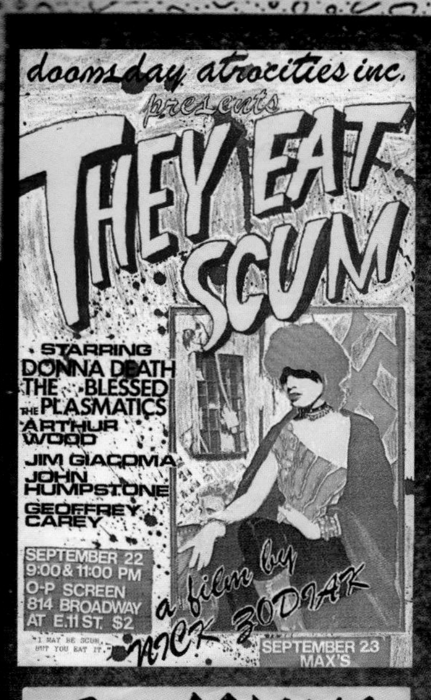

doomsday atrocities inc.
presents
THEY EAT SCUM
STARRING
DONNA DEATH
THE BLESSED
THE PLASMATICS
ARTHUR WOOD
JIM GIACOMA
JOHN HUMPSTONE
GEOFFREY CAREY
SEPTEMBER 22
9:00 & 11:00 PM
O-P SCREEN
814 BROADWAY
AT E.11 ST. $2
a film by NICK ZODIAK
SEPTEMBER 23
MAX'S

NICK ZEDD

STIMULATORS
10 copy's of FIRST RELEASED SINGLE to be raffeld-off
LOUD FAST RULES
TR3
Friday
Feb.15

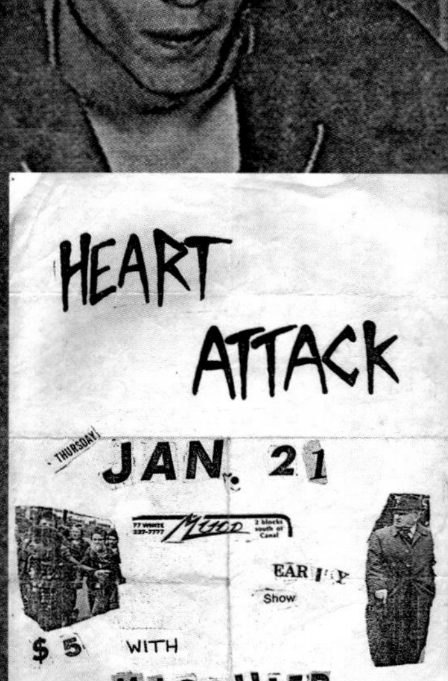

HEART ATTACK
JAN. 21
$5
WITH
MISGUIED

JESSE MALIN

GREENDOORNYC
15 ST MARKS
SATURDAY JAN 15
ALL THIS AND MORE 7$

BEASTIE BOYS
5 RING CIRCUS
FEATURING
REAGAN YOUTH · THE BLESSED
ARTLESS · YOU SUCK
GREAT GILDERSLEEVES 331 BOWERY
THIS SUNDAY · APRIL 24
EIGHT PM

CAN THIS YOUNG ENGLISH LAD REALLY BE PLANNING TO CORRUPT THE YOUTH OF AMERICA?
FIND OUT! AT
max's kansas city
ON Fri. + Sat. - Nov. 10 + 11
APPEARING WITH: THE CRAMPS.
LEVI & THE ROCKATS
BE THERE - OR BE SQUARE !!! - NME.

TAXI DRIVER
MIDNIGHT
FRI JULY 30
& SAT 31
ST. MARKS CINEMA
MOHAWKS HALF PRICE

THE MAD
SUNDAY OCT. 12th.
MAX'S
WEDNESDAY OCT. 8th.
CBGB

THE MAD
SAT MARCH 22
AT
SEDATION
247 W 35th st. Bet. 7th and 8th Ave

from Washington D.C.
BAD BRAINS MEETS THE MAD
BENEFIT CONCERT at
TIER 3.
225 West Broadway
The NIGHT of OCT 15th MONDAY

THE MAD
MAX'S KANSAS CITY
FEB. 22
FRIDAY

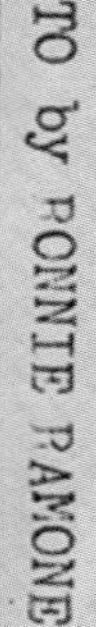

BOTTOM ROW: SCREAMING MAD GEORGE

FOTO by RONNIE RAMONE

SPECIAL TIGER BEAT, HEART-THROB PIN-UP (left to right): JESSE, JAVIER, PAUL

PLASMATICS
SEE LIVE
ONLY BRITISH SHOW
AUG 8
BANNED
HAMMERSMITH ODEON
RECORD OUT NOW ON STIFF
WENDY SAYS 'IF YOU WANT TO SEE ME T-R-A-S-H AN AUTOMOBILE, DON'T MISS THIS SHOW'

COME DANCING

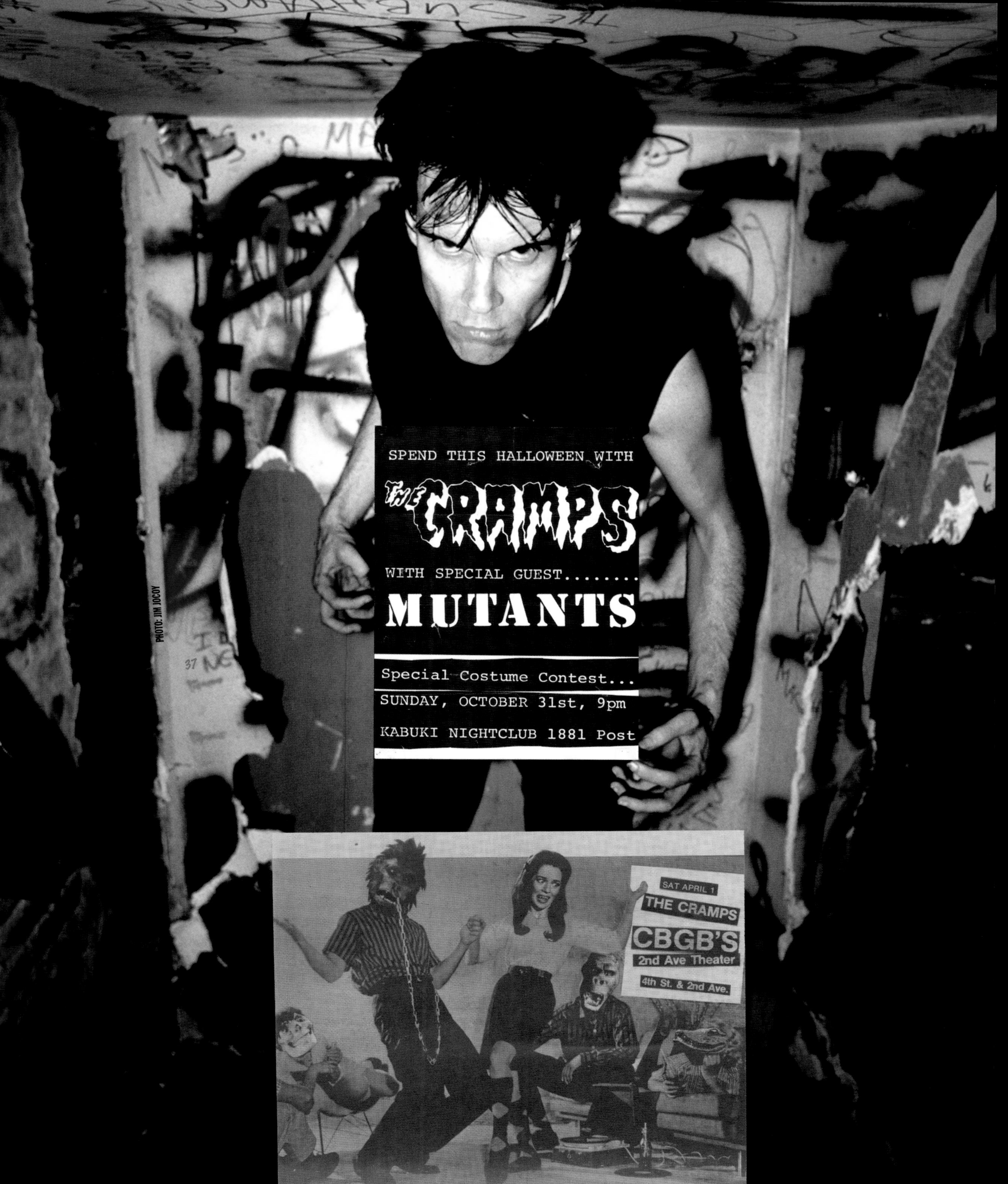
SPEND THIS HALLOWEEN WITH
THE CRAMPS
WITH SPECIAL GUEST........
MUTANTS
Special Costume Contest...
SUNDAY, OCTOBER 31st, 9pm
KABUKI NIGHTCLUB 1881 Post
SAT APRIL 1
THE CRAMPS
CBGB'S
2nd Ave Theater
4th St. & 2nd Ave.
PHOTO: JIM JOCOY

THE CRAMPS
Filthy lyrics,
sexy rhythm,
drinking and
lonely kids—
Does it all
lead to
secret sex
and disease?
DOES ROCK 'N' ROLL
BREED V D?
ASK THE
CRAMPS
AT
MAX'S
KANSAS CITY ON
SAT. NOV. 27
THE CRAMPS
... THE MEN DONT KNOW BUT THE LITTLE
GHOULS UNDERSTAND.
CBGB
FEB. 18 & 19

THIRTY NINE

MIRIAM LINNA

The Cramps asked me to join the band on drums in the Spring of '76. The fact that I had never played any musical instrumentmade me a shoo-in. I spent a year beating the traps for them. The limited-- okay, non-existent-- degree of talent and training within the combo didn't stop the bop until I got derailed and replaced by truly talented and trained Nicky the K, a great guy and well deserving of his shot at the hit parade. That first year in NYC was a full-on hazing into the wild, wild world of sho-biz. And I love that world. Funny how a year in the life boils down to a fading file folder with a few handbills, a business card and some out of focus snapshots.

FRI. SAT. DEC. 29 – 30
MAX'S KANSAS CITY
ROCKABILLY VOODOO
THE CRAMPS

THE CRAMPS
HUMAN FLY / DOMINO
VENGEANCE RECORDS 330 PARK AVE. NY NY 10028

KID CONGO POWERS

Asking me to write about my time in THE CRAMPS (1980-83) is akin to asking someone about their very first childhood sweetheart. My memories are often romantic, full of wonder, and slightly traumatic. Things that happened to me were: °quitting college, °using my first Fuzz pedal °wearing Ivy's latex straight skirt onstage °playing guitar while being hogtied by Lux's mic cord and dragged around the stage night after night on tour °having Nick Knox leap over his drum set and dousing my head with beer when a candle on my amplifier set my much lacquered bouffant aflame °and the scariest event of all-being asked to fill the, pointy high heels of Bryan Gregory after he spooked off in the middle of the night! I guess my romantic notions are a bit different than some others'. The first time I took notice of The Cramps was in an issue of Rock Scene magazine in a "new bands" photo essay on the New York CBGB punk rock music scene. It might have been 1976 or '77. I saw frizzy hair, cat eye sunglasses, black mascara rimmed eyes plus a lot of bone structure and bad attitude. There were boys and girls in the band and the scowls on their faces were highlighted by a supreme arrogance. The few words accompanying the photo mentioned Rockabilly, B Movies and "Surfin Bird". I thought to myself, "Hmmm.. My kind of people" and kept flipping thru the mag. Not too long after that I received a letter from my LA music connection, Trudy, who was in NYC checking out the music scene. In the letter she waxed enthusiastic, even orgiastic, about "THE BEST band I have ever seen", which happened to be THE CRAMPS. I didn't doubt her taste. After all, she took her look from James Williamson of The Stooges, and I had met her at Ramones shows and knew her friends from the pre-punk fanzine, Back Door Man. Fast-forward another few years. By 1980 I had not only become a rabid fan of THE CRAMPS, their records, their artwork, their look and aesthetics, I had become a friend of the band. I had tripped with Bryan Gregory, had been leapt on by Lux Interior, and had even written a song about Poison Ivy in my own Cramps inspired band, The Gun Club. They were everything I had been looking for in a band: sexy, raw, dangerous, funny, scary, smart, stupid, gorgeous and unusual (no bass!). I used the word "orgiastic" earlier in this essay, and that was always the mood at a CRAMPS show. Anything could happen, and usually did. Imagine my surprise when they asked me to join the band!

It was just the beginning of my lesson in music as well as in life. The lesson I learned is that I will never learn my lesson. At least I hope not.

THE CRAMPS
3 WAYS DIFFERENT
FROM A RAZOR
FAN CLUB
322 east 73rd. # 12
NEW YORK N.Y. 1002

CBGB's Oct. 12, 13, 14
THE CRAMPS
ROCKABILLY
VOODOO
ROCK ROCK
ROCK

MYSTERY
GUEST
THE CRAMPS
DATE...

THE
CRAMPS
FANS
KNOW
HOW TO BE COOL
..ITS SO
SIMPLE.

LOVE ME.
THE CRAMPS

D. C.
8. julij ob 20h
menza
ŠN
DJ:2227
gsf, cidm, hc
Washington
D.C.
SCREAM
Design: 2227
2227

As our first trip had brought us to Amsterdam and a besieged crowd of hundreds, which included a large contingent of Italians who had driven 30 hours just to see us play. WOW. We now had made that drive ourselves to Italy to reciprocate in kind. Usually the shows there were held at leftist squats or socialist centers. Few of the mainstream clubs catered to Punk Rock at that time and the socialists latched onto this with zeal, and as well, we were all of like mind and protest. The particular squat we were to play had been targeted by the authorities, as all were from time to time, and unfortunetly they struck at the one we were intended to play they day before the show, and I do mean they blew the fucking roof off. They bombed the place!

So you're thinking..."I'm not going in there...they might come back!!" The air still stunk of gun powder and mace and the sun was shining in hard due to the lack of a rooftop. But with spirit and purpose that got us there...AND the fact that we needed the money, we played! That was kind of our part in rebuilding the place. I had worked on this little castillion like guitar piece along with Dave before the show and that night during the set we stopped right in the middle, at which point we both pulled out chairs center stage and sat down to perform the new number. The crowd went nuts and clapped rhythmically faster and faster and faster to an explosive end! The only light on the stage at the time was the light cast by the beautiful moon shinning through the roof that was no longer there.

FRANZ STAHL

SCREAM SCREAM SCREAM
FROM WASHINGTON D.C.
GOD
HOLLAND
SAB. 22 OTT.
CENTRO SOCIALE LEONCAVALLO
VIA LEØNCAWALLØ 22

STIR

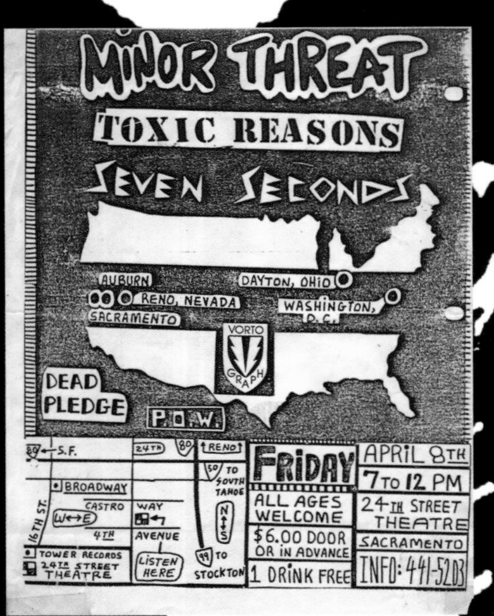
MINOR THREAT
TOXIC REASONS
SEVEN SECONDS
AUBURN
DAYTON, OHIO
RENO, NEVADA
WASHINGTON, D.C.
SACRAMENTO
VORTOGRAPH
DEAD PLEDGE
P.O.W.
FRIDAY
APRIL 8TH
7 TO 12 PM
ALL AGES WELCOME
24TH STREET THEATRE
SACRAMENTO
$6.00 DOOR OR IN ADVANCE
1 DRINK FREE
INFO: 441-5203

HARDCORE
WILSON CENTER 6/25
15th & Irving St. NW, WASHINGTON DC Doors Open 7:00 pm
GOVERNMENT ISSUE • From Boston GANG GREEN
FAITH • ARTIFICIAL PEACE • SCREAM • DEADLINE

GOVERNMENT ISSUE
the SCREAM
FROM D.C.!
FALSE ALARM
from Monterey
Wed AUG. 11
ON BROADWAY

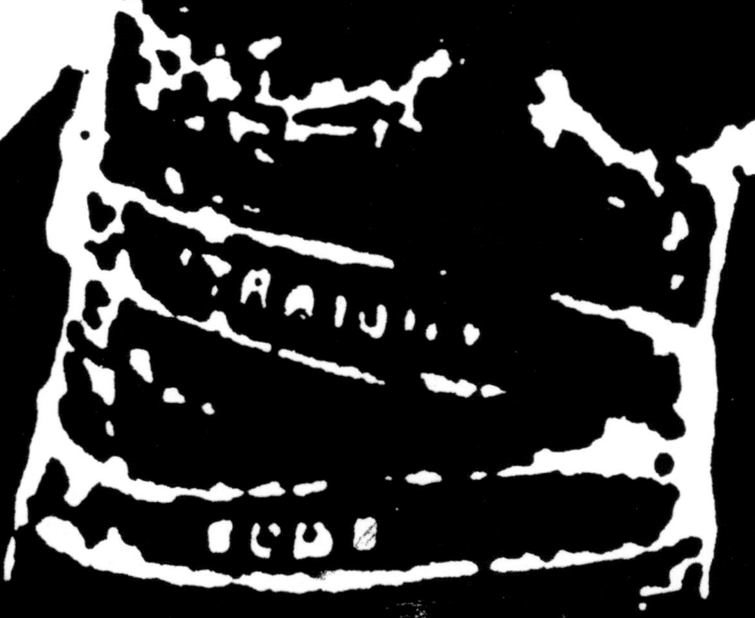

THE SHOW OF THE YEAR!!
MEATMEN
$4.00
W/ THE IDEALS

TUESDAY JUNE 23

RITZ

4.00 COVER

SEX PISTOLS
100 CLUB

100 CLUB
TUESDAY'S IN MAY
11, 18 & 25
100 OXFORD ST.

SEX PISTOLS
T.V. boxing MATCH ALI v DUNN
100 CLUB
SEX PISTOLS PARTY
TUESDAY MAY 25
100 OXFORD ST.
8pm.
LATE BAR, TIL MIDNIGHT
+ SUPPORT TED CARROLL'S rock on disco
Creation, Stooges, Dolls, Teenage

SEX PISTOLS
TUES 15th

100 CLUB
100 OXFORD ST, W1
sartorial
correctness
Sex Pistols
and a CASt (PLAStER)
7.30 till LAtE. bars

PUNK 1
100 CLUB, 100 OXFORD ST
SEX PISTOLS
CLASH
SUB WAY SECT
SUZIE AND THE BANSHEES
AND FROM FRANCE
STINKY TOYS
OPEN 7 PM LATE BAR
ADMISSION £1.50
(£1.00 NUS ETC.)

The
SCREEN
on Islington GREEN
MIDNIGHT

SEX PISTOLS

MON 17th
ADMISSION
FREE.

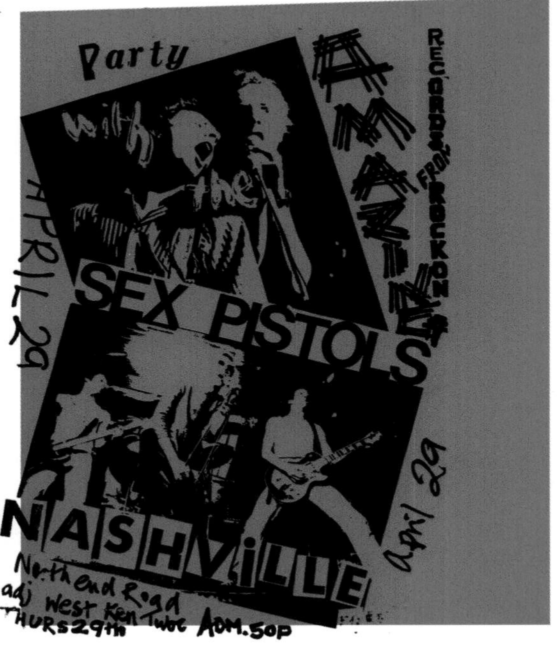

Party
SEX PISTOLS
APRIL 29
NASHVILLE
North End Road
adj West Ken Tube ADM. 50p
THURS 29th
april 29

EL PARADISE
club

BREWER ST W1
Sunday april 4TH
7P.M-2AM

SEX PISTOLS

1976
ANARCHY IN THE U.K. TOUR
SEX PISTOLS
FIRST MAJOR U.K. TOUR WITH SPECIAL GUESTS
THE DAMNED
JOHNNY THUNDER'S HEART BREAKERS
(Ex New York Dolls from U S A)
THE CLASH
TOUR DATES
Tickets From
FRI 3 DEC NORWICH University
SAT 4 DEC DERBY Kings Hall
SUN 5 DEC NEWCASTLE City Hall
MON 6 DEC LEEDS Polytechnic
TUE 7 DEC BOURNEMOUTH Village Bowl
THU 9 DEC MANCHESTER Electric Circus
FRI 10 DEC LANCASTER University
SAT 11 DEC LIVERPOOL Stadium
MON 13 DEC BRISTOL Colston Hall
TUE 14 DEC CARDIFF Top Rank
WED 15 DEC GLASGOW Apollo
THU 16 DEC DUNDEE Caird Hall
FRI 17 DEC SHEFFIELD City Hall
SAT 18 DEC SOUTHEND Kursaal
SUN 19 DEC GUILDFORD Civic Hall
MON 20 DEC BIRMINGHAM Town Hall
TUE 21 DEC PLYMOUTH Woods Centre
WED 22 DEC TORQUAY 400 Ballroom
SUN 26 DEC LONDON Roxy Theatre Harlesden
Students Union, U.E.A.
Kings Hall, Derby
R.E. Cords, Derby, Burton Slect a Disc
Nottingham Record Centre, Long Eaton
City Hall
Village Bowl
Students Union, Leeds Poly
Hime & Adamson, Manchester
Virgin Records, Manchester
Students Union, Lancaster University
Virgin Records
Top Rank, Cardiff
Buffalo Records
Colston Hall
Apollo, Glasgow
Caird Hall
Students Union, Technical College
City Hall – Wilson Peck Records
Usual Agents
Usual Agents
Town Hall
Virgin Records
Woods Centre
400 Club
Roxy Theatre
SINGLES AVAILABLE
THE DAMNED.NEW ROSE HELP (BUY 6)
Available from even your dumbest dealer
SEX PISTOLS. ANARCHY IN THE U.K. (EMI 2566)
Available from your cleverest
TOUR PRESENTED BY ENDALE ASSOCIATES
IN ARRANGEMENT WITH MALCOLM MACLAREN

JOE SIB

It is safe to say that my musical upbringing was a bit strange. I lived on a farm in the mountains of Santa Cruz California until I was about 10 years

old. My only contact with music was what my parents would play in the house and what I heard on a small blue transistor radio my Grandmother gave me. Jerry Vale, Elton John, Vicky Carr and Sinatra were my parents jams and my blue radio was pulling in ABBA, The Carpenters and maybe

if I was lucky a Hall and Oats track. Lucky? Sounds pretty bad when I think about it now, but the strange thing was I loved it. I bought my first

record at a flea market that was held every Saturday in the Sky View Drive-In parking lot. My friends and I decided to split the three bucks to purchase the first release by The Clash. I quickly convinced them that it would be best if I took home "our" new record first. They said "yes" and that was it. That launched my swan dive into punk rock. At this point I was in the 6th grade at Good

school run by the hardest group of Nuns in the Catholic Church

or at least I thought that while I was there. We even had to wear a uniform that consisted of green cords, a white dress shirt and a green sweater. How punk is that? Around this time The Ramones, The Clash and Devo were all in heavy rotation in the Sib household. But, one album still needed to

be acquired... The Sex Pistols "Never Mind The Bollocks". I was convinced that buying this album was basically purchasing a ticket for the "Straight to Hell Express". It was Saturday morning when I took the bus from

my house so I could get to our local record store, The Record Factory, by the time they opened. I quickly made my way over to the 'S' section and there it was. I made the purchase and started the journey

on my turntable quick enough. Then it started, "Is that marching?" I asked myself as the opening chords of "Holidays in The Sun" filled my tiny bedroom. Then, Johnny Rotten came in and I just about pissed my pants. I was lost in a world of sound that my ears had never heard before.

Just the name "The Sex Pistols" had me scared, but now the album cover along with the sound had me completely frozen with fear. Just when I thought Satan himself was going to appear in my bedroom the track "Bodies" kicked in. When the bridge came in and J.R. began screaming "fuck this and fuck that, she don't want a baby that looks like that", I basically jumped on my record

player like it was a live grenade. To hear the word recorded, let alone screamed over Steve Jones wa guitar was

just too much for my sheltered 12 year old mind t I immediately turned off the record and proceede to The Record Factory to return it. I was consum guilt. How could I spend money on something tha wrong but sounded so great? I was confused. I w and filled with punk rock anxiety. I exchanged m "Never Mind The Bollocks" for a Kingston Trio r my Mom. I believed this was the only thing I cou save myself.

For days I couldn't get The Pistols out of my min wouldn't pass without me hearing them in my hea three Pistols songs were scratched onto my brain week of going back and forth I finally gave in

and went back and bought the album again for th time. That same weekend I cut my hair, bleached hydrogen peroxide), "pegged" my Levi's, bought black high top converse, took one of my Dad's "c shirts" and started wearing my new uniform. Tha changed my life and most importantly put me on

and great road of "Rock and Roll". Thanks Sex I

FROM BEYOND THE GRAVE

Sid Vicious ACTION MAN £12·50

THE SWINDLER 8P SEX PISTOLS comic

SOMETHING ELSE
C/W
Friggin' in the Riggin'
FROM THEIR NEW ALBUM........ON VIRGIN RECORDS VD2510
THE GREAT ROCK 'N' ROLL SWINDLE

SEX PISTOLS

ER MIND THE BOLL

we STOCK SEX PISTOLS

ROLLING STONE
CARL BERNSTEIN: CIA AND THE PRESS
The Silkwood Case: Part IV By Howard Kohn
ROCK IS SICK AND LIVING IN LONDON:
A Report on the Sex Pistols
By Charles M. Young
Ronstadt's 'Simple Dreams' By Peter Herbst

SEX PISTOLS
AT WINTERLAND S.F. CALIFORNIA
Jan.14.1979
STATUS

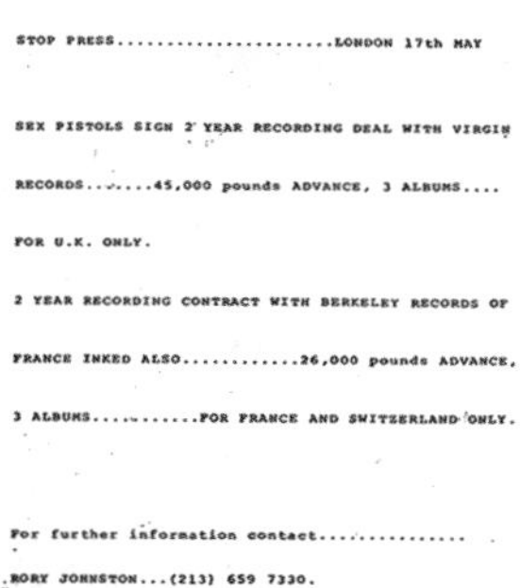

|SEX PISTOLS|

STOP PRESS........................LONDON 17th MAY

SEX PISTOLS SIGN 2 YEAR RECORDING DEAL WITH VIRGIN RECORDS........45,000 pounds ADVANCE, 3 ALBUMS.... FOR U.K. ONLY.

2 YEAR RECORDING CONTRACT WITH BERKELEY RECORDS OF FRANCE INKED ALSO............26,000 pounds ADVANCE, 3 ALBUMS............FOR FRANCE AND SWITZERLAND ONLY.

For further information contact...............

RORY JOHNSTON...(213) 659 7330.

WE STOCK
SEX PISTOLS
WHILST STOCKS EXIST

"PISTOLS LAST SHOW AT WINTERLAND, SAN FRAN"

SEX PISTOLS & SEX AND VIOLINS
FROM
the NERVEBREAKERS
JANUARY 10th. LONGHORN Ballroom 216 CORINTH & ST.?
ALSO See the Nervebreakers At:
FANNIE ANNS JANUARY 9th, 11th, 12th 4714 GREENVILLE AVE.
MUDDA BOOZE 4015 LEMMINZ AV JANUARY 6th & 7th After Hours
Ya'll Come!! No
Art by LADY F. & B. KOEDA

LADY F./ B. KOEDA

SEX PISTOLS
SEX PISTOLS
SEX PISTOLS
GUN CONTROL

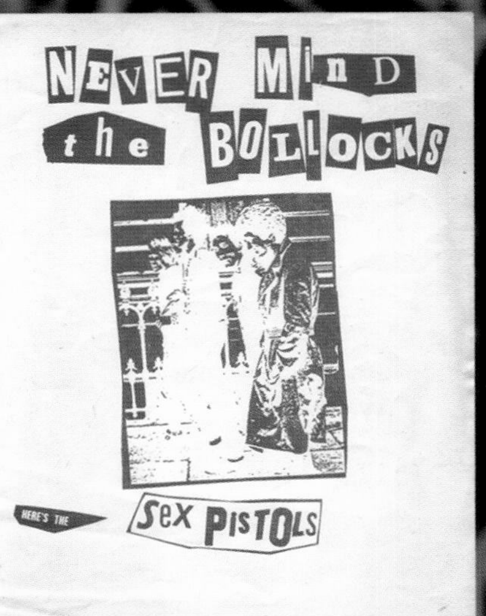

NEVER MIND the BOLLOCKS
HERE'S THE
SEX PISTOLS

MALCOLM MCLAREN SPEAKS TO DOUG WOODS

DW: How do you feel about what punk has become? **MM:** After 25 years, Punk has become a standard, almost dictionary definition of the anti-establishment look used by the establishment. I don't think the underground uses it any more. Now it's a fifty-year- old guy

at an advertising agency or a media empire or a film company. . .In essence everyone from the bank, political parties, airlines, Time Warner and the National Water board are using that aesthetic, the punk look, to look cool. I think that what Punk represented was

anti-fashion. We were out to prove that ugliness could be beautiful. And now, of course, even if they don't know about that rhetoric, or the roots of that aesthetic, they sort of unconsciously think that it belongs to them. Punk has become a popular look. It's no longer earth shattering

new or confrontational. It's very much part of fashion now. In that sense it has lost it's power as an aesthetic.To be both a criminal and an artist at the time was the same thing. Criminals and artists have one thing in common, they both break rules. They can also both change

lives. Punk for me was a moment in which our nihilistic and artistic, gangsterish, behavior was called into design. The design aspect for us was, in a word, failure. Failure as a global pursuit. . . and better to be a flamboyant failure than any kind of benign success. **DW:** You spent time in new york in the early seventies. What were you inspired by while you where there? **MM:** Obviously much. I've always been a kind of hands-on curator. That instinct of selecting ideas that you think you might genuinely profit by, you select. I saw lots of ideas in New York. What was exciting to me was the lonely and postured nihilistic look of the bass player from Television, Richard Hell. That shoe gazing, broken purposeful t- shirt, slightly raggy, hair erupting singing Blank Generation. He was a

great anti-fashion icon. Jonathan Richman was also an influence. There was something about him. I think it was the homegrown, spontaneous, do it your self, look like you're not trying very hard while singing a song with a million mistakes in it thing. It doesn't flow terribly well, but it's okay. It's that haphazard, incorrect, unprofessional manner that I definitely took back home and was inspired by. This New York image was very sexy to me and I had to take it back with me in any shape I could. I felt like Oscar Wilde, some phenomenal entrepreneur, wandering like a philanderer across the

American landscape bumping into these curious images. What I was doing was a form of co-opting, but when I got back to England it took on a new form. The interpretation will always change t he subject. Other images that I remember were from underground shops like the Pleasure Chest. T-shirts found in these, rather daunting

for me, shops full of whips and chains, were great inspiration. They were extraordinary. I brought them back to the Sex Shop and reworked them adding slogans and such. Ultimately, they ended up being worn by kids who became known as punk rockers. **DW:** How did vivienne westwood and the sex shop play into this? **MM:** Vivienne was my girlfriend before the Sex Shop. My first incarnation was called Let it Rock and it opened after I left art school on 1971. Vivienne, at the time, was a schoolteacher. She was very square and a church girl. She was persuaded to stop teaching and come work with me in this store that I had acquired. This was where I was going to create this anti-fashion statement, an extension of my art school where one could run wild and do anything. This was my domain. I would change the law. I would break all the rules and Vivienne would become my conspirator. After a couple of incantations, we arrived at the Sex Shop. It was at this

point that I took a sabbatical and ran off like a mad groupie to follow the New York Dolls. Inadvertently, I became their de-facto manager. This led me to the Lower East Side where I saw Dick Manitoba, bits of the Ramones and bits of Blondie. The only ones that were really on it were Television. Later, I went back to London where my girlfriend was holding court at the Sex Shop and we had these kids that were driving me mad to make them rock stars. . .

with Disc Parade

Great show biz offer:
the result
THE MEN IN BARDOT'S LIFE
YUL BRYNNER
—absorbing new series

MARGARET CLEWS

liar

liar
liar

MALCOLM: ANDY ROSEN

"It's more difficult to be avant-garde today. You couldn't do something like Punk now. People have gotten used to everything."

VIVIENNE WESTWOOD

SEX PISTOLS

Tuesday July 6th

100 CLUB

100 OXFORD ST W.1.

TUESDAY JULY 6

SEX PISTOLS + the Damned

8 – 12pm

LATE BAR

100 CLUB

BANG

SID VICIOUS ACCUSED OF MURDER

Evening
STANDARD

Chelsea Hotel

RM 101 – Erwin Basch, on 10/12/78 early morning, heard loud female screams TIME? Not Home

RM 102 – Vera Mendelsson – on 10/12/78 about 0730 hrs she heard female moans coming from Rm 100 Interview

RM 103 – Loria Garcia – on 10/12/78, she heard a male crying, saying, stop playing, let me in, also heard knocks & kicks on door of Rm 100 – Interview
TIME?

RM 224 – Jake Fleder – Same statement as on D.D.5 Interview

Check Night Bartender at Reynolds Bar 20 St & 2 Ave Re: Sid Vicious being in a fight there at – a week or 2 ago – Show Photo

Rm 228 – Sid looking for Drugs at 0530 Am 10/12/78??

Ritchie Aug 28 Moved in (Oct 2, Changed Room Oct 2 – fire to mattress

on T.V. – Floater phone call to Nor [illegible] – Day after he appeared 9 & 10 Am – [illegible] 3-4 Pm
Male voice – stated "[illegible] like to leave a message [illegible]

KNYB LETS
AM.NY0303039.CA0194200.
28639 FILE 25 PD NEW YORK CITY, NY NOV
TO PD LOS ANGELES CALIFORNIA

RE: NANCY SPUNGEN FEMALE WHITE 20 YRS
VICTIM OF HOMICIDE THIS CITY ON 10/12/78

RE: SID VICIOUS AKA JOHN SIMON RITCHIE MALE WHI

ABOVE SUBJECT ARRESTED FOR HOMICIDE OF ABOVE SUB

THIS DEPT REC'D INFO THAT A T-SHIRT WITH ABOVE V
KNIFE IN STOMACH IS BEING SOLD UR CITY, WITH THE
"SID SAY'S I DID IT MY WAY" OR "I DID IT MY WAY"
TO CHECK AND SEE DATE WHEN MANUFACTURED, COMPANY
WHO AUTHORIZED ABOVE T-SHIRT. ALSO IF POSSIBLE
SAMPLE OF T-SHIRT BE FORWARDED TO NYCPD, 1 POLIC
ROOM 700M, ATTN: DETECTIVE THOMAS 3RD HOM ZONE.
PAID BY NYC DIST ATTORNEYS OFFICE, N Y COUNTY.

PLS REPLY TO OUR TTM 28639.
AUTH INTER-CITY CORR UNIT NYCPD OPR/MCGOWAN
DET THOMAS 3 H/Z

FREE
SID VICIOUS

SID bit OFF more Than HE CouLd Chew
but HE Did IT HIS way

ADDRESSES

NAME JOHN ROTTEN
STREET
CITY CHELSEA
PHONE 352-2917

NAME SOPHIE RICHMOND
STREET
CITY
PHONE 402-0062

NAME JOHN ROTTEN
STREET HOME
CITY FINSBURY PK. N4
PHONE 263-0070

NAME ROGER - SCREEN
STREET
CITY
PHONE 589-3994

57

URE WITH
QUOTO
PT REQUESTS
ADDRESS, ALSO
OULD LIKE A
NY ZIP 10038
SES WILL BE

23 HRS

SID'S PHONE BOOK

ADDRESSES	TELEPHONE
JOHN C.	
6 BRUNSWICK GDNS. OFF KEN-CHURCH ST	221-
KENSINGTON W.8	0392
JORDAN	834-
1016 KING'S HOUSE	8961
ST JAMES CT. BUCKINGHAM GATE VICTORIA SW1	
JOHN H.	
9 HUGON RD SW6	
337-3459	
JULIAN H.	731 2254
JOHN H.	337-3459
JOHNNY THUNDERS	
9 DARBLEY ST.	
5th FL. SOHO W.1	
LONDON	

'eY, siDneY? do yA knOw HoW wE coUld mAkE SuM eXtRa $$ 4 tHe HoliDayS, hUH? dO ya????
eH? . . . yEah suRe, nAncE.
wE NeEd thEsE tYpeS: pUnks, new WavErs, bIkeRs, CoWboYs/cOwgirls, sId ViCious & NanCy SpunGeN LOok-AliKes, loNg-HaiRs
aNd wE NeeD yOU to DreSs in 1978 fAsHionS anD stYle
IF wE cHooSe YoU, yOU'll Be paId $35 fOr eaCH daY yOu wOrK, plUs luNCH!!!!
LoVe KiLLS
wRitTen
aLeX coX &
diRecTed
aLex cOX
— A ZENITH PRODUCTION —

HOWIE PYRO

Johnny Ramone took me to see The Clash at Bonds. I told they'd be great as I'd seen them a few times before. In the middle of the show leaflets were dropped on the audience and a political speech was made… Johnny lost his mind and started to scream 'FUCKIN' COMMIE BASTARDS!', and insisted that we leave…Real performance art…

★ EXTRA ★

Designed by DEADLINE DESIGN, INC.

FOR INFORMATION: (212) 944-6075

BOND INTERNATIONAL CASINO
NEW YORK CITY, MON. JUNE 1, 1981

45TH STREET AT BROADWAY

The CLASH WILL PLAY!

BOND SETS NEW DATES FOR INCONVENIENCED CLASH FANS

TICKETRON TICKET HOLDERS

ALL TICKETRON TICKETS WILL BE HONORED ON ORIGINAL DATES EXCEPT:

ORIGINAL DATE	REVISED DATE:
THOSE TURNED AWAY MAY 28th	EVE. JUNE 4 (THURS.)
MAT. MAY 30	MAT. JUNE 6 (SAT.)
EVE. MAY 30	EVE. JUNE 6

BOND TICKET HOLDERS

ORIGINAL DATE	REVISED DATE
THOSE TURNED AWAY MAY 28th	EVE. JUNE 4 (THURS.)
MAT. MAY 30	MAT. JUNE 13
EVE. MAY 30	EVE. JUNE 13
EVE. MAY 31	EVE. JUNE 12 (FRI.)
JUNE 1	EVE. JUNE 8 (MON.)
JUNE 2	EVE. JUNE 9 (TUES.)
JUNE 3	EVE. JUNE 10 (WED.)
JUNE 5	EVE. JUNE 11 (THURS.)

BOND WILL EXCHANGE ALL TICKETS FOR THOSE FANS WHO CANNOT ATTEND NEW DATES. THANK YOU.

PAUL: EILEEN POLK

ASUC SUPERB FILMS PRESENTS
FRIDAY, FEB.24
$3.00
Rock Night CO-SPONSORED BY KALX
THE CLASH
in
RUDE BOY
URGH!
A MUSIC WAR
D.O.A.
A RIGHT OF PASSAGE
8:30
10:30
6:00
WHEELER AUDITORIUM
FELLINI NIGHT

The CLASH

AZAZEL JACOBS

It was the summer of 1982, and the family was spending it in Colorado. I was given a choice between nine dollars in quarters for the arcade, or my sister taking me to see The Clash at Red Rocks, which was the price of the ticket. When my sister protested so loudly even before I could answer, I knew my choice was made. I was nine years old, a little brat. We set out the day before the show, my sister with another friend the same age as her '13', and a couple in their early twenties that were I guess our chaperones, but also huge clash fans, and we camped out right in front of the entrance all night. I'd say there were as at least thirty other people doing the same, drinking, smoking and hanging out late into the night. I remember some one offering a blowjob to a security guard so that she could get in early. When my ears were covered by an adult I took special notice of that conversation. The next day, we took our places right in the very front. I remember seeing my first Mohawk sitting there in the crowd, the guy would stand up every hour or so and let out a war cry and everyone would cheer. My sisters' friend got smacked in the face for wearing swastika earrings. There was a rumor flying around that the surprise guest warm up band was going to be the Stray Cats. It was a long wait until the bands came on, and once again to my sisters embarrassment, I brought along my Mad Magazines, which turned out to be a big hit, and soon I was passed around along with them. I was safety pinned, hair was spiked, someone put a lock and chain around me that was too heavy. I came out of the punk factory line and suddenly 'not' The Stray Cats began to play and a storm of beer cups and garbage was hailed upon them and they ran for shelter on their third song. I have no idea who the band really was. We waited some more and then it got dark. I remember the slide machines starting on stage. Images of war and rebellion were cast huge upon the stage and then The Clash came out. I think people got a bit pissed that they had to avoid crushing a little kid as they danced, but instead of pushing me to the back, a skinhead put me on his shoulders and he stood right in front of the stage. Strummer was only a foot away from me and I swear I remember him leaning towards me. I had only heard Combat Rock at the time, so those were the songs that stuck, when they played Radio Clash the place went crazy. Allen Ginsberg took the stage for Ghetto Defendant. By the time of the encore I was exhausted and found a place where I could just sit and watch. At that moment at that place is where I saw IT. I remember thinking to myself as I watched, 'this is truth, this is life, this is what its all about'! My parents said I came back a different kid.

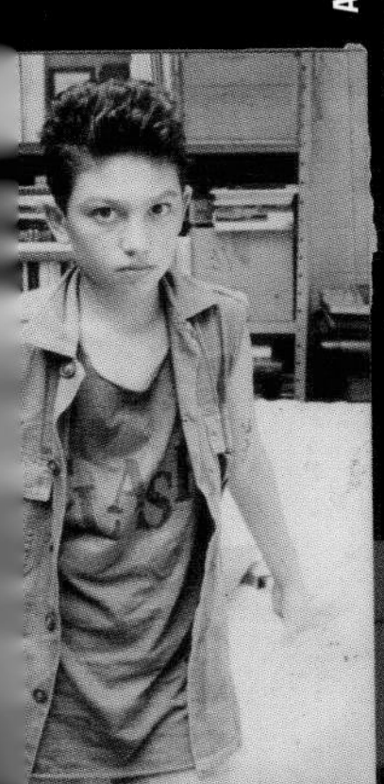

THE CLASH
BLACK
MARKET CLASH

1977
Starts
at The Roxy
41-43 Neal St
Covent Garden
Saturday 1st Jan '77
bar open 8pm-2am
With The CLASH
+ Chelsea + Sounds.
Adm £1-25
2 sets 9:30 and 12:30

on Boxing day The Clash played a small gig for family and friends. It was in a small

club underneath the West Way fly over on the Portabello Road. About fifty people at the most turned up for a very fun enjoyable gig. I was working with

my mates who owned a T Shirt

company known as 5th Column. They were one of the first silk-screen companies on the block at the start of the punk era. I would shoot all the pics and help them with the photo process of

getting images on to the screens. We basically did most of the Punk bands of any worth. Anyway that was the reason we were invited - we were doing all the Clash T-shirts for their upcoming tour. (I did the pics for their original London Calling T-shirt)

At the time the Clash were just another punk band - better than

the Rock Stars they were to become. Funny thing was I shot about 10 rolls of black and white and decided not to develop them. Money was tight in those days - so I would sometimes just not bother processing the film if I felt the band was not worthy of the expense. Looking back on it what an idiot I was. Years (two decades) later

unprocessed film I had left In London at my mum and dads. There they were clearly labeled THE CLASH. I excitedly processed them and to my amazement I realized I had cap tured a precious moment in Rock And Roll history - which might never have been seen. A band in all their

innocent glory - playing to

ANDY ROSEN

into punk history as one of the most prolific Punk Bands ever. Looking back on it now it was a great moment not that I could see it at the time - I was probably stressing

about how I was going to pay for the processing - all my mates were around, a few warm pints, live music,

the punk scene. We all felt part of something, not quite sure what but it felt important and the future didn't matter much

- right then we had enough. (Lucky my never threw out all those old bags of ST I left with her for a few decades)

34—MELODY MAKER, April 30, 1977

There's a wh

Two Nights - at - Of Action.
THE COLLISEUM
MANOR PARK RD HARLESDEN NW10
Saturday 12th March.
The CLASH
Generation X
The Slits.
£1.00 each night
Friday 11th March
The CLASH
Buzzcocks
+
Subway Sect
10.45pm — ONWARDS.
HERE
positive

JOE STRUMMER: ANDY ROSEN

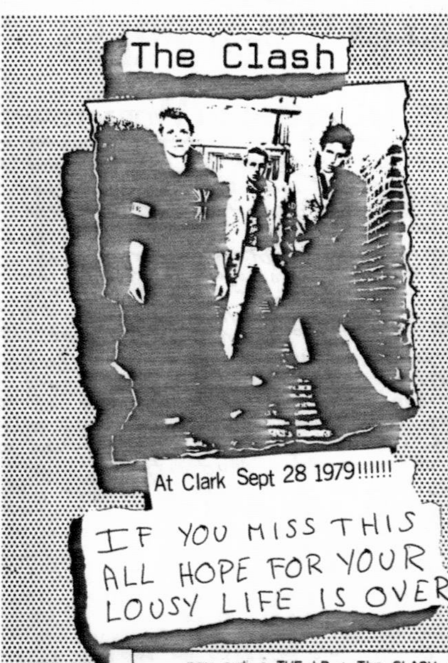
The Clash
At Clark Sept 28 1979!!!!!!
IF YOU MISS THIS ALL HOPE FOR YOUR LOUSY LIFE IS OVER
... now out + THE LP + The CLASH

MELODY MAKER, April 30, 1977—P

e riot goin' on!

en

'new yooth' PRODUCTIONS PRESENT:

"WHITE RIOT IN THE FILLMORE!" WITH

THE BEST BAND EVER, DIRECT FROM ENGLAND!

FEB 8TH THURS. 9:00 P.M.

ALSO: THE ZEROS and NEGATIVE TREND PLUS....

~~$3.00~~ 1839 GEARY and FILLMORE ST.

MINORS OK.

"NEW YOOTH" IS A NON-PROFIT ORGANIZATION. ALL FUNDS GO TO FINDING A NEW HALL FOR ALL BANDS TO PLAY.

Sorcerer Inc. 79.

Punk au BAtaClan

50 Bld Voltaire. Paris 11e. 700 3012

CLASH

Jeudi 29 Septembre
19 h 30

DamNed

6 octobre. 19 h 30

LOCATION 3 FNAC

c K
CLASH
A RIOT OF YOUR OWN!

COLLAGE BY TOMOMI

999
X3
0014

JOE STRUMMER BY X3 BOB LINNEY

X3
0080

JIM PURSEY BY X3 BOB LINNEY

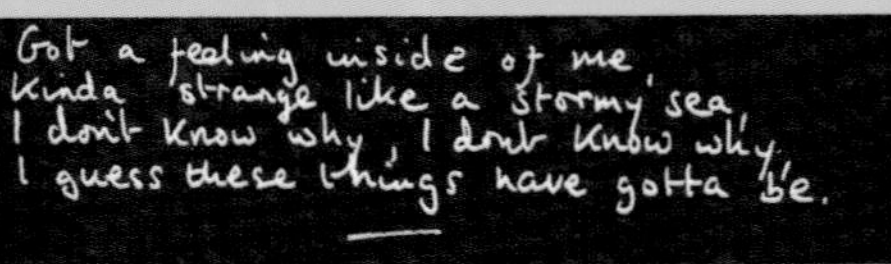
Got a feeling inside of me
Kinda strange like a stormy sea
I don't know why, I don't know why,
I guess these things have gotta be.

No don't you run away that way,
we can come back another day.

Got a new Rose, got her good
Just like I knew that I always would,
Ain't got time to mess around
Got a brand new Rose in town

I don't believe that it's happening to me,
Its not true, why should it be

Goldenvoice
In Association With
Avalon Attractions
Proudly Welcomes
From England
The Damned
Social Distortion
ALL AGES WELCOME FULL BAR WITH I.D.
PALLDIUM 6225 WEST SUNSET BLVD. HOLLYWOOD CALIF. (213)466-4311
MARCH TWENTY FIVE TUESDAY EIGHT P.M. ENDS ELEVEN P.M.
TICKETS AVAILABLE AT
SELECTED GOLDENVOICE OUTLETS PALLADIUM BOX OFFICE
TICKETMASTER

FROM ENGLAND
THE
DAMNED

SAT.
FEB.
13
&NECROS
NEGATIVE APPROACH
$7
CLUTCHCARGO
(CLUTCH CARGO'S) 64 W. ELIZABETH DETROIT

The Damned

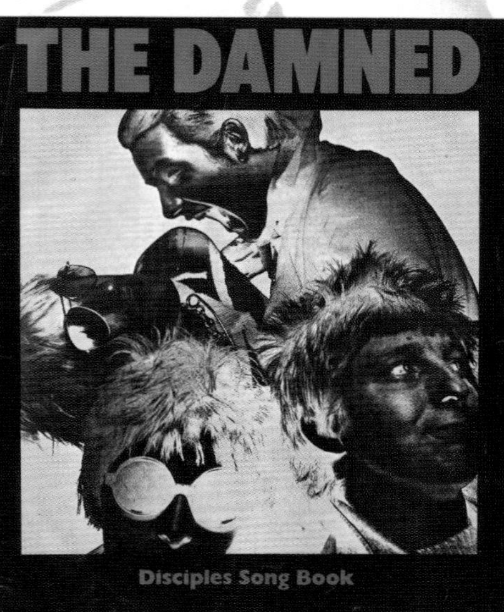
THE DAMNED
Disciples Song Book

GANG OF FOUR

Prism & Cellar Door Productions present
GANG of FOUR
Friday, October 14 · 8pm
Grand Circus Theater · Detroit

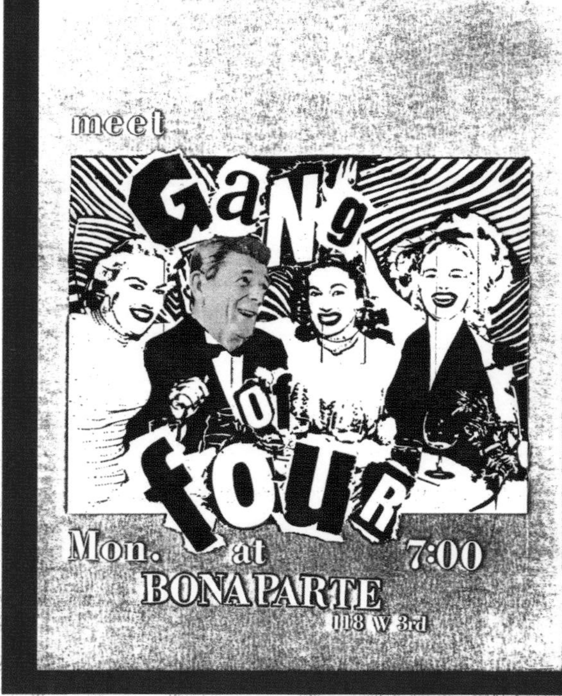

meet
GANg of four
Mon. at 7:00
BONAPARTE
118 W 3rd

CHARGED
G.B.H
MDC
Unruled
SCUM
Spectrum

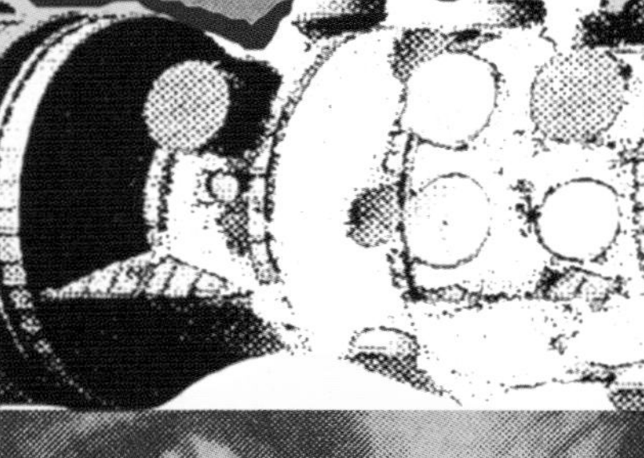

Plate 3.
G.B.H

GOLDENVOICE presents
A SHOW WITH A MESSAGE
'FUCK OFF WANKERS'
THE BRITISH ARE COMING!
THE EXPLOITED
AND
U.K. SUBS
FRI MAY 10
PLUS
AGNOSTIC FRONT
+ Dr Know
+ DON'T NO
OLYMPIC AUDITORIUM
1801 S.GRAND-LOS ANGELES
TICKETS available at and these record stores

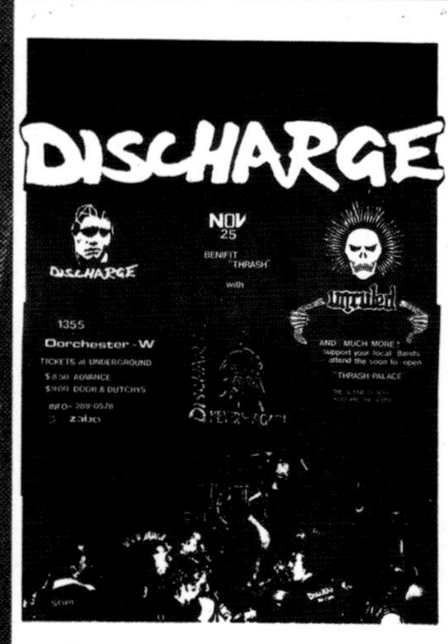

DISCHARGE
NOV 25
BENEFIT "THRASH"
with
Unruled
1355 Dorchester - W
AND MUCH MORE
"THRASH PALACE"

Dec.9
PETER AND THE TEST TUBE BABIES
CRUCIFIX
no policy
SCUM
1355 DORCHESTER WEST INFO-288-0578
TICKETS - $8.50 at UNDERGROUND (CORNER SHERBROOKE & BLEURY)
DUTCHYS - $9.00 - ADVANCE ($9.50 DOOR)

FEBUARY - 7 - 8 PM
D.O.A.
no policy
SCUM
3767 BERRI - THE CHURCH
SHERBROOKE
FREE DOA SINGLE WITH $7.50 ADVANCE TICKET AT DUTCHYS - UNDERGROUND
INFO-288-0578
Get your single at the door

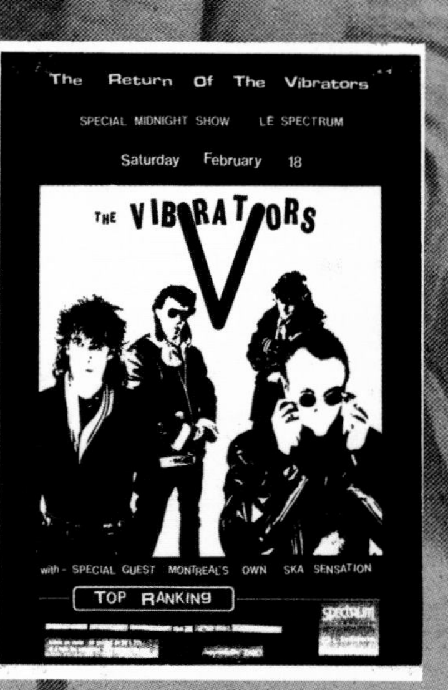

The Return Of The Vibrators
SPECIAL MIDNIGHT SHOW LE SPECTRUM
Saturday February 18
THE VIBRATORS
with - SPECIAL GUEST MONTREAL'S OWN SKA SENSATION
TOP RANKING

FINAL SOLUTION PRESENT, IN AID OF THE CAMBODIA FUND
THE POP GROUP
SCRITTI POLITTI AND D.A.F.
UNIVERSITY OF LONDON UNION, MALET ST, WC1, 7.30PM, FRI. 16TH NOV.
+ THE MIGHTY OBSERVER SOUND SYSTEM
TICKETS £2.00 ON THE DOOR OR IN ADVANCE FROM, SMALL WONDER, ROUGH TRADE, HONKY TONK + LUIGI & THE BOYS (HANWAY ST. W.1) RECORD SHOPS, NEW POP GROUP SINGLE 'WE ARE ALL PROSTITUTES' RELEASED SOON ON ROUGH TRADE RECORDS

SLITS

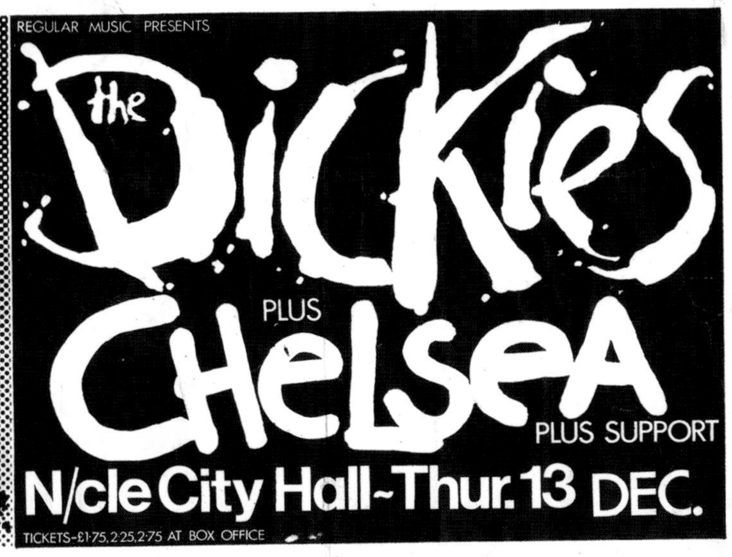
REGULAR MUSIC PRESENTS
the Dickies
PLUS
Chelsea
PLUS SUPPORT
N/cle City Hall~Thur. 13 DEC.
TICKETS-£1·75, 2·25, 2·75 AT BOX OFFICE

GREYHOUND
PARK LANE CROYDON
★ Surrey's Premier New Wave Venue ★

Sunday 12th Feb	SIOUXSIE AND THE BANSHEES
Sunday 19th Feb	WIRE + STUKAS
Sunday 26th Feb	ADVERTS + ALT. TV
Sunday 5th Mar	RICH KIDS
Sunday 12th Mar	MOTOR HEAD
Sunday 1[illegible] Mar	VIBRATORS
Sunday 26th Mar	GENERATION X
Sunday Apr 2nd	Buzz Cocks

PLUS ! Peter Fox Lites and Sounds
LICENSED BARS MEMBERSHIP 7 pm
P.T.O.

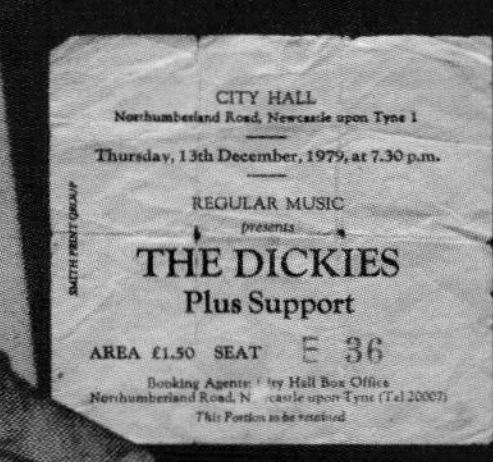
CITY HALL
Northumberland Road, Newcastle upon Tyne 1
Thursday, 13th December, 1979, at 7.30 p.m.
REGULAR MUSIC
presents
THE DICKIES
Plus Support
AREA £1.50 SEAT E 36
This Portion to be retained

THE PLASTICS
Japan Scene
PHOTO: KAORU PUNK IJIMA

松下弘子
SID VICIOUS ANALECTS
[本編中より]
俺はダサい
永遠にダサい
根っからパンクだ
—— SID VICIOUS
ナンシーはシドにとってヘロインの運び屋
ヒマさえあれば注射を打ってた —— JOHN (Vo)
裕福なガキがパンクスになるのは哀れだ
胸クソが悪くなる あいつらは軍隊だ
カッコだけキメてる —— SID VICIOUS
ジョンは私が嫌いでシドから離そうとした
何ヶ月も何ヶ月も —— NANCY SPUNGEN
あいつだけ・・・俺がプレイしたいのは
たった二人だけで。 —— SID VICIOUS
クソ溜めから救うために俺もクソにまみれる
友達のためなら喜んでそうする —— JOHN (Vo)
俺があいつの座を奪い、
新ロットンを狙うと誤解した —— SID VICIOUS
俺はジャンキーとして一生を過ごしたくない
—— SID VICIOUS
みんなシドを愛してたのよ
どこのギグでもシドが一番輝いてた
ジョンなんてカスよ —— NANCY SPUNGEN
何ひとつ楽しくない 地下に住みたい
—— SID VICIOUS
ヴィシャス 哀れな愚か者
—— JOHN (Vo)
発掘映像が語る真実。セックス・ピストルズ最新作!!
NO FUTURE
ノーフューチャー
A SEX PISTOLS FILM
DIRECTED BY JULIEN TEMPLE
FILMFOUR提供■セックス・ピストルズ協力■JERSEY SHORE/NITRATE FILM PRODUCTION製作■ジュリアン・テンプル監督作品
■©FilmFour Ltd. MCMXCIX■原題:THE FILTH AND THE FURY
www.no-future.org
大ヒット公開記念
SPECIAL!!! TALK LIVE開催!!
第一弾 11/17 (fri) 18:50〜
朗読会/出演:三代目魚武濱田成夫
第二弾 11/24 (fri) 18:50〜
トークショー/出演:SORROW川村カオリ他
スペシャルゲストあり
GLEN MATLOCK
AND THE PHILISTINES
Sun.3.Dec. Shibuya ON AIR WEST
Open 18:00/Start 19:00/ADV.¥5,500
大ヒットFUCKIN' 絶賛公開中!!
渋谷道玄坂
ザ・プライム6F
シネセゾン渋谷
☎03 (3770) 1721
連日 11:35 2:00 4:25 6:50
※毎週水曜日¥1,000均一
www.cinemacafe.net/theater/css/
PSYCHO BUSINESS BY HIROKO MATSUSHITA

COMES L.S.D
JELLY

GIG VOL THREE 3

HARD CORE

L.S.D OFFICE

江東区古石場1-5-1

あらのしんじ

Go for Broke!

THE CLAY

RESIST FASCISM

TERRORISTIC GIGS

10,23 SUN 屋根裏
WITH EXECUTE あぶらだこ

11,10 THU 屋根裏
WITH COMES P.C.G

11,13 SUN 屋根裏
WITH GISM ~~COMES~~ GAUZE L.S.D E.T.C...

2:20 (SUN) PM 7:00 ¥600
VOL.2. HARD CORE PUNK GIG
GISM. EXECUTE. COMES. CLAY
KIMONO MY HOUSE

消毒GIG VOL 7
11,15(MON
GAUZE
GAUZE 1周年記念GIG
ゲスト
AXE BOMBER
EXECUTE
AT LOFT
まえうり ¥1000
とうじつ ¥1200
PM 6:30~
PM 10-11

ソドムの市
11.7 薔薇色の夜 VOL 4
AT
渋谷
ヤネウラ
GISM
ソドム
ACHY
オープン 6:30
スタート 7:00
ソドムの
スケジュール

NEWS OF THE PUNK

ノイジング・マシーン
THE COMES GIG

7.15 HOSEI UNIV., BIG HALL
03 (264) 9470
PM 6:30~
500 YEN

7.16 EXPLOSION
03 (267) 8785
PM 6:30~
1200 YEN
ドリンク付

8.4 SHIBUYA YANEURA
03 (464) 6031
PM 7:00~
1500 YEN
ドリンク付

8.14 CHIBA DANCING MOTHER'S
0472 (47) 7045
PM 7:00~
1500 YEN
ドリンク付

GASTANK GIG

8.10 鹿鳴館 9.6 EXPLOSION

DEAR FRIENDS マツムラ ヨシト ヨルハジマデ 0492-42-7696

8.10
6:30
鹿鳴館
OUT OF ORDER GIG
GAUZE
GASTANK
EXECUTE

FLYING
WARHEAD
GASTANK
POWER AND GLORY

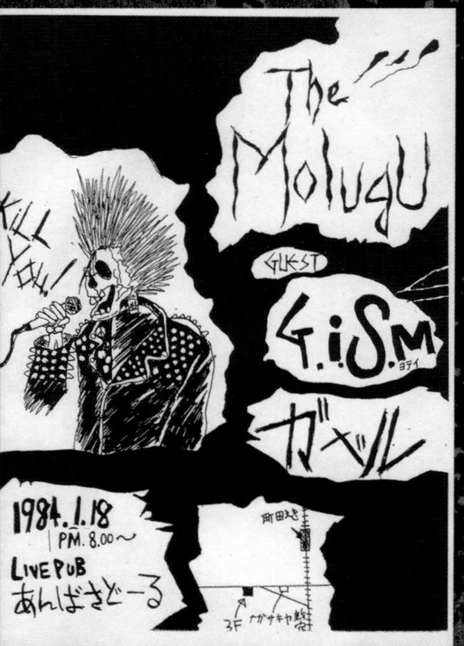

The Molugu
KILL YOU!
GUEST
G.i.S.M
ガベル
1984.1.18
PM.8.00~
LIVE PUB
あんばさどーる
町田え
3F

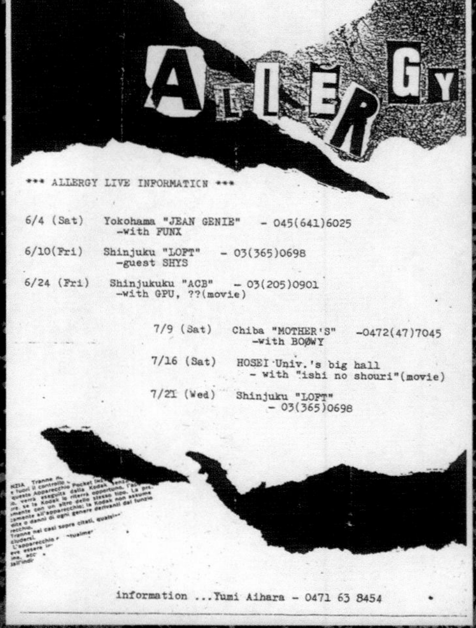

ALLERGY
*** ALLERGY LIVE INFORMATICN ***
6/4 (Sat) Yokohama "JEAN GENIE" - 045(641)6025
-with FUNX
6/10(Fri) Shinjuku "LOFT" - 03(365)0698
-guest SHYS
6/24 (Fri) Shinjukuku "ACB" - 03(205)0901
-with GPU, ??(movie)
7/9 (Sat) Chiba "MOTHER'S" -0472(47)7045
-with BOØWY
7/16 (Sat) HOSEI Univ.'s big hall
- with "ishi no shouri"(movie)
7/21 (Wed) Shinjuku "LOFT"
- 03(365)0698
information ...Yumi Aihara - 0471 63 8454

HARD CORE
GIG
VOL
EXECUTE
GISM
COMES
LSD
11,8
PM 2:00
ヤネウラ

消毒GIG VOL 28

GAUZE
LIP.CREAM
SYSTEMATIC DEATH
S.V.S
LAST BOMB
POISON
DEATH SIDE
DIASTASE
RED ARMY

PAY NO MORE THAN ¥500

5,18(SUN) 鹿鳴館 3:30〜 ¥500

消毒GIG VOL17
1.13(FRY)
目黒CAT CITY
GAUZE
COMES
SYSTEMATIC DEATH
CHAOS U.K.
6:30〜
前売・予約 ¥ 800 +ドリンク
当　日 ¥1000 +ドリンク
GAUZE OFFICE
325-0708

GAUZE
消毒GIG VOL12
6,17(FRI)
鹿鳴館
FACT AND CRIMINAL
GAUZE
TRASH
LSD
6:30〜
前売・予約 ¥1100
325,0708

消毒GIG VOL18 鹿鳴館
CORETIC VALENTINE DAY
2.14(TUE)
GAUZE
COMES
TRASH
SYSTEMATIC DEATH
6:00〜
前売・予約 ¥1300
当　日 ¥1500
GAUZE OFFICE
325-0708

GASTUNK

EXECUTE

7.21 (土) 1984 屋根裏

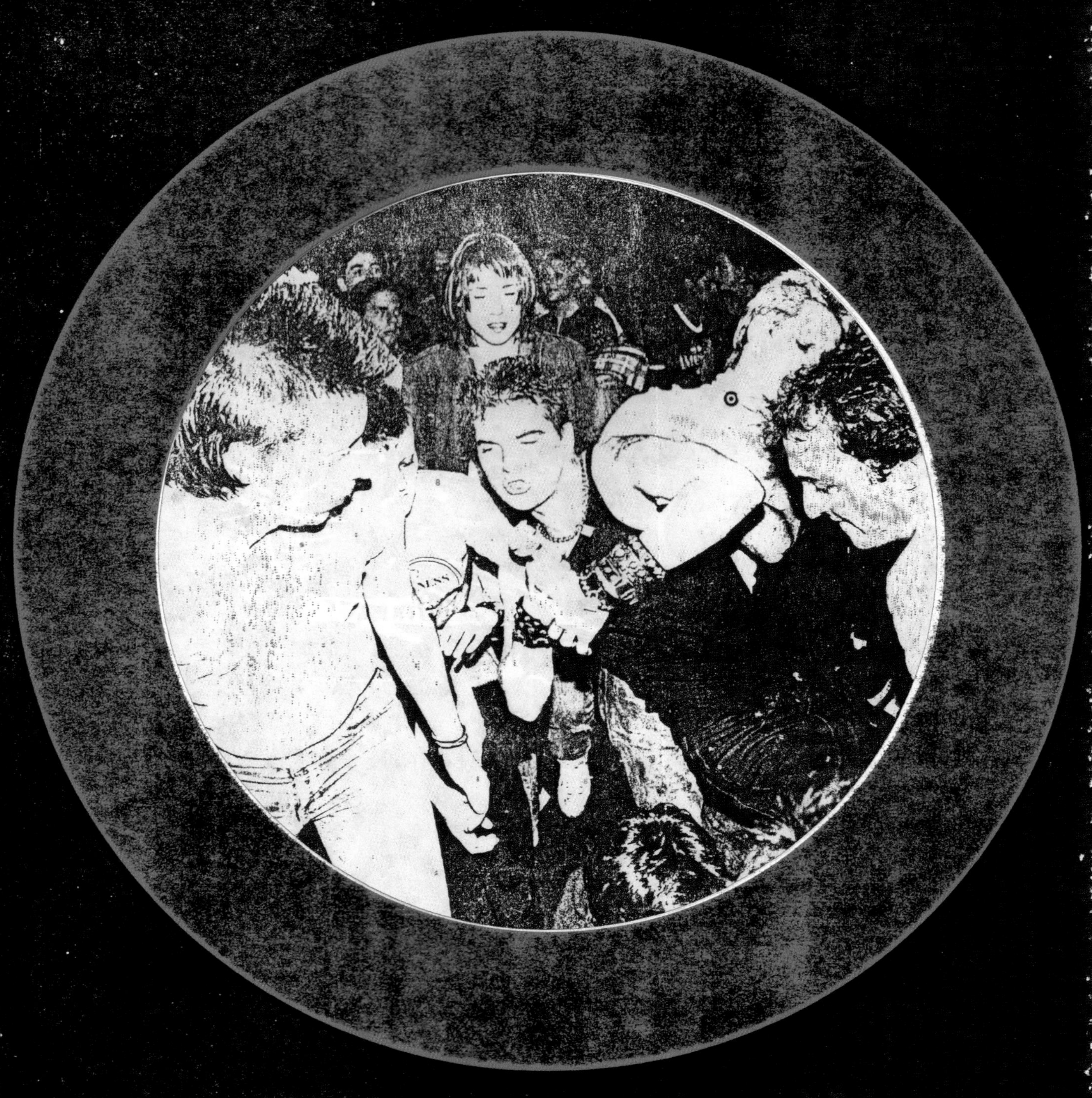

GOOD NEWS
FOR PEOPLE
THE GERMS
THE MIDDLE CLASS
THUR. MAR.13
THE FLEETWOOD
260 N. HARBOR
9PM
REDONDO BEACH

SAT 22ND
Germs G.I.
MIDDLE CLASS
BLACK FLAG
RED CROSS
THUR 27th
U.X.A.
BLACK FLAG
Vidi-ots.
Audio
RED CROSS
HONG KONG CAFE
NO AGE LIMIT
425 GIN LIN WAY - 628-6217

LOVE
KROQ PRESENTS
GERMS
GERMS
AND NEEDLES AND PINS
AT ELKS HALL
MAR 10
DAVE GIBSON 78

DAVE GIBSON

More than a pain
HAVE YOU THE NERVE TO FACE
THE MIGHTIEST MONSTER OF ALL!
WITH THE EXTERMINATORS
KRAY-ZEE HOMICIDE
AT THE ZOO
MONDAY DEC. 12 9:00 PM
EYES WILL POP AS FRIENDS GASP!
1724 E. McDowell $1
THE FIRST SIN WAS COMMITTED THERE!
...BUT THEY'RE STILL BLASPHEMING GOD!!!
THE CONCLUSIVE ACT OF MAN'S CRAZY HISTORY!
MASS MURDER OF BELIEVERS !!!
SATAN RELEASED ???
you need Death
SHOCKING MENACE
So much to do, so much to see at such little cost.

ORIGINAL ART BY DON BOLLES (PRE-GERMS!)

GERMS
(G.I.)
SATURDAY SEPT. 22ND
The sound of the 80's
MIDDLE CLASS AND
BLACK FLAG
HONG KONG CAFE
(213) 628-6217
425 GIN LING WAY, CHINATOWN, L.A.

THE WEIRDOS

plus THE
germs
OCTOBER 7-8
1977
$3.00
MABUHAY GARDENS

The Germs need
a Drummer!
Call Pat: 826-5712

What God Means to Me . . .
The GERMS
FRIDAY AND SATURDAY
JULY 14
JULY 15
at the
WHISKY

DON BOLLES

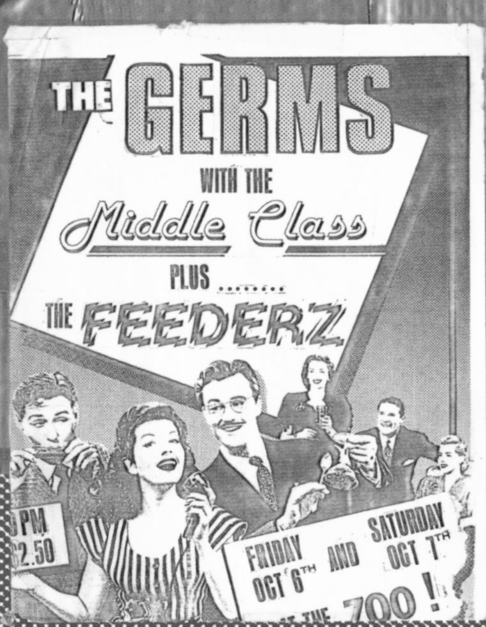
THE GERMS
WITH THE
Middle Class
PLUS ....
THE FEEDERZ
9PM
$2.50
FRIDAY OCT 6TH AND SATURDAY OCT 7TH
AT THE 700!

JON MORRIS

PAT FEAR PLAYING WITH THE GERMS AT THE HONG KONG CAFE. PAT SMEAR HELPING DON BOLLES ON DRUMS.

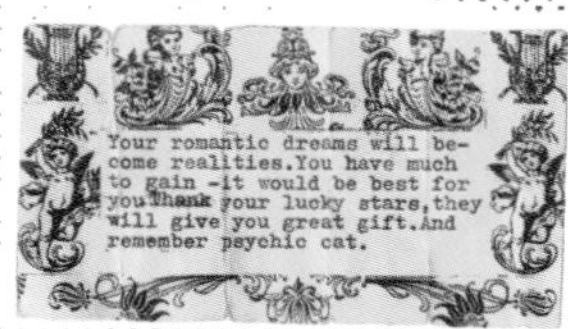
Your romantic dreams will become realities. You have much to gain -it would be best for you Thank your lucky stars, they will give you great gift. And remember psychic cat.

EVERYBODY NEEDS MILK
EVEN CAROL DODA'S

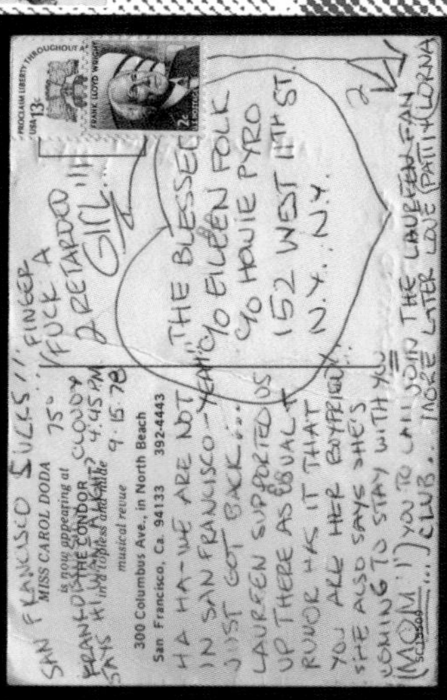
MISS CAROL DODA
is now appearing at
THE CONDOR
musical revue
300 Columbus Ave., in North Beach
San Francisco, Ca. 94133 392-4443

L.A. WEEKLY
Free
The Publication of News, People, Entertainment, Art and Imagination in Los Angeles
August 3-9, 1979 Volume 1, Number 35
Michael Ventura: Peter Weir's Genius
Big Boy Medlin: Surviving Manhattan
Who Is Darby Crash Anyway?
Critic Contest Winners Page 8
Inside: L.A.'s Biggest Guide to Movies, Music & Fun

GERMS

GERMS
HELTER SKELTER

UPBEAT.
GERMS
"MC" TOMATA DUPLENTY
BAGS
contROllers
middle CLASS
A SOCIAL BLAST!
Adolescent eruptions
APRIL 21
8:00 P.M.
LARCHMONT
HALL
118 LARCHMONT, HOLLYWOOD

MOTHER'S DAY
May 11, 1980
ROLLER DERBY
AT
FLIPPER'S
ROLLER BOOGIE
STA. MONICA & LA CIENEGA
STARRING
THE GERMS

"See You All at Okie Dogs"
DARBY CRASH

Support the Scene
GERMS
CONTROLLERS
L.A. SHAKERS
DETOURS
Fri. May 19th
$3.00
8 pm.
LARCHMONT HALL
118 Larchmont
Hllywd.

C FROM LA X WITH EXENE
RUSE & U 100
ISLAND XMAS PA
D DAY 5 SPO

HOW I
LEARNED MY LESSON

FREE THE DAVE
CLARK 5!!

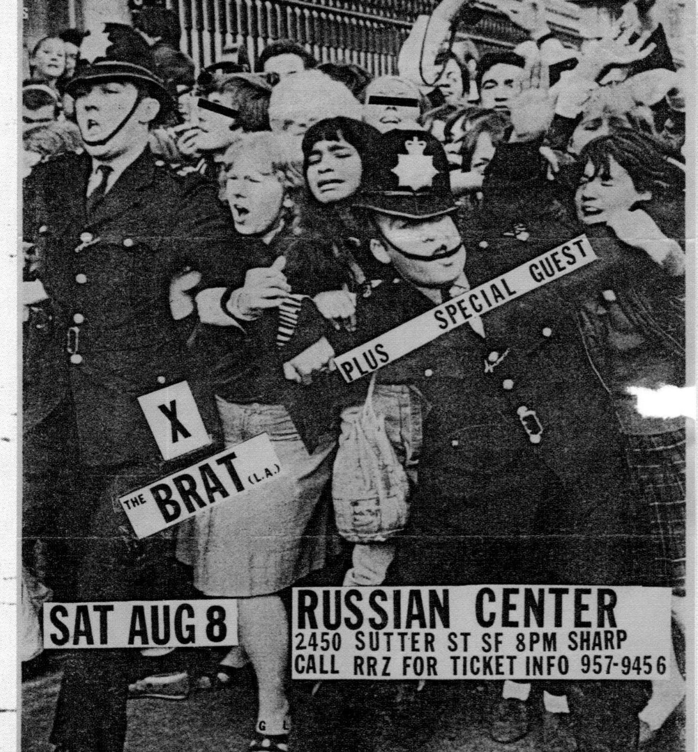
PLUS SPECIAL GUEST
X
THE BRAT (L.A.)
SAT AUG 8
RUSSIAN CENTER
2450 SUTTER ST SF 8PM SHARP
CALL RRZ FOR TICKET INFO 957-9456

X's SECOND ALBUM ON Slash RECORDS IT'S WILDER TO GIVE THAN TO RECEIVE
WILD X GIFT
13 MUSICAL CHARMS
NOV 17 18 CLUB FOOT X
NOV 17 18 CLUB FOOT X
NOV 17 18 CLUB FOOT X
NOV 17 18 CLUB FOOT X
XXXXXXXV

Adventurous Attraction

XIII

XIII

at the FLORENTINE GARDENS

with the GEARS and GREEN ON RED

FRIDAY, AUGUST 28th 1981

5951 HOLLYWOOD BLVD. $5.00

at 7:30 pm for info call: 464–6166

R.S.D·AZT

RICHARD DUARDO

A.S. SPACE

Presents

X

with Special Guests

SUNDAY, MARCH 25, 1984

AT 8:00 PM

IN THE CSUN GYMNASIUM

TICKET PRICES— $8.50 WITH CSUN ID

$10.50 GENERAL

TICKETS AVAILABLE AT THE A.S. TICKET OFFICES IN THE STUDENT UNION AND SPEECH/DRAMA BUILDING

TURNS IT INTO A HONEYMOON SCREAM

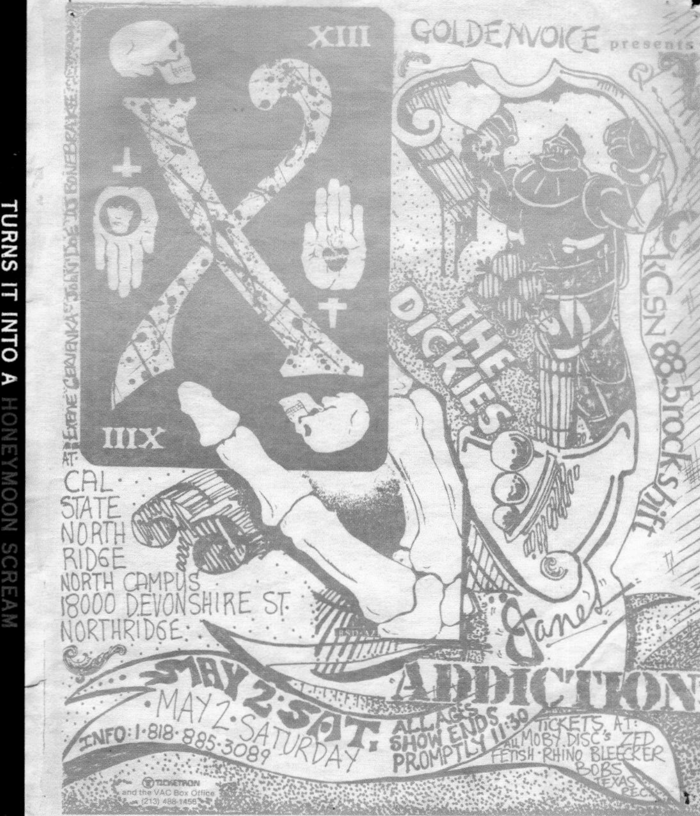

GOLDENVOICE presents
XIII
X
THE DICKIES
KCSN 88.5
AT CAL STATE NORTH RIDGE
NORTH CAMPUS
18000 DEVONSHIRE ST.
NORTHRIDGE
Jane's ADDICTION
MAY 2 SAT.
MAY 2 SATURDAY
INFO: 1-818-885-3089
ALL AGES
SHOW ENDS PROMPTLY 11:30
TICKETS AT:

AND YANKED OUT MY HAIR

X

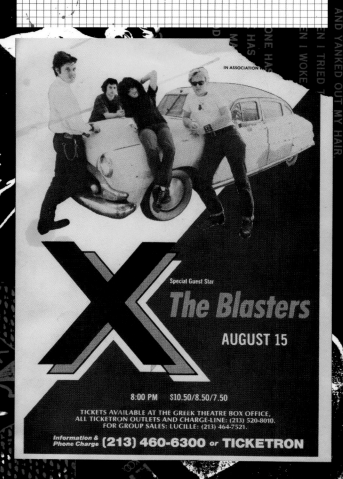

Special Guest Star

The Blasters

AUGUST 15

8:00 PM $10.50/8.50/7.50

TICKETS AVAILABLE AT THE GREEK THEATRE BOX OFFICE, ALL TICKETRON OUTLETS AND CHARGE-LINE: (213) 520-8010. FOR GROUP SALES: LUCILLE: (213) 464-7521.

Information & Phone Charge (213) 460-6300 or TICKETRON

X IN PERSON TO PUT THEIR JOHN DOE ON YOUR L.P.

SAT., MAY 10

VINYL FETISH

606 N. LA BREA

935-1300

SPECIAL X LP PRICE $4.99

2 - 5 P.M.

BE IN A MOVIE
WITH
DEVO
AT THE
Roxy
MON. AUG. 28 6:00PM
DRESS DEVO!!
YOUNGER THE BETTER!!

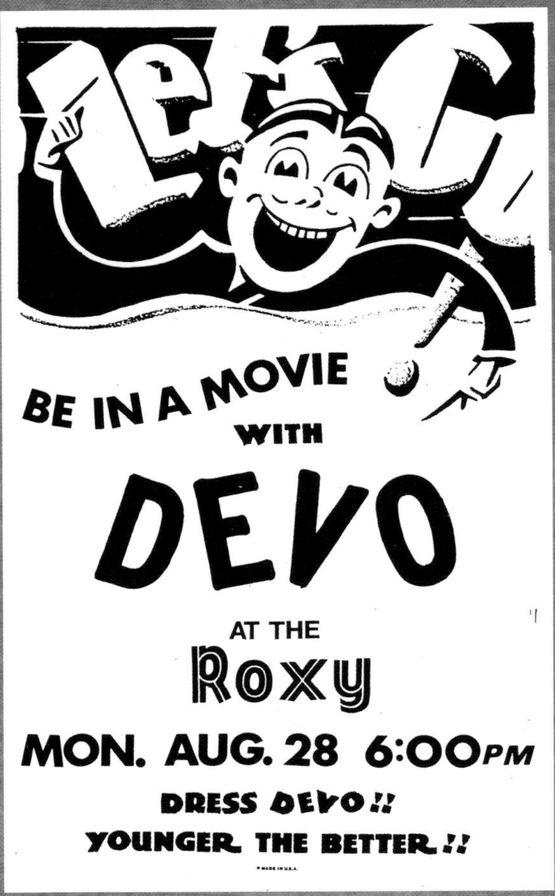

DEVO
REVERSE

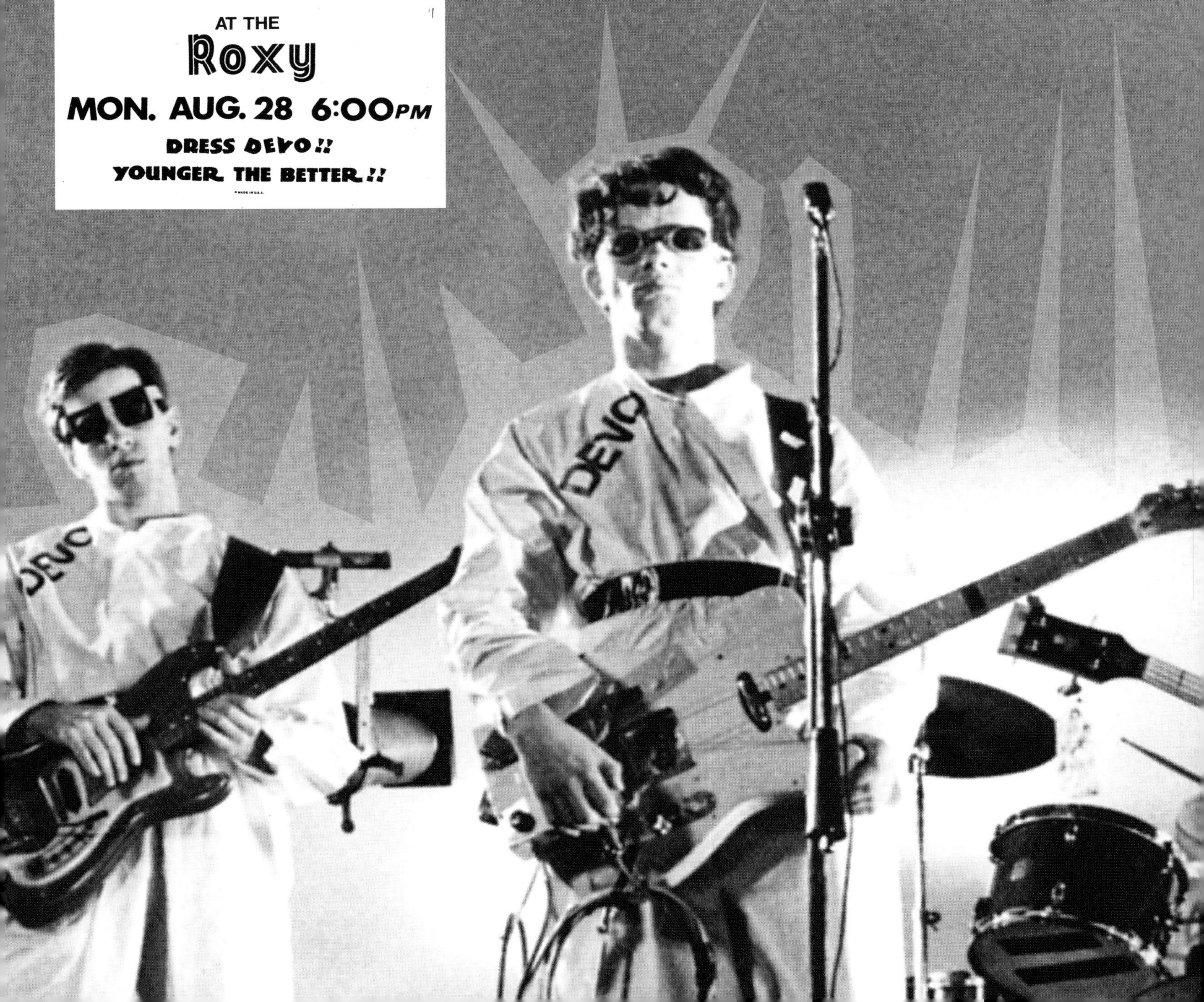

INNERVISIONS & LITTLE WING PRESENT
oh, no! it's
DEVO
CIVIC CENTER MUSIC HALL
FRIDAY DECEMBER 3 8PM
TICKETS ON SALE NOVEMBER 13th. RESERVED SEATS. ADVANCE TICKETS AVAILABLE AT RAINBOW RECORDS (OKC & Norman), RECORD TOWN (Crossroads Mall), ALL BIG DADDY RATS CLOTHING STORES and CAR TUNES (Stillwater)

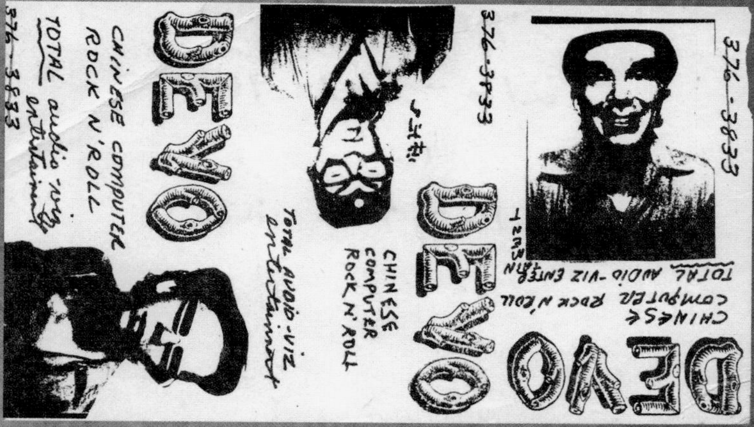

DEVO
CHINESE COMPUTER ROCK N' ROLL
TOTAL AUDIO-VIZ ENTERTAINMENT
376-3833

HALLOW'EEN 1977
MASQUE
at · the
MASQUE
Controllers; probably the Berlin—
Brats, ZEROS (subject to confirmation) Kipper Kids will phone back,
X if they're not sick!
$2.50
A GARANTEED...
SUPER SPECIAL
SUPRISE!! no one, & I mean no one can guess what the fuck it is. (+ urban warfare, & autopsy IF THEY EXIST)
7:30 pm 1655 N CHEROKee HOLLYWood
$2.50
ANTI-DISCO
dead boys
at
bomp records!
PUNK
THE LEGEND OF NICK DETROIT
BOMP
HIGHLAND AVE
THE MASQUE
WEIRDOS
DEVO
PUNK FASHION SHOW
HOLLYWOOD PALLADIUM
FRIDAY SEPT 23, 7:30 P.M.
RAMONES

TRUDIE

In 1977 it was possible for four unemployed teen girls to rent a single apartment with kitchen in Hollywood yet barely possible to scrape together the $175 rent. That didn't leave much for gin, Shermans and Ding-dongs so we lived off the generosity of other young escapees from suburbia, soon to be known as "L.A. punks" for whom our pit was a central gathering spot and crash pad. A recent gift was the marble tombstone with graveyard dirt still attached. There were also visits from various big-city burn-outs a few years older and young transplants from other states who would live at our place while joining bands. We had a fold-out couch besides the bed and both were able to hold four people each, everyone else found a spot on the floor, in the one chair or the bathtub. Spazz Attack, Rock Bottom, Kid Congo, the Gogos, the Zeros, Dickies, Screamers and Germs all found room to sleep and/or live for a time here. This is Mary Rat's corner meaning her collection of posters and flyers are on the walls. I am tossing a doll with a noose into the air while holding a knife. G.I.Joe is being hung by the neck on the window grate. Just visible on the left is the home of our snakes Stiv and Sid. The book "The Family" is on the TV. The photo is by Jules Bates whose photos are unique for his use of a large format camera which gave them wide-angle deep focus.

DAMNED
NEW ROSE
SPEED QUEENS
RIK L RIK
AND MORE
VEX
SCREAMERS
BEST
TWISTEDROOTS
NOV. 26 ANTICLUB
SHADOW MINSTRELS
REDD KROSS
SUPERHEROINS
DEC. 3 COVE THEATRE
45 GRAVE
CHRISTIAN DEATH
GO-GO'S
HONG KONG CAFE
JAN. 18-19
ALLEY CATS at the Whisky
mit der Flesh Eaters & Consumers
June 20th 'n 21st
Seal of approval
DE DE TROIT sings SOLO...
w/ SPECIAL GUESTS
6 PM
FRI JAN. 30
CHRIS D.
6:00
CATHAY DE GRANDE
HOLLYWOOD
THE FLESH EATERS
TEX & THE HORSEHEADS
LONGRYDERS
FRI. FEB. 11
ON KLUB
3037 W. SUNSET

RODNEY BINGENHEIMER

I was a kid from the 60's. I'm finally an adult witnessing a cool scene.

The Punk Rock scene. Let's make the scene was a record I did with Lita Ford of the Runaways and produced by Dan and David Kessel. They were sons or Barney Kessel who worked with Phil Spector. They played on many Spector productions including John Lennon's 'Rock and Roll' LP, Cher, Leonard Cohen etc. They would always go out with and protect Phil. . .they were big guys. They loved the Ramones and my show 'Rodney on the Roq' cuz I would be playing all the new music, the Punk Rock. They pushed me to do my own record. I wrote the lyrics and they did all the music. I would yell a line like 'All the kids on the Sunset Strip listening to the Ramones on the radio' (which was outrageous at the time) then Lita would yell out the names of Punk clubs that the Runaways played. It came out on Razor Records. The Photo was done in a photo studio with a couple of models, and of course Trudy. Trudy was the queen of the Punk Rock girls from the Masque. My show started end of August 1976. The first record I played was the Ramones, they were my first guests in the studio also. I really liked the Avengers a lot as well as the Damned and the Clash. I had the Damned and Blondie both in the studio at once.

Tapes are floating around. I always took phone calls on the air so kids could talk to them. A lot of the bands recorded special for the Rodney on the Roq LP's, Red Kross, Minutemen and Adolescents.

I WANT RODNEY BINGENHEIMER'S LET'S MAKE THE SCENE WITH THE PICTURE SLEEVE

"LET'S MAKE THE SCENE"

RODNEY BINGENHEIMER

FRAGILE
HANDLE WITH CARE

PROMOTION COPY

His New Single...
On RAZOR RECORDS!

FROM DAN & DAVID KESSEL
RAZOR RECORDS/DEEP SLEEP
BOX 3751 HOLLYWOOD, CALIF. 90028

TO THE PRESIDENT
THE WHITE HOUSE
WASHINGTON D.C.
USA

AIRMAIL
PAR AVION

FOURTH CLASS MAIL

Razor Records Deep Sleep P.O. Box 3751 Hollywood Calif. 90028
Executive Coordination: Chimera

photo: Johnathan Postal

SLASH PAGE ELEVEN

29

ORIGINAL ART BOARD / SLASH MAGAZINE

...YOU GODDAMN KIDS!!!
Love, GEZAX

YOOOOU GODDAMN KIDS!!!
Love, GEZA

For me, the whole punk rock thing came out of a horrible vacuum that they call the '70's. From about 1972-1976, I'd been hitchhiking up and down California's west coast trying to get people interested in a style of atonal improvisation I called "X Music". I was all X-happy in those days. I had read the Autobiography Of Malcolm X and even though I was white I "got it" and wanted to drop my slave name too. Finally, in Santa Maria (a small central California cow town that's permanently stuck in the 1950's), I found some other philosopher-musicians who became my first weird aggro noise band. We started a band called "Band X" (no relation to X). We used to pore over Greg Shaw's editorials in BOMP magazine, articles where he would get all gloppy-eyed over the idea of a rebirth of garage bands playing primitive 3-chord songs. Well, guess what? Apparently the Ramones and Sex Pistols were reading those things too and starting bands too. So punk rock began. A certain American president named Jimmy Carter had other plans. He gave the record companies a giant 10-to-1 tax break, but only if they signed NO PUNK ROCK. In other words, it became really profitable to LOSE money. If you knew your tax laws you could even make money "losing" it on coke and hookers! If a label "lost" a couple of million on, say, Meat Loaf, they could write off TEN TIMES the investment! HAHAHAhahahah. Yup, there's your free speech, buddy, and a bird's -eye lens into the Dark Truths behind '70's and '80's music. No, I'm not makin' that up—truth really IS stranger than fiction. The labels began

GEZA X

grinding out these incredibly expensive records and not signing anything new. That's why we ended up making our own records DIY styley. Duh. Okay, so I was bumming around LA in 1976. You know, the place where if you turned an amplifier up past 2, you would get booted out of every "singer-songwriter showcase" and "open mike jam" in town? Unless, of course, you were blastin' disco... but seriously, disco was NOT as cute and funny as it looks on those retro shows. It was downright, uh, ridiculous and boring. So we were feeling our ribs like starved animals for those theoretically soon to arrive, primal 3-chord garage bands playing loud and bad like Uncle Greg promised. Then I saw the Ramones at the Whisky a GoGo and it was ON. Okay, there were only 10 people in the audience but it was a pivotal moment because there were a lot of proto-punks at that show. Loud amps. WOW! I got invited to a Weirdos/Screamers show soon after that. WOW, more amps! I joined a band called the Bags (yes, we really wore paper bags on our heads—mine had bloody tampons dangling on it. PS It's not really that easy to play a guitar that way.) Then I moved into this rehearsal hall called The Masque, which became my stomping ground. We did a lot of amazing punk shows there. Then I joined a band called the Deadbeats, an amazing art-noise-jazz band that did bloody surgery on mannequins and shit like that. That's also how I started producing records. It was so easy. I was interested in recording and spread the word that I was a "producer"—but I had no idea what the word meant. One day Darby said: "You're a producer-produce us." Slash Magazine put the record out and that's how they became Slash Records. Ta daa... everything kinda went like that back then.

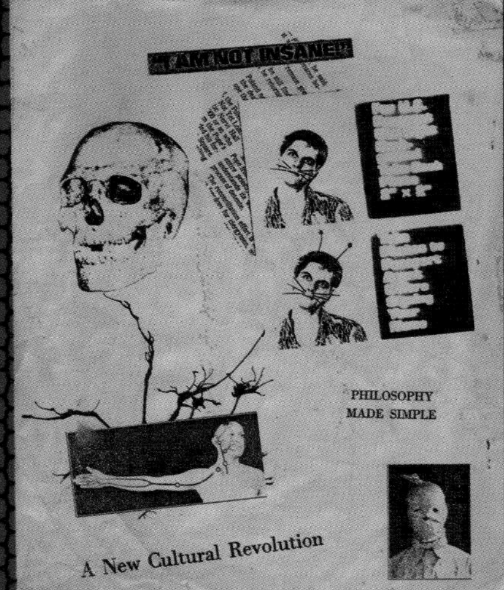
I AM NOT INSANE!
PHILOSOPHY MADE SIMPLE
A New Cultural Revolution

TWISTED ROOTS
AT THE Whisky July 15
SPECIAL GUEST GEZA X
ALSO PHRANC
VOXPOP
PRIMAL TRIBAL

NO MORE PUNK ROCK
GEZAX
SUBURBAN LAWNS
B PEOPLE
STARWOOD JAN.13,1981

STEVEN MCDONALD

My brother Jeff and I started Redd Kross when I was 11 and he was 14. We originally called the band the Tourist because we lived in Hawthorne, CA, which is a good 3, or 4 miles inland from the coast. In our even younger years we would spend our summer days at the beach and if you didn't live a stones throw from the sand you were berated by local surfers and called a "tourist". We liked this idea of being outsiders and not part of the surfer power set. We liked being Tourist. When it was time to do our first recordings I was the only person in the band that had an actual job. I delivered a local Newspaper with a somewhat conservative slant called the Daily Breeze.

Although there was a 17-year old in the band, I, an 11-year old, would pay all studio costs for our original demos. Before we were studio ready we met another local band that we felt a kinship to. They were called Black Flag. Even though Black Flag were basically as unknown as we were at the time, they were much older than us, and lived in an abandoned church in Hermosa Beach. Although they were nice and encouraging to us we essentially had to audition to hang-out with them. They invited us to one of their rehearsals. We sat on the dirty beer soaked floor and watched them go through their set. After they were done, they handed their guitars to us, and said "OK Tourist, lets see what you can do". I remember they liked us, especially our punk rock cover of "I want to hold your hand". They didn't like our name though... and they didn't like our drummer either, for some reason. When we found out there was already a new wave band in England called the Tourist we quickly agreed to change our name to something that would sound good on a bill with Black Flag... we settled on Red Cross.

REDD KROSS
IS COMING

R. REYES

RED CROSS
AT
HONG KONG CAFE
NOV 1st
MAU-MAUS & BLACK FLAG
URINALS and SPITTIN TEETH
NOV 2nd
CROWD & 391 FROM S.F.
AND THE CARTRIGHTS

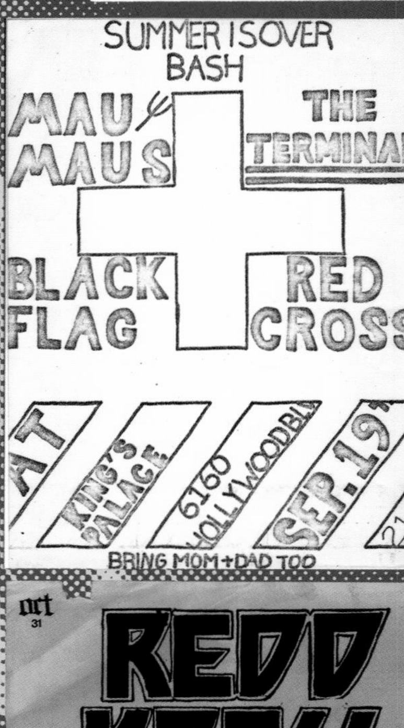
SUMMER IS OVER
BASH
MAU MAUS
THE TERMINAL
BLACK FLAG
RED CROSS
AT
KING'S PALACE
6160 HOLLYWOOD BL
SEP. 19
BRING MOM + DAD TOO

PAT FEAR

REDD KROSS
the UNCLAIMED!
a rare appearance by
the carrie nations
WHITE FLAG
plus SPOCK
$5
GRAND PRIZE TO BEST KISS or MENUDO COSTUMES
FREE KISS ALBUM

RED CROSS: DAVE MARKEY

REDD KROSS
AND
WHITE FLAG
PLUS SUPRISE GUESTS!
WEDNESDAY
JULY
13th
AT 8:00
THE NEW
SHAMUS O'BRIAN'S
20001 N. Tyler St.
N El MONTE
213) 443-9376 or 575-9122
FROM L.A. take 60 Fwy East to
Santa Ana Ave → go North on Tyler St.
to Corner of Tyler & RUSH St. and
see LINDA BLAIR take on Hitler

FRI. JULY 3
RED CROSS
WASTED YOUTH
DEEP 6
SOCIAL DISTORTION
DISPOSALS
OVERKILL
DOORS OPEN AT 7:30
$4.00 cheap!
NO AGE LIMIT
BRING I.D. FOR BEER
AT
BARDS
APOLLO
4417 W. ADAMS
ADAMS AND CRENSHAW
ONE BLOCK SOUTH OF
THE SANTA MONICA FWY.
PHONE: (213) 737 9042
*WASTED YOUTH
10 SONG EP
OUT SOON!
BRILLIANT ARTWORK DANIEL SPIRA

RED CROSS
SACCHARIN TRUST
OVERKILL
YOUTH BRIGADE
SALVATION ARMY
NO AGE LIMIT
THURSDAY
JULY 23
AT
ALPINE VILLAGE
IN THE BARN
TAKE HARBOR FWY TO TORRANCE BLVD OFFRAMP

BENEFIT FOR THE MOTION PICTURE → "DESPERATE TEENAGE RUNAWAYS"

REDD KROSS

A WE GOT POWER FILM

white flag

NIP DRIVERS

PLUS SPECIAL SURPRISE GUESTS!

FRI. DEC. 30

AT THE CATHAY DE GRANDE

9:00 PM

DAVE '83

PHOTO: JORDAN SCHWARTZ

FLYER: DAVE MARKEY

SIN 34

SIN 34

AMERICA,AMERICAN
Dont talk about equality,
Dont talk about democracy,
Dont tell me about anarchy,
You dont know what you say,
CHORUS,
Government bullshit thats all i hear,
Nothing of sense,nothing new,
Peace and warfare just dont mix,
Propoganda that makes me sick.

You tell me we're right tell me they're wrong,
Whose to know what's really going on,
I hate them as much as you do,
But when they die,we'll die too.

CHORUS.

no more bullshit,no more lies,we only want truth,
we only want our lives,no one wants war,no one
wants death,i dont want to die,i just want to live,
no facism,no jail for innocents,no police brutality,
no stupid,wars,more social welfare,think about your
people,think about americans,think about america.

AMERICA,AMERICAN,AMERICA.

CHILDREN SHALL NOT BE HEARD
Help me,here i am,i pay attention to you,
I scream,look at me,thats something you never do,
How can i listen to you when you block me out,
This is not suppose to happen,you dont know what
im about.
The church standerd thought you obey them though,
I refuse to follow anyone that i dont know,
I decide whats for me i dont ask anyone else
ITS SO EASY FOR YOU TO ASSUME ILL PUT MY LIFE IN
YOUR SHELF.
CHORUS
I dont need your help here i go im through with you
I leave without your help thats something you'd
never do.
This is my time i've gained your time is nearly out
I CAN WALK AND THINK ON MY OWN BEYOND YOUR DEEPEST
DOUBT.

WHO NEEDS THEM
Who needs police
pushing us around,
FUCK THEM ALL
Who needs authority
telling us what to do,
FUCK THEM ALL
Who needs parents
running our lives,
FUCK THEM ALL
Who needs anyone
but myself,
FUCK THEM ALL
No one needs to run my
my life,
I know whats wrong and
whats right,
I can do what i want
all i can say,
FUCK THEM ALL.

SAY WE SUCK
Say we suck,Who cares.
Dont need you,So what.
All your comments,Dont mean
shit.
Play how we want,We'll rip.

To our face you smile
and stare,
Wont talk shit you dont
dare,
Rip our flyers cross out
our names,
We wont play your stupid
games.
CHOURS
Always putting us down
Playing punk is our sound,
No rock star attitudes,
Your jelousy is what it
boils down to
CHOURS.

NOTHING MAKES SENSE,
Everyday theres a problem,
Dont know what side to choose,
Cant figure out right from wrong,
"Oh god"im so confussed,
Sometimes i got it figure out,
Then the next thing i dont,
Everythings so complicated,

Only Love
Played with my head,
Made me believe,
What you said was true,
That i was the only girl for you.

I said i wouldnt care,
Id go out and have lots of fun,

DAVE MARKEY

SIN 34
SIN 34
AMERICA, AMERICIAN/ WHO NEED'S 'EM?/ SAY WE SUCK/ CHILDREN SHALL NOT BE HEARD/ NOTHIN' MAKES SENSE/ ONLY LOVE/ LIVE OR DIE

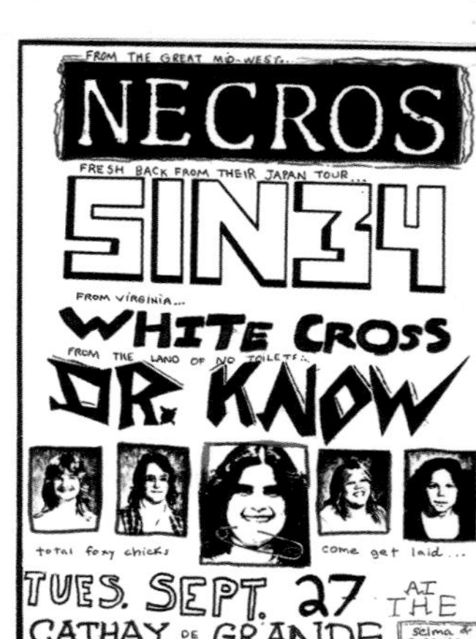
FROM THE GREAT MID-WEST...
NECROS
FRESH BACK FROM THEIR JAPAN TOUR...
SIN 34
FROM VIRGINIA...
WHITE CROSS
FROM THE LAND OF NO TOILETS...
DR. KNOW
total foxy chicks
come get laid...
TUES. SEPT. 27 AT THE
CATHAY DE GRANDE
selma & argyle HOLLYWOOD

DAVE MARKEY

DAVE MARKEY

I had the name Sin 34 for a punk rock band in my head since age 15 in 1979. I'd even created a logo for it centered around a crucifix with S on the left side of the top center of the cross, the center being the "I" and N on the right, same with the 3 and 4 on the bottom of cross. It sounded real cryptic, but in actuality it was just a UHF television station based in Los Angeles-Spanish International Network, channel 34 In addition to making up fake punk rock bands (some of the names were hilarious), I would also make up fake punk-rock clubs just to entertain myself. Long before I ever ventured out into the actual punk scene in Hollywood, or beyond, I had an alternate universe in my mind of what "the punk scene" actually was. In some ways it was more interesting than reality. It would be a couple years before I decided I was going to be a drummer and make "Sin 34" a REAL band.

SIN34

SAT JAN 22
T BIRD ROLLERDROME
8252 WHITTIER BLVD.
1 mi. W of 605 Fwy, 3 mi. N of 5

AND:
SOCIAL DISTORTION
MAU MAUS
FUCK UPS (from S.F.)
URBAN ASSAULT (from S.F.)
MEN IN BLACK
& MORE

5 HOUR MAGAZINE Actress Betty White. Also: weight-loss; the punk life style. (Repeat; 60 min.)

When police asked the crowd to disperse, some of the punk rockers apparently became upset and threw rocks and bottles at police

"Kids can't afford $25 for fancy hair styling," said Sal Ericcio, a Washington, D.C., barber.

DAVE MARKEY

SIN 34

SIN 34-TAPE and EP Yowza! This is a great tape from some kids in Santa Monica CA whoknow how to play the tunes! Send 'em a dollar and a blank tape and you'll get 7 fast songs, a picture & the lyrics. Oh yeah, the singer is a girl who really handles it pretty well, ya know? Get this one fer shure mon! Dave Markey 2607 Broadway, Santa Monica, CA 90404. These dudes have an ep out too called "Die Laughing" on Spinhead Records (2265 Westwood Blvd, Suite #541, la, ca 90064) Get it too and listen to it while making love to a kangaroo...Other places to hear Sin 34-Charred Remains cassette Compilation, "You Ordered It" compilation album put out by Clem Fisher, and finally another LA HC comp called "Sudden Death"...Watch out Partridge Family!

PARANOIA 10.82

WGP 10.82

SIN 34

DIE LAUGHING

DAVE MARKEY

SIN34

...DUCTIONS PRESENTS
WITH! Julie Dave Mike Phil
DEBUTING THIER NEW LP!

SVDB
DECRY
Drew Bernstien invented mod, ska ska ska!
S&M PRODUCTIONS
SCATTERED FEW
AND SPECIAL SURPRIZES
MONDAY, AUGUST 1ST
8:30 PM
AT $4.00
ROXANNES
131½ HUNTINGTON DR. IN ARCADIA
TAKE 210 FWY EAST
GET OFF ON HUNTINGTON DR.
GO RIGHT. IN BETWEEN 1ST AND 2ND STREET. GO AROUND BACK.
FREE! PARKING
Go to BACK ALLEY PARKING NEXT DOOR
INFO (213) 355-4438
SVDB-TWO SONGS ON UPCOMING "DESTROY L.A. COMP L.P."
SIN 34 "Do You Feel SAFE" LP out Now!

PAT S.V.D.B.

SIN34

DO YOU FEEL SAFE?

NEW 15-SONG LP

SIN 34 Die Laughing EP also available

MAIL ORDERS: LP-$6 EP-$2 (PP) overseas add $1

SPINHEAD records
2265 westwood blvd. #541
L.A. CA. 90064

DIST. BY Rough Trade, Faulty, Greenworld, Systematic & more

DAVE MARKEY

DAVE MARKEY and MIKE "NOT" ROTH at the PUNK SHACK by JORDAN SCHWARTZ

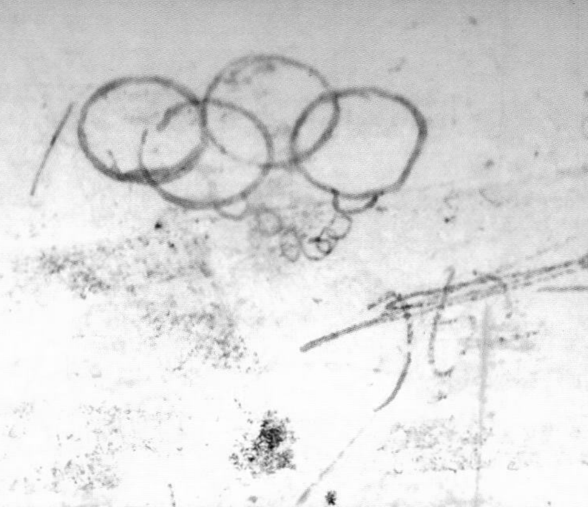

PAT FEAR

'Twas 1979 I believe, and Jello B. Afro and I were in the "big city"- Hollywood, (to see the Germs most likely, as Jello only went to LA to see them, or Black Oak Arkansas, and they definitely weren't playing the Hong Kong Café that night...). Walking around before the gig, we spotted a weathered poster featuring a remarkably well drawn pencil sketch of an insanely intimidating cop...with a huge bulging "nightstick" in his trousers. We took the poster down, which was an ad for pencil artist Timothy Anderson's exhibition, but had no idea what to do with it, (except to definitely NOT put it up on our bedroom walls in our parents' homes, where we, being teenagers, still lived) so it got stuck in a box somewhere with KISS posters and Germs flyers. Fast-forward to 1984. White Flag had already taken a tongue in cheek pro-police and anti-communist stance, having parodied Black Flag's famous "Police Story" T-Shirt, (which had pissed off a LOT of cops) with our "good cop" version, (that cops actually LIKED, and often mail ordered from our label!), and our famous "Com-

WHITE FLAG
WHAT IRONS WILL ENSHACKLE WHITE FLAG SHALL SET FREE

PAT FEAR

45 GRAVE
ANTI · DR. ND
D.I.
AND BELIEVE IT OR NOT........
WHITE FLAG
T-BIRD ROLLER RINK IN PICO RIVIRA
ADMIT ONE
FRIDAY, JAN. 21
DOORS OPEN AT 7:30
L.A. TAKE 605 N. (OR 5 FROM LA) TO WHITTIER BLVD. GO WEST TO T-BIRD ROLLER RINK 8252 WHITTIER BLVD. IN PICO RIVIRA
INFO: (213) 851-1700

PAT FEAR

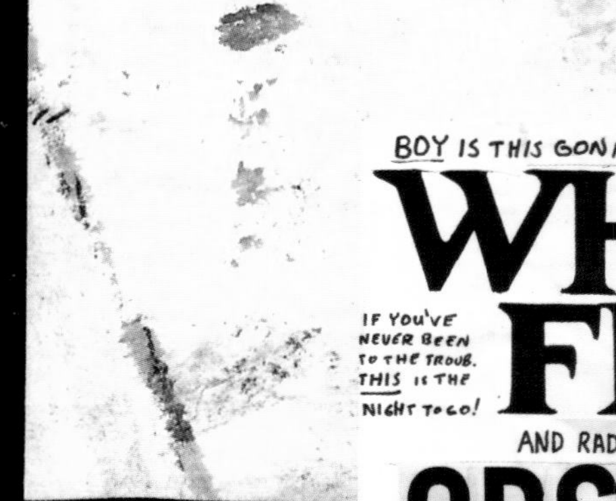
BOY IS THIS GONN
WH
FL
IF YOU'VE NEVER BEEN TO THE TROUB. THIS IS THE NIGHT TO GO!
AND RAD
OBS
PLUS MORE HEAV
Troubadou
9081 Santa Moni
AND BECAUSE THIS
WHITE FLAG WANT
$2
WHITE FLAG

munists Suck, Cops are Your Friends" buttons. Needing more new mock-rock fascist imagery, we recalled the poster, and made it into stickers, using the cop art, and a quote from a fan letter we'd received from the then communist Poland stating, "What Irons Will Enshackle, White Flag Shall Set Free". Then, when we toured the US for the first time that year, we used the same image for the tour shirt, which sold rather well.

Subsequently, we received a plethora of fan-mail from around the country, saying cops were hassling kids about wearing our tour shirt with (quoting a Florida Deputy) "that faggot LAPD cop" on it. Puzzled, we did some research, (which consisted of going into the Pleasure Chest in Hollywood and ASKING a clerk...this was long before the Internet) discover that the cop in the drawing was one Chuck Romanski (RIP), the single most hated COP in the world; hated BY OTHER COPS. Officer Ro-

WE ARE GOING TO KILL YOU
TEST PATTERN
HONG KONG
DECEMBER
ROCK
RISE
PIGS
TEST PATT
DIE!

BILL BARTELL

DRUMMER
WANTED
PUNK
PUNK

FOR ALL ORIGINAL HARD ROCK BAND. WE ARE AN ESTABLISHED GROUP WITH A GREAT DEMO AND LOS ANGELES MAJOR CIRCUIT GIGS LINED UP. WE ARE TIRED OF OUR PENDING SUCCESS BEING SLOWED BY JERKS THAT HAVE TO ASK PERMISSION TO PRACTICE AND HAVE TO BE HOME BY A CERTIAN TIME OR THEY " GET IN TROUBLE". WE ARE A SERIOUS FOUR PIECE (THREE AT THE MOMENT) RANGING IN AGE FROM 18 TO 20. WE HAVE ALL EQUIPMENT, CREW AND BOOKING AGENTS, AND HAVE RAISED AN INTEREST with INDUSTRY EXECUTIVES. YOUR AGE IS NOT IMPORTANT AS LONG AS YOU DON'T LOOK LIKE YOU'VE BEEN AROUND MUCH LONGER THAN WE HAVE. IF YOU ARE WILLING TO PRACTICE FIVE NIGHTS A WEEK AND ARE INTERESTED IN BECOMING A MAJOR ACT GIVE US A CALL. IF YOU WANT TO PLAY YOUR FAVORITE TED NUGENT OR DEVO SONGS DON'T BOTHER, BECAUSE WE DON'T PLAY PARTIES. If you have it in you, if you're willing to do anything to make it with ~~HEAVY METAL HARD ROCK~~ PUNK

CALL: BILL: (714) 653-5484
MARTY: (714) 653-4481
DEAN: (714) 684-3596
BRUCE: (213) 656-3386 (Booking agent- call if you have too)

PUNK

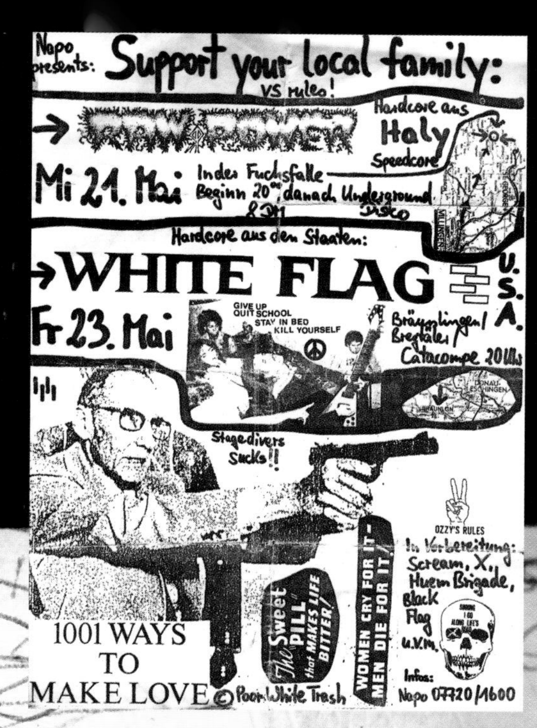

Napo presents: Support your local family:
vs rules!
Hardcore aus Italy
Speedcore
Mi 21. Mai In der Fuchsfalle
Beginn 20⁰⁰ danach Underground Disco
Hardcore aus den Staaten:
→ WHITE FLAG U.S.A.
Fr 23. Mai
Bräunlingen/ Breitale/ Catacompe 20 Uhr
GIVE UP QUIT SCHOOL STAY IN BED KILL YOURSELF
Stagedivers Sucks!!
OZZY'S RULES
In Vorbereitung: Scream, X, Huem Brigade, Black Flag u.v.m.
Infos: Napo 07720/1600
1001 WAYS TO MAKE LOVE
©Poor White Trash
The Sweet PILL that MAKES LIFE BITTER!
WOMEN CRY FOR IT MEN DIE FOR IT

OZZY YOUTH PRESENTS
WHITE FLAG
WHITE FLAG KILLS AIDS ON CONTACT
AND WÜRM
FEATURING CHUCK DUKOWSKI of BLACK FLAG
THE MENTORS
PLUS MANY SUPRISES!
CARD HOLDING S.M.F.'s GET IN FREE!
-AT-
CATHAY DE GRAND
1600 ARGYLE (AT Selma) HOLLYWOOD
RIGHT BEHIND THE PALLADIUM (213) 461-4076
WED. AUG 3

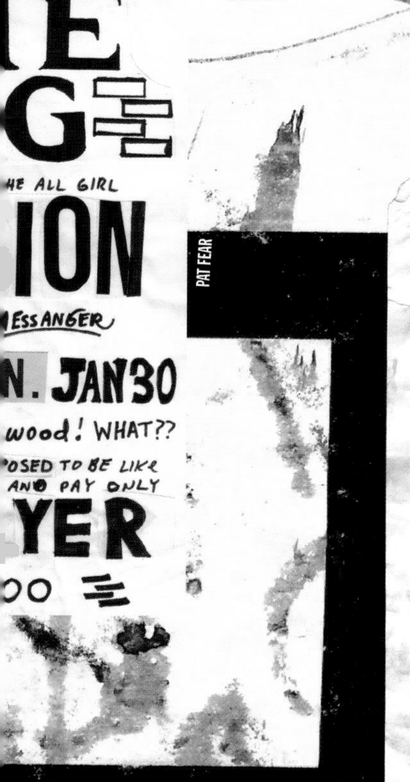

STING!!
REMEMBER ELKS LODGE ?
TE
FLAG
HE ALL GIRL
ION
ESSANGER
N. JAN 30
wood! WHAT??
POSED TO BE LIKE
AND PAY ONLY
YER
OO

PAT FEAR

BLACK FLAG
GREG CHUCK B. HENRY CHUCK D. DEZ
with
WHITE FLAG
FROM SUNNYMEAD
JULY 31 7 p.m.
Rickenbosh Turkey Hatchery
2634 Old North Road, HEMET
$ 4.00 at door night of show
Wedding Reception Guests free with invite
directions (714) 652-5554

ROCK AND ROLL
PARTY!
PANIC
and
TYRANT
with KASHMIR and Full House
in their triumphant return from England, the bad boys of Rock and Roll
TEST PATTERN
this FRIDAY, JAN 15, 8:00
THE RITZ
NO AGE LIMIT
PARTY!
2958 UNIVERSITY
ANOTHER FINE EVENT FROM DIPLOMAT PRODUCTIONS

admit one

RED KROSS + WHITE FLAG

April 24th

9pm $4

The Brewery

WHITE FLAG

had apparently been a closeted gay LAPD officer, (and former Marine MP) who had decided to resign after a particularly hairy brush with uring a burglary. Seeing unemployment looming, he also saw dollar signs, ntacted the high-end gay porno publication COLT, and arranged to do a e

ession with them, in his LAPD uniform, WHILE ON DUTY, the day he resigned. Re-christened "Clint Lockner", he became one of the most fa- ay porn stars of all time. Needless to say, he was NOT very popular with ner coworkers when the pictures came out, and apparently in the 70's, eelings were universal among the world's police forces. Unwittingly, while

attempted to annoy sophomoric neo-communist punks, we inadvertently off the cops (who had loved our previous "cop shirts"), in probably the possible way... much to the chagrin of the band, not to mention our fans by -Shirts! Sorry kids. . . but it makes a good story!

RAYMOND PETTIBON

les seldoms
J.F.A (of Phoenix) and-
BLACK FLAG
Friday, Nov. 6
at Backstage
Also: Seldoms-
Phantom Limbs
Saturday, Oct. 17
also at Backstage
Be early

PRESENTS
at The Hideaway
BLACK FLAG
GEZA X
ALL I WANT TO DO IS DIE IN PEACE.
THE CIRCLE JERKS
STAINS
DESCENDENTS
and special guests
MAD SOCIETY
$4
FRI SEPT. 19 8:30

D.O.A.
LEGAL WEAPON
APR. 3
AT
VEX
2706 E. BROOKLYN

SACCHARINE TRUST
SALVATION ARMY
MINUTEMEN
RED BERET

$4.00
Harbor Frwy. to Torrance Blvd. off ramp
san diego frwy.
harbor frwy.
Alpine
torrance blvd.
9 p.m.
Thurs. Nov. 5
Alpine Village
at the Heimathus in Torrance

S.I.R
Studios
Presents
SAT. NOV 27
D.O.A
BLACK FLAG
WASTED YOUTH

UGH-AHHH-OOO
45 Grave
The Red Rockers
ZELLA AND THE BLACKS
NO AGE LIMIT!
9:00
$5.00
THURSDAY NIGHT
MARCH 5
WHISKY A GO GO
IN HOLLYWOOD

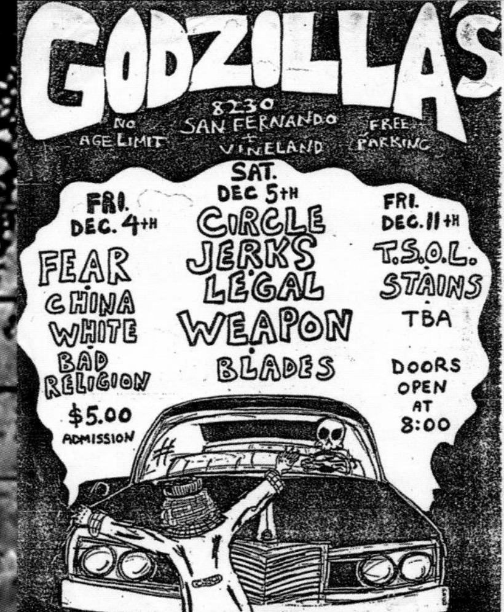

GODZILLA'S
8230 SAN FERNANDO + VINELAND
NO AGE LIMIT
FREE PARKING
FRI. DEC. 4TH
FEAR
CHINA WHITE
BAD RELIGION
$5.00 ADMISSION
SAT. DEC 5TH
CIRCLE JERKS
LEGAL WEAPON
BLADES
FRI. DEC. 11TH
T.S.O.L.
STAINS
TBA
DOORS OPEN AT 8:00

fri. feb 24
GOLDENVOICE presents
FEAR
Circle Jerks
VANDALS
SIN 34
TOXIC REASONS
Afflicted
OLYMPIC AUD.
1801 S. Grand
fri. feb 24
TICKETS $8.50 AT DOOR $7.50 IN ADVANCE

TEX AND THE HORSEHEADS
DC3
AND
DOBERMAN
FRIDAY
APRIL 26th.
AT THE GOLD MINE
REDONDO BEACH
732 NO. CATALINA (NEAR P.C.H.)
(213) 376-3032
21 OR OVER

SHAWN KERRI

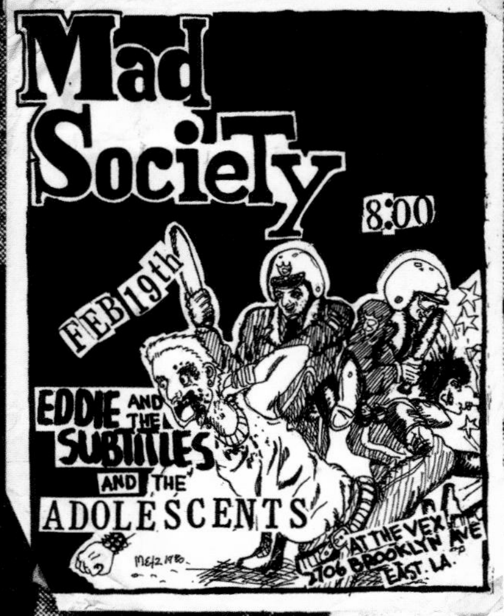
Mad Society
8:00
FEB 19th
EDDIE AND THE SUBTITLES
AND THE
ADOLESCENTS
AT THE VEX
2706 BROOKLYN AVE
EAST L.A.

METZ

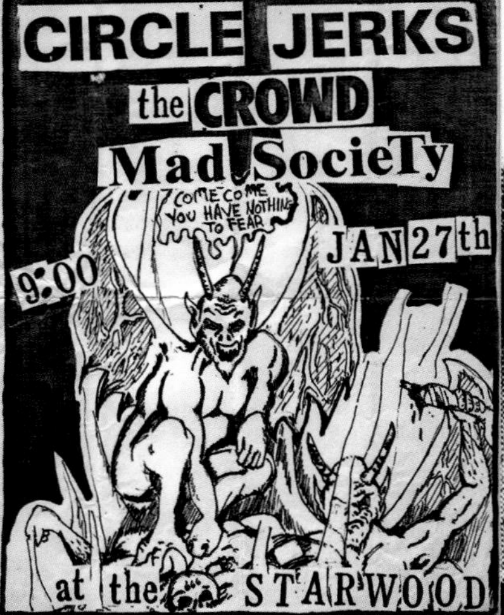
CIRCLE JERKS
the CROWD
Mad Society
COME COME YOU HAVE NOTHING TO FEAR
9:00
JAN 27th
at the STARWOOD

METZ

THE PLUGZ
BLACK FLAG
nov.28
8pm–2am
CIRCLE JERKS
MAD SOCIETY
VEX
LIVE
VERN AUD.
Prod.
2811 E. OLYMPIC BLVD.
E.L.A.
$5.00

the vex
$5
7/1 FRI.
MAU-MAUS
SOCIAL DISTORTION
STAINS
MINUTEMEN
SACCRINE TRUST
SIN-34
URBAN GURRILLAS
ESSENTIALS
CREWD
$3.50 JULY 3 SUN
ARTICAL OF FAITH
REALLY RED
STALAG 13
AFFLICTED
7/9 CIRCLE JERKS
7/22 & 23 BLACK FLAG
7/2 SAT
$4
DECENDENTS
SUICIAL TENDENCY
NIG-HIST
PLUS GUEST
2580 n. soto
222-5600

BOBBY LANE

FORBES

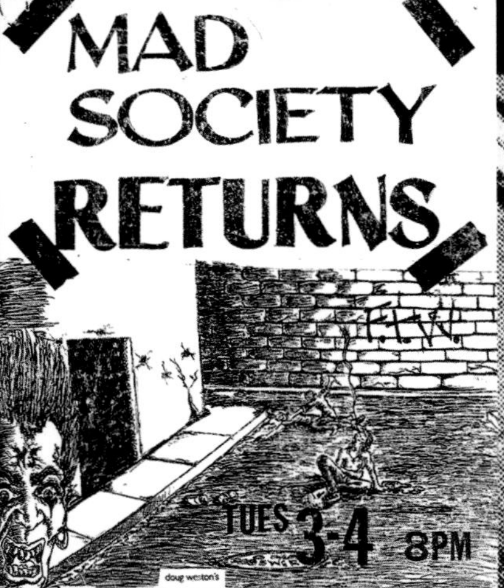
MAD
SOCIETY
RETURNS
TUES 3-4 8PM
doug weston's
Troubadour

The only
L.A. PUNK
Art Show
APRIL 18-30
C.A.S.H.
1953 Cahuenga
Hollywood, Ca.
(213) 462-9083
RECEPTION
Sunday, Apr. 18,
5:00 - 10:00pm

J. MESSER

DEADORALIVE
BATTALION OF SAINTS
youth Brigade
redscare
catch-22
friday
may
28
$5
northpark
lions club
3927
utah
Bobby Lane '82
"Mother is that you?"

STAINS
AT THE NEW
VEX
THIS WEEK
WITH
OZZIHARES
THE CROWD
RED CROSS
-TUESDAY-
JULY 7th
845 W. WASHINGTON AT OAK
LOS ANGELES
ALSO AT BARD'S -APPOLLO
$4.00
WITH
45-GRAVE-OVERKILL
CAUSTIC CAUSE
-THIS FRIDAY-
JULY 10
4417 W. Adams

THIS SATURDAY
June-20
STAINS
PHONE
722-2222
AT STAGE 1
E.L.A.

STAINS
WITH
MINUTEMEN NIG-HEIST
SACCHARINE TRUST
SAT. MAY 23-AT
STAGE ONE
EAST LOS ANGELES
3259 E. BROOKLYN ST.
ALSO WITH
CHINA WHITE - MAD SOCIETY
TUES. JUNE 16-AT
-STARWOOD-
2 MILES WEST OF
8151 SANTA MONICA BL.

YOUTH PARTY PRESENTS
SATURDAY FEB. 20th at GODZILLAS
MAU-MAU'S
LIVE MUSIC · PERFORMANCE · DANCE
UXA
ALL-STAR BAND
WITH
ALICE BAG ·
TRACI LEA · PHRANC ·
TIFFANY KENNEDY
(EX-CASTRATION SQUAD ·
EX-BAGS · RED CROSS)
GEZA X ·
RICK WILDER ·
+ MORE
RED CROSS
THE MORAL DECAY
PRIORITY
PLUS MUCH MORE!!!

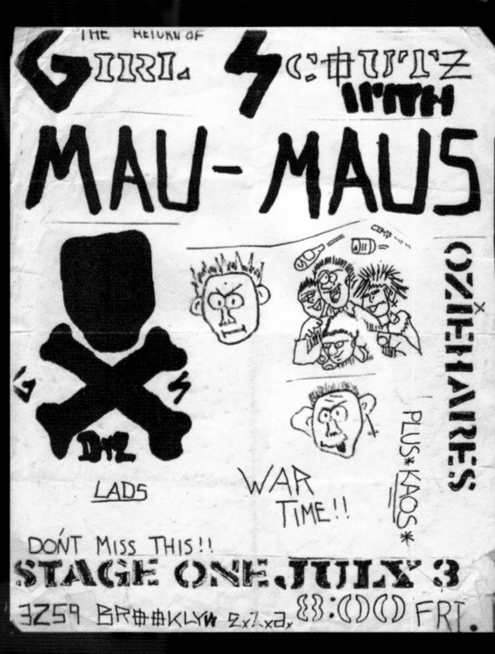
THE RETURN OF
GIRL SCOUTZ
WITH
MAU-MAUS
OZIEHARES
LADS
WAR TIME!!
PLUS KAOS
DON'T MISS THIS!!
STAGE ONE JULY 3
3259 BROOKLYN
8:00 FRI.

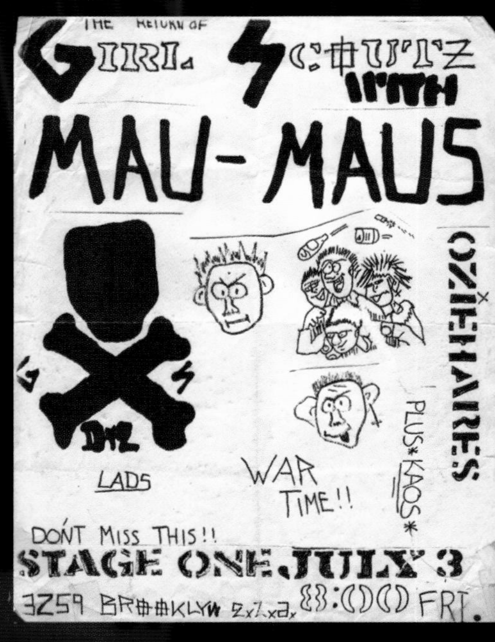

STAGE ONE PRESENT IN CONCERT
MAU-MAUS
GIRL SCOUTZ
THE RETURN OF THE NEW GIRL SCOUTZ
DOORS OPEN AT 8:00 PM
$5.00 AT THE DOOR
$4.00 with Flyer
JULY 3 Fri.
STAGE ONE
3259 BROOKLYN
OPEN BAR
·ALL AGES WELCOME·
PLUS:
OZIEHARES
KAOS
July 3
722-2222
Flyer #1 1981

STAGE ONE PRESENTS IN CONCERT
MAU-MAUS
TO SLAM OR NOT TO SLAM THAT IS THE QUESTION
RETURN OF THE NEW
GIRL SCOUTZ
KAOS
PLUS
ANGRY SAMOANS
TICKETS AT THE DOOR
STAGE ONE HAS FOOD!!!
OPEN BAR
ALL AGES
DOORS OPEN
FRI. JULY 3
8:30-2
STAGE ONE
722-2222 FOR DIRECTIONS + INFO

THU. JUNE 24
MAU MAU'S
PENGUINS
VENUS & UNIT 3
GRANDIA ROOM
5657 MELROSE
$5
$1.00 OFF W/ FLYER

MAU-MAUS + MINUTEMEN
CH. 3 + SEDITIONARIES
+ INVISIBLE CHAINS
SAT. Nov. 13
ONLY TWO DOLLARS!
ONLY TWO DOLLARS
8:00
105 PARK ROW
VENICE
MAIN
WINDWARD
PARK ROW
PACIFIC
AND IT'S ONLY TWO BUCKS!
ONLY TWO DOLLARS

PEPSI the OKI DOG

DRED SCOTT
Culture Death Dance?
Gun Club
urinals
CLUB 88
FRIDAY
MARCH 6

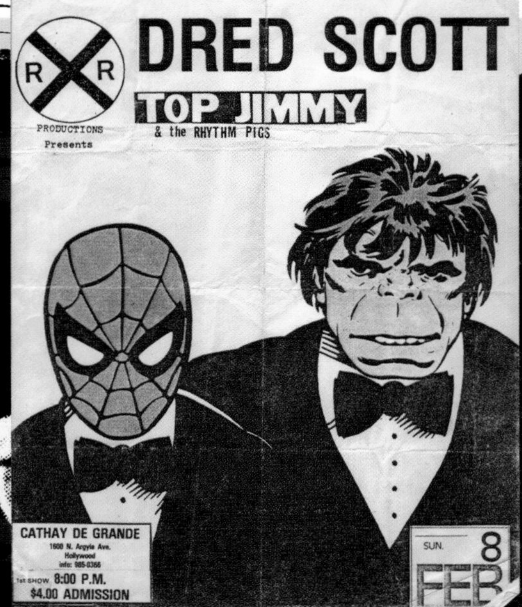
R X R
PRODUCTIONS Presents
DRED SCOTT
TOP JIMMY
& the RHYTHM PIGS
CATHAY DE GRANDE
1600 N. Argyle Ave. Hollywood
1st SHOW 8:00 P.M.
$4.00 ADMISSION
SUN. 8 FEB

BLACK RANDY & THE METRO SQUAD
HUMAN HANDS
SPEED QUEENS
© 1980 KERRY JACKSON
STARWOOD
12/30
KERRY JACKSON

TOP JIMMY and the RHYTHM PIGS
OCTOBER......81
SAT. 3rd FLORENTINE GARDENS
BLASTERS, US, GEARS, JIMMY & the MUSTANGS, GIGOLOS·
5951 HOLLYWOOD BLVD. 464-6166 BETWEEN GOWER & BRONSON
MON. 5th CATHAY DE GRANDE SAVE THE WHALE SELMA & ARYGYLE
BENEFIT FOR GIL "T" — "GIL IS GUILTY" — OR A SLOB IS A SLOB!!
"KEEP GIL-MU OUT OF OUR OVERCROWDED JAILS" - JERRY BROWN
PILES OF HOLLYWOOD STARS - WE KNOW EM ALL, BUT THEY WON'T ADMIT IT!
SAN FRANCISCO
FOR SALE — USED BRIDGE
FRI. 9th MABUHAY GARDENS
SAT. 10th BERKLEY SQUARE
FRI. 16th WHISKY A GO GO w/ X WILD!
WELCOME HOME · JOHN · EXENE · ZOOMS · D.J. · KIT LYDIA
MON. 19th CATHAY DE GRANDE w/ Silvertones FROM SAN FRANCISCO
TOP JIMMY & NADINE SPOTTED IN TAHITI ////—— 13 X 69 ——
858·1931 NOON TO FIVE
GO TO S.F. AND GET ON THE GUEST LIST ____! AND A BEER!!
I HEARD A RUMOR THAT LEE VING AND DERF SCRATCH ARE A DUO
AND LIVE TOGETHER IN 'FRISCO. THEIR MUSICAL DUO IS CALLED
THE "SWINGING SWINGLES"......RUMOR HAS IT....LOS SLOBOS NEWS.

PINK'S SINCE 1939 CHILI DOGS BURGERS FRENCH FRIES

MICHAEL ETTER

On one hot, smoggy, Orange County summer day like any other in Nineteen Eighty I was introduced to Punk. In the bedroom of my friend's big sister,(all pink and flowery with every sort of stuffed animal and rainbows bla bla bla... she was older and cool for sure, but still had all the remnants of the little girls room that she grew up with), my friend asks me "You ever heard of any of THIS music before?" It felt as if he was

asking me something dangerous like "You ever done drugs or made out with a girl before?" The question made me nervous. What was I in for? What do I say? He knew I had no idea what he was talking about as he pulls out the 45's from their sleeves. I could tell by the smirk on his face I was about to be hit with a nice hard punch of something I never expected... like rapid fire... The Damned into the Buzzcocks into The Clash into The Sex Pistols into more and more and more. It kept coming and at 13 I couldn't get enough... wave after wave of Black Flag, Circle Jerks, DEVO, the Germs, and more. In those brief moments in time I was destroyed. It was like a switch clicked permanently into a new position in my brain and I loved it. I remember, soon after, this guy who lived up the street from me came up to me, (he had one of those stupid, peach-fuzz mustaches and wore a cap that had the word 'Fog' on it... you know fog... on his

hat...), and said, 'Punk Sucks Dude'. He knew I was getting into Punk and figured he could somehow put me in my place with such an intelligent use of words. I just paused in amazement. Then I thought 'is that supposed to be a put down', 'is that all he has to say'. I wanted to go off on this guy and say something even better like, 'what the fuck do you know you stupid Burnout'. But I didn't. Somehow with that one idiotic

FEAR
WITH
OVERKILL
SATURDAY
AUG
29
AT THE
CUCKOO'S NEST
1714 PLACENTIA, COSTA MESA

SAT OCT.
THE 3RD
AT THE
LEGENDARY
CUCKOOS
NEST
STARTS
AT
9:00
CHINA WHITE
-AND-
THE
BLADES
RED SCARE
SYMBOL
SIX

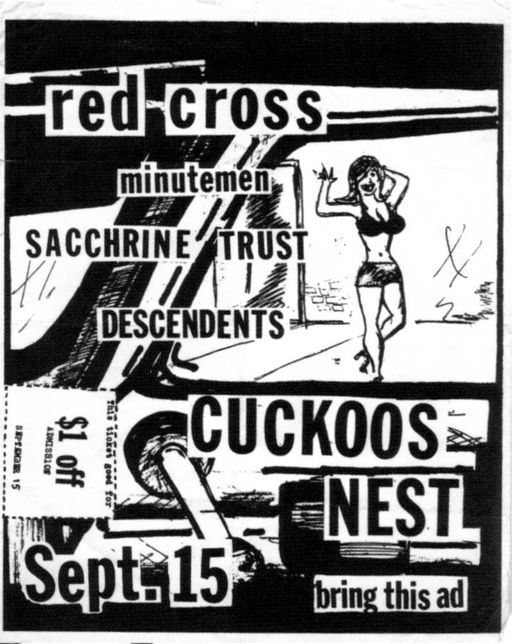
red cross
minutemen
SACCHRINE TRUST
DESCENDENTS
CUCKOOS
NEST
Sept. 15
bring this ad
$1 off

45 GRAVE

Heinrich Hoffmann

NO AGE LIMIT!

WASTED YOUTH SAT. Sept. 5

Cuckoo's Nest

of his, as quickly as that switch clicked into a
e, I knew the line was drawn. I was not HIM!
that he thought Punk sucked was just a bonus
nd enough for me to just grin and walk away. I
d all my Rock albums that day. Using them as

and launching them into obscurity in the field
e street. Styx, Boston and all the rest smashed
black pieces. I jumped in feet first. All this new
re Punk, Punk, Hardcore, New Wave, Post
Whatever...It was all great. It served no real pur-
be subtitled. As long as it was 'anti rock' it

k Rock to us at that time. It was new and it felt
as mine. It had attitude and innovation and it
lent that there was something great happening.
ng original. It could thrive based on the simple
Do It Yourself! The Mount Olympus of bloated
ods with huge corporations attached to them and
stoid, kimono-wearing, narcissist rockers could

not even understand it much less stop it. It was so fast upon them they couldn't

even get it. It was ours. Thousands of kids were re-born inside older sisters bedrooms across the world just as I was. With record albums strewn across the floor... our young minds exploding, trying to decipher clues from the new language making it our own. Passed off to us by an older brother, sister, cousin or friend it was twisted into something new. Listening to 45's, reading fanzines, taping Rodney's show every Sunday Night, drinking, skateboarding all day, talking about music non-stop and learning how to play when we weren't talking about it or listening to it, starting bands, putting out music, designing all our own record covers and flyers, it was enlightenment and freedom. I took it all in. It saved me from my own adolescence. It was dangerous and exciting like

nothing else I've ever known. Its all here, chronicled in the flyers like those that hung on telephone poles made to be torn down and re-posted on my bedroom walls, now stashed in an old Milwaukee's Best box in the closet. They now resurface to be used as inspiration to the unexploded mind still waiting. It isn't the ONLY thing...It isn't definitive and it isn't over. This was our history. Now, what's next?

SUBURBAN LAWNS

Sunday

July 15

CUCKOO'S NEST

714 Placentia COSTA MESA

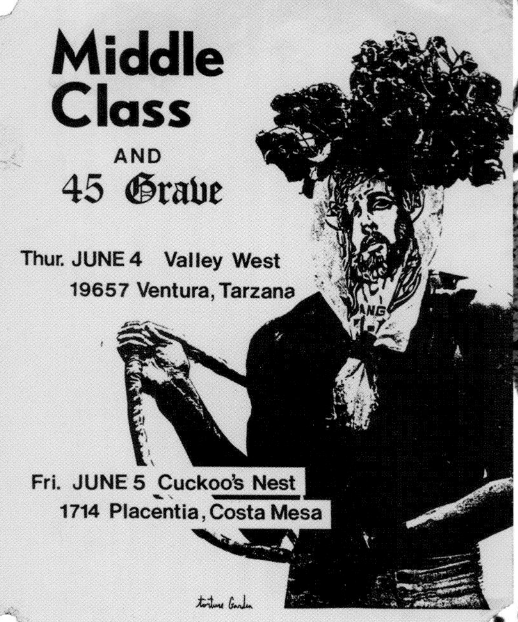
Middle Class
AND
45 Grave
Thur. JUNE 4 Valley West
19657 Ventura, Tarzana
Fri. JUNE 5 Cuckoo's Nest
1714 Placentia, Costa Mesa

RAUS!!
FEAR
+
CHEIFS
STILL MORE BEER WITH
CUCKOO'S NEST
SAT.
JULY 17

CIRCLE JERKS
FRI. FEB. 6
CUCKOOS NEST
WITH CHINA WHITE & LEGAL WEAPON

THE MisFits
From New York City
The Cuckoo's Nest
This Friday 27 Nov
1714 Placentia
Costa Mesa
Info-4974469
Info-6450390
PUNK ROCK RULES
From 'ollywood Take the 5 Freeway to the Long beach Southern Freeway 405 Freeway south to Harbor blvd turn right then turn right on 18th or 19th which ever comes first and Find Placentia
Circle One
Raw Sewage
File 17
The Scientists

CUCKOO'S NEST

CucKoos NeSt
presents
LOST CAUSE
© 1981 Reick Davis Prod
NO AGE LIMIT
AUG 11
DOORS OPEN 8 PM

"SOCIAL DISTORTION"
ED-E and the SUBTITLES
The DE-de troit BAND
SHATTERD FAITH
THIS SATURDAY
CUCKOO'S NEST
1714 PLACENTIA-COSTA MESA
SEPT 19TH
NO AGE LIMIT
BRING I.D. FOR BEER
safe substitute for cash
Mainliner

ADOLESCENTS
LEGAL WEAPON
AND
45 GRAVE
Saturday, Febuary
21 ST
at
THE COOCOO'S
NEST
1714 Placentia
COSTA MESA
info. «714-645-0393»

MINUTEMEN
D. Boon 84
SEX PISTOLS
DIO
DEAD HEAD
MINUTEMEN
LPX2
BE SURE TO CATCH THEIR CAMPAIGN TRAIL 84 TOUR
DOUBLE NICKELS ON THE DIME
ON SST
DOUBLE NICKLES ON THE DIME
ANGRY SAMOANS VEX 9 O'CLOCK
SACCHARINE TRUST
FRI. AUG. 5
MINUTEMEN
and
OTHERS
SACCHARINE TRUST
DON'T NEED FREEDOM
ANGRY SAMOANS
222-5600
Minute Men
100 Flowers
Modern Torture
Fri. November 19th
Anti Club
8 P.M.
4658 MELROSE (at Helen's Place)

D. BOON by DAVE MARKEY

Circle Jerks
PLUS
AL'S BAR
DEC 27!
"Social-Distortion"
MINORS FUCK OFF!!
NO PIGS
NO GUES ASSHOLE

Circle Jerks
AT
Dancing WATERS
FRIDAY Aug 20

KEITH MORRIS AND MOM

FROM LOS ANGELES
CIRCLE JERKS
FRI. DEC. 13
TICKETS $6 ADV. $7 DOS.
Plus ACTIVE INGREDIENTS and VALE OF TEARS
JOCKEY CLUB
633 YORK NEWPORT KY.

CIRCLE JERKS
On the Battlefield
Shocking Truth
Parents Are Too Permissive
Clinging to a Log
Collecting Manure
Medical Problems
Get Rid of Dirt,
Polio, Horror, Abuse,
Stains and Odors
How to Get More Respect
East L.A.
CLUB
2706 E. Brooklyn Ave L.A 90033
FRI. MARCH 27

THE CIRCLE JERKS
THE GERMS
EDDIE AND THE SUBTITLES
TUES 26TH FEB.
THE CROWD AND THE CHEIFS
THE GREAT GATSBY ON THE (BEAUTIFUL) REDONDO PIER
TAKE ME!
$3.00 CHEAP ENOUGH FOR YOU STINGEY ASSHOLES
18 AND OVER (BRING FAKE I.D.S)
I closed my eyes and dreamed of a better world
CIRCLE JERKS FLYER #2

RAY PETTIBON

CIRCLE JERKS
STINGERS
RHINO 39
RUNS
FRI· DEC· 19
$ 4.00
CIRCLE JERKS LP. AVAILABLE ON FRONTIER RECORDS

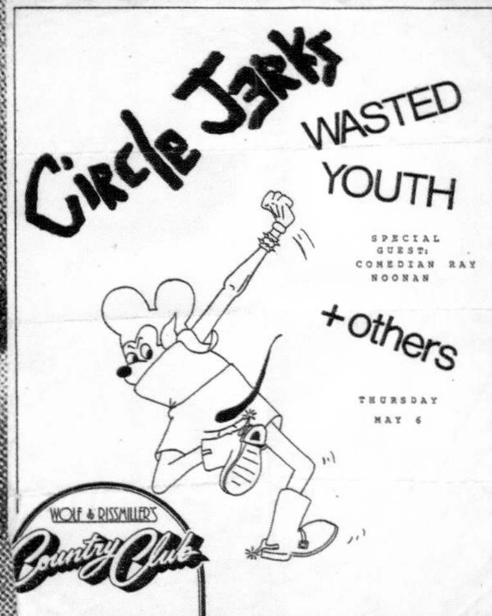
Circle Jerks
WASTED YOUTH
SPECIAL GUEST: COMEDIAN RAY NOONAN
+others
THURSDAY MAY 6
WOLF & RISSMILLER'S
Country Club

A NIGHT OF SHEER INDULGENCE
GOLDENVOICE PRESENTS
SOCIAL-DISTORTION
SAT MARCH 30
INFO: 213-749-5171
REDD KROSS
PLUS FLYING IN FROM BOSTON FOR THEIR LAST EVER APPEARANCE
SS DECONTROL
MAD PARADE
UNIFORM CHOICE
OLYMPIC AUDITORIUM
1801 S GRAND · LOS ANGELES

MIKE NESS by BRUCE KALBERG

I can remember how long I spent combing my hair for this show. I must have used half a can of grease. I changed my shirt five times, I had

boots on and duct taped the laces so they wouldn't come undone. My jeans had the perfect cuff. My palms were

sweating. I couldn't eat. I knew what I was in for or at least I thought I knew. You see I was going to my first Social Distortion show.

I was fourteen and this was one of many rite of passages that we do to earn our rights as young punks. Everything about my look was more about fitting in than vanity. I didn't want to draw any attention to myself which is funny because when I rolled around town that's what I got but

not here. This was a gladiator show. I was still two blocks away from The Catalyst in Santa Cruz which is where I

grew up, and you could hear the loud bikes and cars coming down the street. This was my wet dream to be at a punk show with older punks and I couldn't wait to be one. The cars

were almost as loud as the drunk punks out front. There were some real menacing looking biker guys that were standing in front of their bikes and skate punks laughing. All I am telling myself is to be cool, look down. Don't get noticed. As we are being let in you can smell the sweat and alcohol and I am getting this feeling like when you're too small to

ride a roller coaster and the person sizes you up and nixes you. I walk in and the place is already wet with sweat, I think I must have missed the opener doing my hair or something because it was hot as fuck already. Punks were pushing past me to smoke or get more drinks, I was trying to get as close as possible. I am getting drinks spilled on me, older punks are now trying to touch my hair and fuck with me as I make my way to the front.

JAY DIOLA

I remember wishing that I could say something but I was scared, I couldn't, I just wished I looked so tough that no one would fuck with me but again I was in a training ground and everyone is trying to start shit and that's what they're there

for. When the lights dimmed there was no going back. Beer is showering me and people are pushing up to the front, I am just trying to keep myself up front. Mike comes out looking

real cool. He has on wrap around dark glasses, a wife beater, tattoos blazing and some dark jeans. He starts with 1941 and I was just trying to see as everyone starts to mash into each other. I feel tough just being there. The Catalyst is a converted narrow bowling alley so looking up you can see

people looking down into the pit. I am mixing it up with the punks in the front and the band sounded really good. I decided it was time to get in the pit so I

nove back a couple of people and punks are rushing up and over the kids in the t and over me as I move back. I can now see punks are bloody. As I turn to watch I get pushed into the pit, I can feel the arms, fists, elbows, and heads just barely missing. This is it, the release of fear. I am straightedge and

always have been. This is it, confronting, knowing and being present at that moment. I let my hands down in front of me and was just dancing around the circle. I got a foot on the back of my calf and I went down, trying to hold the guy in front of me I got kicked in the ribs twice before I got pulled up. I was so

excited, I was in it, being punk getting kicked made me feel alive. Then I notice

those biker guys just posted up in the center of the pit with chains in their hands. I was scared shitless but so hyped by the story I was going to be able to tell those hat weren't there. I got pummeled in the back and got the back of someone's head nto my cheek but that was it. I was bruised up but made it. It was so empowerng I remember how proud of the bruises I was... fucking stupid.

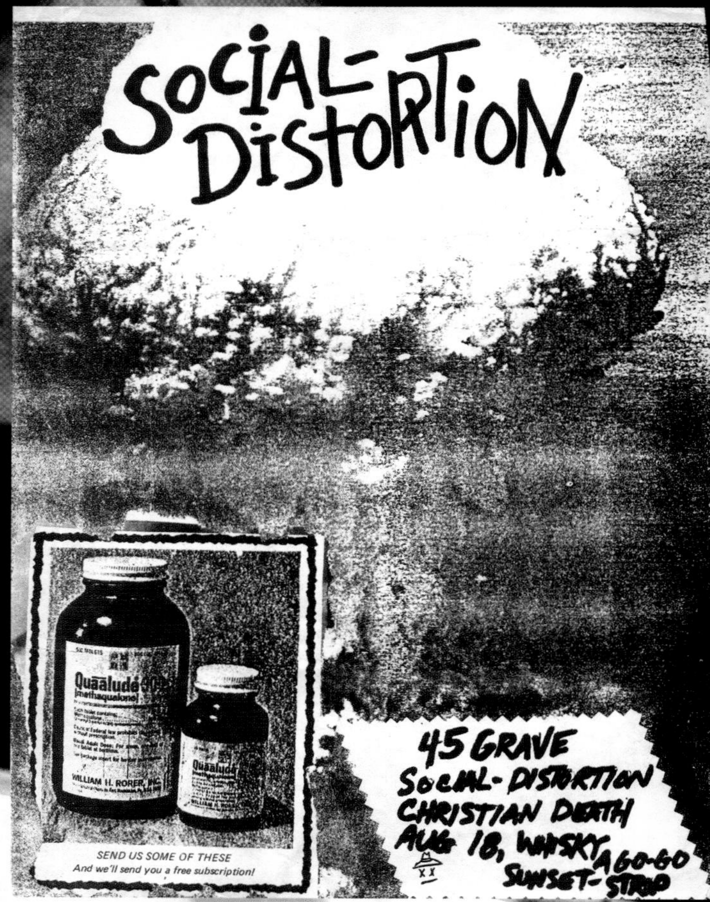

SOCIAL-DISTORTION
SEND US SOME OF THESE
And we'll send you a free subscription!
45 GRAVE
SOCIAL-DISTORTION
CHRISTIAN DEATH
AUG 18, WHISKY A GO-GO
SUNSET-STRIP

MICHELLE MARINI

Thanksgiving NIGHT

The
VANDALS

THE VANDALS

Plus THE JONESES

ON CLUB

STEVO!

T.S.O.L.

SANDI

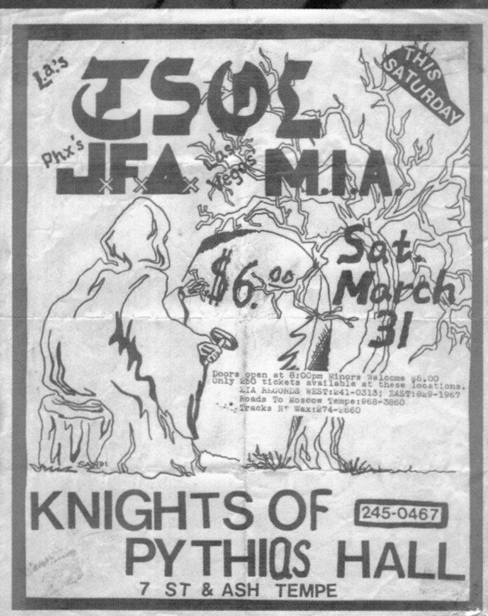
THIS SATURDAY
T.S.O.L.
Phx's J.F.A.
M.I.A
$6.00
Sat. March 31
Doors open at 8:00pm Minors Welcome $6.00
Only 250 tickets available at these locations.
ZIA RECORDS WEST:241-0313; EAST:829-1967
Roads To Moscow Tempe:968-3860
Tracks N' Wax:274-2660
KNIGHTS OF PYTHIAS HALL
245-0467
7 ST & ASH TEMPE

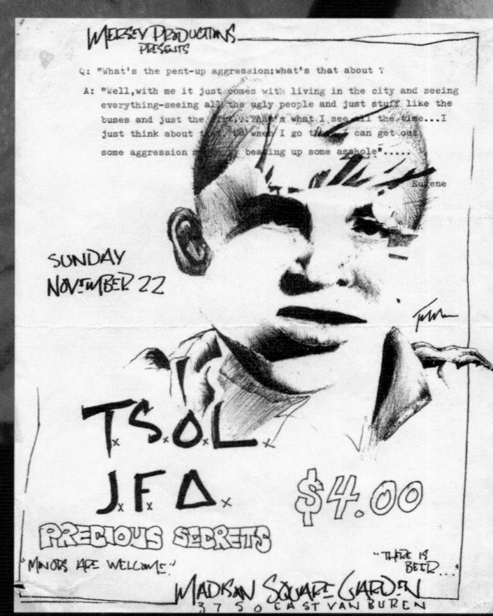
MERSEY PRODUCTIONS PRESENTS
Q: "What's the pent-up aggression:what's that about ?
A: "Well,with me it just comes with living in the city and seeing everything-seeing all the ugly people and just stuff like the buses and just the ... That's what I see all the time...I just think about ... when I go ... can get out some aggression ... beating up some asshole".....
Eugene
SUNDAY NOVEMBER 22
T.S.O.L.
J.F.A.
$4.00
PRECIOUS SECRETS
"MINORS ARE WELCOME"
"THERE IS BEER..."
MADISON SQUARE GARDEN
37 S. O EAST VAN BUREN

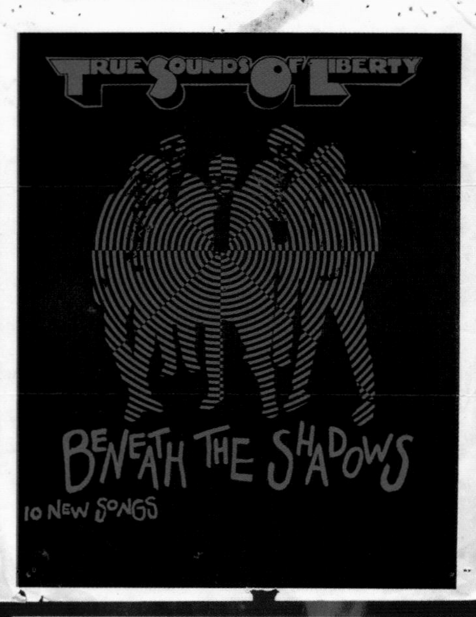
TRUE SOUNDS OF LIBERTY
BENEATH THE SHADOWS
10 NEW SONGS

t.s.o.l.
AGENT ORANGE
EASTER
D.I.
JUNE 27
FRI,
DOGGY STYLE
FENDERS BALL ROOM
521 E. FIRST ST. LONG BEACH
(213) 435-2838

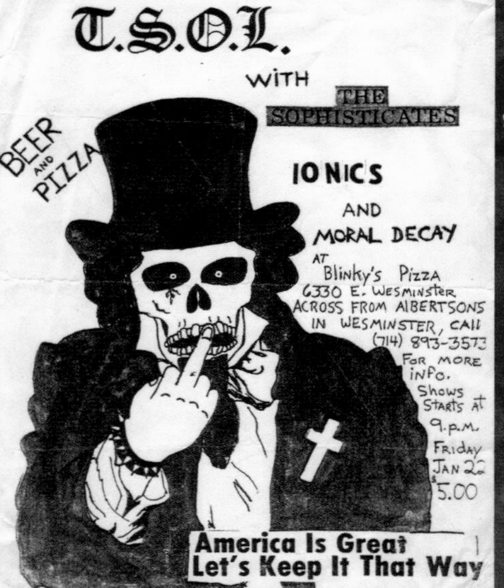
T.S.O.L.
WITH
THE SOPHISTICATES
BEER AND PIZZA
IONICS
AND
MORAL DECAY
AT Blinky's Pizza
6330 E. Wesminster
ACROSS FROM ALBERTSONS
IN WESMINSTER, CALI
(714) 893-3573
FOR MORE INFO.
SHOWS STARTS AT 9 P.M.
Friday JAN 22
$5.00
America Is Great
Let's Keep It That Way

RRR

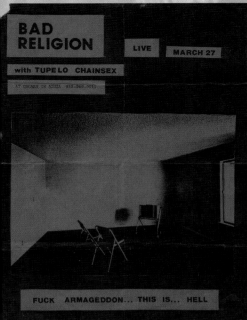

BAD RELIGION
LIVE
MARCH 27
with TUPELO CHAINSEX
FUCK ARMAGEDDON... THIS IS... HELL

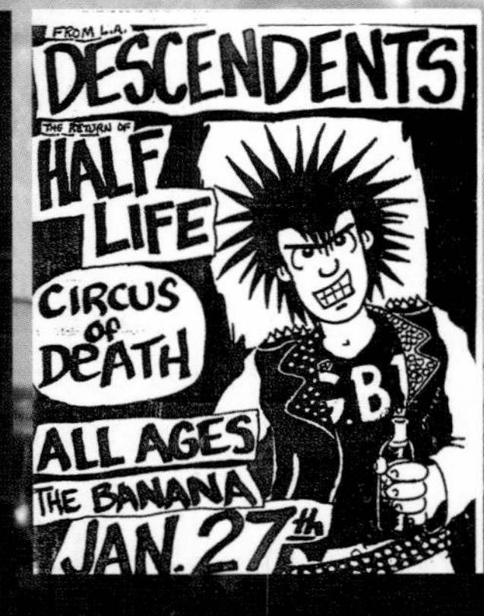

FROM L.A.
DESCENDENTS
HALF LIFE
CIRCUS OF DEATH
ALL AGES
THE BANANA
JAN. 27th

WASTED YOUTH PRESENTS
I CAN'T WAIT,
WASTED YOUTH
IS PLAYING
GODZILLAS
WHEN
I'LL TELL ALL THE GIRLS
JAN. 30th
NO AGE LIMIT
FAKE I.D. FOR BEER

BAD RELIGION
SLAM 81
OCT 17
FEAR T.S.O.L.
CHINA WHITE
MANY MANY MORE
DOORS OPEN 12:00 NOON GET THERE EARLY
OVERNIGHT CAMPING AVAILABLE $6.50 ADVANCE $8.50 AT THE GATE
(for info)
424-7911

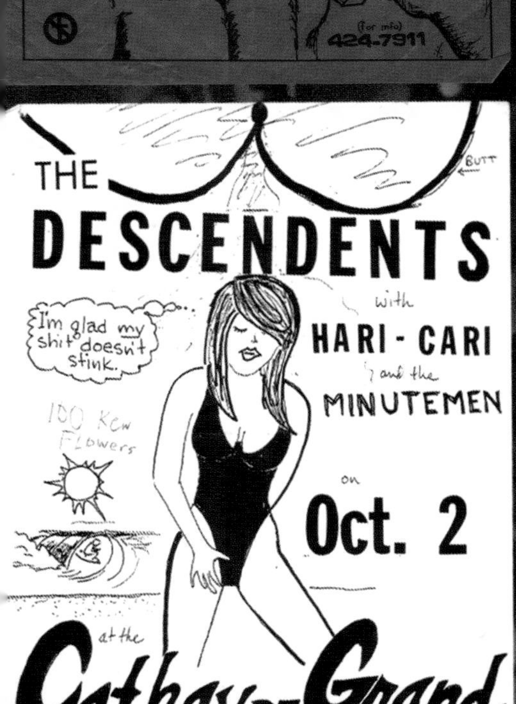

BUTT
THE
DESCENDENTS
with
HARI-CARI
and the
MINUTEMEN
I'm glad my shit doesn't stink.
on
Oct. 2
at the
Cathay de Grand.

WASTED YOUTH
WITH THE CIRCLE JERKS
WASTED YOUTH
10 SONG L.P.
OUT SOON!
AUG.3 AT THE WHISKY
WASTED YOUTH
FLYER NO. 8

BAD RELIGION GIG IN T.J. PHOTO: KURT PORTER

WASTED YOUTH FLYER NUMBER 8

BLACK FLAG

EDDIE AND THE SUBTITLES

THE MINUTEMEN

STARWOOD Tuesday November 18th

THE DEAD KENNEDYS

AND

THE CIRCLE JERKS

WHISKY A GO-GO

TUES. AUG. 19

BLACK FLAG

MARCH 6th & 7th

AT THE MABUHAY

TONIGHT
AT
TOOL & DIE
BAD POSTURE
LOS OLVIDADOS
HELLATIONS
FANG
UXB
$3.50 STARTS AT 12:00
974 VALENCIA ST.

FINALLY!
DISCHARGE
ALSO
SPECIAL GUESTS
D.O.A.
AND
BAD BRAINS
THE LEWD
THE FARTZ
CRUCIFIX
SATURDAY OCT 1 9PM
OAKLAND AUDITORIUM ARENA
ADVANCE TICKETS AT ALL BASS OUTLETS

caustic cause

CATHAY DE GRANDE

DEC 15

a polka party to remember

fear
circle jerks
45 grave
mentors

Polish
auditorium
4434 crenshaw

saturday
January 10
9:00 P.M.

lots of cheap brewski available

SAT. NOV. 20

ON BROADWAY

BLACK ATHLETES

RANK & FILE

DOA

BLACK ATHLETES

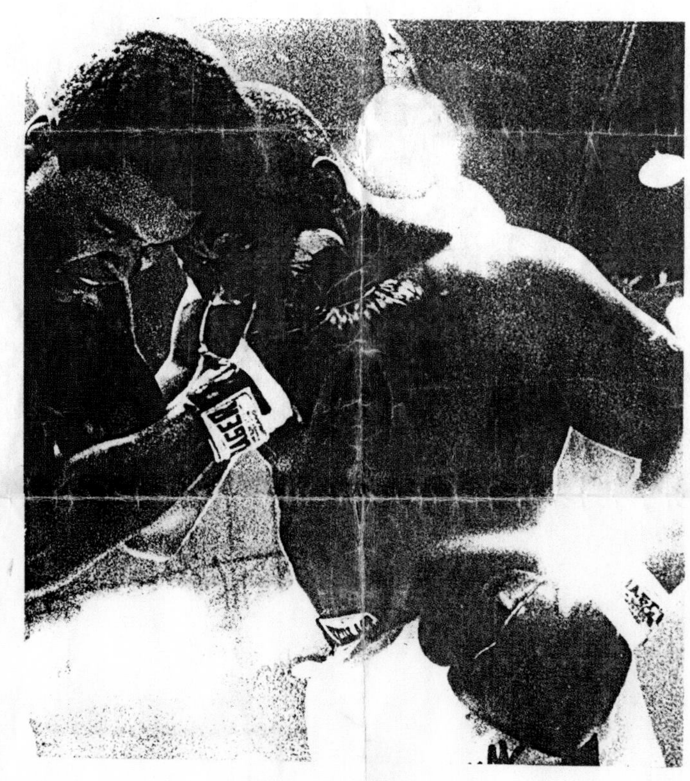

ON BROADWAY

SAT. NOV. 5

BROKEN
BONES
FROM ENGLAND
+
THE DRAB
from SAN JOSE
+ OTHERS TO BE ANNOUNCED
AT RUTHIES INN
IN BERKELEY
JAN. 17 9:00 p.m.
$6.00
FUN FOR ALL

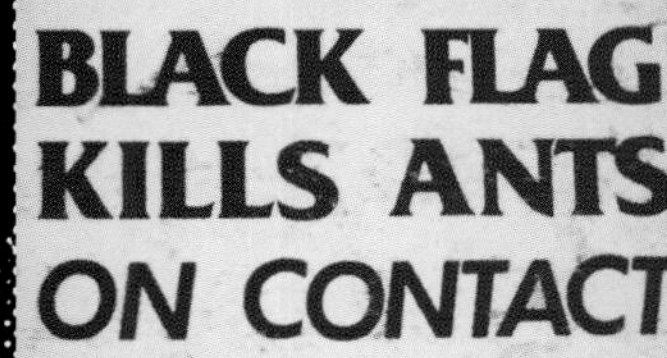
BLACK FLAG
KILLS ANTS
ON CONTACT

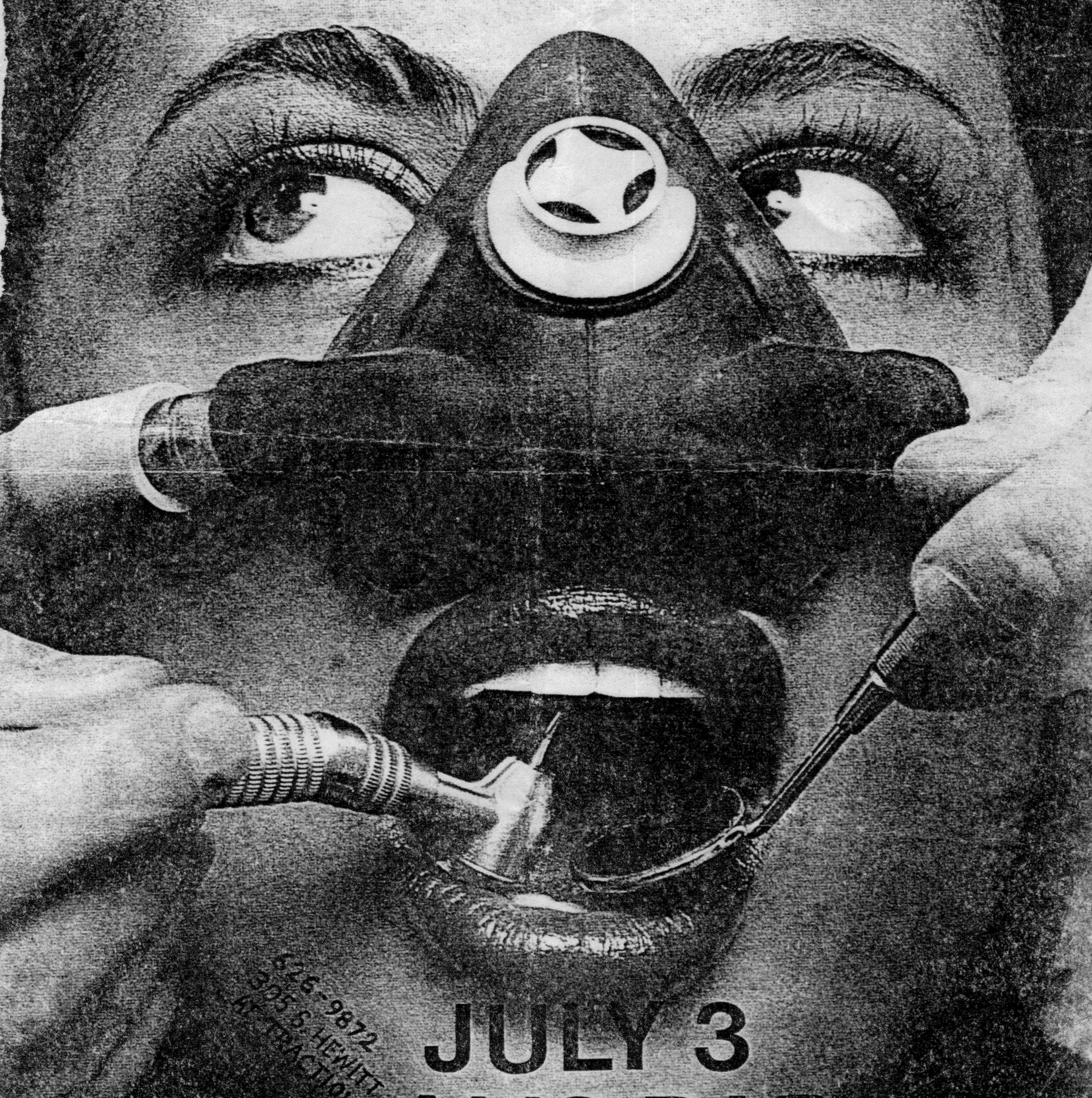
BPEOPLE
LEGAL WEAPON
626-9872
305 S. HEWITT
AT TRACTION
JULY 3
AL'S BAR

CONSUMERS:
TV
GENERATION OF NOW
consumers:

DEADBEATS
WHISKY
MAY 26–28 Fri–Sun
EXPAND THE FRONTIERS OF SIMULATION

NEW ORDER

BPEOPLE

·perkins palace nov 6·

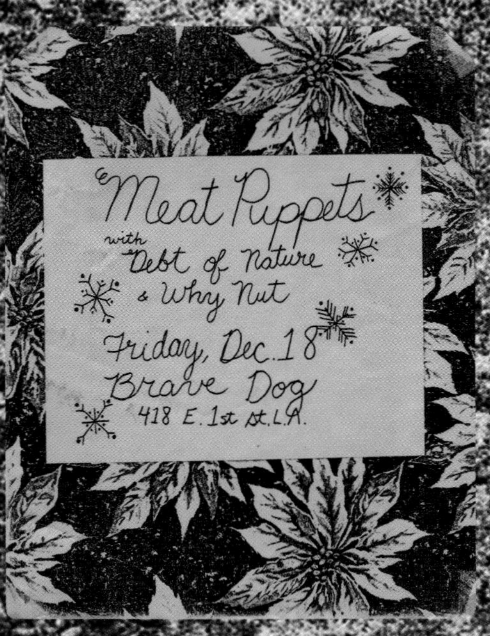
Meat Puppets
with
Debt of Nature
& Why Nut
Friday, Dec. 18
Brave Dog
418 E. 1st St. L.A.

D.N.A
BPEOPLE
PLUS
THE OMLITS
SAT SEPT 6 · 9PM
HONG KONG CAFE

FROM NEW YORK
SLASH RECORDING ARTISTS
VIOLENT FEMMES
THURS MAY 5
GEEZERS
only $4.00
DECADANCE
NIGHT CLUB
4001 EAST VAN BUREN 244 9242

MUTANTS
X
ALLYCATS
330 GROVE ST
MAY 11

FRIDAY july 17TH
CHEIFS
FROM L.A.
NUTRONS
violent crime
anti trust
$4
8PM
DEAD OR ALIVE
DEAD OR ALIVE
DEAD OR ALIVE
DEAD OR ALIVE
DEAD OR ALIVE
DEAD OR ALIVE
FAIRMONT HALL 3670 FAIRMONT AVE

NUTRONS - PRE BATTALION OF SAINTS

VOX POP!
MEAT PUPPETS
CATHAY
DE GRANDE
WED. SEPT. 9
ELVIS, thee King, He liveth yet?
BLUE MOON OF KENTUCKY KEEP ON SHINING

AARON WHITE

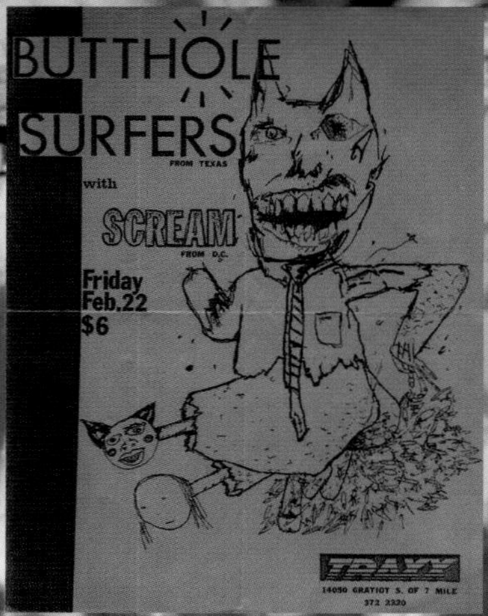

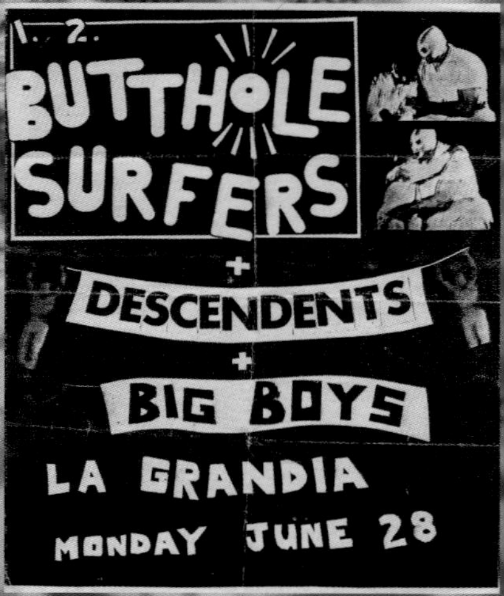

FROM LOS ANGELES
DESCENDENTS
WITH
DAG NASTY
(NEW LP OUT ON DISCHORD)
and
Justice League
(from CA)
Enjoy!
DESCENDENTS
Enjoy!
JULY 18th
8pm
$7.00 IN ADVANCE
$7.50 At the Door
COMPLEX
1239 9th St nw
wash dc
PHONE: 682-0474
RECORDING: (301)-320-2991
TICKETRON

AARON WHITE

Back in the mid eighties myself and Craig Ibbarra used to do most of the flyers in the Harbor Area but we never had money to do the layout or for simple materials. The times before computers you know! We had a Fanzine called the "Toilet Times" that called for Scratch off letters because it was way too fucking much shit to hand letter! So I stuffed about 400.00 dollars worth of those plastic letter sheets down my Dickies bought a Thrifty's ice cream and headed for the door, unfortunately it was witnessed by a guy upstairs through a mirror window and I got swarmed in the parking lot. You would think some little skate punk stealing office supply wouldn't be that big of a deal, take it back and let me go on my way. This became a huge victory for the conservative Thrifty's to get even with the strange punk youth of the times! They called the cops and the drama continued. I did get out of Harbor Patrol but hours later after they decided to fuck with me and call me a fag! All I know is, they were the ones with the MUSTACHES!

BUTTHOLE SURFERS
FLAMING LIPS
DECLARATION OF LOVE
KOZIK 88
HOUSTON
NUMBERS
300
WESTHEIMER
713·526·6551
APRIL 27
AUSTIN
RITZ THEATRE
320 EAST 6TH
512·479·0054
APRIL 28
DALLAS
ARCADIA
2005
GREENVILLE
214·823·3363
APRIL 30
TICKETS FOR HOUSTON & DALLAS SHOWS AVAILABLE AT RAINBOW TICKET MASTER
FRANK KOZIK
Butthöle Surfers

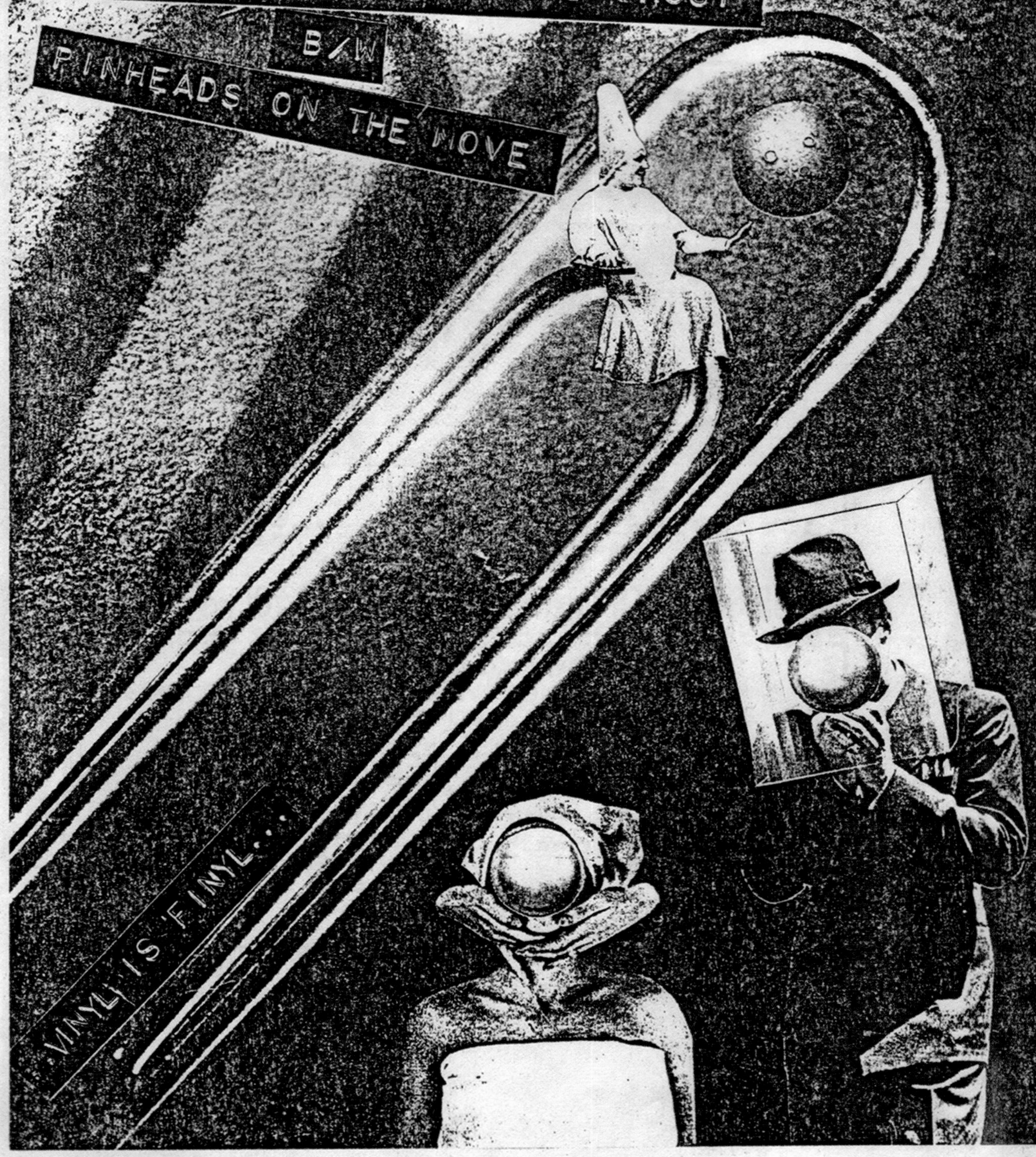
TUXEDO MOON/ THE '45'..
JOEBOY /THE ELECTRONIC GHOST
B/W
PINHEADS ON THE MOVE
VINYL IS FINYL...

moog
TUXEDOMOON

EUREKA THEATER PRESENTS
TUXEDOMOON
&NOH MERCY (formerlyontherag)
DEC.2,MIDNIGHT,DEC.3,TEN P.M.
$3,EUREKA THEATER 2299 MARKET

TUXEDO
MOON
MARCH
2/3
CONTAMINATED
symbiosis
MASQUE

TUXEDOMOON
Electronic Fun!
steven brown
blaine reininger
winston tong

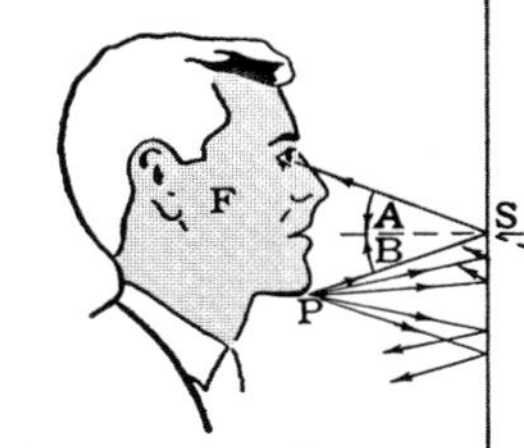
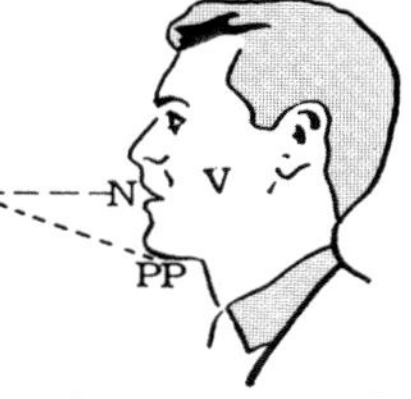

TUXEDOMOON
F
A
B
S
N
V
P
PP
M
3-27
3-28 hurrah's
4-1 mudd club
4-3 max's
OFF THE DEEPEND TOUR '79
4 SONGS,12 INCHES OF ELECTRONIC VINYL,
PUT IT WHERE IT'll DO THE MOST FOR YOU. EP 45RPMs

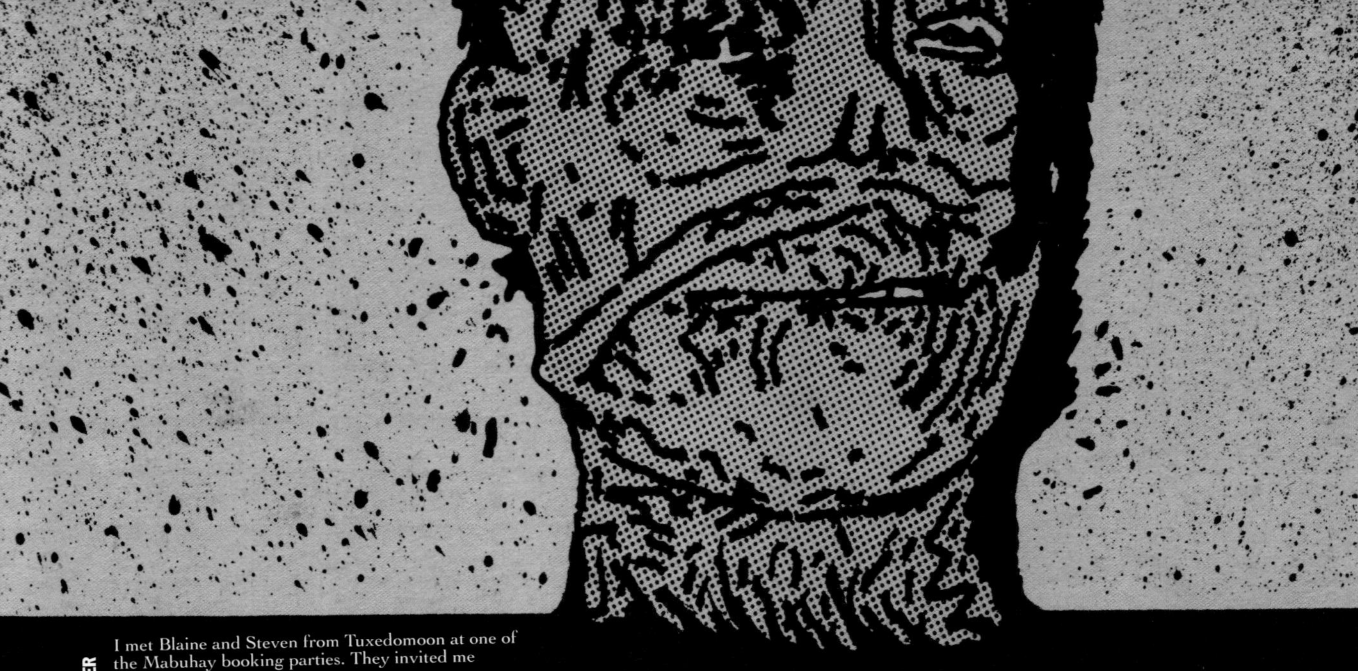

MICHAEL BELFER

I met Blaine and Steven from Tuxedomoon at one of the Mabuhay booking parties. They invited me

to come record at their studio with them. I did and wound up staying to join the band and record the first Tuxedomoon E.P. soon afterwards.
I met Patrick Miller when Tuxedomoon moved into his basement on Valencia St. to rehearse. He was

primarily a visual artist, making what he called his "Big Head"

M I N I M A L M A N

paintings and stenciling the image all over town. He also made these very cool sculptures he called "Nail Dogs". He made them for specific people he liked. He would ask you for hair, nails, skin or

whatever he could get you to give him and then incorporate them into your "Nail Dog".

Minimal Man was originally formed with Cole

and Bond from Factrix backing Patrick. Their first show was with Tuxedomoon at The Eureka theatre. I think Winston Tong made the posters. Minimal Man performed with Film Loops behind them that Patrick edited

together from found footage. It was a mesmer-

izing performance I'll never forget. I used to enjoy collaborating with Patrick whenever I could. He helped me record the Sleepers second 7 inch Mirror/Theory (which we did at his flat) and also helped me get the sessions going for Tuxedomoon's second E.P. Scream With A View which we started in his basement and then finished at The Residents studio. It was also in his basement(where the Shadow came to pay a visit and stayed for a week) on Valencia St. that I helped write and record his album The Shroud

which had his big head image as the cover...I only remember us doing a few performances of that record. Patrick was an extremely brilliant and multi-talented artist. I'm at a loss for words to describe how

much he is missed. I need to dust off my nail dog.

MINIMAL MAN
NERVOUS GENDER
GHOULS + WILMA
MAY 9 + 10 SAT+SUN
SOUND OF MUSIC 885-9616
162 TURK ST. S.F. $3.50

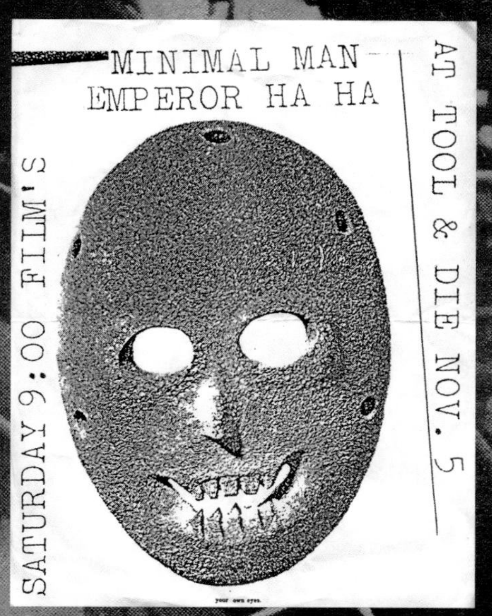
MINIMAL MAN
EMPEROR HA HA
SATURDAY 9:00 FILM'S
AT TOOL & DIE NOV. 5

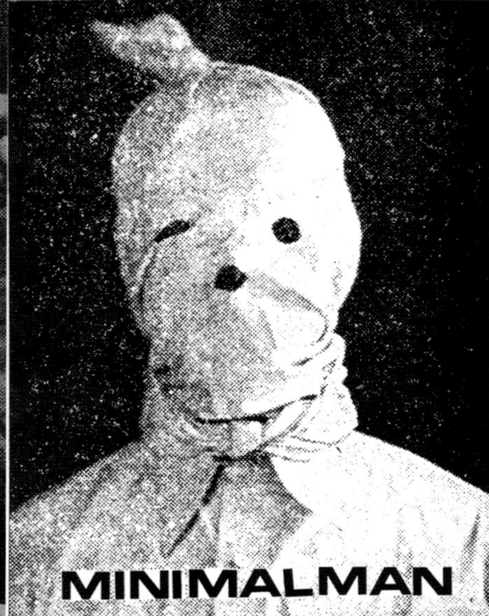
MINIMALMAN

AND TUXEDOMOON
AUGUST
24
FRIDAY
DEAF CLUB
530 VALENCIA

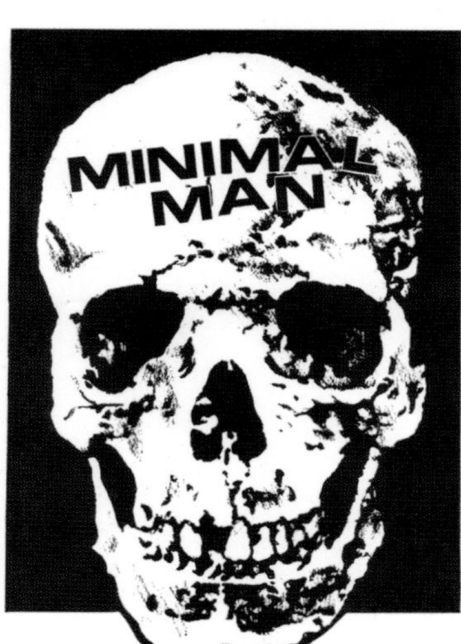
MINIMAL
MAN

AND PINK SECTION
MIDNIGHT AUG 3-4
EUREKA THEATER
16 ST AT MARKET

TSOL
MINIMAL MAN
CRUCIFIX

FRI. SEPT 25 9PM
ON BROADWAY THEATER
435 Broadway 398-0800

ALL FLYERS: PATRICK MILLER

FAULTY PRODUCTIONS
PRESENTS

BAD POSTURE &

MAD

with
RIBSY
&
KARNAGE

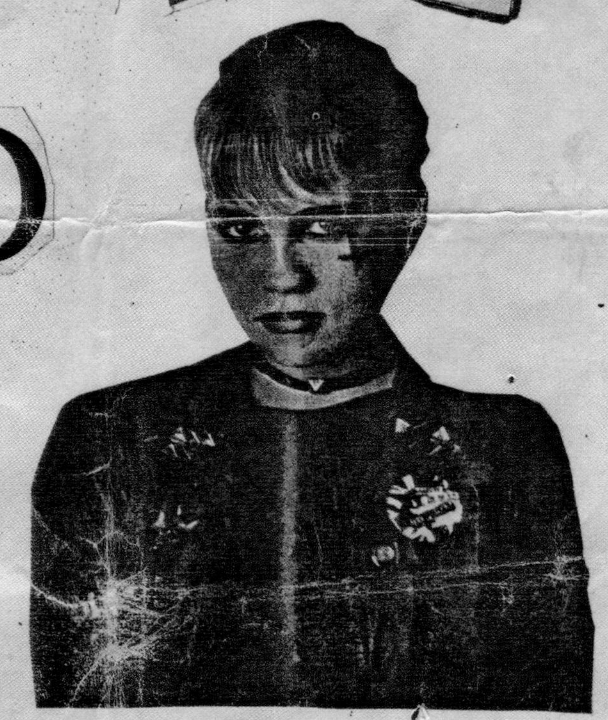

Dec. 23 at THE
AMERICAN LEGION
14TH & K ST Sac.

ROSS McDUFFY

U.S. No 1
SELECT
50 LBS.
NET WT.
(22.7 Kg)
STIFFS
PRODUCE OF U.S.A

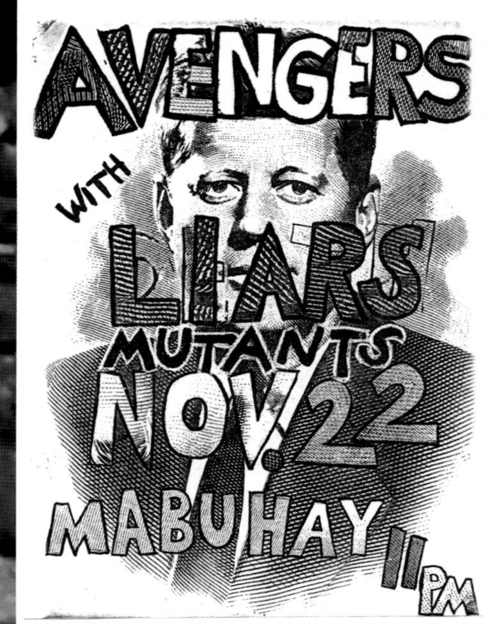

AVENGERS
WITH
LIARS
MUTANTS
NOV. 22
MABUHAY
11PM

Psyclone Presents
BEERS
20
15
THE NUNS AND CRIME
WEDNESDAY MARCH 16
SHOWS AT 11 and 12
$2.00 at the DOOR
MABUHAY GARDENS 443 BROADWAY S.F.
JAMES STARK

©77
JAMES
STARK

the OFFS
&
CRIME
MABUHAY Gardens
Friday July 28

The OFFS
RANK & File
UxA
SUNDAY
We are LOOKING for YOU this SUNDAY.
JULY 9
330 GROVE
4-9PM $1.00
It's for you!

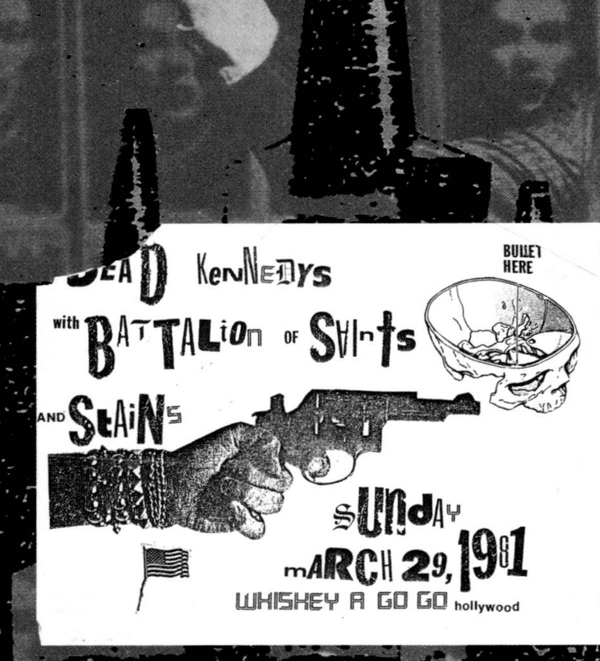
DEAD KENNEDYS
with BATTALION OF SAINTS
AND STAINS
BULLET HERE
SUNDAY
MARCH 29, 1981
WHISKEY A GO GO hollywood

JELLO FOR MAYOR!

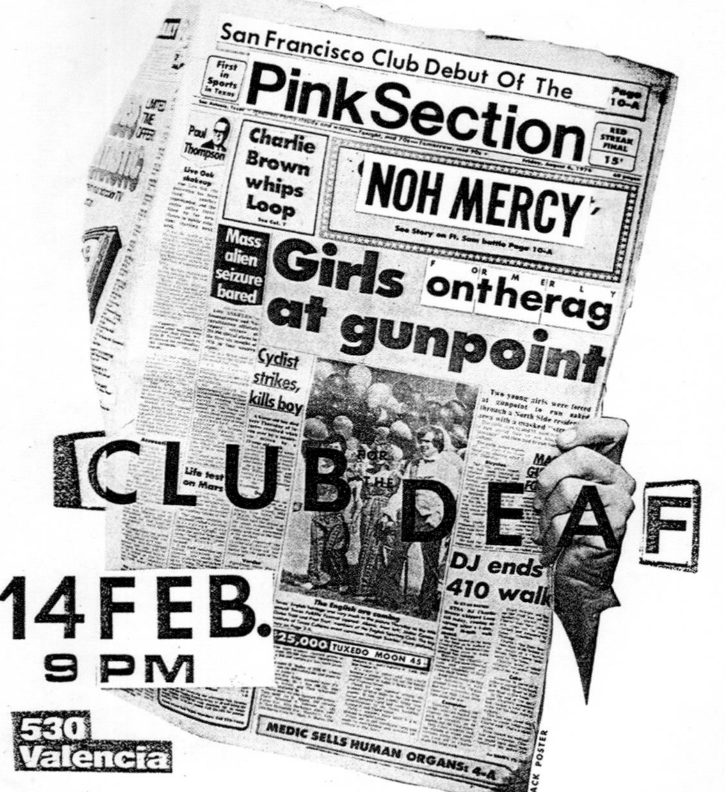
San Francisco Club Debut Of The
Pink Section
Charlie Brown whips Loop
'NOH MERCY'
Mass alien seizure bared
Girls FORMERLY ontherag at gunpoint
Cyclist strikes, kills boy
CLUB DEAF
DJ ends 410 walk
14 FEB.
9 PM
25,000 TUXEDO MOON 45
530 Valencia
MEDIC SELLS HUMAN ORGANS: 4-A
JACK POSTER

THE AVENGERS &&&&
THE DILS
.1
.5 .10 .7
.9 .2
.8 .4
.3 .6 .11
.13
.12
WITH:
NEGATIVE TREND & UXA
MABUHAY Gardens
SAT.&SUN
28TH &29TH JAN.

MUTANTS
45 GRAVE
PUDS
HALF ChUrch
sät.
november
14
435 on broadway
slides by Jill von Hoffman
THE AVENGERS
POWELL GARAGE
1350 CALIF ST.
THE AVENGERS
STREET PUNKS & X-RAY-TED
Thursday
AUG 25
MABUHAY Gardens
443 Broadway
956-3315
11pm
DEAD KENNEDYS
T.S.O.L
BAD BRAINS
7 SECONDS DOMINO THEORY
sat. March 20
8:00 PM
$600 All Ages
ELITE CLUB Fillmore - Geary
Alternative Tentacles
94103

B.W.

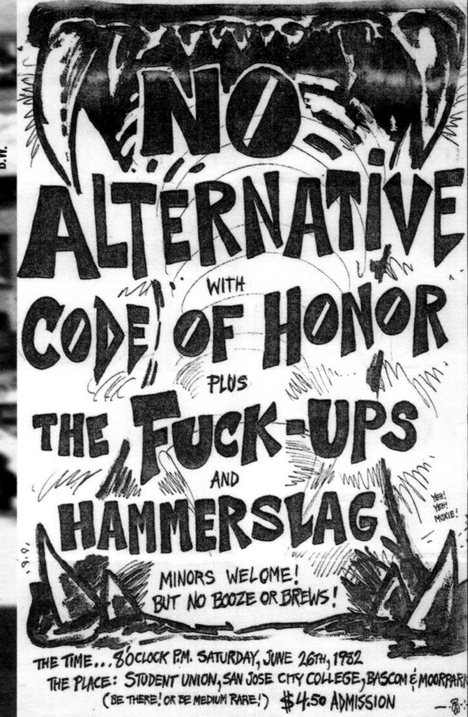
NO ALTERNATIVE
WITH
CODE OF HONOR
PLUS
THE FUCK-UPS
AND
HAMMERSLAG
MINORS WELOME!
BUT NO BOOZE OR BREWS!
THE TIME... 8 O'CLOCK P.M. SATURDAY, JUNE 26TH, 1982
THE PLACE: STUDENT UNION, SAN JOSE CITY COLLEGE, BASCOM & MOORPARK
(BE THERE! OR BE MEDIUM RARE!) $4.50 ADMISSION

GRIM REALITY

BY MURRAY

DELLA CHAFFEE

HAUSER BROTHERS

There's a time for playing it safe and a time for...
THE HAUSERS 2nd Annual Blow Out
WOTTA SHOW!
WITH
the Fuck-Ups
also
PERSONALITY CRISIS
EXECUTIONER
LIVING 2 ABERTIONS
RIBZY
$3.00
SAT 6.83 3:00

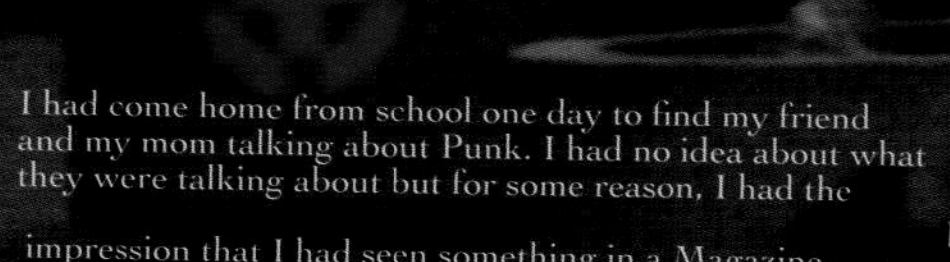

I had come home from school one day to find my friend and my mom talking about Punk. I had no idea about what they were talking about but for some reason, I had the

impression that I had seen something in a Magazine. Then one evening, I opened up New West magazine

(a Bay Area culture magazine at that time) and I slammed into a picture of Johnny Rotten. The photo was taken back stage at the Winterland show. Their last show. Right about that time I was beginning to get into bands visually.

I had become sensitive to what you could do with merely a look and a graphic. That image in

New West made me go out and hunt for more images. It had a huge impact on me. Punk's appeal was the thing that allured me for quite a few years. It was

worth changing my life for. The only real feeling I h so far. Then my friend Bob played me Stiff Little Fi gers' - Nobody's Heroes. That along side "Listen"

by Generation X made me decide that I wanted to s in a band. The allure was growing. In the city (San Francisco) I would go out and see the Fuck Ups an or Social Unrest play. They worked the best for me

They looked like the feel. Discharge on stage tweak me a little as well. Ribzy was always different. Soci Unrest's "Making room for Youth" single had the chords, better than anything else around here. Tha record really sang. Creetin was an entity. Hearing voice peek out a mic over the band's ripping was

inspiring. With the Sex Pistols it was the descendir chords that got me! Also, I loved the Destroy shir made me giddy. It was like a Hieronymus Bosch su hero logo. Finally I could wear something that lool

like music and history smashing together. Kinda lik

the feel you might be able to get if you crossed one of thos old BBC World at War programs and a video of a Ballard story. I was way too serious. I guess it made me feel like all the music I was getting into was alive and actual at any instant. Now I was broadcasting the music while wearing something about it. It still has very real deliberate feeling

JASON HONEA

PRODUCTIONS PRESENT
HALF CHURCH
FRIDAY, JUNE 7TH
10 PM 18 & OVER
WITH FONTANELLES
AND VERY SPECIAL GUESTS
MABUHAY GARDENS
443 BROADWAY, SAN FRANCISCO
(415) 956-3315

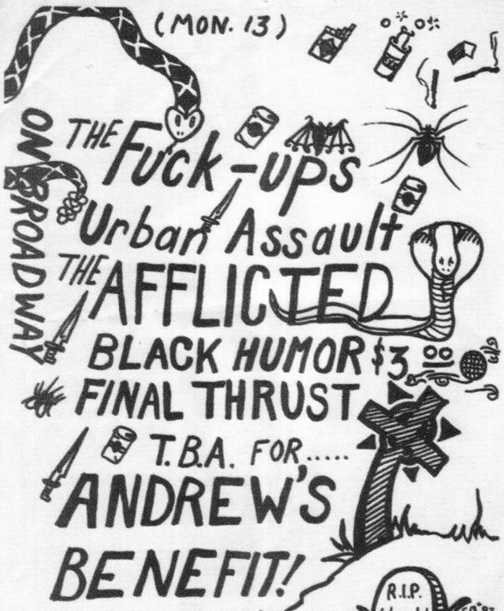
(MON. 13)
ON BROADWAY
THE FUCK-UPS
Urban Assault
THE AFFLICTED
BLACK HUMOR
$3.00
FINAL THRUST
T.B.A. FOR.....
ANDREW'S BENEFIT!
R.I.P.

MABUHAY
FRIDAY
AUGUST 31
FADE TO BLACK
OUR LADY OF PAIN
NAPALM BEACH
THIEVES CROSS

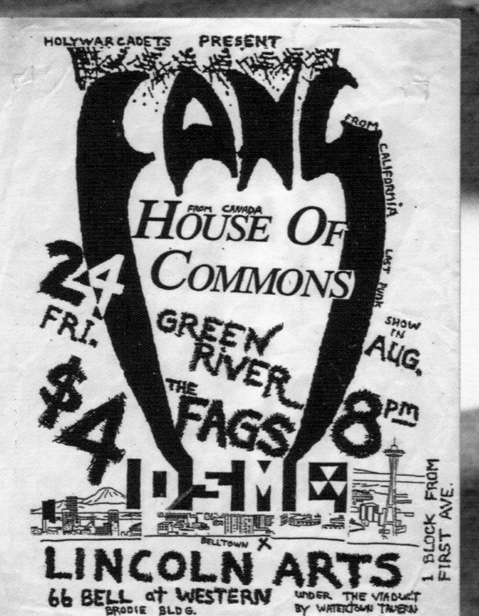
HOLYWAR CADETS PRESENT
FANG
FROM CALIFORNIA
FROM CANADA
HOUSE OF COMMONS
24
FRI.
GREEN RIVER
SHOW IN AUG.
THE FAGS
$4
8pm
LINCOLN ARTS
66 BELL at WESTERN
BRODIE BLDG.
UNDER THE VIADUCT
BY WATERTOWN TAVERN
1 BLOCK FROM FIRST AVE.

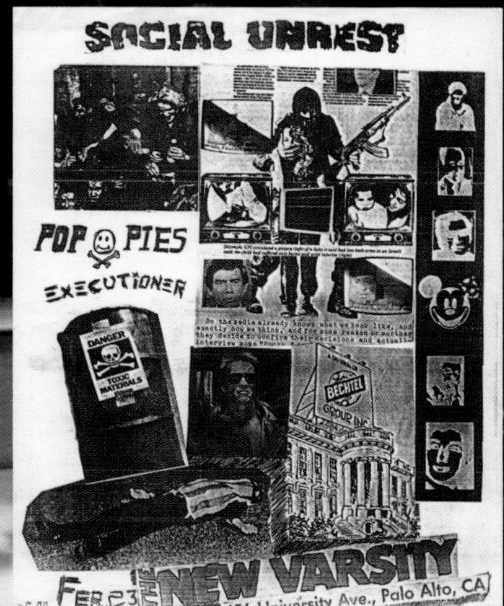
SOCIAL UNREST
POP PIES
EXECUTIONER
FEB 23
NEW VARSITY
456 University Ave., Palo Alto, CA

SOCIAL UnREST
CRUCIFIX
EXECUTIONER
TWIST & SCREAM
P.L.H.
D.B.R.
× MINORS WELCOME
4$
SAT FEB. 5
AT "THE" BARN IN LIVERMORE
7:00 P.M.
580
CEMETERY
SHOPPING CENTER
LIBRARY
THE BARN

JAMES S.D.

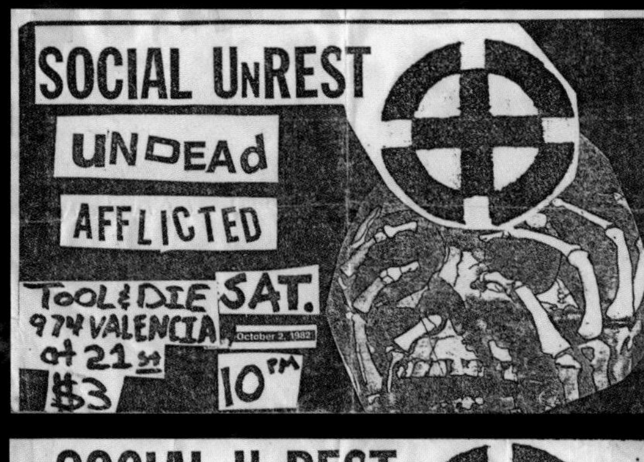
SOCIAL UnREST
UNDEAD
AFFLICTED
TOOL & DIE
974 VALENCIA
at 21 st
$3
SAT.
October 2, 1982
10 PM

MARK MONTI

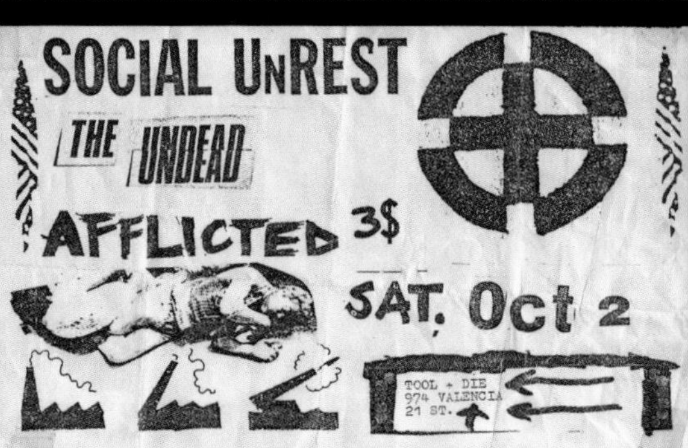
SOCIAL UnREST
THE UNDEAD
AFFLICTED
3$
SAT, Oct 2
TOOL + DIE
974 VALENCIA
21 ST.

MARK MONTI

SOCIAL UNREST
PLH
EXECUTIONER
TWIST AND SCREAM
CRUCIFIX
9 PM SAT.
the BARN
LIVERMORE
DRUNK with POWER!
580 EAST
LIVERMORE CENTRAL EXIT
Cemetery
Shopping center
Library
× the BARN
N
W
E
S
17

SOCIAL UNREST
RIBSY AND CIVIL DEFENSE
15TH SEPT
FROM THE 408 AREA CODE!!!
VIDAL'S
UNION + CALIF...
5 BUCK A PERSON
8 BUCKS A COUPLE ...DOORS OPEN AT 7:30pm

GRIM REALITY

DAVE BURKS

Spring 1983 was the best of times. As a band we had put in the time, practice, sweat and effort to get to the level all young bands seek. Just trying to make it. This did include a bit of thieving of musical instruments in order to get there, but, to us, it was all part of the Punk Ethic. By the summer of 83' we were well on our way. One instance in particular made me realize it. I was getting dropped off for our gig at the Tool and Die in the City (San Francisco) and immediately after exiting the car, three little punk girls grab me and escort me to the nearby alley and present me with a gift. A Big-Assed bottle of Cheap-Ass wine! This is great! In between chugs and belches, we talked of the evening ahead and about the scene and bands etc. The next thing I know its time to play and I am sloppily mounting the rinky-dink stage and getting ready. Before I can catch my breath we bust through the first two songs like lightning. Then it hits me like a ton of bricks. 'Man I'm gonna puke!' I leap behind the guitar amp and let it out, barely wiping my mouth, struggling to my feet, and 'One Two Three Four' into the third song and the words fly out of my mouth like nothing happened.

EXECUTIONER
Love At First Sight

"GREAT..."
"SPECTACULAR.."
JAN.18th1986
EXECUTIONER
FRONT-LINE
& RETALIATION
"PREPARE TO BE ASTONISHED"
MURPHY AVENUE CINEMA 735-9251
$7
$4
-9pm-

JOE SIB

RIPPER MAG BENEFIT:
STARRING
BAD POSTURE
FREE BEER
MAD
RIBZY
eXECUTIONER
GREAT SCOTT! RIBZY HAS ACQUIRED SUPER-POWERS, AND HE'S USING THEM AGAINST US!
AT: ON BROADWAY
435 BROADWAY
SAN FRANCISCO
TIME: AUGUST 31 TUESDAY 9:30
PRICE: $3
Featuring RIBZY "The SUPER BAT-HOUND!"

EXECUTIONER
pop o pies
feb 23
NEW VARIETY
THE RIDER OF DEATH, S. DALI, 1935

DAVE BURKS

PHIL MEANS

EXECUTIONER
REALITY
FEAR FOR YOUR LIFE
THE ANSWER
TALK OF THE WORLD
FREE AND INNOCENT
IN JAIL
this is your reality.

EXEcutioner
Lives!!!
Live...
JUNE 2nd
at The
ON
BROADWAY
+
Live
Killing Joke
YEA!
Loud Music
LACK OF PAIN

EXECUTIONER by DANNY HERNANDEZ

DENISE VAUGHN

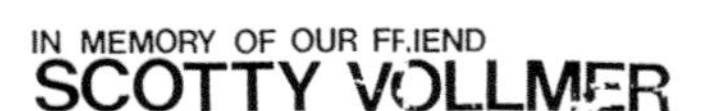

IN MEMORY OF OUR FRIEND
SCOTTY VOLLMER

CLUB X WORKS/S.J. KFJC
PRESENT
A BENEFIT PERFORMANCE BY HIS FRIENDS...

THE BONE SHAVERS
FRONTIER WIVES
THE INJUNS
THE KINGPINS
McRAD
ODD MAN OUT
RIBZY w/ DERRICK
S.J.'S FRONTLINE
SHOCKWAVES
SWING PARTY
WHIPPING BOY
WHISTLIN' BULLETS

SUN. MAR. 13, 1988
STAGECOACH INN
610 COLEMAN AVE. SAN JOSE
DOORS OPEN 1PM
MAIN SHOW 2:30 - MIDNITE
WALK ON ACOUSTICAL PERFORMANCES FROM 1PM TO 2:30
$5.00 DONATION AT THE DOOR
ALL PROCEEDS GOING DIRECTLY
TO THE VOLLMER FAMILY
(408) 377-1170 CENTRAL INFO. LINE
NO ALCOHOL PLEASE

THE FINAL NIGHT IN THE SKATETOWN BUILDING
CLUB X
SAT. JAN. 26
MOVING PARTY
WITH A SPECIAL EARLY LIVE SHOW
FEATURING
RIBZY
AND SPECIAL GUEST
MISTAKEN IDENTITY
NO ADDED COST
DOOR OPENS 7:30 FOR LIVE SHOW
REGULAR DANCING BEGINS AT 9:30
NO ID REQUIRED
MAILING LIST P.O. BOX 6692 SAN JOSE, CA 95150

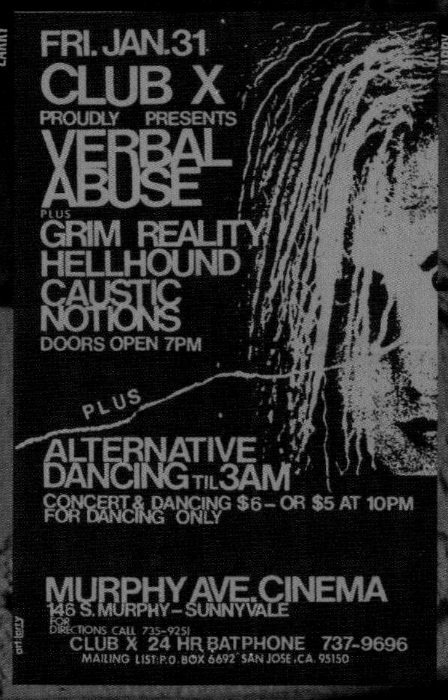

FRI. JAN. 31
CLUB X
PROUDLY PRESENTS
VERBAL ABUSE
PLUS
GRIM REALITY
HELLHOUND
CAUSTIC NOTIONS
DOORS OPEN 7PM
PLUS
ALTERNATIVE DANCING TIL 3AM
CONCERT & DANCING $6 - OR $5 AT 10PM FOR DANCING ONLY
MURPHY AVE. CINEMA
146 S. MURPHY - SUNNYVALE
CLUB X 24 HR BATPHONE 737-9696
MAILING LIST P.O. BOX 6692 SAN JOSE, CA. 95150

DEVIATIONS AND CLUB X
PROUDLY PRESENT
8 BANDS, 8 DOLLARS
THRASHIN' IN THE YEAR 1986 WITH
SOCIAL DISTORTION
AND THE VANDALS
PLUS
DR. KNOW
CAPITOL PUNISHMENT
MISTAKEN IDENTITY · JUSTICE LEAGUE
DEATH TRAP · LEGION OF DOOM
FRI. JAN. 3RD 5:30 TIL MIDNITE
SAN JOSE CONV. CNTR.
CONCERT HOTLINES: 737-9696, 73PUNK-O

SAT. JAN. 25
THE DRAB
Prepare For Some Action!
THE BARFING DOGS
BREATHLESS
Plus Special Guest!
MURPHY AVENUE CINEMA 735-9251
8:30 P.M.
4$ All Ages.
Washington
Town Center

FACTION

THE FACTION TOUR 1985
with THE DRAB
JUNE
16 San Jose
17 Los Angeles
18 Phoenix
19 Santa Fe
20 Dallas
21 Houston
22 Memphis
23 Nashville
24 Atlanta
25-28 Florida
29 Winston Salem
JULY
1 Norfolk
2 Virginia Beach
3 Baltimore
4 Atlantic City
5 Stamford
7 New York
8 Allentown
10 Cleveland
11 Grand Rapids
12 Chicago
13 Milwaukee
14 Des Moines
15 Lincoln
16 Kansas City
17 Denver
18 Salt Lake City
19 Reno
The Faction-Dark Room 12 inch $7 ppd I.R. Records Suite 109-222
15466 Los Gatos Blvd, Los Gatos Ca, 95030. Booking 408-356-1939

GROWING PAINS
A compilation from Scum Jose
featuring;
the FACTION
UNAWARE
EXECUTIONER
GRIM REALITY
FACTION PRODUCTIONS
the BRUCES
RIBZY
TIME: Winter of '83
PLACE: Silicon Valley
WHY: Noth'n else to do.
Whipping Boy
Los Olvidados
A FACTION PRODUCTION
COVER ART BY GAVIN O

CLUB CULTURE
418 FRONT ST.
SANTA CRUZ
PRESENTS
DRAB WITH
RAGE &
LONELY CROWD,
ARMISTICE
CAUSTIC NOTION
PARTY
LOCAL S.J. BANDS
MARCH · 22 FRI
$3
425-9468 for more info.
All ages welcome!

the DRAB

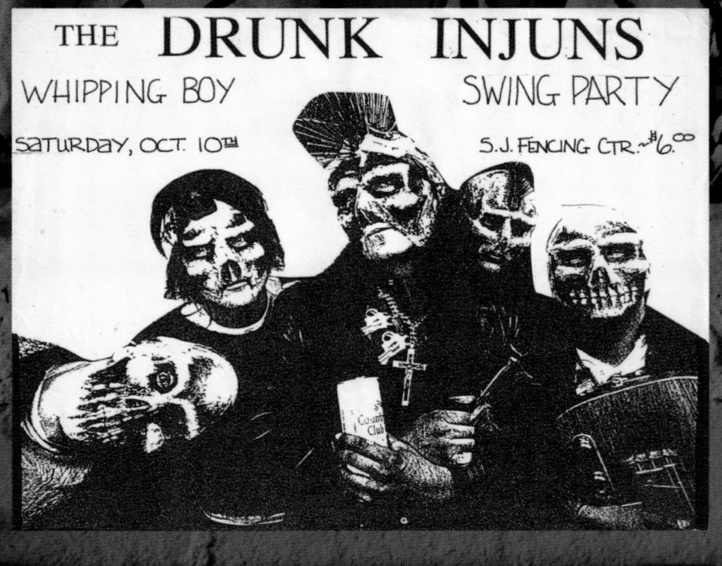

THE DRUNK INJUNS
WHIPPING BOY
SWING PARTY
Saturday, OCT. 10TH
S.J. FENCING CTR. ~ $6.00

A STUPID PET TRICK CALLED:
The FORGOTTEN
MARCH 15TH
COME INTOXICATE
at: VIKING CENTER AT WEST VALLEY COLLEGE
8:00 PM FREE
The Basement holds 3,000 pairs of shoes and BEER & FRY and JELLY BIRD EGGS & DOLL BODIES

FROM THE
PAT TOVES
After living in San Francisco and New York over the years the general attitude when I tell people I grew up in the suburbs is one where I'm supposed to feel some kind of humiliation. The truth is, thanks to early 80's Hardcore/Punk, I wouldn't have traded growing up in San Jose for anything. Besides, my friends and I knew more of what cool events were going on in "the City" than those who claimed to have been "big city born and raised". It was pre-MTV/pre-Information Age- a time when people were creative on their own and fought to hold onto it. That held especially true in little unknown San Jose and countless other small towns. And although not many bands came out of there, the few that did were better than most and would still blow people away to this day (Los Olvidados, Ribzy, and Executioner to name a few). Regardless, it's great to see so much of Punk still alive and so influential on the pop culture of today. It sucks that no one realizes that it's from the least likely areas and towns where much of it came from.
NO AID TO THE CONTRAS!
CONCERT AND RALLY FEATURING SAN JOSE'S OWN
RIBZY
SATURDAY, SEPT. 26
FREE
Rally: 1:00 p.m. Prusch Park Story & King Rds. SAN JOSE
Candlelight Vigil: Friday, Sept. 25, 7:30 p.m. Congressman Konnyu's Office 10080 N. Wolfe Rd, Cupertino (Across from Sears) Only Bay Area Representative to vote for Contra aid
RESPECT NICARAGUA'S SOVEREIGNTY
Speakers: Dolores Huerta, Vice-President, United Farm Workers Marta Alicia Rivera, Salvadoran Trade Unionist Brian Wilson, Veterans Fast for Life
Performers: Kamanchaka Teatro de los Pobres Robin Flower and Nancy Vogl Ribzy
These actions are part of nationwide demonstrations against the U.S. war
For More Information: South Bay Mobilization, 408-293-2902 or 408-224-8262
* Organization for Identification Purposes Only
CDC/DEVIATIONS PRESENTS:
D.O.A.
CANADA
RIBZY
SAN JOSE
STARK RAVING MAD
NEW YORK
UGLY AMERICANS
NORTH CAROLINA
THURS MAY 16 CLUB CULTURE $6
all ages * 7-11 p.m.
THE ... SER BR...
Presents:
Their 2nd Annual with
RIBSY
FROM SAN JOSE
The Fuck-Ups
FROM S.F.
LIVING ABORTIONS
FROM SAN JOSE
EXECUTIONER
FROM SANTA CLARA
PERSONALITY CRISIS
ALSO FROM S.F.
AUG. SAT. 6th SUMMER OF 83 AFTER NOON 3:00 P.M. DOWN TOWN SAN JOSE
13
RIBZY
For info. write:

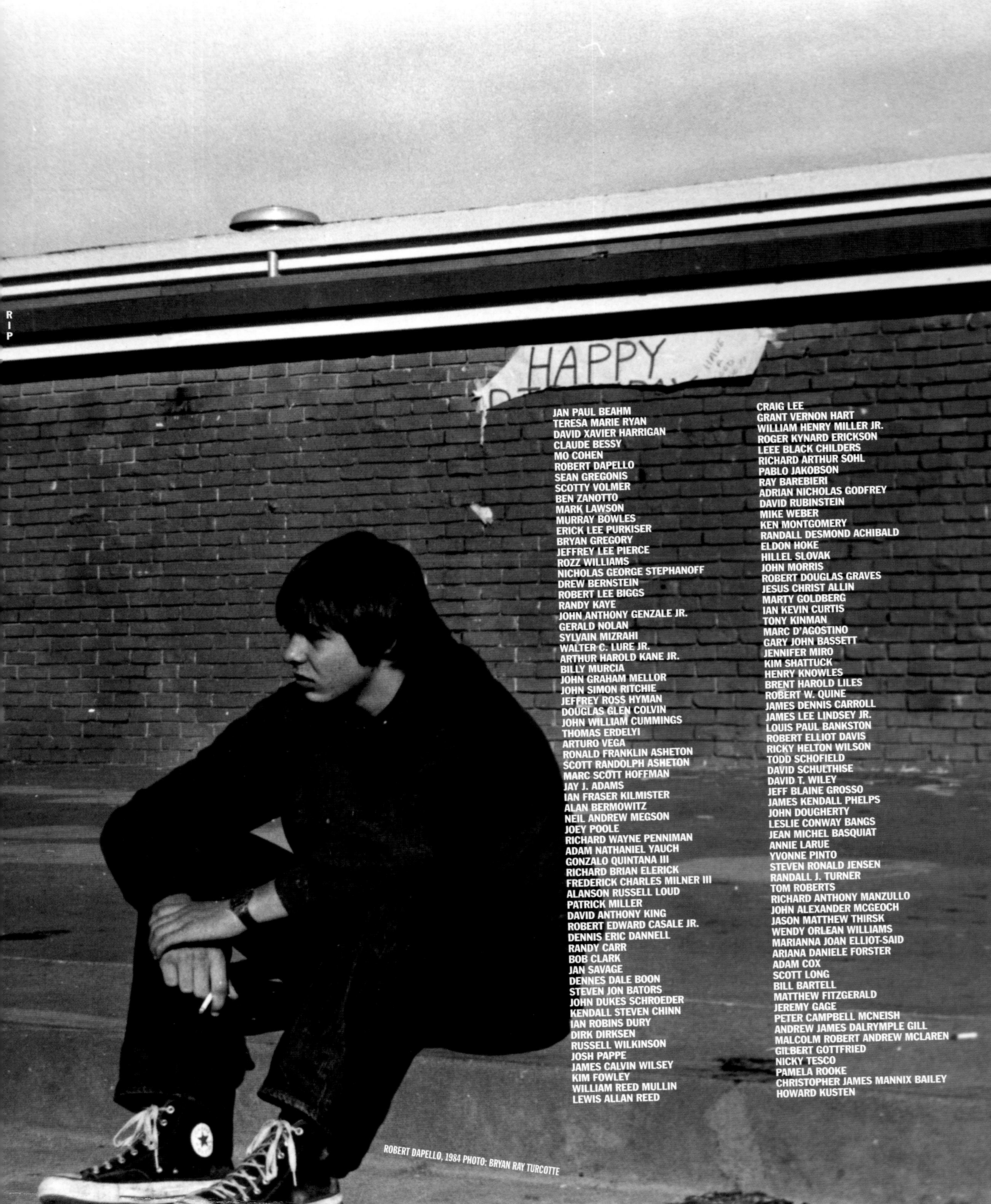
HAPPY

JAN PAUL BEAHM
TERESA MARIE RYAN
DAVID XAVIER HARRIGAN
CLAUDE BESSY
MO COHEN
ROBERT DAPELLO
SEAN GREGONIS
SCOTTY VOLMER
BEN ZANOTTO
MARK LAWSON
MURRAY BOWLES
ERICK LEE PURKISER
BRYAN GREGORY
JEFFREY LEE PIERCE
ROZZ WILLIAMS
NICHOLAS GEORGE STEPHANOFF
DREW BERNSTEIN
ROBERT LEE BIGGS
RANDY KAYE
JOHN ANTHONY GENZALE JR.
GERALD NOLAN
SYLVAIN MIZRAHI
WALTER C. LURE JR.
ARTHUR HAROLD KANE JR.
BILLY MURCIA
JOHN GRAHAM MELLOR
JOHN SIMON RITCHIE
JEFFREY ROSS HYMAN
DOUGLAS GLEN COLVIN
JOHN WILLIAM CUMMINGS
THOMAS ERDELYI
ARTURO VEGA
RONALD FRANKLIN ASHETON
SCOTT RANDOLPH ASHETON
MARC SCOTT HOFFMAN
JAY J. ADAMS
IAN FRASER KILMISTER
ALAN BERMOWITZ
NEIL ANDREW MEGSON
JOEY POOLE
RICHARD WAYNE PENNIMAN
ADAM NATHANIEL YAUCH
GONZALO QUINTANA III
RICHARD BRIAN ELERICK
FREDERICK CHARLES MILNER III
ALANSON RUSSELL LOUD
PATRICK MILLER
DAVID ANTHONY KING
ROBERT EDWARD CASALE JR.
DENNIS ERIC DANNELL
RANDY CARR
BOB CLARK
JAN SAVAGE
DENNES DALE BOON
STEVEN JON BATORS
JOHN DUKES SCHROEDER
KENDALL STEVEN CHINN
IAN ROBINS DURY
DIRK DIRKSEN
RUSSELL WILKINSON
JOSH PAPPE
JAMES CALVIN WILSEY
KIM FOWLEY
WILLIAM REED MULLIN
LEWIS ALLAN REED
CRAIG LEE
GRANT VERNON HART
WILLIAM HENRY MILLER JR.
ROGER KYNARD ERICKSON
LEEE BLACK CHILDERS
RICHARD ARTHUR SOHL
PABLO JAKOBSON
RAY BAREBIERI
ADRIAN NICHOLAS GODFREY
DAVID RUBINSTEIN
MIKE WEBER
KEN MONTGOMERY
RANDALL DESMOND ACHIBALD
ELDON HOKE
HILLEL SLOVAK
JOHN MORRIS
ROBERT DOUGLAS GRAVES
JESUS CHRIST ALLIN
MARTY GOLDBERG
IAN KEVIN CURTIS
TONY KINMAN
MARC D'AGOSTINO
GARY JOHN BASSETT
JENNIFER MIRO
KIM SHATTUCK
HENRY KNOWLES
BRENT HAROLD LILES
ROBERT W. QUINE
JAMES DENNIS CARROLL
JAMES LEE LINDSEY JR.
LOUIS PAUL BANKSTON
ROBERT ELLIOT DAVIS
RICKY HELTON WILSON
TODD SCHOFIELD
DAVID SCHULTHISE
DAVID T. WILEY
JEFF BLAINE GROSSO
JAMES KENDALL PHELPS
JOHN DOUGHERTY
LESLIE CONWAY BANGS
JEAN MICHEL BASQUIAT
ANNIE LARUE
YVONNE PINTO
STEVEN RONALD JENSEN
RANDALL J. TURNER
TOM ROBERTS
RICHARD ANTHONY MANZULLO
JOHN ALEXANDER MCGEOCH
JASON MATTHEW THIRSK
WENDY ORLEAN WILLIAMS
MARIANNA JOAN ELLIOT-SAID
ARIANA DANIELE FORSTER
ADAM COX
SCOTT LONG
BILL BARTELL
MATTHEW FITZGERALD
JEREMY GAGE
PETER CAMPBELL MCNEISH
ANDREW JAMES DALRYMPLE GILL
MALCOLM ROBERT ANDREW MCLAREN
GILBERT GOTTFRIED
NICKY TESCO
PAMELA ROOKE
CHRISTOPHER JAMES MANNIX BAILEY
HOWARD KUSTEN

ROBERT DAPELLO, 1984 PHOTO: BRYAN RAY TURCOTTE

JASON HONEA

I loved the Destroy shirt. It made me giddy. It was like a Hieronymus Bosch superhero logo. Finally I could wear something that looked like music and history smashing together.

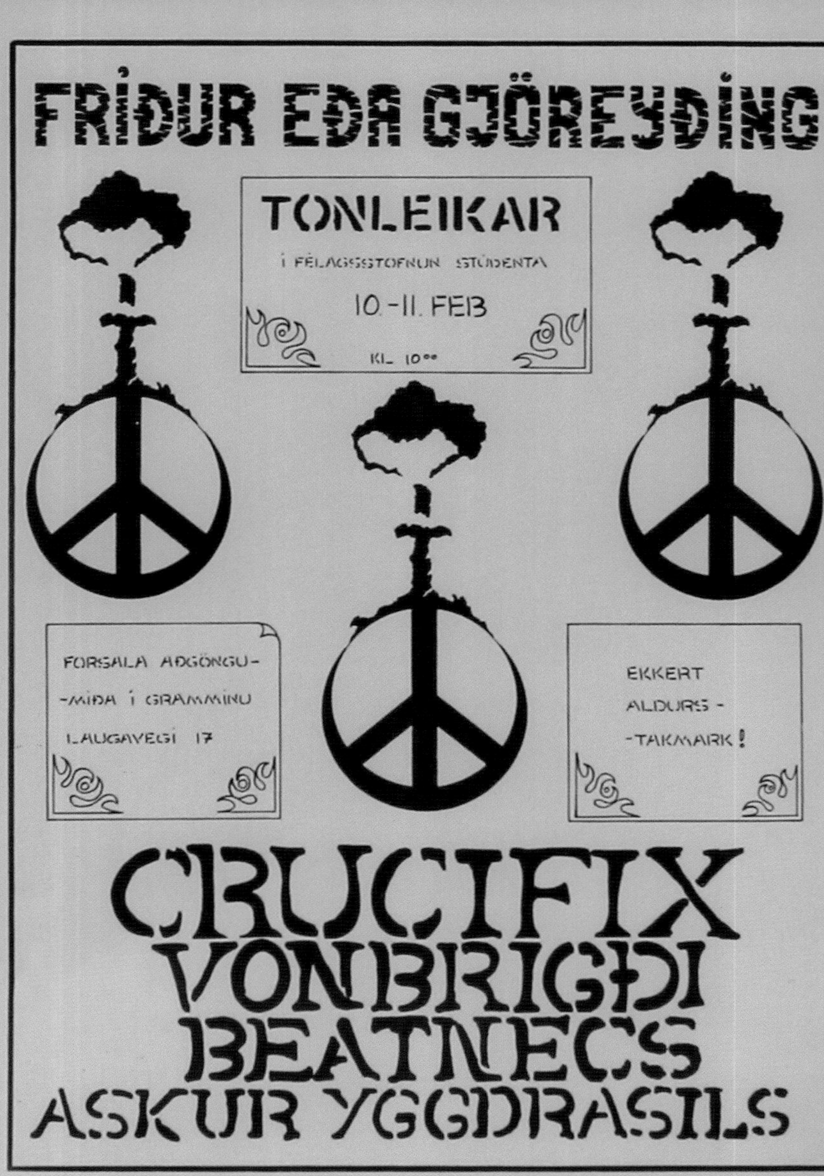
FRIÐUR EÐA GJÖREYÐING
TONLEIKAR
Í FÉLAGSSTOFNUN STÚDENTA
10.-11. FEB
KL. 10°°
FORSALA AÐGÖNGU-
-MIÐA Í GRAMMINU
LAUGAVEGI 17
EKKERT
ALDURS-
-TAKMARK!
CRUCIFIX
VONBRIGÐI
BEATNECS
ASKUR YGGDRASILS

CRUCIFIX IN NYC by LISA DEANN

Crucifix

POSTCARD FROM THE ROAD

uth = A group of hardcore 13 yr. awn of Lincoln Jr. High glaring r of flexyourhead...we

"wow...their scene looks rad"... Godzilla's... 2. 1982+Nuclear that wanted to hear music and a movement that reflected how e world! We were weirdo teens the right channel. 3. 1982+Fly- ovement I knew I belonged to... uldn't go to a show, I could at and look at ill artwork by Marc

nead...Rick Clayton... 4. 1982+ n Old Man Shirts = Suicidal hand-drawn shirts by R. Clay- a rite of passage for Suicidal- as like Wes Humpston drawing your deck.... 5. 1983+Police Heads = The Exploited Riots...

lidn't sit on the floor and get my d in! What gave the cops the us and tape over their badge ? Eight of us got away in a and the news said we were the

wood = Cathy De Grand...Now this was my club....I experienced some of the illest shows there like S.T., Stalag 13, Necros...I worked there (i thought i was some kind of bouncer)...

that was fun...Tex used to actually flow my 14-year-old scrub-ass beer....One night I tried to pick a fight with the singer of Battalion of Saints...Thank god he just laughed and pushed me away...I can't forget how they tried to do matinee shows like CBGB's...They didn't last long, but Black Flag played one and only about

15 heads showed...They performed balls out

one of their best shows! I could go on more but I'll stop.... 7. 1983+Crass = No to sexism... No to racism...No to apartheid...No to animal torture...Yes to becoming politicized @ a young

age...Yes to being a vegetarian...Yes to respect-

ing anything crass...All the bands they put out...Yes to wearing all

black ...Yes to eating @ veggie soup kitchens...Yes to realizing I control my destiny...Yes to D.I.Y. action! 8. 1984+My Mom Having Enough = She thought hardcore was something a young black male should not

be into...So @ the age of 15 Mike & I (from NOFX...I was their first roadie when 5 people went to their shows) drove up to S.F. for the Eastern Front Hardcore Festival...Before I left, my mom said if I leave, don't come back... So I didn't...I moved into a flat in the Castro

with Drew Bernstein (from

America's Hardcore, Crucifix & now the owner of Lip Service)... He taught me how to silkscreen

when I was 13...He silkscreened tees for bands like the Meatmen, Stretch Marks, Suicidal) ....I forsook my mother's love for hardcore...I held down a job, went to school (my best year in high school - I got straight B's), and started a peace punk band,

Diverse & Effective...Drew became my legal guardian (he actually had pretty good parenting skills)...he was strict about me doing my homework...

I totally immersed myself into the Bay Area peace punk scene...At the end of the day 7 months after I had moved to S.F., my mother came to visit me...I was wearing 8-hole Doc's, skin-tight black jeans, an Indian skirt , Black Sabbath & @ least 20 bangles on each arm...After she saw me, she said, "Sean you look great...I've never seen you look more beautiful"...Then she came to my flat and cooked a massive meal for all kinds of weirdos...my friends! 9.

1984+Summer = The summer of hate, S.F. skins...Bay Area skins...Skinhead Hill...Racist bastards...I was supposed to be beaten up on sight by any skin... Why? Because I stood up to them on the Maximum Rock n' Roll radio show and beat them in a debate...I just strangled them with their own racist thoughts and made them feel dumb so they wanted to break my bones...They

never got that chance because I went to shows dressed as an African exchange student...Don't get me wrong we still had fun that summer in spite of them! 10. 1984+Post Punk = The Birthday Party...Joy Division...March Violets...Killing Joke...Southern Death Cult etc...This music was speaking to me a whole lot more, plus the girls

were hot...I was reaching that age...I started to gain a fashion sense...By the time I moved home in 1985, I was really into Post Punk and moving

towards Rasta...I STILL LOVE

CRUCIFIX
(U.S.A.)
hardcore
en
pandemonium
BABYLON
HENGELO
Zat 18 FEBR.
21.30 uur
entree 7.50

CRUCIFIX
SOCIAL
UNREST
PLH
TREASON
DO YOU CARE?
SAT. JULY 9th
TOOL
& DIE
974 VALENCIA S.F.
MINORS WELCOME

CRUCIFIX
DISCHARGE
WAR?
45 GRAVE
THE
LEWD
SAT. OCT. 2ND
FLORENTINE
GARDENS
HOLLYWOOD
HOLLYWOOD BLVD

CRUCIFIX
1981
SOCIAL UNREST
WITH...
LIVING ABORTIONS
&
VERBAL ABUSE
MARCH 11
AT DE ANZA COLLEGE
ONLY $4
MINORS WELCOME
NO ALCOHOL

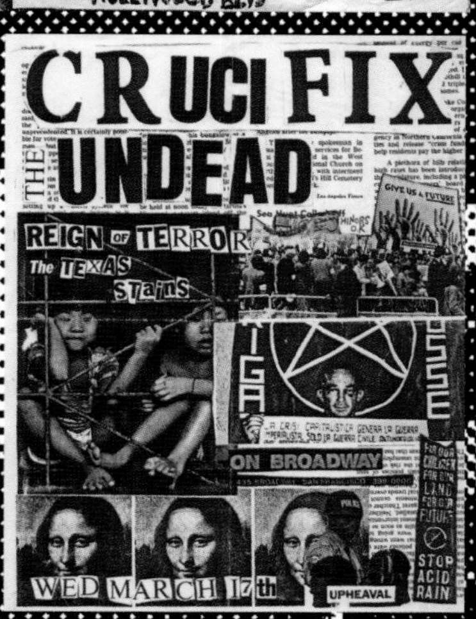
CRUCIFIX
THE UNDEAD
REIGN OF TERROR
The TEXAS STAINS
ON BROADWAY
STOP ACID RAIN
WED MARCH 17th
UPHEAVAL

CRUCIFIX
SOCIAL
UNREST
TRIAL

FRIDAY
JULY
13TH
FILM 'ARMY'
WILL BE SHOWN
MINORS
WELCOME
9:00
PM
$4.00
TAKE 38 GEARY
GET OFF AT PRESIDIO
WALK TWO BLOCKS
RED STUCCO BUILDING
ON RIGHT HAND SIDE
AT BOOKER T WASHINGTON
COMMUNITY CENTER
800 PRESIDIO AVE AT SUTTER ST SF

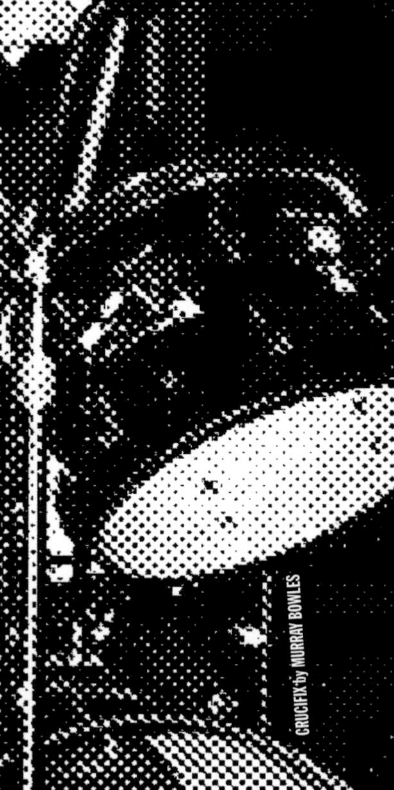

CRUCIFIX by MURRAY BOWLES

DE PIEK

DATUM 17 FEB

CRUCIFIX

sup. act. B.G.K.

HELLEBARDIERSTR. 11-13 VLISSINGEN TEL: 16791

AANVANG ~ 20.30 ENTREE ~ f 7,50

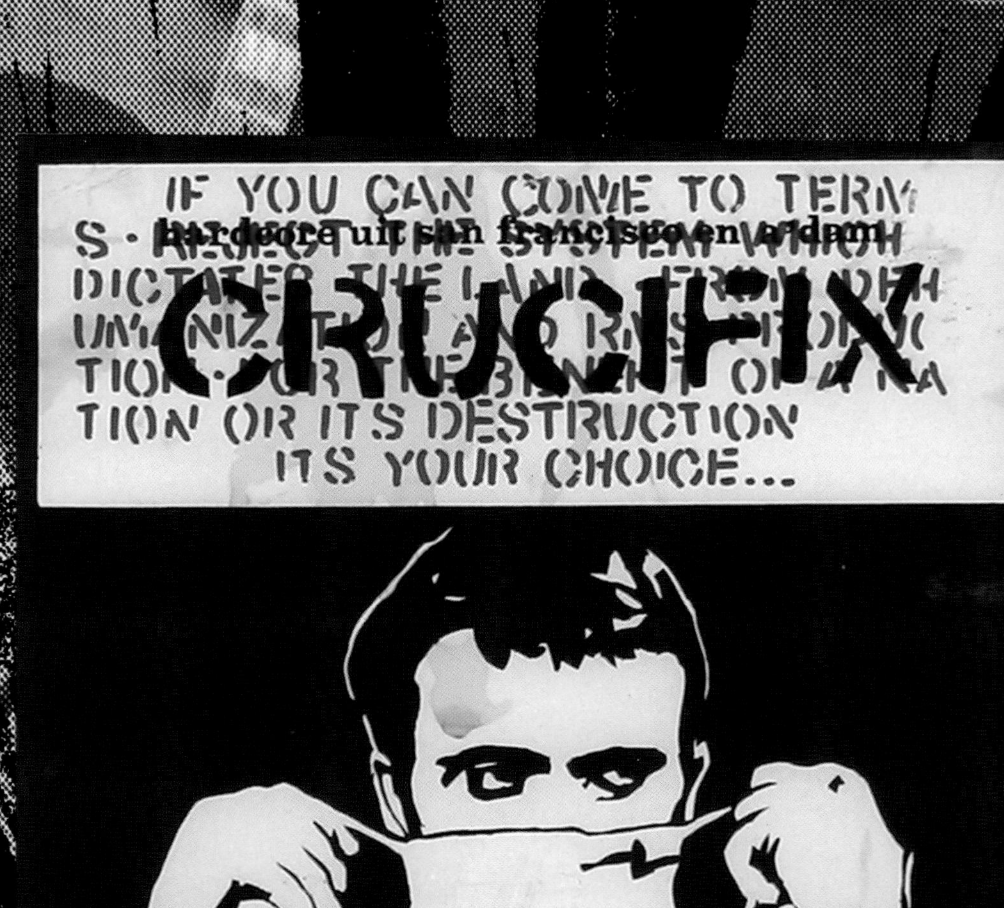
IF YOU CAN COME TO TERMS
hardcore uit san francisco en a'dam
CRUCIFIX
TION OR ITS DESTRUCTION
ITS YOUR CHOICE...
NO PIGS
UMANIZATION AND RMS PRODUC
TION · FOR THE BENEFIT OF A NA
20 19 feb
21.30
entree 6.50 b.z.k.
vvk: elpee
VERA
CRUCIFIX

CRASS LOGO BY DAVID ANTHONY KING
1:30

FIGHT WAR
NOT WARS
FRI WILD REGGAE BUNCH · ARSENAL
CONTORTIONS · CRASS
JUNE 30 · JULY 1
BLESSED · GYNAECOLOGISTS
SAT CONTORTIONS · CRASS
· CUANDO NINE 2ND AVE BY HOUSTON 9 PM $3 BAR

ANNIE ANXIETY

I'd seen the posters for their shows long before having ever heard of CRASS or their music. The graphics stuck out because they were so austere. Our local revolution was much more technicolor.

Bohemia in New York City, at that time being the world to us, was in reality a little ghetto. I met Steve from CRASS on my stoop on 5th street a few days before their NYC shows. It was hot as hell and I was out smoking a cigarette when he came over and sat down. It was 2am but we hung out and rode the ferry. I went to their Cuando show: they seemed like nice enough people, though I couldn't quite tell them apart. They were all dressed in black paramilitary drag and were very serious. Penny stuck out as being warm. CRASS played with some good pals and mentors The Blessed, whom I mothered as they were 16 and I was 17, and The Contortions, which should've been a good bill as they both had that atonal offbeat no wave thing going on. The night was strange. The hall brightly lit, was like being at a tense junior high school dance, or a Puerto Rican social club with two bands desperately out of context. The cultural differences were glaring. The punk scene in NYC was much more Warholian juvenile delinquency. Our revolt was in the way we survived. The English scene, or CRASS' thing, was much more political. Anyway, something struck a chord in me and I ended up living with CRASS.

My friends back in New York read the words Dial House on my letters home and assumed was in rehab.

CRASS
CHRIST : THE MOVIE
3 FILMS:
AUTOPSY 1979
CHOOSING DEATH 1982
YES SIR I WILL 1984
8:00P
ROOM
THURS 17 OCTOBE
INTERN ONAL COMMUNITY CENTR
MANSFIELD ROA
PENNIES IN THE
CARL SWANBERG
FIGHT WAR NOT WARS
WAR WOMAN FEAR WAR MAN FEAR
FUCK WAR CUNT FEAR MAN
"Get well soon," the Prince said. And the heroic soldier replied: "Yes, sir, I will."
THE SUN, Thursday, December 2, 1982
FILE: STRICTLY CONFIDENTIAL

Name THATCHER.Margaret Hilda.
True Name Margaret Thatcher Interviewed: Date: *** By: ***
Alias: The Iron Lady. Court: *** County:
*** Offense: Murder on the high sea. Murder,
Date of Birth: 13th Oct 1925 Age: 57. GBH in N.Ireland & Brixton,Toxteth etc
Race: White. Innumerable crimes of theft from the
Nativity: Grantham. public.Various crimes of deception. etc
Citizenship: Great Britain. Plea: *** Admitted: ***
Marital Status: Married. Min Exp. *** Max Exp.
Residence (Legal) 10 Downing St.London. Detainers: NOT AS YET DETAINED.
Co-Defendants: HESELTINE.Michael. PYMM.Francis.

HM GOVERNMENT 122054 1984

PREVIOUS CRIMNIAL HISTORY:

This woman,having been personally responsible for the deaths of several hundred young men aboard the Argentinian ship 'General Belgrano',now appears to be suffering from severe 'GUILT PSYCHOSIS','PARANOIA' and 'MEGALOMANIA'.It is evident however that,although in milder forms, these conditions existed prior to her act of MASS MURDER.
Murderers will,to appease their consciences and to justify to themselves the rationality of their actions,use force far in excess to that required simply to kill.They are also invariably motivated by their sense of guilt to commit further murders. Taking this into account,it is almost certain that given the opportunity this woman will kill again. Her obsession with a 'Russian Threat' indicates classic symptoms of 'PARANOIA'.She firmly believes that 'THEY' are out to 'GET HER'.This condition makes her bellicose,volatile and exceedingly dangerous,as does her 'CHURCHILLIAN MEGALOMANIA'. She is known to quote Churchill at times of stres in much the way that the 'Yorkshire Ripper' quote GOD.She appears to be suffering delusions of grandeur concerning both herself and her 'nation' She is surrounded by a GROUP of PERSONS known to be suffering from similar complaints and who have shown themselves WILLING TO COMMIT SIMILAR CRIMES SHE IS HEAVILY ARMED AT ALL TIMES and will strike out under the slightest pressure.
She is desperately in NEED OF HELP and MUST BE STOPPED before she becomes RESPONSIBLE for a GROSS CRIME AGAINST HUMANITY that by her own PUBLIC CONFESSION she is both capable of and willing to commit.....THE DEATH OF MILLIONS.

FORM 99/4/79

I am **not** he, nor master nor lord, no crown to wear, no cross to bear, in stations. I am not he, nor shall be, war-lord of nations. These heroes have run before me, now dead upon the flesh-piles, see? waiting for their promised resurrection; there is none. Nothing but the marker, crown or cross, in stone, upon these graves. Promise of the ribbon was all it took, where only the strap would leave it's mark upon these slaves. What flag to thrust into this flesh, rag, bandage, mop, in their flowing death. Taken aside they were pointed away, for god, queen and country, now in silence they lie. They ran before these masters, children of sorrow, as slaves to that trilogy, they had no future. They believed in democracy, freedom of speech, yet dead on the flesh-piles I hear no breath, I hear no hope no whisper of faith, for those that have died for some others privilege. Out from your palaces, princes and queens, out from your churches you clergy you christs, I'll neither live nor die for your dreams, I'll make no subscription to your paradise.

MAN MADE POWER MAN MADE PAIN
DEADLY REIGN
DONT BE A M.I.A.
CRASS
ANARCHY
FIGHT WAR NOT WARS
DESTROY POWER NOT PEOPLE
DOUG WOODS, AGE 14

THE HOUSE THAT MAN BUILT
DISARM OR DIE
CONFLICT
no more than 180p

GOLDENVOICE presents... FROM ENGLAND...
THE SUBHUMANS
SCREAM
SUN. MAY 19
SUNVALLEY
SPORTSMANS HALL
11050 LORNE
INFO: 818-767-9293
CAUSTIC CAUSE
JUSTICE LEAUGE
+ JOHNNY AND THE DINGBATS
DOORS OPEN AT 7:00
NO BAD VIBES ALLOWED
TICKETS $7.00 AT DOOR...
ZERO
B.Otis '85

B. OTIS

SUNDAY AUG.11 1985
CONFLICT
GOVERNMENT ISSUE
THE ICONOCLAST
Final Conflict
THE END
THE BITTER END
AT
FENDERS BALLROOM
521 E. 1ST ST. LONGBEACH
8:00
$5.00

Final
Conflict

0012-13	**FINAL CONFLICT** - "Ashes To Ashes" Lp	6.50
	FINAL CONFLICT - T-SHIRTS	8.00

CANADIAN ORDERS ADD 50¢
FOREIGN ORDERS ADD $3.00

PUSHEAD P.O. BOX 701 SAN FRANCISCO, CA 94101 U.S.A.

THE CHILDREN THEY'LL NOT UNDERSTAND

WHAT ARE WE GONNA BE DOING NOW IT'S 1985 ?

CONFLICT

NO BUSINESS AS USUAL

VENUE:

DATE:

TIME:

PRICE:

LET'S GIVE THEM WHAT THEY DESERVE!

FREAK RECORDS

I HEAR THE CRYING, FEEL THE E

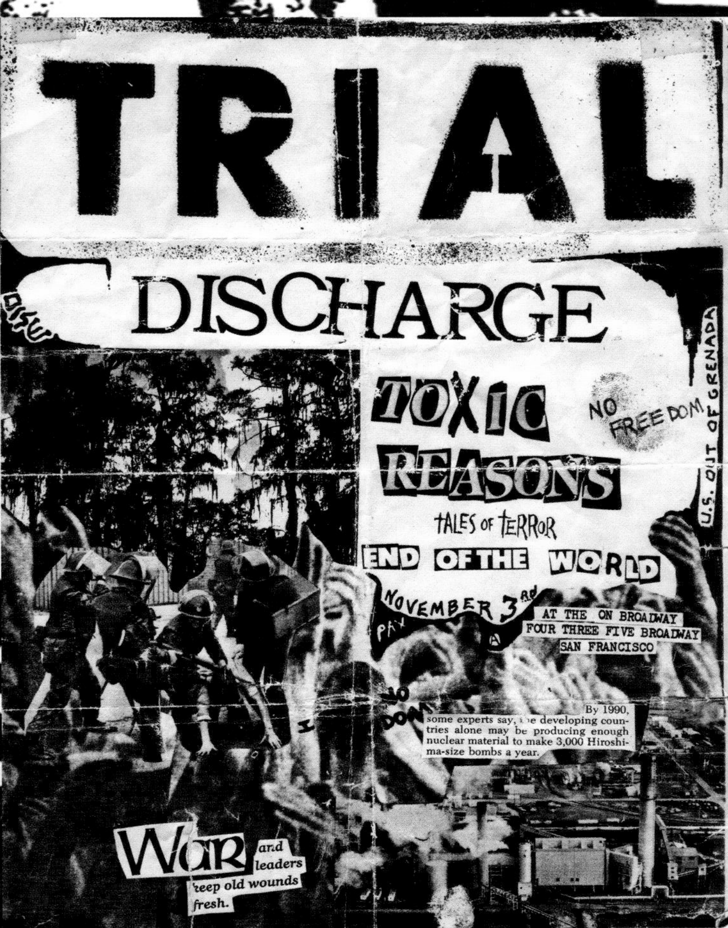

TRIAL
DISCHARGE
TOXIC REASONS
NO FREEDOM
U.S. OUT OF GRENADA
TALES OF TERROR
END OF THE WORLD
NOVEMBER 3rd
AT THE ON BROADWAY
FOUR THREE FIVE BROADWAY
SAN FRANCISCO
By 1990, some experts say, the developing countries alone may be producing enough nuclear material to make 3,000 Hiroshima-size bombs a year.
War and leaders keep old wounds fresh.

TRIAL
PLH
CRUCIFIX
SLEEPING DOGS
EXECUTIONER
JUNE 23, 1983
MINORS WELCOME
AT THE ON BROADWAY.
BE YE MEN OF VALOUR
WE DON'T WANT YOUR WAR - IT'S NOT THE ANSWER...
SAN FRANCISCO

FEEL THE HATE THAT HAS NO

TRIAL

APRIL 22ND AND 23RD.

ON BROADWAY

FRIDAY WITH

WHITEHOUSE

NEGATIVE LAND

MINIMAL MAN

PROBALISTS

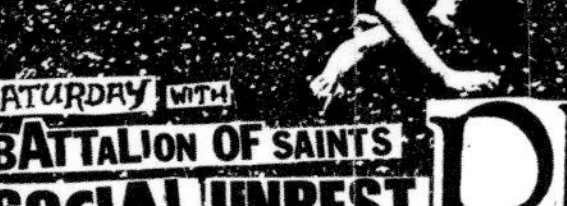

SATURDAY WITH
BATTALION OF SAINTS
SOCIAL UNREST

PLH

PLUS GUEST

JEEZ.. WHATTA DEAL
GOLDENVOICE
7 BANDS $5.00 that's cheap
SUNDAY... AUG. 11
FROM ENGLAND
CONFLICT
THEIR final show in U.S.
DOORS OPEN AT 7:00
INFO: 213-435-2838
total ANARCHY DUDE..
ICONOCLAST
GOVERNMENT ISSUE
FINAL CONFLICT
BITTER END
THE EDGE
AND DIATRIBE
B. OTIS 85
FENDERS
521 1st St. LONG BEACH
B. OTIS

SEE THE HEAVENS YET DESCEN

TREASON

C-2-D

barely human

ANIMALS HAVE FEELINGS TOO.

9pm

Benefit to keep the place open

sunday FEB 26 1984

Sleeping Lady Cafe

58 Bolinas Rd. Fairfax 456 2044

NG, TOUCH THE

BE THE LAST

BE THE LAST

TRIAL MCMLXXXI

HARDKORE KONSERT PÅ BLITZ

PILESTREDET 30 C

FREDAG 28·11·86

KL 20.00

FRA BRISTOL U.K

DISORDER

DISTORTION TILL DEAFNESS

INNGANG 30 K.R.

T.M.B. FRA TRONDHEIM

+ NOISE NOT MUSIK +

HELP END
WORLD HUNGER
flux of pink indians

ICONS OF FILTH

WHOEVER PUTS HIS HAND ON ME TO GOVERN ME IS A USURPER AND A TYRANT. I DECLARE HIM MY ENEMY

Pierre-Joseph Proudon

ZOUNDS!

JOHN JOHN JESSE

This was the time of the Reagan era and much of the world was living in a state of constant fear of a nuclear war. It was a political time and many punk releases began to feature cut and paste pictures of Ronald Reagan on their covers, often with a bull's eye target on his forehead. Republicans seem to bring out the protest in your everyday citizen. It was hard not to be political back then. We moved into squats and fought with cops. We were angry and young and it felt like NOTHING could ever stop us. Punk art started out raw and to the point and quickly evolved into a cohesive recognizable style that we all identified with. I loved Jamie Reid's work with the Sex Pistols, Winston Smith's with the Dead Kennedys and Gee's for Crass. I loved the cut out and paste style of the flyers and records. I loved the ink drawings by artists like Pushead and Mad Marc Rude. Nausea formed out of necessity for me. I dreamed of gigging after watching bands like GBH and The Exploited on tour as well as seeing locals like The Bad Brains, Agnostic Front and Reagan Youth. I had something to say and the world needed to hear it. I found others who shared my ideology and musical tastes and formed a band. My influences were a lot of the UK bands and some NY hardcore of that time as well as anyone who was as pissed off as me, as punk rock as me, and hated cops and the government as much as me. The only member back then who had any band experience was Victor (known as Vic Venom). He had played for KGB, Hellbent, Sacrilege and Reagan Youth. He whipped us into shape and we soon developed our own sound. A whole lot of tight, fast punk, some tribal dirges and a little bit of metal thrown in. We gigged locally as part of the NY hardcore scene. We played with Bad Brains, Agnostic Front, Ludichrist, and Sick Of It All. Not long before, there were hundreds of punk rock kids but no punk bands. We had to do it ourselves. We put on benefits in squats and abandoned lots and soon enough hundreds of kids flocked to these gigs. We became a voice for our movement and scene in the lower east side. This was around 1986. We recorded a few records and toured extensively throughout the States and Europe until we finally called it quits in 1992. It's hard to keep a band together that long and all stay friends.

Unity is hard. In archetypical punk fashion, we self-destructed. Back then we had no idea if Nausea would have an impact 20 years later with newer generations of punks. We lived in the moment and did what came naturally to us. Our music and message came from deep in our hearts and was passionate and real in every way. I am VERY proud that our message of anarchism, autonomy, animal rights and squatting still lives on and has continued to influence others. Peace.

NAUSEA
NAUSEA

JOHN JOHN JESSE

NAUSEA
ALL COPS ARE BASTARDS, YES THIS IS TRUE. I HATE THE STENCH OF MUSTACHE THAT REEKS OF THE MEN IN BLUE.
A.C.A.B.
with: BAD BRAINS
PLUS MORE SUPRISE GUESTS
SNFU LEEWAY WARZONE
at the Ritz 11st bet. 3rd & 4th aves
doors open at 8pm sharp
SAT DEC 27
MERRY ANTI-CHRISTMAS!

NAUSEA
FREE
LIVE AT CENTRAL PARK
IN THE BANDSHELL
70th St. ENTER ON 5th AVE.
ALL DAY FESTIVAL STARTS AT 12PM MIDAY
with: FALSE PROPHETS
the toasters
ROUGH IDEA
STETSASONIC MC'S
PLUS MUCH MORE
BE THERE SUNDAY MAY 1ST
1988
BLIND VIOLENCE... BLIND HATES...
YOUR BLIND PATRIOTISM IS BREEDED FOR THE STATE.
rock against racism

NAUSEA SFA
ABSOLUTION
GO!
THE RADICTS
public nuisance
AND MORE
ANIMAL RIGHTS BENEFIT
SATURDAY
APRIL 29TH
5:30 PM
and film, food, info, art
PYRAMID CLUB 101 AVE A
5$ suggested donation
BE THERE OR BE SQUARE

NAUSEA
CHRIST ON A CRUTCH
PSYCHO
ANIMAL CRACKERS
SAT AUGUST 18 - 3PM
AT ABC-NO-RIO
156 RIVINGTON ST.

SQUAT OR ROT
PRESENTS
AT: 537 EAST 13TH STREET
7PM SHARP
SAT. APRIL 15TH
WITH
the RADICTS
public nuisance
FROM CONNETICUT...
SEIZURE
SFA
REZISTURZ
StiSism
BLOODSUCKERS FROM OUTERSPACE
NOBODY'S HEROES
AND
WORLD DISCRIMINATION
ONE YEAR ANNIVERSARY
ADMISSION: DONATION

ALL FLYERS THIS PAGE: JOHN JOHN JESSE

NAUSEA
INHERIT THE WASTELAND

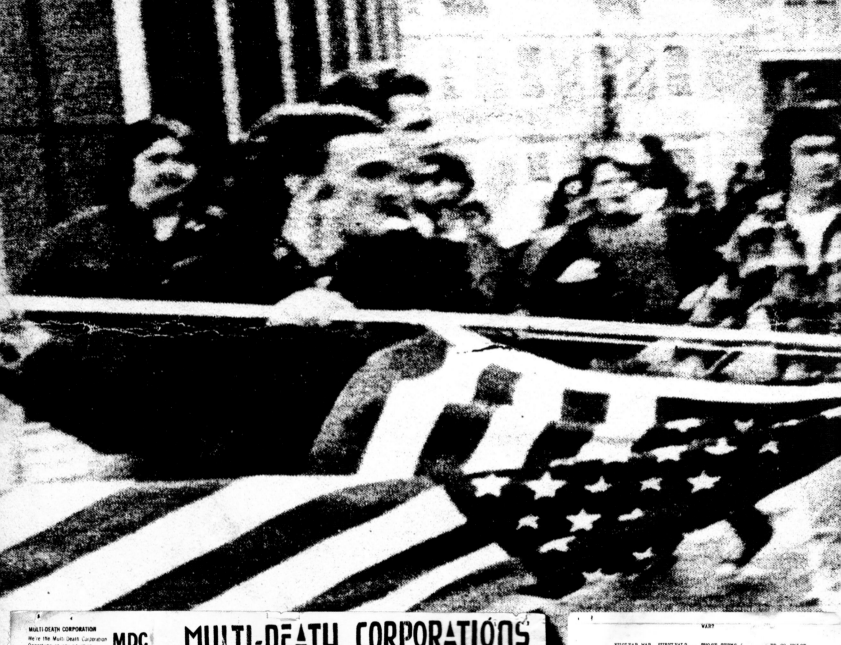

MULTI-DEATH CORPORATION

MDC

MULTI-DEATH CORPORATIONS

We're the Multi Death Corporation
Opportune on any situation
Our only concern capitalization
And world economic domination
Profits are made from global starvation
Russian roulette for the world population
We need terror and repression
For third world exploitation
Generals plot extermination
Bank on death and devastation
Sick control manipulation
From the Multi-Death Corporation

Promises of free expression
CIA assassination
State Department no explanation
Bought and sold legislation
TV "news" half information
America prays in isolation
Sick control and manipulation
From the Multi-Death Corporation

WAR?

NUCLEAR WAR, SURVIVAL?... THOSE TERMS [illegible] ER CO-EXIST. AFTER ANY NUCLEAR WAR NOTHING AND NO [illegible] EXIST. WAR IS WAR, BEING JUST ANOTHER HISTORICAL [illegible] H, WHATEVER THE CAUSE MAYBE. NUCLEAR WAR IS A [illegible] ERENT STORY, NOT WAR, NOT VICTORY, BUT [illegible] O MEAN COMPLETE DESTRUCTION... THE END OF [illegible] FE AS WE KNOW IT... WORLDWIDE INCINERATION! NUCL [illegible] SHOULD NOT ATTEMPT TO CO-EXIST WITH LIFE... LI [illegible] EATH IS DEATH...

NAGASAKI, HIROSHIMA, WERE MER [illegible] ALL EXAMPLES OF 2 MORBID EXPERIMENTS... THE NUCLEAR FIREPOWER EXISTING TODAY IS RIDICULOUS... ENOUGH TO DESTROY THE EARTH A THOUSAND TIMES, BUT WORLD LEADERS STILL FEEL WE NEED MORE, FOR NEGOTIATIONS,... "WE HAVE MORE THAN YOU DO,"..."WE CAN BLOW YOU UP, US, AND EVEN THE MOON ALONG WITH US"... IT MAKES YOU WONDER IF THESE SO CALLED POLITICIANS REALLY HAVE SUPPOSED "COLLEGE EDUCATIONS"... IT DOES NOT TAKE AN EDUCATION TO GAMBLE WITH HUMAN LIFE, ANY MORON COULD PLAY, AS THEY SAY "RUSSIAN ROULETTE"...

NO MATTER WHAT ANYONE HAS TO SAY, TO STAND BEHIND NUCLEAR DEFENSE SERVES NO PURPOSE, EXCEPT FOR DEATH AND COMPLETE DESTRUCTION. IT SIMPLY CANNOT BE STRESSED ENOUGH, HOW POTENTIALLY DANGEROUS ANY FORM OF NUCLEAR POWER OR DEFENSE IS. PEACE AND NUCLEAR ANYTHING COULD NEVER SENSIBLY GO TOGETHER! WHICH BRINGS US TO PUNK ROCK, AND HOW CONCERNED PUNKS CLAIM TO BE TOWARDS NUCLEAR WAR,... ARE THEY?, OR IS IT JUST FASHION TO CLAIM THEY ARE AGAINST IT... HOW MANY PUNKS DO ANYTHING BUT BITCH AND COMPLAIN ABOUT IT, OR JUST MERELY PAINT SYMBOLS ON LEATHER JACKETS THAT REPRESENT A PROTEST AGAINST NUCLEAR WAR, BUT REALLY MAKE ANY REAL DRASTIC ACTIONS TOWARDS IT... 99% OF ALL SOCIETY WILL NOT TAKE ANYTHING SERIOUSLY THAT IS ONLY A PAINTING ON A LEATHER JACKET,... IN ORDER TO MAKE YOURSELF CLEAR, WITH THE ATTITUDE MEDIA AND SOCIETY HAS TOWARDS PUNKS, YOU HAVE A CHOICE... PUNKS CAN EITHER START BEING MORE SERIOUS ABOUT THEIR GOALS, AS IN A REAL PROTEST TOWARDS NUCLEAR WAR, AS IN DOCUMENTATION AND PETITIONS, RATHER THAN RALLIES THAT MERELY SHOW OFF HAIR-DOO'S, THE PUNK LOOK AND OBNOXIOUS BEHAVIOUR... OR... YOU CAN JUST FORGET ABOUT WHAT YOU CLAIM TO BE CONCERNED ABOUT... AND GIVE THE MEDIA, PUBLIC, LAW ENFORCEMENT, AND SOCIETY JUST WHAT THEY EXPECT, AND WANT. THEY'RE STILL CONVINCED PUNKS ARE SIMPLE MINDED, SADISTIC, NIHILISTIC, AND COMPLETELY DESTRUCTIVE... EITHER GIVE THEM WHAT THEY WANT, OR BE SERIOUS ABOUT YOUR STATEMENT, DON'T JUST PAINT IT ON YOUR JACKET... AS MANY PUNKS AS THERE ARE EVERYWHERE, WE COULD REALLY DO SOMETHING ABOUT THE THINGS WE'RE SUPPOSEDLY SO SERIOUS ABOUT, RATHER THAN BEATING EACH OTHERS BRAINS OUT... AND PROVING PEOPLE RIGHT, THAT FEEL WE SHOULD BE ABOLISHED. NOT JUST THE ISSUE OF NUCLEAR WAR, BUT ALL THE ISSUES PUNKS ARE SUPPOSEDLY SO SERIOUS ABOUT... OUR GOAL IS TO GET PEOPLE TO WORK TOGETHER, AND MAKE THINGS WORK...

ANY POSITIVE OR NEGATIVE COMMENTS
WRITE US

FINAL CONFLICT
P.O. BOX 2334 - 1834
CYPRESS, CA. 90630-1834

Final
Conflict

Final Conflict
WAR?
WAR?
WAR?
WAR?
The threat is spreading, and the phantom proliferators lead the way

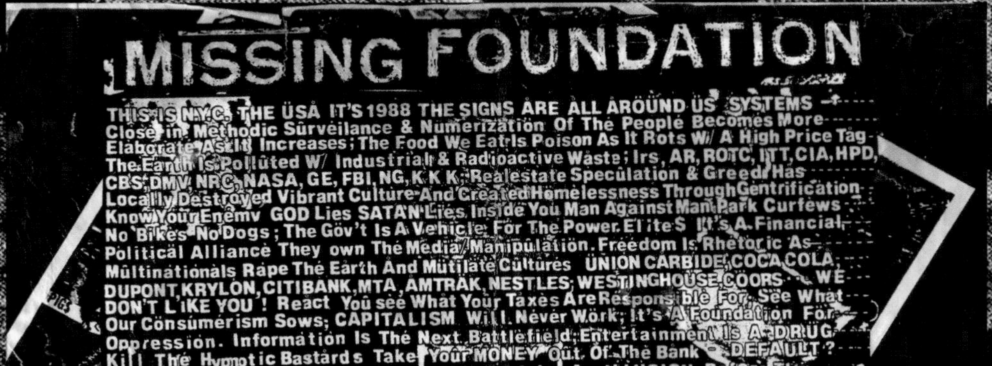

MISSING FOUNDATION

THIS IS N.Y.C. THE USA IT'S 1988 THE SIGNS ARE ALL AROUND US SYSTEMS
Close in Methodic Surveilance & Numerization Of The People Becomes More
Elaborate As It Increases; The Food We Eat Is Poison As It Rots W/ A High Price Tag
The Earth Is Polluted W/ Industrial & Radioactive Waste; Irs, AR, ROTC, ITT, CIA, HPD,
CBS, DMV, NRC, NASA, GE, FBI, NG, K.K.K.; Realestate Speculation & Greed Has
Locally Destroyed Vibrant Culture And Created Homelessness Through Gentrification
Know Your Enemy GOD Lies SATAN Lies Inside You Man Against Man Park Curfews
No Bikes No Dogs; The Gov't Is A Vehicle For The Power Elite$ It's A Financial
Political Alliance They own The Media/Manipulation. Freedom Is Rhetoric As
Multinationals Rape The Earth And Mutilate Cultures UNION CARBIDE, COCA COLA,
DUPONT, KRYLON, CITIBANK, MTA, AMTRAK, NESTLES, WESTINGHOUSE, COORS WE
DON'T LIKE YOU ! React You see What Your Taxes Are Responsible For; See What
Our Consumerism Sows; CAPITALISM Will Never Work; It's A Foundation For
Oppression. Information Is The Next Battlefield; Entertainment Is A DRUG
Kill The Hypnotic Bastards Take Your MONEY Out Of The Bank - DEFAULT ?
We Are At The DEMISE Of Mankind - HOPE Is An ILLUSION Before The
WORLD We Face TOday ---- Militarism, Sexism, Cultural Homogenization,
Police States, Propaganda, Disinformation, Systematization; The System In One Of
It's Forms, Has Or Is Classifing You. If You Are Outside Of It You Are A Threat To
The System. THIS IS GERMANY "IT'S 1933 - GOOD LUCK" RACISM, NATIONALISM,
FINANCE - THEN - NOW 50 YRS OF NOTHING

DON'T LOSE SIGHT OF THE BIG PICTURE
WATCH WHO YOU WORK FOR
BE CAREFULL OF THE FOOD YOU EAT
DON'T SELL YOUR LEASE / HOMES
BE CAREFULL WHO YOU TALK TO — DON'T VØTE
DON'T GIVE UP — DEVALUE PROPERTY — DO NOT RELENT

LIBERTY UNDER SIEGE

CRUCIFIX
SOCIAL UNREST
PLH
TREASON
SAT. JULY 9th
TOOL & DIE
974 VALENCIA S.F.
DO YOU CARE?
MINORS WELCOME

ACTIVISM+

A WHOLE NEW WAY OF LIFE

REVOLT

supreme power?

from power, will

Young rebels

Old Order

self-expression

the individual

PROTEST

TUPELO chain sex

SPOT THE DIFFERENCE

©SELMA RECORDS 1985

JOIN A PEACEFUL, LEGAL DEMONSTRATION AT THE $1000 A PLATE REPUBLICAN PARTY FUNDRAISING DINNER, HOSTED BY RONALD REAGAN

5 to 8 pm SOUPLINE AVAILABLE FOR THOSE WHO CANNOT ATTEND THE GOP DINNER.

CENTURY PLAZA HOTEL. 5pm
Thurs, Aug 22

PHOTOMONTAGE/MARK VALLEN, SHOCK BATTALION

END APARTHEID/STOP RACISM AT HOME! * STOP U.S. INTERVENTION IN CENTRAL AMERICA, MIDDLE EAST, AND ELSEWHERE! * STOP U.S. AND ISRAELI AID TO SOUTH AFRICA! * STOP SEXISM AND DISCRIMINATION BASED ON SEXUAL ORIENTATION! * FUND ENVIRONMENTAL AND HUMAN NEEDS! * STOP ATTACKS ON LABOR, ON UNIONS, AND UNDOCUMENTED WORKERS! * DEFEND THE RIGHT TO SAFE AND LEGAL ABORTIONS.

FEED THE HUMAN RACE, NOT THE ARMS RACE

HINCKLEY FOR PRESIDENT

He's had a shot at the man. . . Let's give him a shot at the job.

And Jodie for Vice.

Hinckley for President Campaign c/o 1338 Haight St., SF, CA 94117

ROCK
AGAINST
REAGAN
FROST

The ROCK AGAINST REAGAN Tour comes to L.A.
October 30th, 10am – 5pm
At the Federal Building 11000 Wilshire Blvd. Westwood
With THE MINUTEMEN · THE HUNDREDTH MONKEY · STICK AGAINST STONE · SHATTERED FAITH · and THE F-BEATS · Plus Speakers and more ....FREE!

Rock Against Reagan is sponsored by the Youth International Party, Rock Against Racism, CARD Youth Caucus, Squatters Anonymous, Sleepy Hollow Direct Action Commitee, Iowa Socialist Party, Rainbow Family for World Peace, and Long Island SHAD, among others.

For more info call: California Marijuana Initiative (213) 902 -WEED

FROM THIS...
TO ...THIS!
WHAT CAUSED IT?
PUNK ROCK!!

FRONTIER

JESSE MALIN

The early 80's was a time when I was becoming a young man. I was forced to become politically aware, not only through the music I was listening to, but at the very possibility that I could become drafted into the military to fight a war in Central America, that my country probably had no business being in anyway. I began to feel the pressure and presence of police when I rode the subway trains to school, or at night to punk shows. I was given attitude, chased, threatened, and on a couple occasions even hit with a billy club. I believed these confrontations were a direct result of the way I dressed as a "punk rocker". Kids at school laughed at me, kids in my local neighborhood had a similar reaction, and I grew to question what was considered "normal". As a young child I had been aware of some of our previous presidents like Jimmy Carter, and Richard Nixon, but in those adolescent days, President Ronald Reagan's image seemed to be ever present with his jellybeans, goofy slogans, and a John Wayne image. But, as I started to listen more, I realized there was something scary going on here. The nuclear arms race seemed to be like some macho game of Monday night football, with our planets mortality on the line. His ties with Religious Right fundamentalists like Jerry Fallwell and the moral majority seemed to give no evidence of any separation between church and state. When he announced that ketchup would count as a vegetable in the four food groups in our country's school cafeterias, I knew for sure that this guy was a retard, or maybe he was a genius, and the rest of us Americans were idiots eating it all up.

I realized that a big part of being a politician was being an actor, but this guy who made b-films like Bedtime for Bonzo, and the Killers, was running our country. I remember when Reagan was shot, watching it on TV, and hearing Alexander Hague repeat over, and over again, "I'm in control now. I'm in control now." After reading books at school like George Orwell's 1984, and the year actually coming soon, it really felt like we were being controlled by some blinding media machine. I had read how President Kennedy had spoke years before about "Global Unification" (whether he meant it or not) this was clearly not the case with our happy cowboy and his friends. Listening to bands like The Dead Kennedy's, CRASS, and The Clash, opened my eyes to what was really going on with our country's secret wars in Central America, and how the arms race was just a big business endeavor for multi-national corporations, and how freedom of speech was something you had until you tried to use it (Lenny Bruce to Jello Biafra). Their music raised my consciousness, and led me to alternative media such as, public radio, magazines, movies, and eventually public demonstrations in Washington, DC. My family would call me a Communist and constantly ask, "Who on a soapbox in Greenwich Village is brainwashing you!" Though the Reagan Administration offered us hardcore punk musicians a plethora of ammunition to channel into songs. This lyrical concept would eventually become a cliché as much as slam dancing, safety pins, and swastikas. By the end of his term, Reagan seemed to be becoming more and more senile, and our Vice President George Bush senior's agenda (especially in foreign policy) especially seemed to be becoming more and more frightening. There's an old Woody Allen quote that "Tragedy plus time equals comedy." I recently re-learned that in America, tragedy plus time, can equal hero. I was recently sitting in a Chicago hotel room watching the news coverage of Ronald Reagan's death and funeral. The whole country seemed so devastated and sad. People were commending him like he was the greatest president ever. At first I was shocked, but in these days of George Bush, jr. and his stuttering, grimacing fascist idiocy, Ronald Reagan appears to be almost human. Rest in peace Ronnie.

U.$. OUT OF CENTRAL AMERICA
March & Rally
SAt, mARch 24th
Corner of OLYMPIC and BroadWay, noon.
rally 3:00 olvera st. bandstand

ARE YOU REAGAN YOUTH?

AMERICAN
BIBLE BELT

JOHN YATES

ASSHOLE

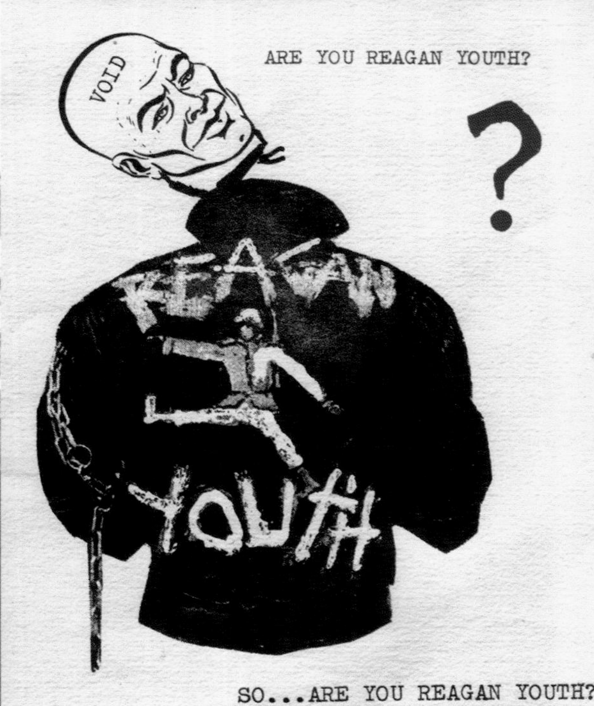
ARE YOU REAGAN YOUTH?
VOID
?
REAGAN
YOUTH
SO...ARE YOU REAGAN YOUTH?

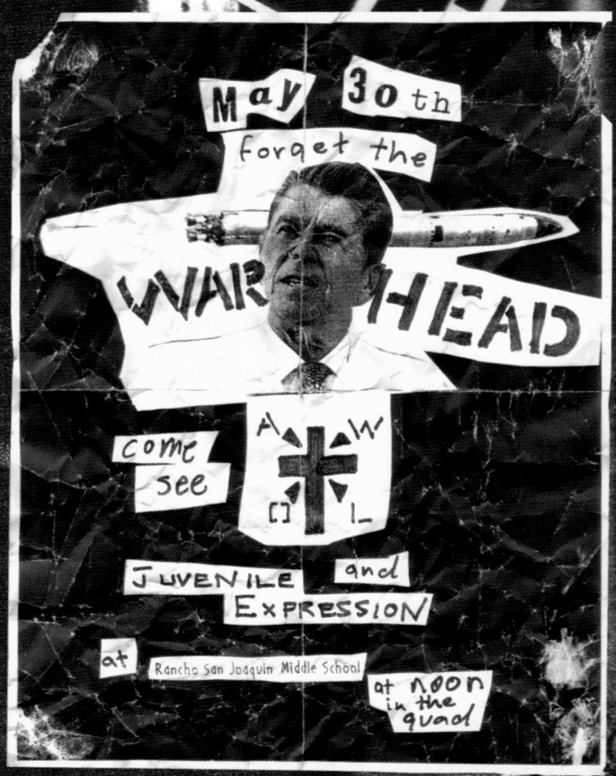
May 30th
forget the
WAR HEAD
come see
AWOL
JUVENILE and EXPRESSION
at Rancho San Joaquin Middle School
at noon in the quad

MICHAEL ETTER

REAGAN YOUTH

************1985 REAGAN REGIME RESURRECTION PIN-UP**********

MESSAGE FROM THE
PERIAL WIZARD . . .

ou are proud of being white
ou are tired of black insults
ou want to improve yourself
ou have time to spare
ou are a person of action
ou are between ages 10 & 17

YOU BELONG
IN THE
KLAN YOUTH CORPS

"Ground Zero"?

Q: If I could follow that up: Can you just envision any circumstances under which we would be sending U.S. combat troops to El Salvador?

The President: Well, maybe if they dropped a bomb on the White House, I might get mad. . . .

From the transcript of President Reagan's news conference at the White House on February 18, 1982.

YOUTH: ACHTU

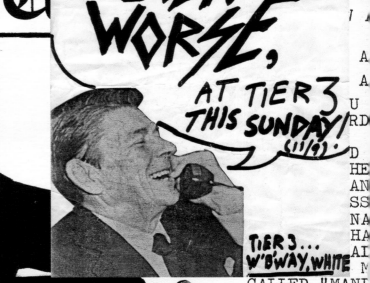

HELLO, JIMMY? IT's "EVEN WORSE," AT TIER 3 THIS SUNDAY! (11/9).
TIER 3... W'B'WAY, WHITE

ATLANTIC AND CAPE MAY CO. KLAN
KLAN IDEAL
STATE
SCHOOL
CHURCH
HOME

ATTENTION!

YOU! YES YOU

CALLED "MAND
OF AMERIKKKA

A MANDATE? A
FOR FUCKING

LEFTOVER TURKEY FOR A COUNTRY
SAT. NOV. 28
HEY BUDDY GOT THE TIME?
THAT'S GONNA THE BIRD
max's kansas city
213 PARK AVE. SOUTH AT 17th STREET
STEPHAN IELPE
FALSE PROPHETS
VON LMO
"THE LAST SUPPER"
??????????

IT CAN'T HAPPEN HE

DEAD KENNEDYS
CONTRACTIONS
D.R.I.
and GREAT BAND FROM 415 RECORDS
also WIG TORTURE
plus
ANTI-KKK SLIDESHOW
VIDEO FROM AUSTIN, TEXAS

FRI. NOV. 11 9PM $6
ON BROADWAY
435 Broadway, S.F.

BENEFIT FOR JOHN BROWN
ANTI-KLAN COMMITTEE

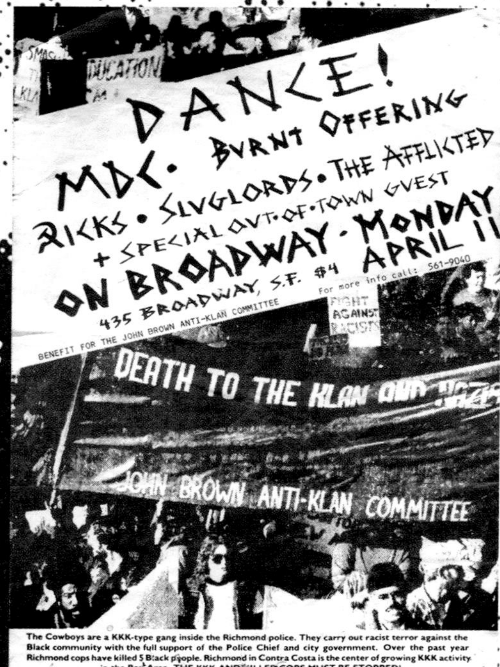
DANCE!
MDC • BURNT OFFERING
RICKS • SLUGLORDS • THE AFFLICTED
+ SPECIAL OUT-OF-TOWN GUEST
ON BROADWAY • MONDAY APRIL 11
435 BROADWAY, S.F. $4
For more info call: 561-9040
BENEFIT FOR THE JOHN BROWN ANTI-KLAN COMMITTEE
FIGHT AGAINST RACISM
DEATH TO THE KLAN
JOHN BROWN ANTI-KLAN COMMITTEE
The Cowboys are a KKK-type gang inside the Richmond police. They carry out racist terror against the Black community with the full support of the Police Chief and city government. Over the past year Richmond cops have killed 5 Black people. Richmond in Contra Costa is the center of growing KKK activity in the Bay Area. THE KKK AND KILLER COPS MUST BE STOPPED!

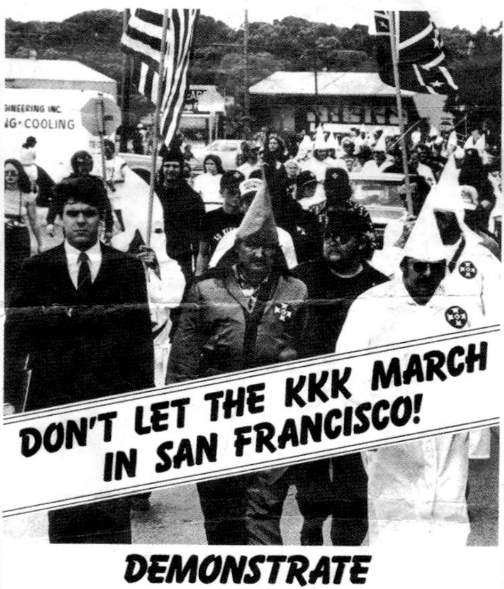
THE KLAN IS PLANNING
TO HOLD A RACIST, ANTI-GAY MARCH
AT THE DEMOCRATIC CONVENTION.
DON'T LET THE KKK MARCH
IN SAN FRANCISCO!
DEMONSTRATE
TUESDAY JULY 17 NOON

REAGAN YOUTH
NAUSEA
apple
CBGB and OMFUG
315 Bowery (at Bleecker) (212)982-4052
—HARDCORE MATINEE—
JULY 4
SAT.
independance
DAY REVIVAL

ONE500NE

ANTI-KLAN BENEFIT

//SUNDAY, SEPTEMBER 23//4-10 PM//
//D.A. WARD STUDIO/220 S. ROSE/DOWNTOWN L.A.//

BODY COUNT//THE ICONOCLAST//BASIC BLACK//ROBIN RYAN//
//THE BLACK NOTES//HOLLYWATTS//POETRY//ANTI-KLAN VIDEOS
& FILMS//SPEAKERS//MUSIC//FOOD// //$3 DONATION//

ROSE ST
1st
2nd
Alameda
220
3rd

//BENEFIT FOR THE CENTER FOR BLACK SURVIVAL
& JOHN BROWN ANTI-KLAN COMMITTEE//
/SPONSORED BY JOHN BROWN ANTI-KLAN COMMITTEE//213/464-8381

Fuck
White Supremacy

GWB / 2007

BUSH
Lied My Son
Died

DON'T BE THE
LAST SOLDIER
TO DIE IN THE
WAR!

BUSINESS,
AS U.$.UAL

ANTI-WAR ART EXHIBITION
NOON to 10pm daily. JULY 27 - AUG 13.
CORDELL HALL, 1020 VICTORIA AVE.
Corner of Lincoln Blvd & Victoria Ave. in Venice.

U.S. OUT OF EL SALVADOR
June 5, 1981
Friday nite
8 P.M. in
Monarch
Hall
at LA Valley
College
5800 Fulton Avenue
Van Nuys, CA
Ventura Fwy to Coldwater
North to Burbank Blvd
West to Fulton,
North to LAVC
entrance
THE PLUGZ
ALICE BAGS BAND
PHRANC
BENT
$5
$3 for LAVC
students with paid I.D.
For more info call: 241-77
Committee in Solidarity with the People of El Salvador
BENEFIT FOR CISPES

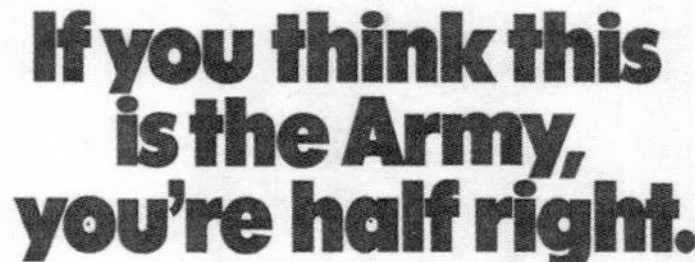

If you think this
is the Army,
you're half right.

CHRIS D.

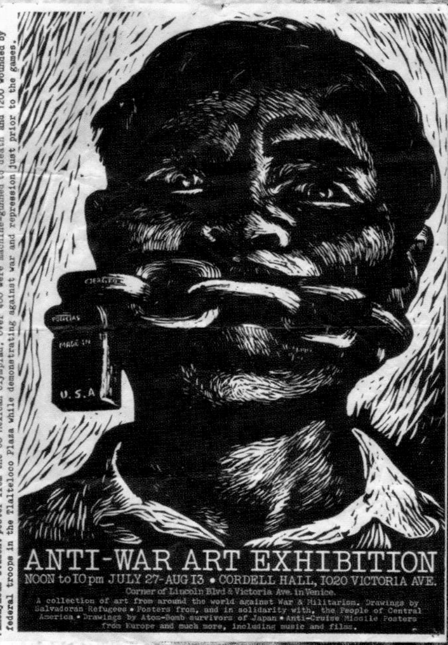

ANTI-WAR ART EXHIBITION
NOON to 10 pm JULY 27-AUG 13 • CORDELL HALL, 1020 VICTORIA AVE.
Corner of Lincoln Blvd & Victoria Ave. in Venice.
A collection of art from around the world against War & Militarism. Drawings by Salvadoran Refugees • Posters from, and in solidarity with, the People of Central America • Drawings by Atom-Bomb survivors of Japan • Anti-Cruise Missile Posters from Europe and much more, including music and films.

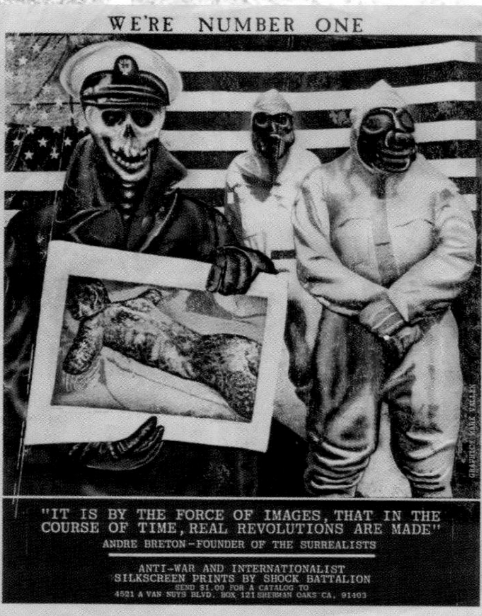

WE'RE NUMBER ONE
"IT IS BY THE FORCE OF IMAGES, THAT IN THE COURSE OF TIME, REAL REVOLUTIONS ARE MADE"
ANDRE BRETON - FOUNDER OF THE SURREALISTS
ANTI-WAR AND INTERNATIONALIST SILKSCREEN PRINTS BY SHOCK BATTALION
SEND $1.00 FOR A CATALOG TO
4521 A VAN NUYS BLVD. BOX 121 SHERMAN OAKS CA. 91403

WHY WASTE TIME?
JOIN THE 1984 OLYMPIC MARCH
off to die in WORLD WAR 3
before THE GAMES Even end
MON aug 6 4 PM at Hollywood & Highland

From the athletic field to the battlefield. You've been getting programmed with the message for a week now, so who needs to hear another week of it. USA #1. USA kicks ass. USA = beauty, truth, and beautiful god given grace and bodies.

The endless closeups of the American flags as our boys and girls show the world who the real superman is. Thousands of preprogrammed happy face idiots shed tears on cue and wave flags on command as the home team occupies the floor. The athletes are "combatants", "stationed at the court", Bobby Knight, the basketball team's "general", says he's never fired a shot for his country (yet) so he's doing the next best thing.

Who needs a scorecard? The "teams" are identified for tv viewers with little helpful notes like "Here's Belgium, home of the Allied Military Command Center in Europe", or "Here's Costa Rica, the only nation in Central America without an army, and some people think they need one."

Then of course there's the "team" that didn't show. In "normal" times competing imperialist blocs duke it out on the sports field to promote the superiority of their empires. But this year Ivan won't meet GI Joe in the Olympics. Between the state sponsored "Ban the Soviets" atmosphere, and "we're not boycotting, we're just not coming", both sides are showing that they can't risk a defeat in the Olympic medal count that might disrupt their momentum in the race to the Nuclear body count.

But hey, never mind that the Soviets aren't coming. And so what if the stadiums have empty seats visible on tv, the FBI, LAPD and CIA thought police are tripping over each other in an effort to intimidate people and that the spirit of kill kill kill pervades the games. If you're REALLY a patriotic American, nothing matters except that these are the GREATEST GAMES in the GREATEST COUNTRY ever no matter what.

TV told us that the opening ceremony (a celebration of chauvinism as stupid as it was reactionary) was "the greatest pageant ever." America is singing "we love it". And in the happy finale, a steroid nation marches off behind real generals proud and stupefied, sucked in via sports and spit out into the nuclear battle zone.

Among their problems with pulling this off is the emergence of a disloyal rebel force among today's youth. It rose up out of the streets of San Francisco during the Democratic Convention chanting "Reagan - Mondale, which will it be? Either one means World War 3" and "Heads they win, tales you lose... glad we have the right to chose." It broke thru the press blackout on disgust for the Olympics when the LA Times reported punks in Hollywood spit on the torch when it passed through. Its a voice that needs to shatter the atmosphere in LA during the Olympics!

The whole world is watching LA '84. The Revolutionary Communist Youth Brigade is calling on rebel youth, and extending a particular invitation to people here from other countries, to take advantage of that. Why wait? Join the "1984 Olympic March off to Die in World War III" before the games even come to their patriotic orgasm end. Meet at Hollywood and Highland, Monday at 4 PM and march off to "register" to die at the Hollywood Army recruiting station at 6301 Yucca. Appropriate dress please!

revolutionary communist youth brigade (RCYB)

WAR FEVER
the official disease of the 1984 olympics

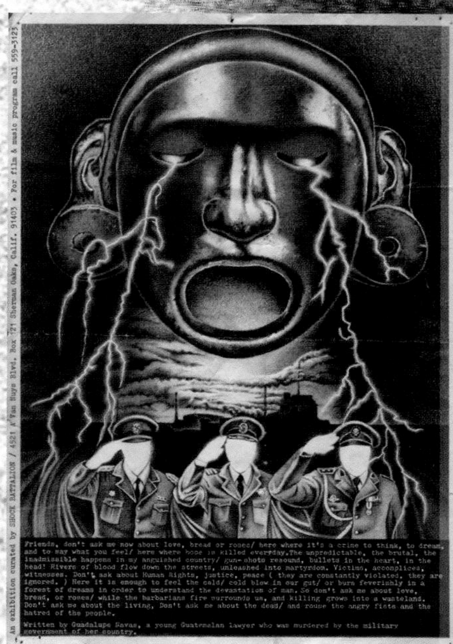

Friends, don't ask me now about love, bread or roses/ here where it's a crime to think, to dream, and to say what you feel/ here where hope is killed everyday. The unpredictable, the brutal, the inadmissible happens in my anguished country/ gun-shots resound, bullets in the heart, in the head! Rivers of blood flow down the streets, unleashed into martyrdom. Victims, accomplices, witnesses. Don't ask about Human Rights, justice, peace (they are constantly violated, they are ignored.) Here it is enough to feel the cold/ cold blow in our gut/ or burn feverishly in a forest of dreams in order to understand the devastation of man. So don't ask me about love, bread, or roses/ while the barbarians fire surrounds us, and killing grows into a wasteland. Don't ask me about the living, Don't ask me about the dead/ and rouse the angry fists and the hatred of the people.
Written by Guadalupe Navas, a young Guatemalan lawyer who was murdered by the military government of her country.

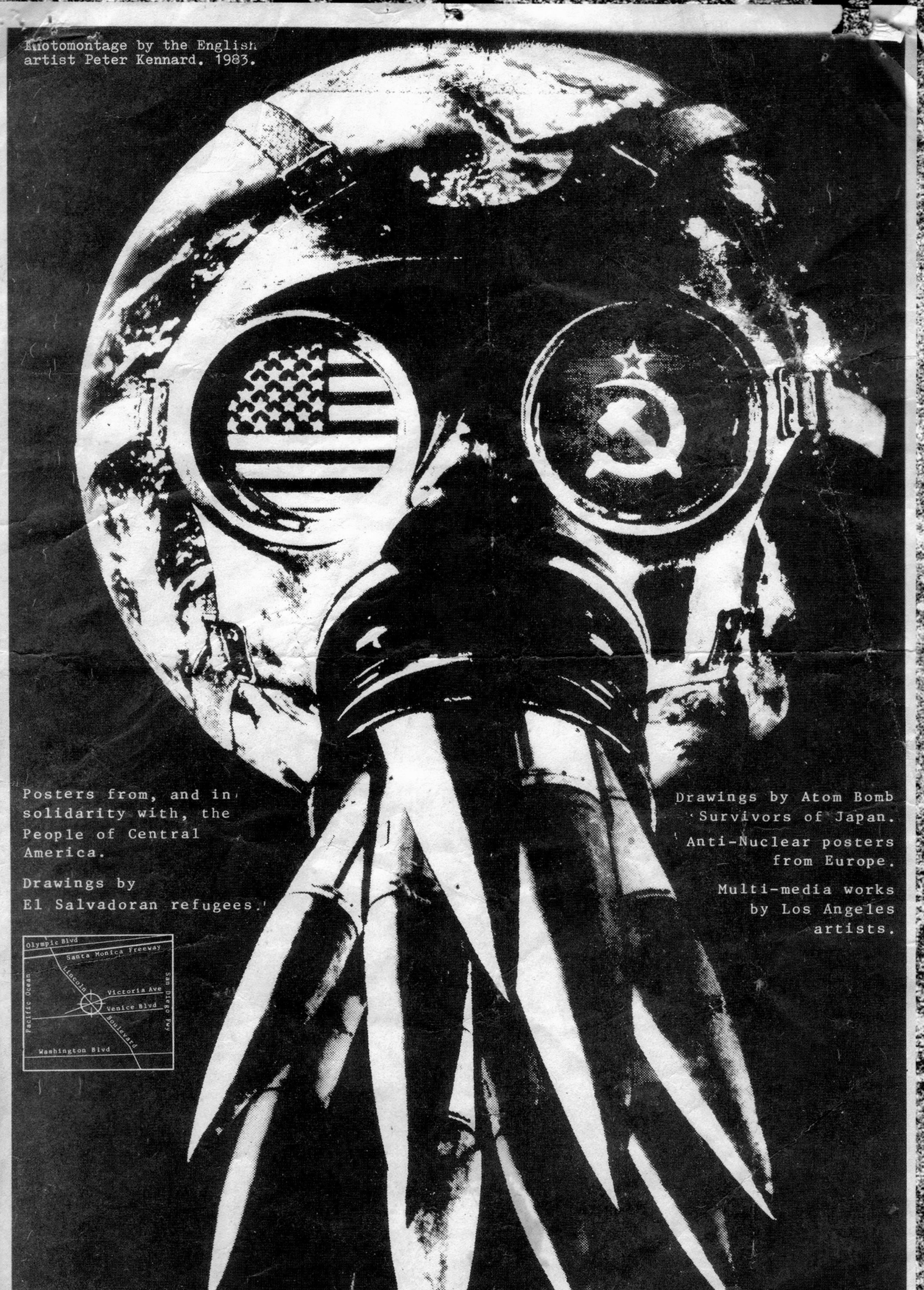
Photomontage by the English
artist Peter Kennard. 1983.
Posters from, and in
solidarity with, the
People of Central
America.
Drawings by
El Salvadoran refugees.
Olympic Blvd
Santa Monica Freeway
Lincoln
Victoria Ave
San Diego Fwy
Pacific Ocean
Venice Blvd
Boulevard
Washington Blvd
Drawings by Atom Bomb
Survivors of Japan.
Anti-Nuclear posters
from Europe.
Multi-media works
by Los Angeles
artists.

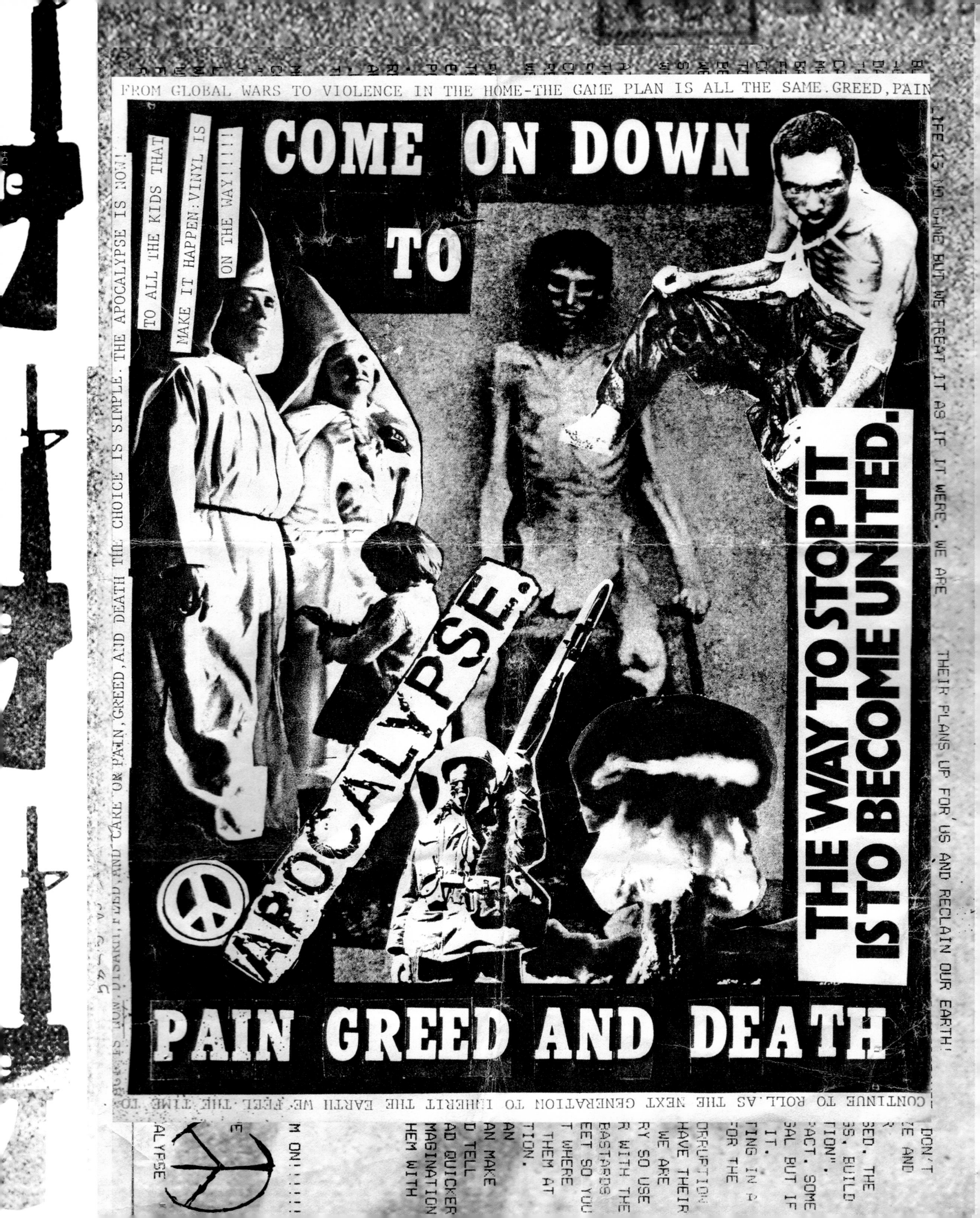

FROM GLOBAL WARS TO VIOLENCE IN THE HOME-THE GAME PLAN IS ALL THE SAME.GREED,PAIN

LIFE IS NO GAME BUT WE TREAT IT AS IF IT WERE. WE ARE ... THEIR PLANS UP FOR US AND RECLAIN OUR EARTH!

CONTINUE TO ROLL.AS THE NEXT GENERATION TO INHERIT THE EARTH WE FEEL THE TIME TO

... CAKE OR PAIN,GREED,AND DEATH THE CHOICE IS SIMPLE. THE APOCALYPSE IS NOW!

TO ALL THE KIDS THAT MAKE IT HAPPEN:VINYL IS ON THE WAY!!!!

COME ON DOWN TO

APOCALYPSE

PAIN GREED AND DEATH

THE WAY TO STOP IT IS TO BECOME UNITED.

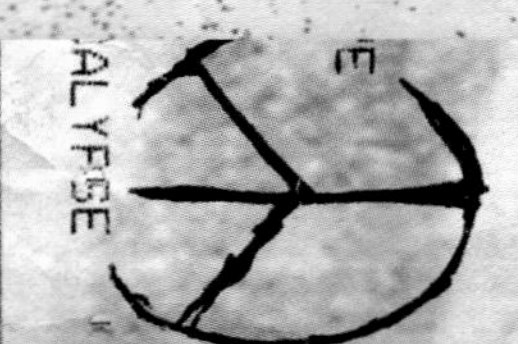

ALYPSE

NO BUSINESS AS USUAL–APRIL 29

PREVENT WORLD WAR III–

NO MATTER WHAT IT TAKES!

…AL OFFICE: No Business As Usual, 3309½ Mission St. #127, …cisco, CA 94110 Phone (415) 550-8506 or (415) 550-1530

LOCAL OFFICE:

Enronergizer Bunny
PULPit
BY ROBBIE CONAL
0 VOLTS
EXPIRES
NOV. 5, 2004

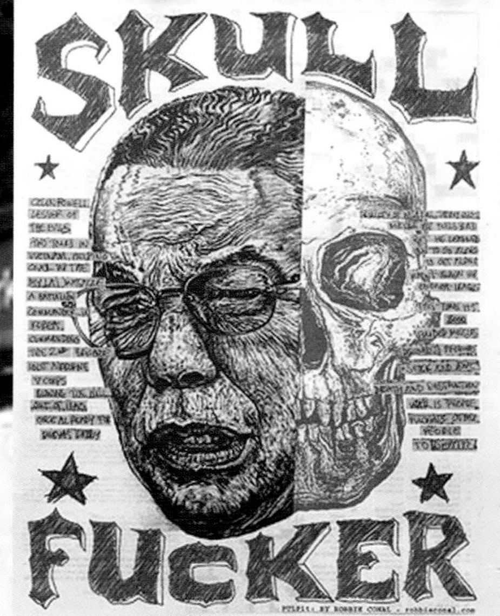
SKULL
FUCKER

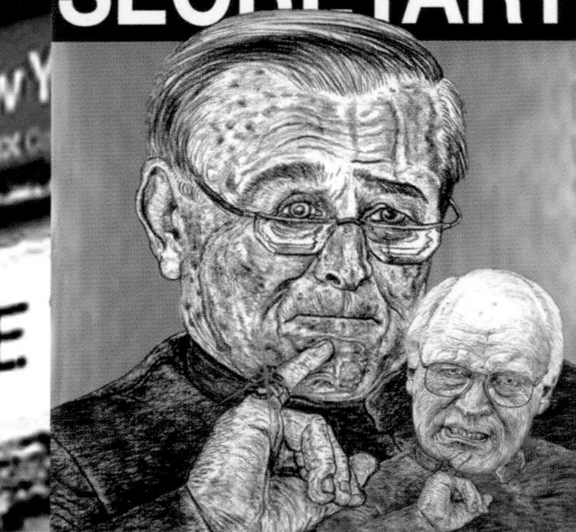
SECRETARY
OF OFFENSE

ROBBIE CONAL

I love to draw and paint - scratching on a piece of cloth (canvas) with a burnt stick (charcoal) to make an image appear out of nothing is like magic (of course, sometimes the magic works and sometimes it doesn't). Smooshing oil paint around on fabric is positively (or negatively) primal, like covering your mom's living room drapes with your shit (just one example, nothing personal). But when real shit happens - like ugly old white guys in suits and ties with too much power over us and the rest of the world abusing it in the name of a mere rumor, like representative democracy (well, for kids growing into their voting rights in, say, the year 2000, it's a distant echo of a rumor), making art about it becomes imperative. You gotta do something, with whatever skills you've got. Even if it's just cathartic - get rid of all those evil vibes. There isn't much of anything good about becoming an artist in contemporary American culture - you ain't gonna make your first million being an artist and your parents are gonna hate having spent their life's savings on your so-called education so you can go starve in a storefront and work as a clerk in a video store or waitress in a diner (or these days, be a peon in a big corporate graphics department, doing cheesy photoshop effects for idiots) olds trying to take over their Kindergarten class. And, if you have a sense of mischief, you can provide people with a little counter-infotainment in the process. I'm not the only one doing this. A group of ambitious D.C. punks trumped me so bad once: In July 1987 I was so pissed off about Ed Meese, Ronald Reagan's Attorney General, who was being investigated by two special prosecutors at the same time (Wedtech and Iran Contra), that I did a poster about him called, "Something Fishy." My little guerrilla street-postering army and I put it up all over LA, the Bay Area and New York in the next few months. By December, we wrangled our DC crews (disaffected law clerks, students, artsy types, the great "Lesbian Avengers", etc.) and we hit the streets of the nation's capital. It was just before Christmas—we were in a festive mood. The "heh-heh-heh" factor was kicking in: as in "this is gonna be so cool, people on the streets are gonna be shocked and dig us the most ...heh-heh-heh." (Actually, without the "heh-heh-heh" factor in this kind of art-making, it's hard to get it up at all. You gotta at least think it's gonna be cool; there's no other pay-off.) It must have been about midnight when we swooped into Dupont Circle with hundreds of "Some thing Fishy" Meese posters, buckets of glue and brushes. All we could see were giant three color all text posters plastered [illegible] where: "MEESE IS A PIG." What the fuck?Somebody - actually it must have been a gang of some-bodies - had beaten us to the punch. I was mystified, somewhere between annoyed and elated. There was a paragraph of text beneath the headline, ending with the words, ""Let's make this odious little weasel resign right now." Meese is a pig and he's a weasel—whatever! When I got back home to LA, there was a mailing tube waiting for me (with no return address). Sure enough, a "MEESE IS A PIG" poster. With a little hand scrawled note: "We like your work, hope you like ours." I loved it! I had been so out-punked! Turns out, of course, that it was Jeff Nelson (of Minor Threat and later Fugazi) and about 3 dozen of his DC punk cohorts who had gotten the piggies up over town the night before. That poster is legendary. The sequel, "EXPEF AGREE MEESE IS A PIG!" and the t-shirts are also the stuff of guerrill legend. Great work! Funny thing is, everywhere I go people still come up and tell me how much they dug my "MEESE IS A PIG" [illegible]

CONTRA
DICTION

LITTLE
NO SEX IS GOOD SEX.
WHITE LIES

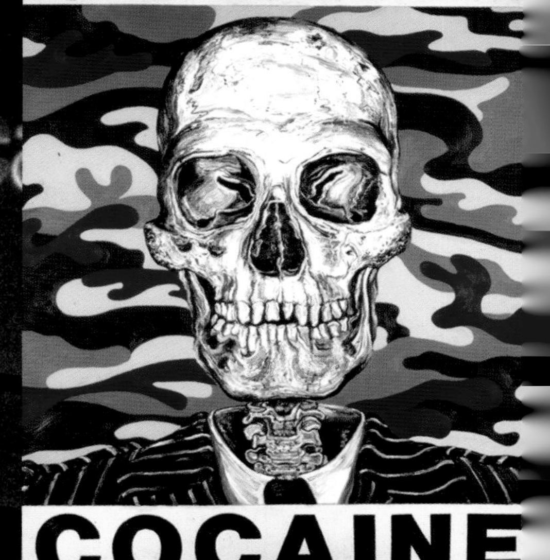
CONTRA
COCAINE

SHMECKLE
SOUR WILLIE
SWEET WILLIE
IN A PICKLE
PULPit
BY ROBBIE CONAL

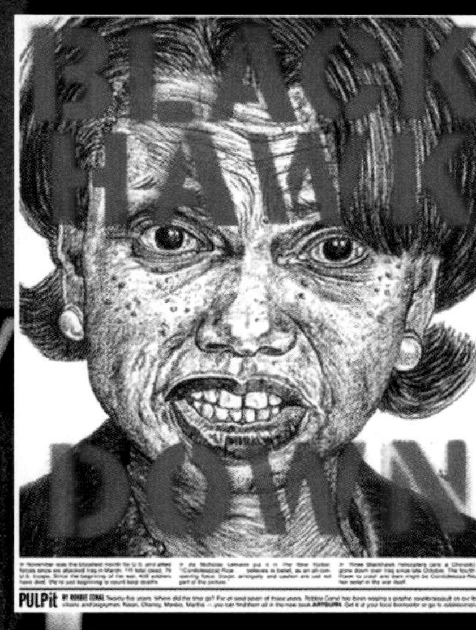
BLACK
HAWK
DOWN
PULPit

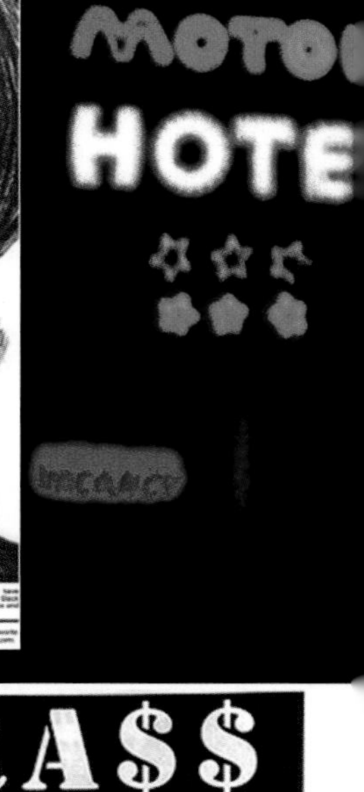
MOTO
HOTE

ERECTILE
PULPit
ISSUES

SECRETARY
F OFFENSE

SEX
DRUGS
ROCK&ROLL

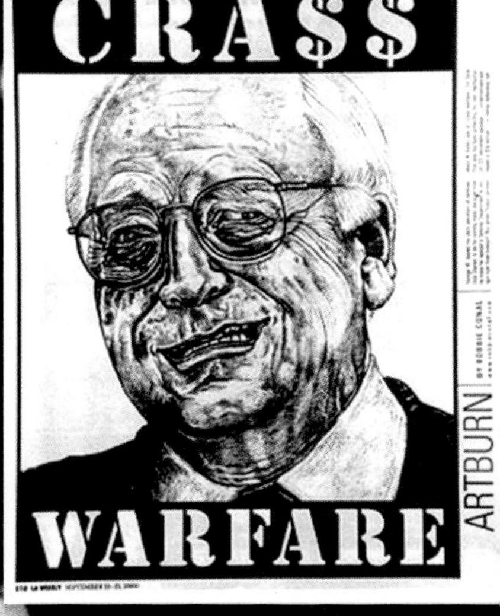
CRA$$
WARFARE
ARTBURN
BY ROBBIE CONAL

KNOW THE MEDIA
CHANGE THE MEDIA
BE THE MEDIA
JOURNAL
U.S. AIR FORCE
Gook
NO CONNECTION
VIETNAM, MARCH 1966
god+war=resolve
ALL ART by ADBUSTERS

Every ten years or so, the United States needs to pick up some small crappy little country and throw it against the wall, just to show the world we mean business.

– Michael Ledeen, former Reagan administration intelligence officer and current fellow at the American Enterprise Institute for Public Policy Research.

'zines

"Alaska's only Alternative"

WARNING

FREE

number 6
sept.-oct.

IN THIS ISSUE: BLACK FLAG/SHOCKS/WARNING CONCERT II/OUTSIDE SCENE/LOCAL SKATERS/REVIEWS, COMICS & MORE

DON'T GET LOST IN THE CROWD

read it all or not at all

ALASKA!

INTERNATIONAL ANTHEM

NIHILIST NEWSPAPER FOR THE LIVING

Vol.I.No3. 30p. 421984

THE BIRTH OF A NATION

BECAUSE I LOVE YOU SO MUCH
I HAVE CREATED YOU TO EMBRACE
EVERY LITTLE PART OF YOU

THEY sever the cord brutally
in their life-giving hands.
A filthy habit.
Red-hot,it is thrown to the
side and slides,clammy-hot,
beneath the table.
The knife is placed between
us.
The initiation rite is com-
plete.Only the cry cuts the
head,to bury deep and linger.
They have laboured long to
separate the other.In their
duty,we are left to lie
alone,gently breathing.
It lays pulsating beneath
the table.It was never de-
tached enough.
It hangs,parasitic,to the
body.
The serpent moves,to embrace,
it is the death knot of our
dutiful love and obedience.
The shedding was an illusion.
In their eagerness to give
us life,they gave us theirs.
The initiation rite was
wrong,was death.
The baby drops into the bin,
beneath the table.
The serpent lives,to define
our death.It grows so pale,
it is hard to distinguish.
The teaching is complete
when all trace has vanished.
Only the marks remain.
Only the remains are felt.
Joyfully we step from the
room,to celebrate our loss.
The serpent grows warm.It
fattens and pulls us closer.
The FAMILY.
The room.
We are all contained within
its walls.The conditions
are set.There is no escaping
the blood.It is thicker than
water.Thick,sticky and black.
We are forced to kneel
through the weight of it.
YOU are MY mother MY father.
YOU are MY son MY daughter.
YOU are MY husband MY wife.
YOU are MINE.
I am YOURS.
The serpent is not dead,it
is only sleeping.
The nightmare is the force
of its reality.We are
tightly bound by the vision.
We must learn to submit,not
to survive.
The serpent pulls tighter.
We must be willing to
possess and be possessed.
Beneath the table,the
withered cord pumps,cold,
laying like some discarded
snakeskin.
The air thickens.The density
is suffocating.There is no
room to see.
Life is life never realised.
Tighter.Tighter.
We must,finally,sublimate
all love and life for theirs.
There can be no meeting.
The serpent writhes in its
joy of life.We can not
breathe.It pumps a sickening
air in its attempt to regain
the submission.It tightens
still and the cry is heard.
The knife is between us.

WORLD EXCLUSIVE

INSIDE! EVEREST, SINGLE-HANDED. AN ACCOUNT OF THE FIRST SOLO ASCENT

BEAT IT!
DAMNED
DEAD BOYS
83
PERE UBU
VERLAINE
MUMPS
82
JOHN CALE
JERRY HARRISON
& NOT MUCH MORE
81
FIRST EDITION
STIV BATORS
BEAT IT! 2
AKRON IS FULL OF SPUDBOYS...
DEVO
DICTATORS
DEAD BOYS
NEW RECORDS
MISC.
$1.00 1977
SEPTEMBER
4
BEAT IT
ELVIS COSTELLO & THE ATTRACTIONS
1.00
3
THE JAM
DR FEELGOOD
T. HEADS
HOT RODS
DEVO
MUMPS
BOB GORDON
IGGY
J. RICHMAN
BEEFHEART
REVIEWS
ETCETERA
BEAT IT!

'BEAT IT!' BY JULIA GORTON

'77 SUMMER OF NO FUN
(its all over)
NO
instant artifact of the new order
VOL.1 no2
50¢
VOL1 NO 1 INSTANT ARTIFACT OF THE NEW ORDER
NO MAGAZINE IS GOOD ENOUGH FOR YOU!
Lead singer wanted for New Wave
Call J
BUY IT NOW
WHEREVER YOU CAN FIND IT.
ZIG-ZAG
WAYNE COUNTY NOT GUILTY!!!

AN ORIGINAL
PUNK
$1.25
#15
"INTERNATIONAL" PRODUCTION
MUTANT MONSTER
BEACH PARTY
STARRING
CO-STARRING
SPECIAL GUEST
Joey Ramone
Deborah Harry
Andy Warhol
Peter Wolf
August
with Peter Frampton
Annette Funicello
John Cale
Chris Stein
"A STUDY IN TERROR"

NEW YOR

PUNK
$1.25
ROLLING STONES!
DAVID JOHANSEN
ALICE COOPER
THE TRUTH ABOUT THE KENNEDY ASSASSINATION
BUDDA BUDDA
CHUCK WEPNER VS IDI AMIN
CLASH

Punk
85¢
RAMONES

FLESH AND BONES
$2.50
#8
Tater Totz
Sloth
Hawkwind
Hickoids
J.D. King
Sound garden
Gary Panter

JEFF O.

PUNKROCK
Think mink
dictators rule
sex pistols shoot
OOh! That iggy
nasty Criminals
DeVO, jam, Weirdos & sirius
COLOR POSTERS
Exclusive: HOW To be a PUNk for all You Sophisticates

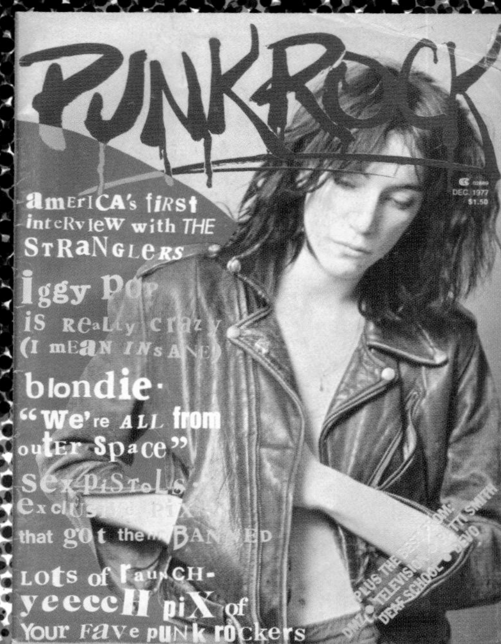

PUNKROCK
DEC. 1977
$1.50
america's first interview with THE STRANGLERS
iggy pop is really crazy (I mean insane)
blondie "We're ALL from outer Space"
that got them BANNED
lots of raunch-yeeccH piX of Your fave punk rockers

FLESH+BONES

JEFF O.

$1.25/75p.UK

OCKER

Vol. 2, No. 1 $1.50

ALL THE YOUNG DUDES

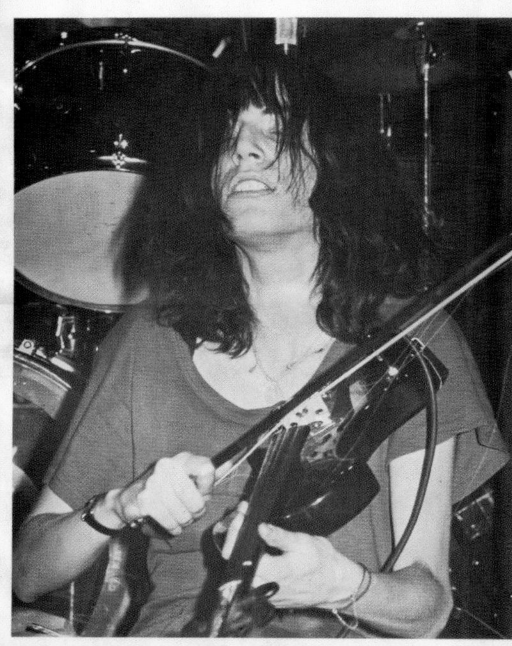

Vol. 1, No. 6 $1.50

ALL THE YOUNG DUDES

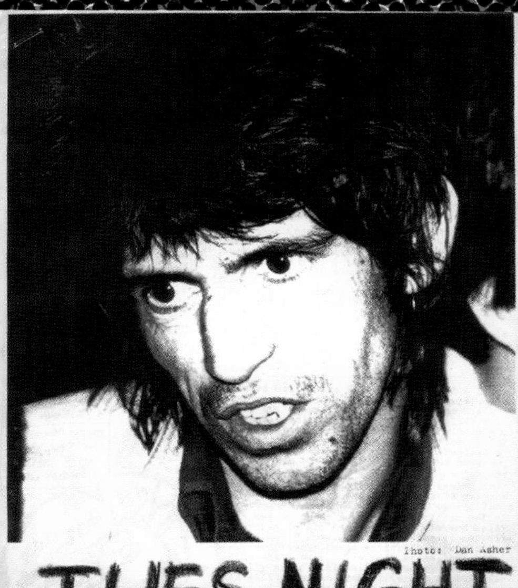
Photo: Dan Asher

TUES. NIGHT

NEW YORK CITY SEPT. 27 1977

NEW YORK CITY SEPT. 20, 1977
TUES. NIGHT #4
TOM VERLAINE

Sept. 13, 1977 New York City #3
TUES. NIGHT
photo:Patti Kane

"'A song so mystical and calm, so full of certainties....'Thus did a poet describe the music of a bird he had heard singing in a tree. In ________ — ____ ______ choirs of singing birds, rich, rare and rhythmic, are combined with some especially delightful man-made music to form a totality as singular as it is appealing. There is no truer music than the sounds of nature, pure and deep.

~ Faith Crumpacker (MGM SE4442)

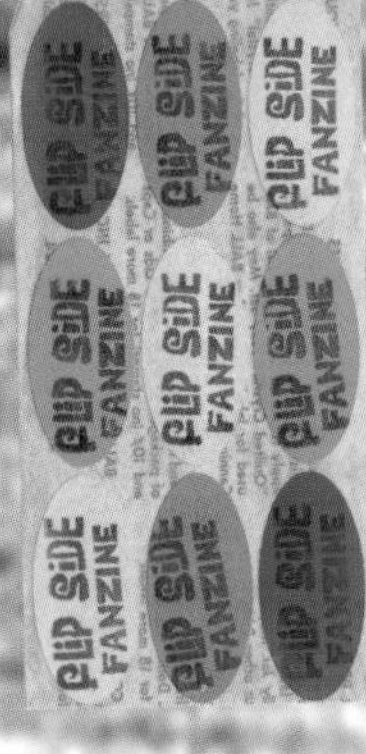
FLIP SIDE FANZINE
FLIP SIDE FANZINE
FLIP SIDE FANZINE
FLIP SIDE FANZINE
FLIP SIDE FANZINE
FLIP SIDE FANZINE
FLIP SIDE FANZINE
FLIP SIDE FANZINE
FLIP SIDE FANZINE

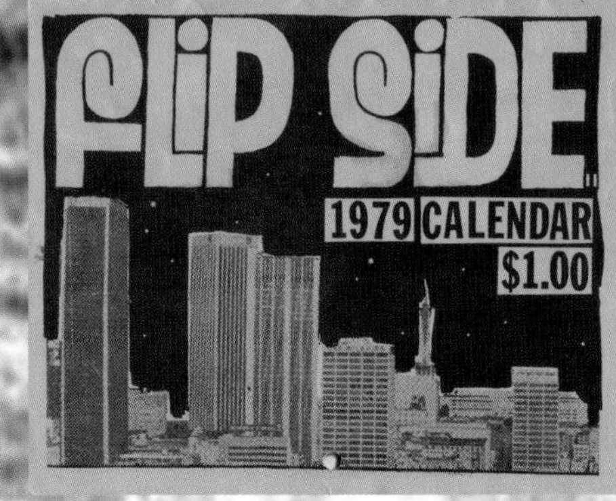
FLIP SIDE
1979 CALENDAR
$1.00

LOS ANGELES
FLIP SIDE
25c
FASHION SHOW
DEAD BOYS
INTERVIEWS:
DAVE TROUT of the weirdos
ZIPPERS
MORE!

FLIPSIDE NUMBER THREE!

THIS IS MESSED UP! I'M GONNA WRITE..
FLIP SIDE!
44
$1.00
YOU GUYS ARE GONNA BE SORRY NOW- WOE!!
WHITE FLAG
GET OUTTA HERE SISSY!
THE NEXT DAY...
DEAR AL AND HUD, EVERYTIME I SOB: GO TO A SHOW- I GET BEAT-UP!!
INTERVIEWS THIS ISSUE: SECOND WIND, RAS ZEBRAS, REPLACEMENTS, MIKE STONE CLAY REC., ENTROPY, NOTA, MAD PARADE, DECRY, JOHNNY AND THE DINGBATS, CIRCLE ONE
WHY OH WHY CAN'T PUNKS UNITE? WHEN WILL THE VIOLENCE END?!
WHATS HAPPENED TO THE SCENE?!
THE LETTER ARRIVES AT FLIPSIDE!
AL, HERES ANOTHER 'WHATS HAPPENED TO THE SCENE' LETTER!
WOW! THAT MAKES ONE THOUSAND THIS WEEK!
MEANWHILE AT THE SHOW...
I'M TIRED OF ALL OF THIS SHIT! I'M GONNA ______!
STORY/ART LEE

LOS ANGELES
50c
FLIP SIDE
DICKIES
BEATLES
CONTROLLERS
SHOCK
DEADBEATS
MORE!

FLIP SIDE
32
$1
IN THIS ISSUE:
MINUTEMEN
SIN 34
JOHANNA W.
JEFF DAHL
BATALLION of SAINTS
CHELSEA
JAM
CONVICTED
+ MORE

FLIP SIDE
20
75¢
I'VE GOT THE WORLD UP MY ASS
HALLOWEEN ISSUE WITH - THE CIRCLE JERKS - WEIRDOS - ADOLESCENTS - EDDIE - SOCIAL DISTORTION - POSH BOY AND MORE!

LOS ANGELES
FLIPSIDE
75¢
IN THIS ISSUE: THE OO-OOS.....THE DILS.....SANDY PEARLMAN.....GARY PIG'S TORONTO...ALLEYCATS...
BRENDAN VS. THE DILS.....SAN FRANCISCO...SNUKY...RODNEY'S CHART...GOSSIP, AND ALL THAT

ted Flipside Fanzine in 1977,
new nothing about the pub-
s, only that we wanted an

passion for the burgeoning
v wave genre. Jumping blind-
ld of the printed media, we
les to adhere to, so we

r own style. We grew up
Creem, Rock Scene, and
Press, but we couldn't write
s their staffs. We could,
, talk around a record
nd type our conversational
that way. We weren't on

's good side, so in order to
headlining act, we'd grab
ts to see the opening bands
about the concert. Being
unfashionable Eastside
ngeles meant we had no
ge of the other members
ne, thus we could be very
our assessment of them as

nd as performers. In short,

othing to lose, so we could
y honest, a trait we tried
or close to 25 years. Our

way of distribution was to drive clear across town to put five copies in a store's magazine rack to sell them on consignment. We'd return to the store

to drop off the next issue,

collect our nickels and dimes, and head back home. It wasn't the most cost-effective means of distribution, but it was the only way at that time to get our 'zine a little shelf space. Running Flipside was time consuming but it was a great learning experience for novices like us. When you loved the music, enjoyed hanging

with your friends, and had the feeling you were involved in promoting something very

special, it made everything worthwhile. I wouldn't have changed a thing.

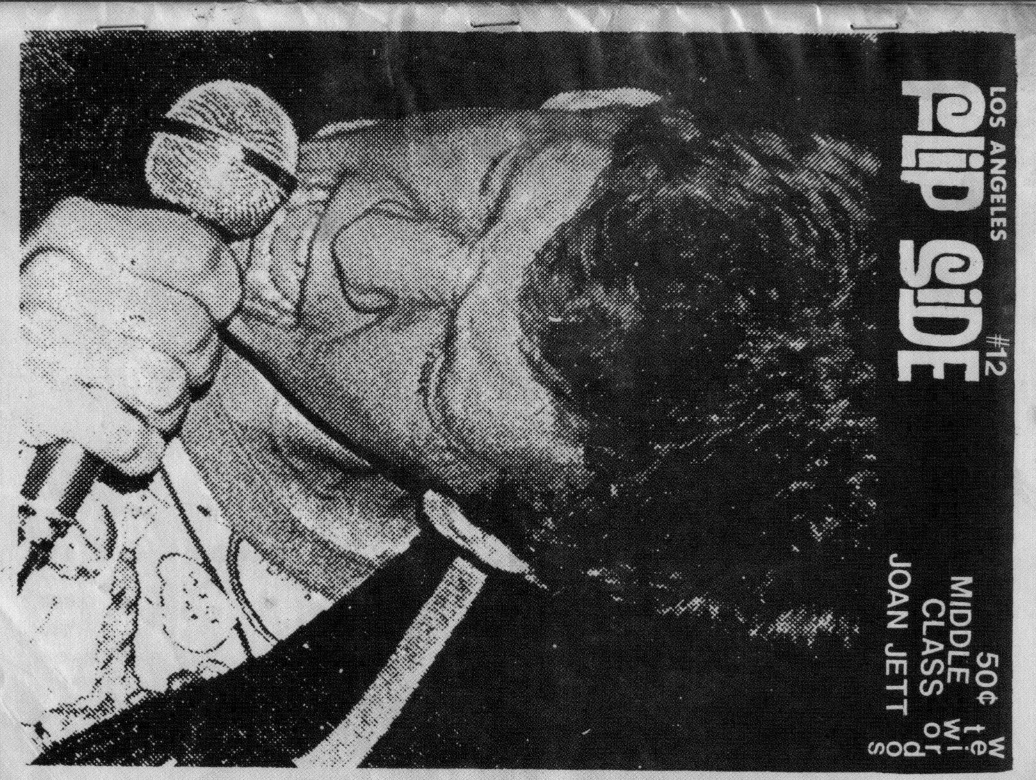
LOS ANGELES
FLIP SIDE
#12
50¢
MIDDLE
CLASS
JOAN JETT

LOS ANGELES
FLIPSIDE
#15
75¢
INSIDE:
GERMS
FLYBOYS
MODS

LOS ANGELES
FLIP SIDE
25¢
SPASTICS
Rodney Bingenheimer
BACKSTAGE PASS
runaways
masque
MORE!

LOS ANGELES
FLIP SIDE
25¢
WEASELS
GERMS
IGGY
MORE!

LOS ANGELES
FLIP SIDE
25¢
EULOGY
PUNK ROQ
GERMS
CLASH
MORE
NEW!

MAXIMUMROCKNROLL
No. 28
SEPTEMBER '85
$1.00
NEW RIGHT
INTELLIGENCE
CONNECTIONS
GOD BLESS AMERICA
by
IRVING BERLIN
The 700 Club
Plus: ICONOCLAST/ANTI-SCRUNTI FACTION/ACTIVE INGREDIENTS/GRB/KINA/POLICAL ASYLUM/FRITES MODERN/OTTAWA & More!!!!

#28 COVER: WINSTON SMITH

MAXIMUMROCKNROLL

VOL. 1 NO. 1

MDC
MILLIONS OF DEAD COPS

MINOR THREAT

VICIOUS ^ CIRCLE

JUVENIL JUSTICE

CHURCH POLICE

S/M NIGHTMARE

RIP RRZ?

AND

GOD FORBID,

POLITICS

NORTHERN

CALIFORNIA

COVERAGE

BI- monthly

$1.00

VOL. 1 NO. 1

LOBOTOMY
75¢
#3
THE BRAINLESS MAGAZINE
LIVE!RAMONES,RUNAWAYS,DILS,SCREAMERS...
IOTSA SEX PISTOLS JUNK,SLANDER,LIBEL,
SIZZLING GOSSIP,AND--OUR PRETTIEST
LOBOTOMATE YET!!!(AND MORE!)

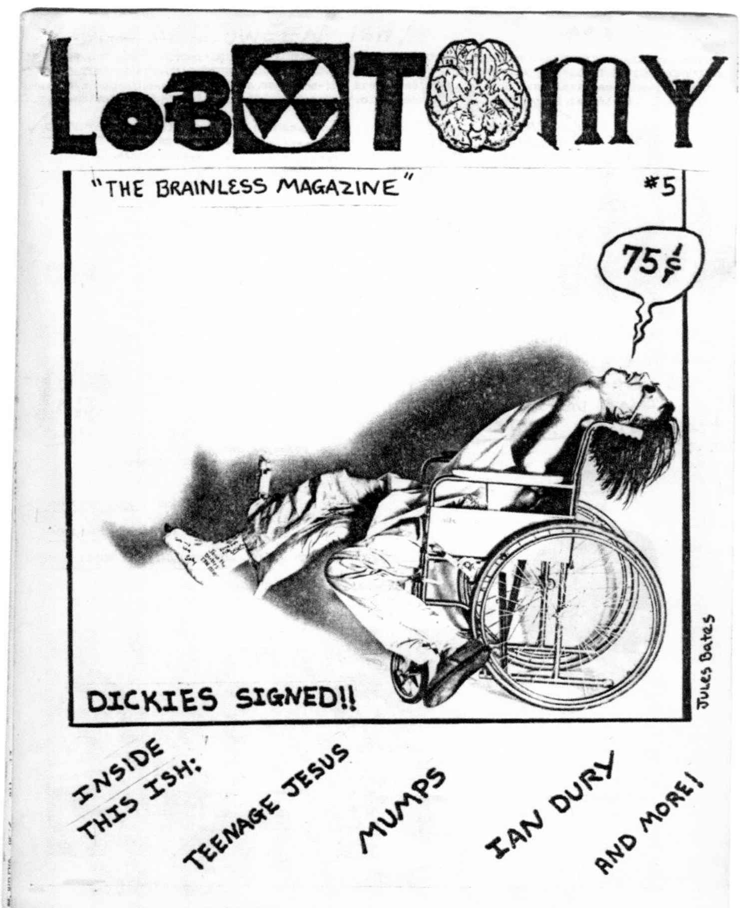
LOBOTOMY
"THE BRAINLESS MAGAZINE"
#5
75¢
DICKIES SIGNED!!
JULES BATES
INSIDE THIS ISH:
TEENAGE JESUS
MUMPS
IAN DURY
AND MORE!

LOBOTOMY
VOL.II, NO.3
'the brainless magazine'
.85
GO GO'S
DAVID LYNCH
EXTREMES
999
jam
rockats
and
more!
CALIFORNIA
NF 339

LOBOTOMY
Vol.2
The Brainless Magazine
No.4
.85
Damned
u.k. news
senders
X
village people
n.y news
music and totally unrelated subjects

RANDY KAYE & PLEASANT GEHMAN

SEARCH & DESTROY
No. 1 $1
Search and Destroy
JOHNNY ROTTEN
JOHNNY ROTTEN
L I V E S

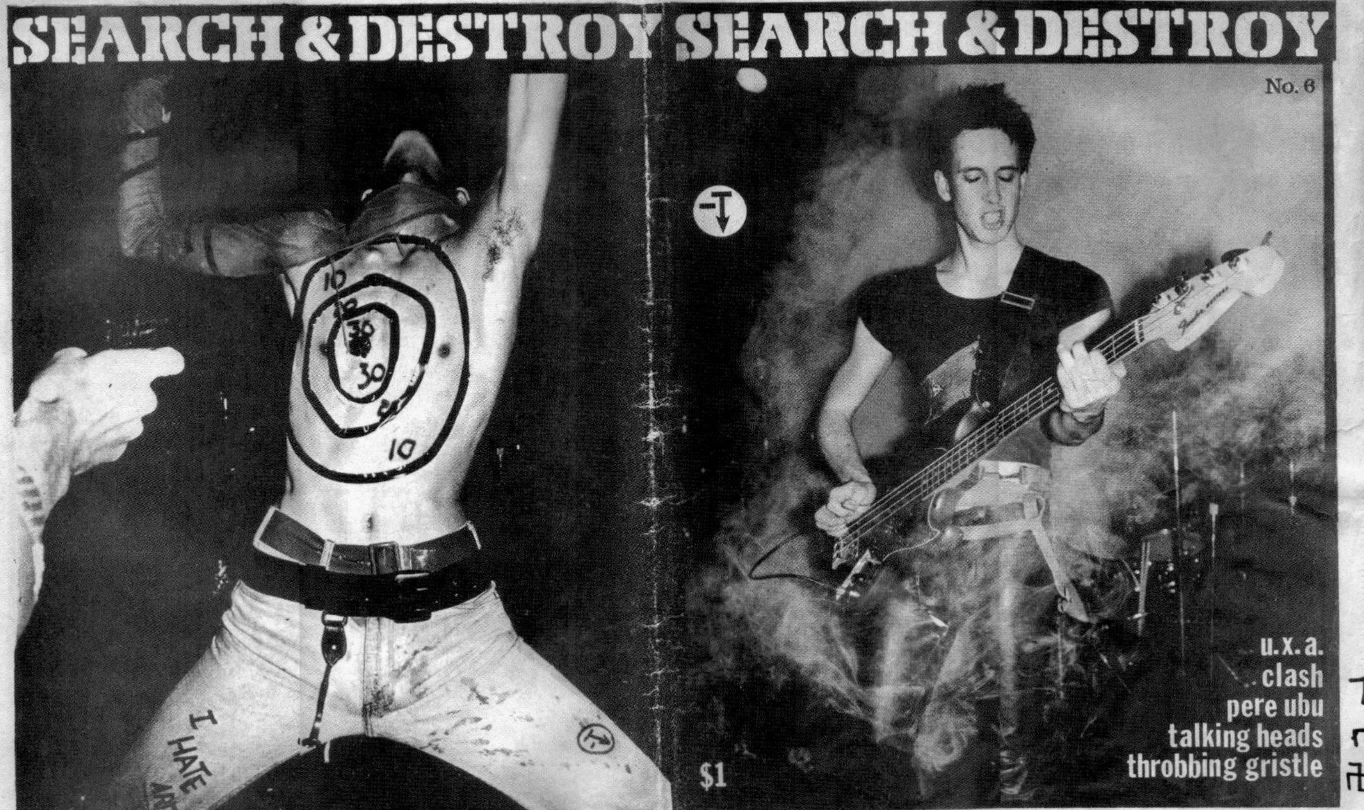
SEARCH & DESTROY SEARCH & DESTROY
No. 6
10
30
10
I HATE ART
u.x.a.
clash
pere ubu
talking heads
throbbing gristle
$1

PRACTICING TO DRAW SWASTIKAS?

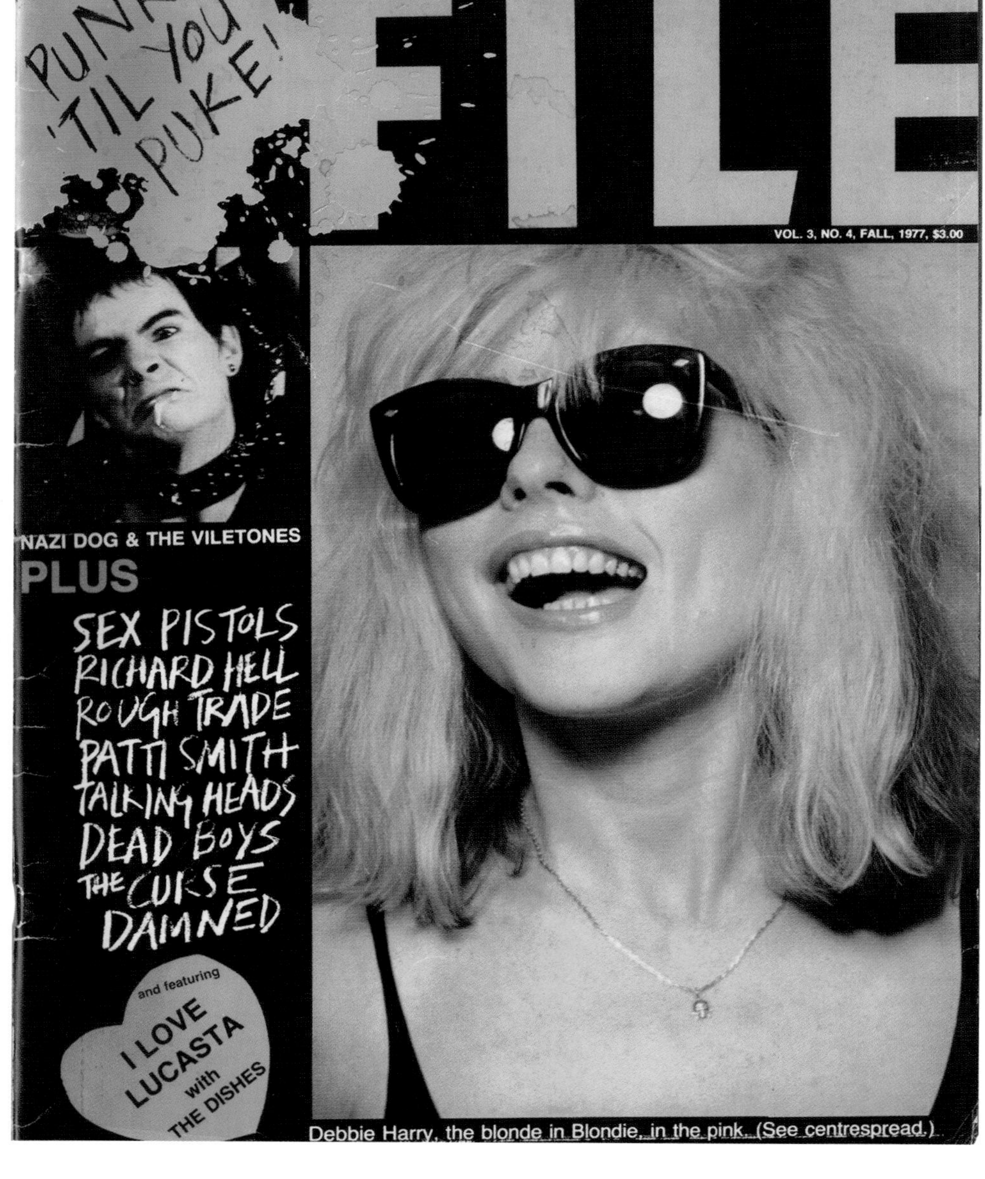
PUNK 'TIL YOU PUKE!
FILE
VOL. 3, NO. 4, FALL, 1977, $3.00
NAZI DOG & THE VILETONES
PLUS
SEX PISTOLS
RICHARD HELL
ROUGH TRADE
PATTI SMITH
TALKING HEADS
DEAD BOYS
THE CURSE
DAMNED
and featuring
I LOVE LUCASTA with THE DISHES
Debbie Harry, the blonde in Blondie, in the pink. (See centrespread.)

VAGUE

Virgin

#21 : CYBER-PUNK : £3.50

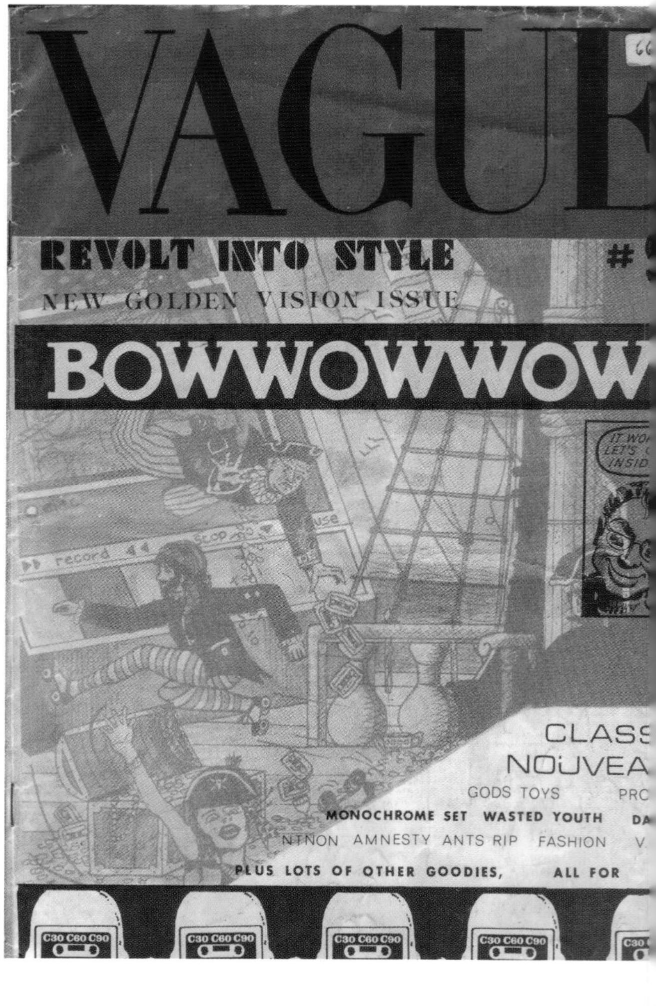

VAGUE

REVOLT INTO STYLE

NEW GOLDEN VISION ISSUE

BOWWOWWOW

CLASS

NOUVEA

GODS TOYS

MONOCHROME SET WASTED YOUTH

NTNON AMNESTY ANTS RIP FASHION

PLUS LOTS OF OTHER GOODIES, ALL FOR

C30 C60 C90

PATTI SMITH GENERATION X
SEX PISTOLS WILKO JOHNSON
POP GROUP THE AVENGERS SUB-
WAY SECT MOTORHEAD DESTROY
ALL MONSTERS WHIRLWIND

ZIGZAG
Nº89 Nov'78
40p $1·50
JOHNNY THUNDERS
RAMONES
DICTATORS
STIFF'S TRAIN TOUR
inside: 28 page
SMALL LABELS CATALOGUE '78

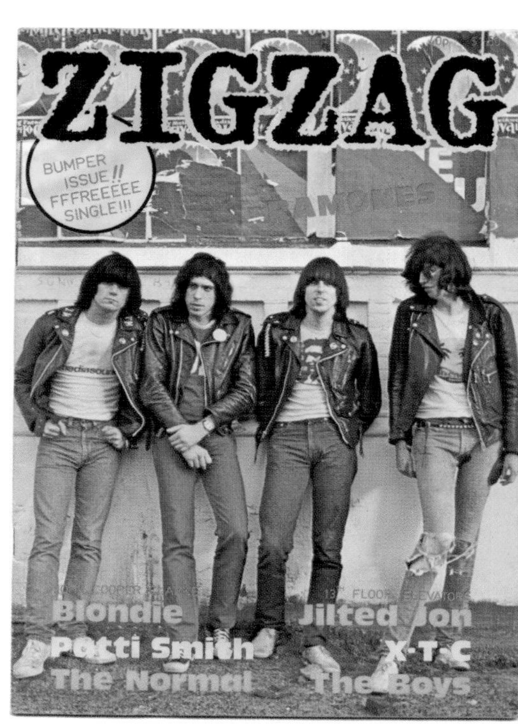
ZIGZAG
BUMPER ISSUE!! FFFREEEEE SINGLE!!!
Blondie
Patti Smith
The Normal
X·T·C
The Boys

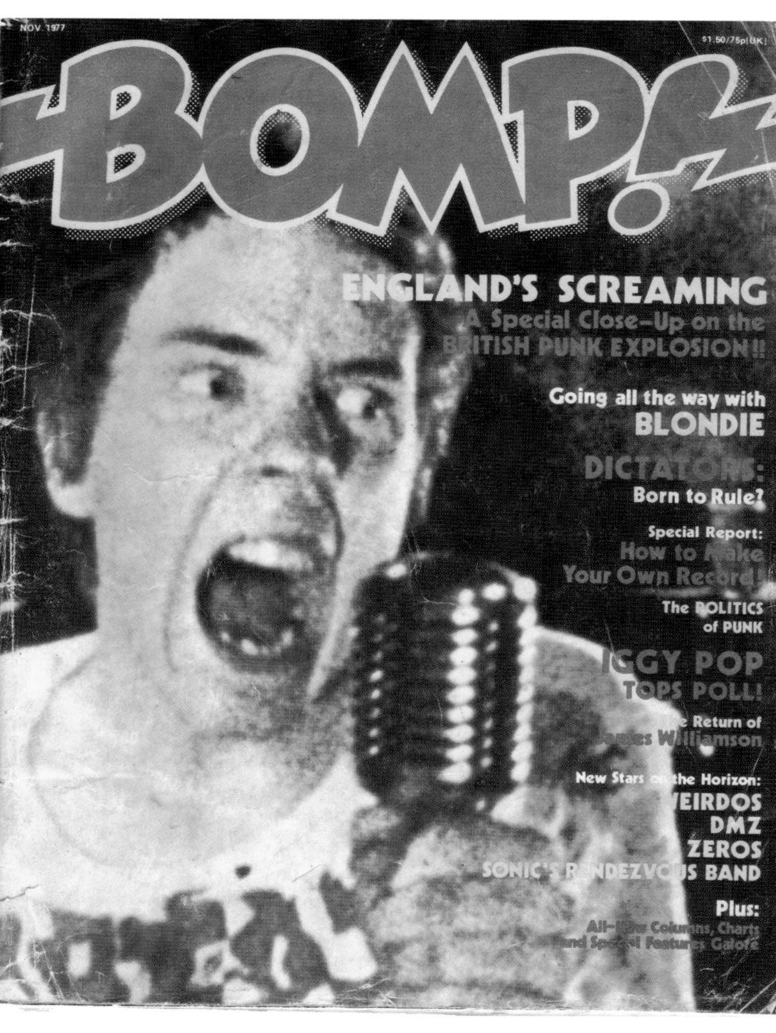
NOV. 1977
$1.50/75p(UK)
BOMP!
ENGLAND'S SCREAMING
Going all the way with
BLONDIE
Born to Rule?
Special Report:
The POLITICS of PUNK
IGGY POP
TOPS POLL!
DMZ
ZEROS
Plus:

DER SPIEGEL
C 7007 CX
Nr. 4
32. Jahrgang · DM 2,50
23. Januar 1978
CAMB MA PRICE
KEY
3 $2.00
PUNK
Kultur aus den Slums:
brutal und häßlich

THE MORGUE'S COPY
BLACK MARKET
FANZINE
FIRST ISSUE
APRIL '85
FEATURING INTERVIEWS WITH
TEX AND THE HORSEHEADS
AND LOCAL PUNKS
DIATRIBE
AND
REVIEWS
A COMIC BY LEE
MISC. BULLSHIT
MORE MISC. BULLSHIT

BLACK MARKET
INTERVIEWS...
SAMHAIN,
CHRISTIAN DEATH,
TUPELO CHAINSEX
AND! THE TESTICLE HEAD INTERVIEW!
COMIC BY... LEE
ISSUE #2
JUNE/JULY '85

BLACK MARKET 3
INTERVIEWS!
D.O.A.!
MAD MARC RUDE!
POEMS
COMICS
AND
MORE!
A STORY BY LEE
LEE '85

SUBURBAN VOICE
NO. 17
$1.00
DESCENDENTS
DEAD MILKMEN
DIRECT ACTION
BRIAN WALSBY
MINUTEMEN

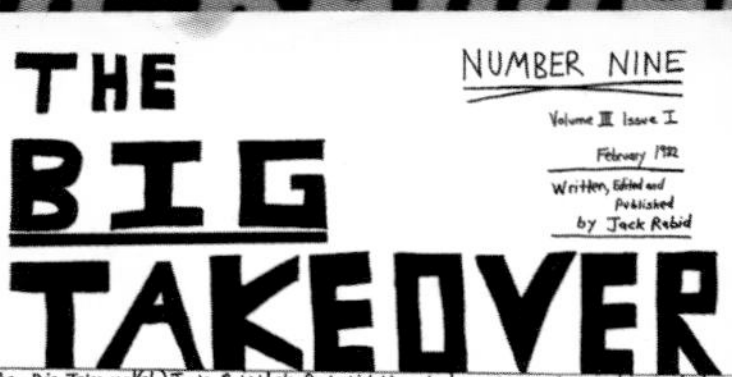
THE BIG TAKEOVER
NUMBER NINE
Written, Edited and Published by Jack Rabid

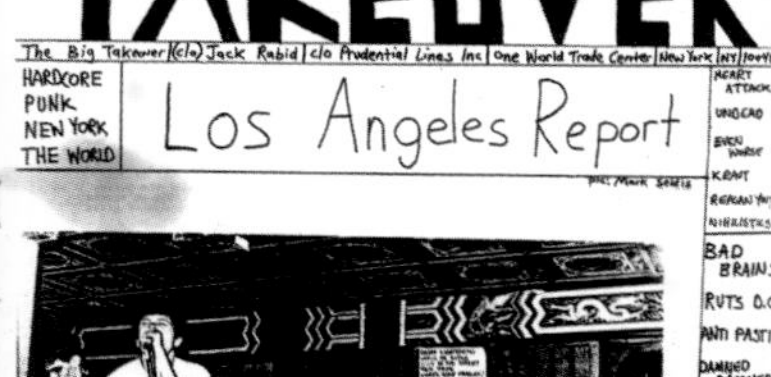
HARDCORE
PUNK
NEW YORK
THE WORLD
Los Angeles Report

The Circle Jerks, Los Angeles, California

The Big Takeover
#8
Volume 2 Issue 6 Late November, Early December 1981

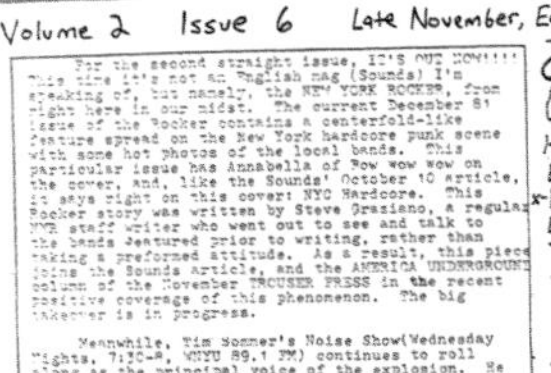
CIRCLE JERKS
UNDEAD
HEART ATTACK
BLACK FLAG
BUZZCOCKS
EVEN WORSE
T.S.O.L.
999
DAMNED
FEAR
WASTED YOUTH
BAD BRAINS
NOISE SHOW
NOISE NEWS
DAMAGED GOODS
ROCKER ARTICLE
UPCOMING SHOWS

THE BIG TAKEOVER
KILLING JOKE
MUSIC W/ HEART/NEW YORK/THE WORLD.....
ALSO INSIDE:
R.E.M.
SALEM 66
142 NEW RECORDS ???
AND LOTS MORE...!

SUBURBAN VOICE
NO. 27/$1.50

MURPHY'S LAW
DR. KNOW
IGNITION
EYE FOR AN EYE
POISON IDEA
UNIFORM CHOICE

THE SOUTH BAY
RIPPER
2
75¢

666
UNDER TONES
KERRY LOEWEN
PETER BLOOM
SAUCERS AND MORE!

RIPPER
75¢
#5
VKTMS
SOCIETY DOG
ANGRY SAMOANS
MAXIMUM ROCK'N'ROLL

RIPPER
#6
75¢
THE LEWD
WASTED YOUTH
BLACK FLAG
AU PAIRS
RIBSY
TSOL

MAXIMUM ROCK N ROLL PRESENTS
$1.50
IF LIFE IS A BOWL OF CHERRIES
WHAT AM I DOING IN THE PIT ?
A PHOTOZINE BY MURRAY BOWLES

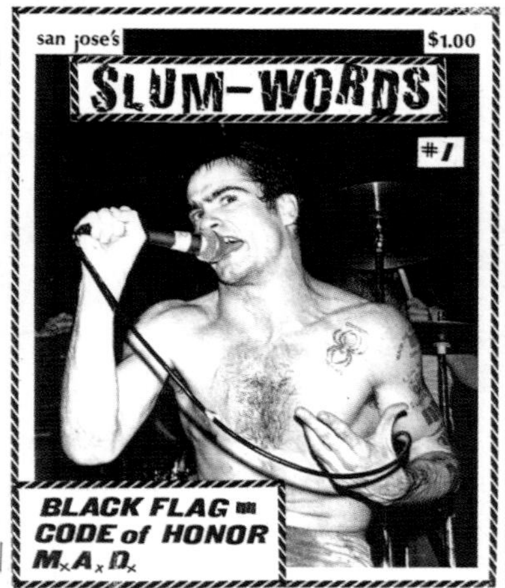
san jose's
$1.00
SLUM-WORDS
#1
BLACK FLAG
CODE of HONOR
M.A.D.

SLUM-WORDS
$1.00
NO. 2
NEGATIVE APPROACH
IRON CROSS
LOS OLVIDADOS

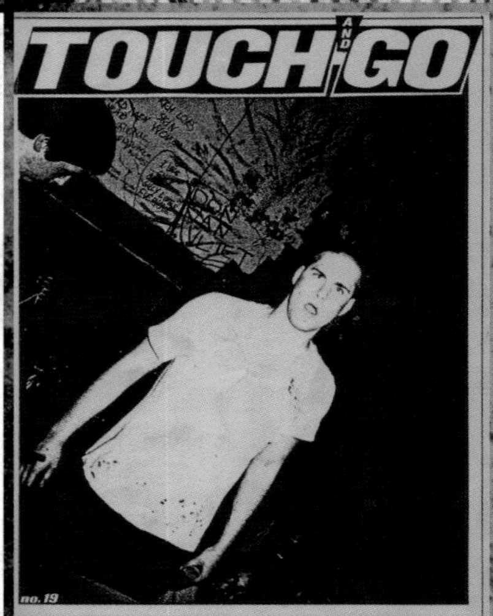
TOUCH AND GO
no. 19

TOUCH AND GO
no. 22
$1.50

Takeover read OK to me, at least better than I expected as I was a teenager then, though some of them looked so terrible! #8 is by far the worst looking issue we ever did, as I clearly had zero art skills in those pre-computer days, and learned on the go. The best bands then did that too. They didn't have to wait until they were as "skilled" as Emerson, Lake, and Palmer to kick up a great racket and I didn't need art skills. In the end the real rock n' roll is what gets remembered, the stuff that had visceral and raw-edged

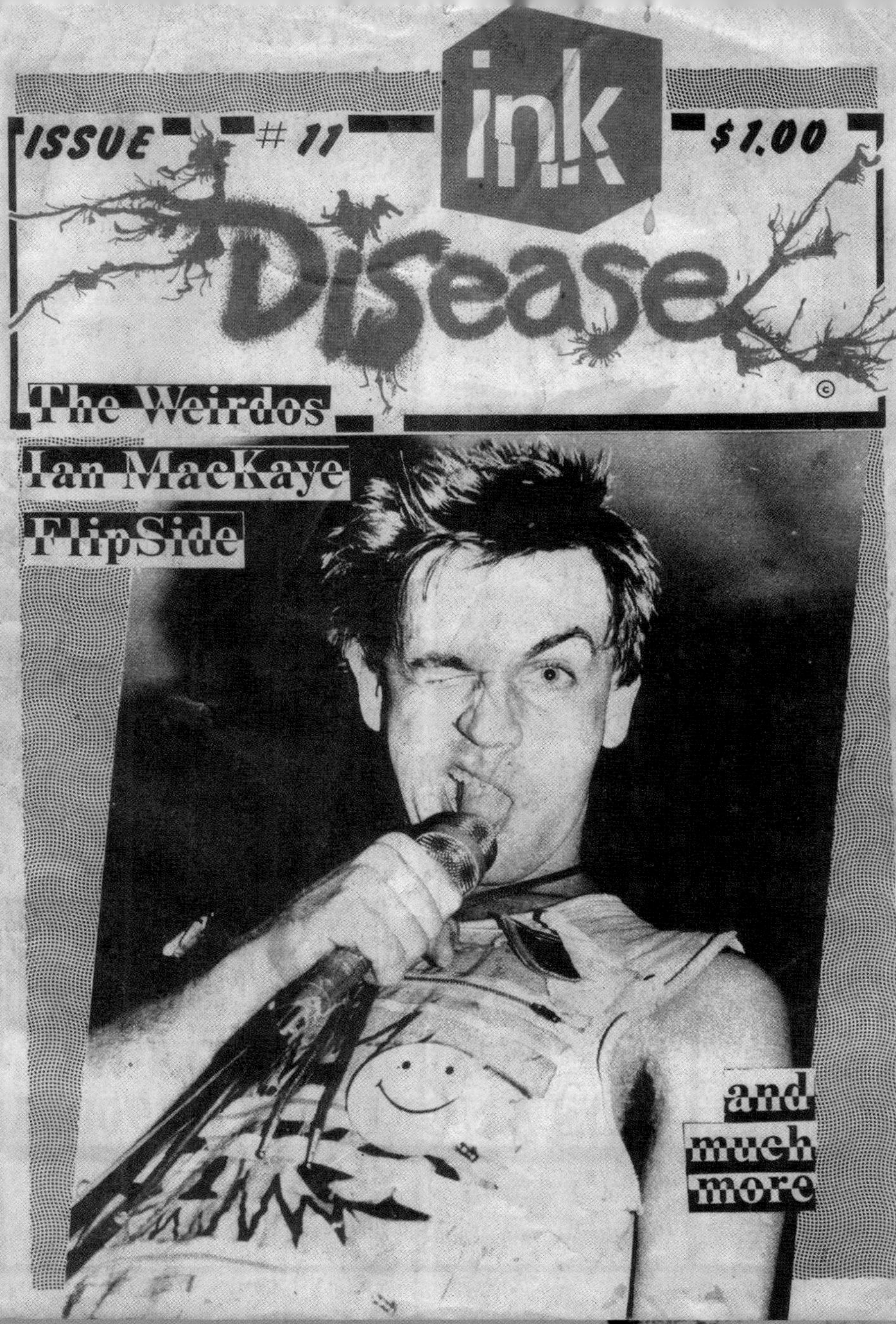

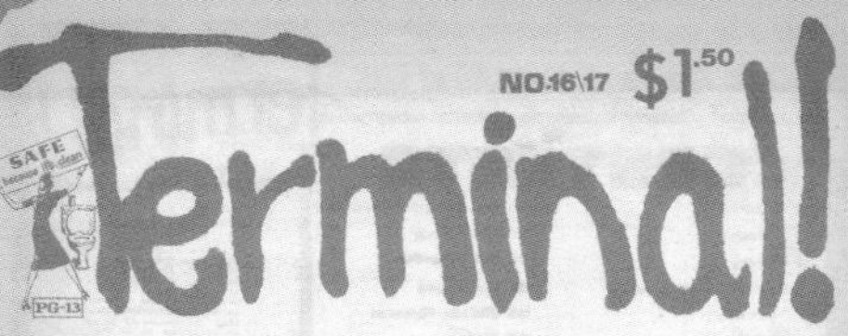

ISSUE # 11

ink Disease

$1.00

The Weirdos

Ian MacKaye

FlipSide

and much more

impact. It wasn't obvious to the majority then and it still isn't completely now. We are real professional these days but I still like the old issues better. You just can't beat the sense of belonging to a genuine alternative-to-crap inspired-arts community.

Terminal!
NO.16\17 $1.50
DOUBLE ISSUE
BLACK FLAG
EINSTURZENDE NEUBATEN
RAT AT RAT R
MINUTEMEN
BILL BRUFORD
HOLGER CZUKAY
TRIGGER & THE THRILL KINGS
HÜSKER DÜ
DAVID BORDEN
ALFRED JARRY
TEST DEPT.
LIVE SKULL
LOS LOBOS
BUTTHOLE SURFERS
VIOLENT FEMMES
DANCE FACTOR
AND MORE!

send $2.00 & .50¢ ($1. overseas) for postag

MY RULES / Glen E. Fried

WE GOT POWER

yearbook '82

88 pages · First four issues complete · Only $2. !

CIRCLE ON
wasted
BAD R
Red Cro
BLACK
DOA
CH3
saccharine trust
J.F.A.
husker du
its
inor threat
tSOL
+more
ALSO:
·'81+'82 GIG & RECORD REVIEWS·
·SCENE REPORTS·
·BEST BAND NAMES·
·SCAMMING·
ride the wild surf with so. cal's
WE GOT POWER no.3
$1
DoA
hates
misfits
saigon
ch.3
JFA
NO crisis
Jack tsol
toy surprise inside
Also:
scamming
U.S.' SCEEN-NEWZ
reviews
games
keith morris
& MORE!
WE GOT POWER!
magazine SOUTHERN CALIFORNIA no. 2 $1.00
if you Hate it... change IT !!!
henry
godzilla's
Red Cross
saccharine trust
nervous gender
SPOT
OVERKILL
brave dog
fer yourz
THE TAN
Reviews
anti pasti
atoms · 999 ·
sub humans
FEAR
+more
PHOTOS · CARTOONS · FUN & GAMES
party or go home
WE GOT POWER
number 5
$1.25
NECROS
circle JERKS
flipper
SIN 34
POLice Raidz
WHAT A GOOD IDEA
LA RAID
SUCKS MONTHLY
AUGUST 1983
FREE SMALL PLASTIC EXPLOSIVE INSIDE!
LA NEWS
VIEWS
REVIEWS
INTERVIEWS
Avoid Hell: Turn From Sin. Trust Jesus Christ (GOD) As Your Lord & Savior.
BLACK FLAG
STELLA
FACIAL HAIR
INSIDE TOTAL ANARCHY MAN, TOTALLY
Introducing
SUCKS
monthly
JUNE 1983
When you put it on...something happens to you.
Brand New LA mag!
Intro issue!
Buy this ass-hole!
MR.T DEMONSTRATES PUNK VIOLENCE

THIS PAGE: DAVE MARKEY

PIX!
Super Punk
KISS
BREAK UP!!??
NO. 1
$1.
no SKA
germs
darby crash
GANG OF 4
AC/DC
TEST PATTERN
DEATH PATROL
SEX PISTOLS
FUN FAX!!
SUPER CONTEST:
win
PAT'S
GUITAR!
999
GEN-X
FAX!
CLASH

I made 'Super Punk' at work behind my bosses back. Although I sold a few at Poseur, I mostly gave them away free at shows since

they didn't cost me anything to make. I never did a follow-up issue.

Fallout
$1.50
rat art
1981 urban olympics
The Contractions
HOW GOD GIVES US PEANUT BUTTER
DR. JOHN GOFMAN
PLUTONIUM PLAYERS
WHAT IT'S REALY LIKE TO BE DEAD
№ 4
"ACT LIKE NOTHING'S WRONG" Winston Smith 1981

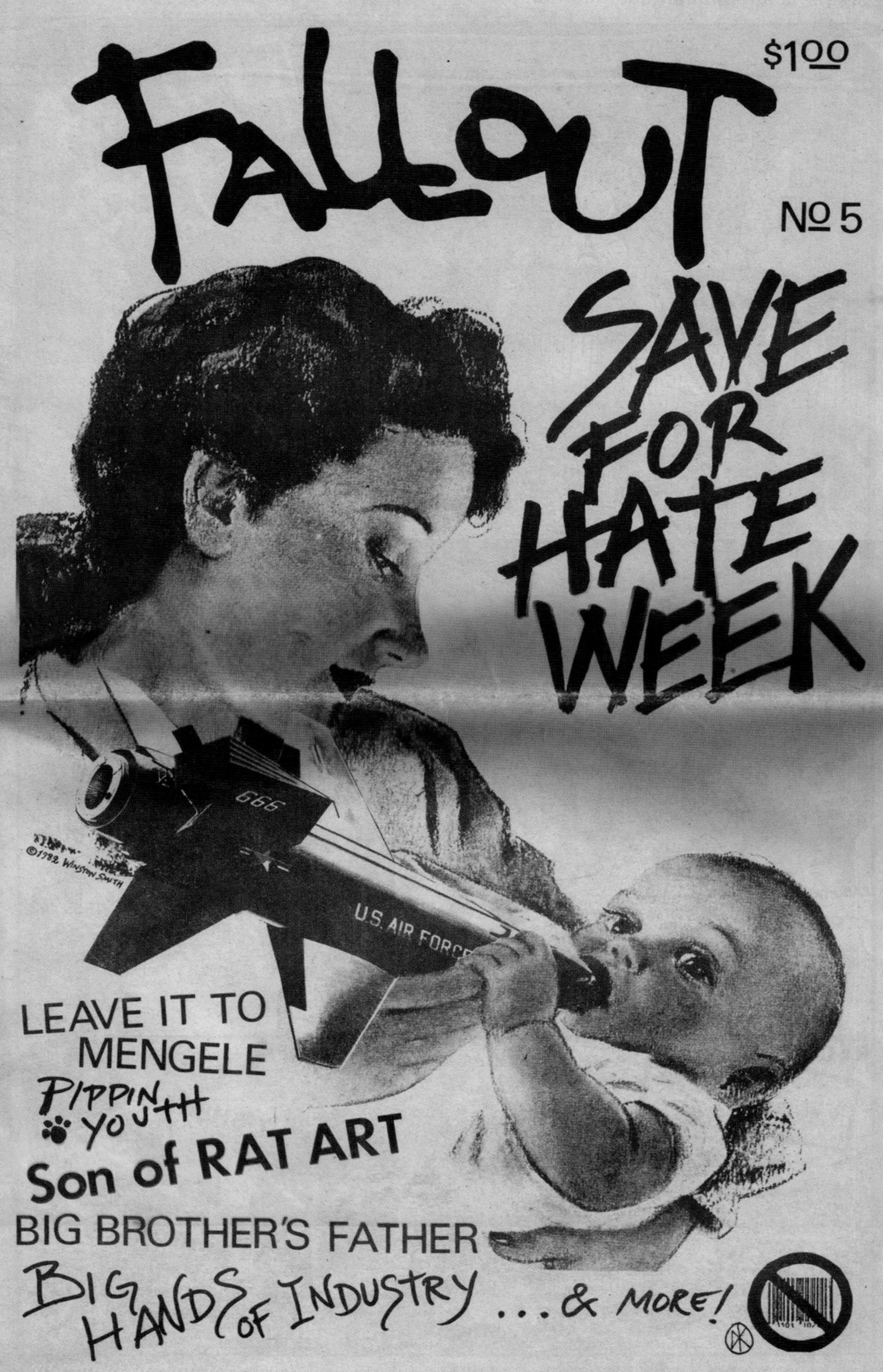
FALLOUT
$1.00
No 5
SAVE FOR HATE WEEK
666
©1982 Winston Smith
U.S. AIR FORCE
LEAVE IT TO MENGELE
PIPPIN YOUTH
Son of RAT ART
BIG BROTHER'S FATHER
BIG HANDS OF INDUSTRY ...& MORE!

May 28th, 1977 US 95c/Canada 55c 15p
new MUSICAL EXPRESS
WHAT'S THE TONGUE DOING LOOKING LIKE THIS?
SPECIAL GRATUITOUS
SEX PISTOLS
OVERKILL ISSUE
PAGES 1, 3, 7, 8, 12, 23, 58, 59, 60.
SO WHAT ARE THE
GRATEFUL DEAD
DOING ON PAGE 28?

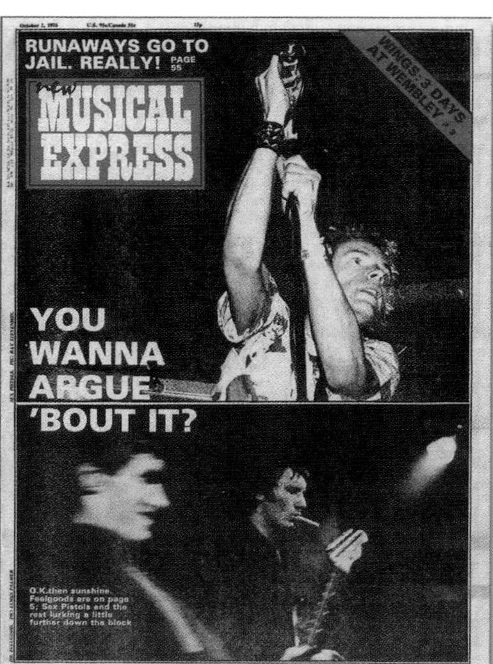
RUNAWAYS GO TO JAIL. REALLY! PAGE 55
new MUSICAL EXPRESS
WINGS: 3 DAYS AT WEMBLEY
YOU WANNA ARGUE 'BOUT IT?
O.K. then sunshine. Feelgoods are on page 5; Sex Pistols and the rest lurking a little further down the block

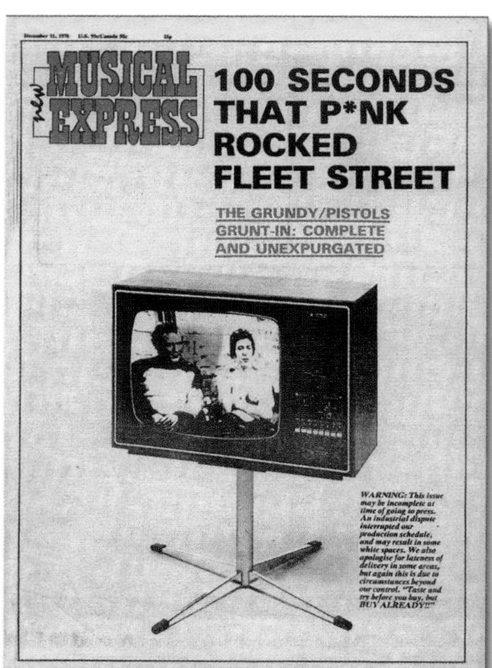
new MUSICAL EXPRESS
100 SECONDS THAT P*NK ROCKED FLEET STREET
THE GRUNDY/PISTOLS GRUNT-IN: COMPLETE AND UNEXPURGATED
WARNING: This issue may be incomplete at time of going to press. An industrial dispute interrupted our production schedule, and may result in some white spaces. We also apologise for lateness of delivery in some areas, but again this is due to circumstances beyond our control. "Taste and try before you buy, but BUY ALREADY!!"

US $1.10/Canada 60c 18p
new MUSICAL EXPRESS
COOK & JONES
THE LIFE AND CRIMES
The Sex Pistols Chronicles P.25-28

U.S. $1.50 (by air)/Canada 80c 20p
NEW MUSICAL EXPRESS NME
PETER GREEN
The Lost Years
EXCLUSIVE INTERVIEW
By Steve Clarke
THE PRIVATE LIFE OF PUBLIC IMAGE
By Danny Baker

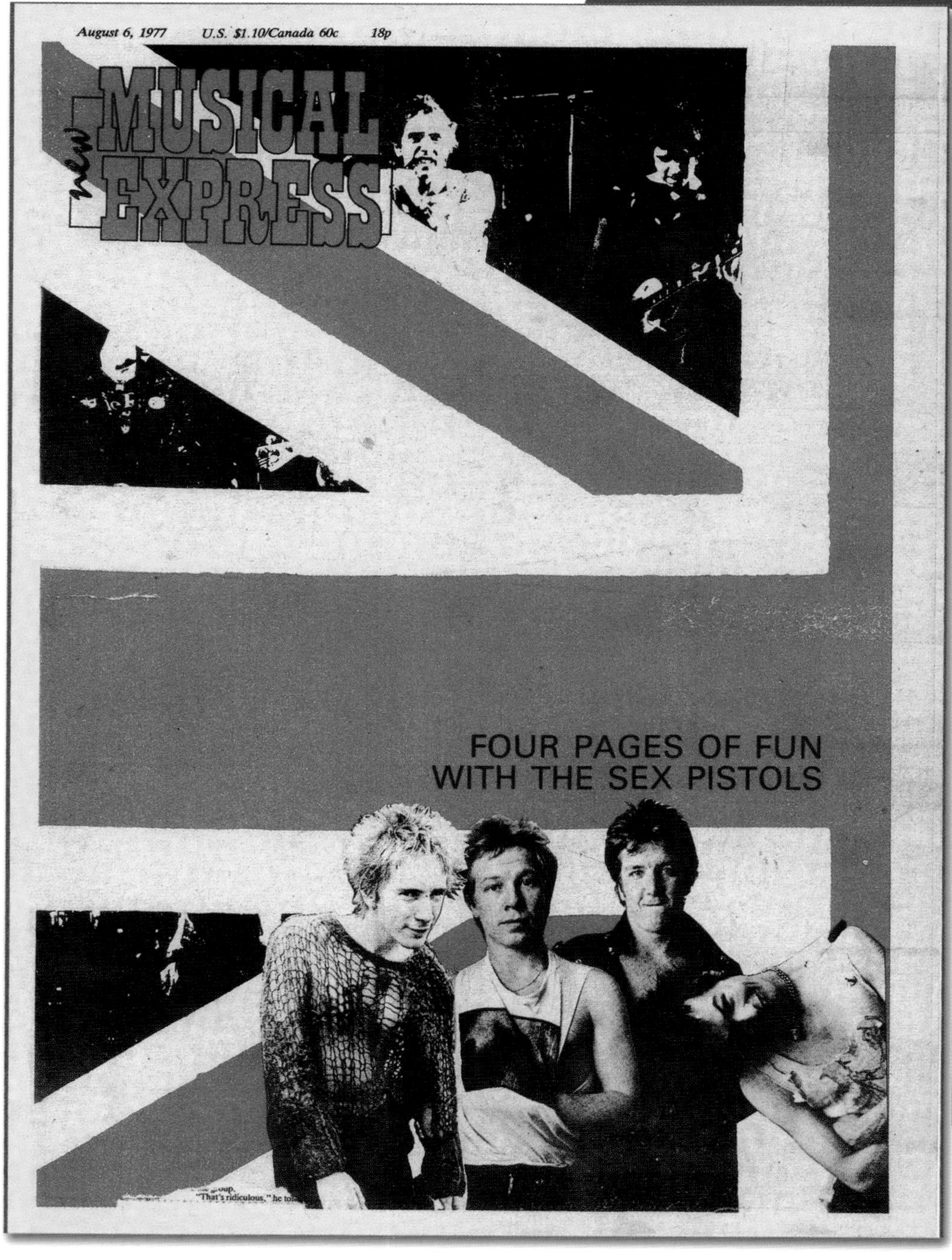

August 6, 1977 U.S. $1.10/Canada 60c 18p

new MUSICAL EXPRESS

FOUR PAGES OF FUN
WITH THE SEX PISTOLS

...group.
"That's ridiculous," he to...

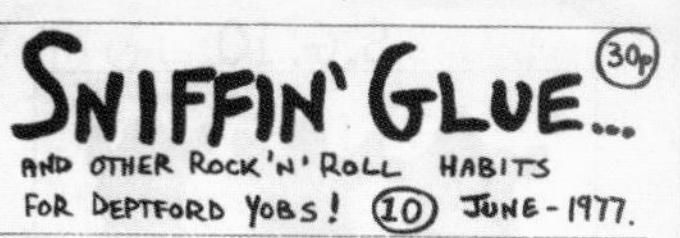
SNIFFIN' GLUE...
30p
AND OTHER ROCK 'N' ROLL HABITS
FOR DEPTFORD YOBS! 10 JUNE-1977.

CHELSEA + JOHNNY MOPED

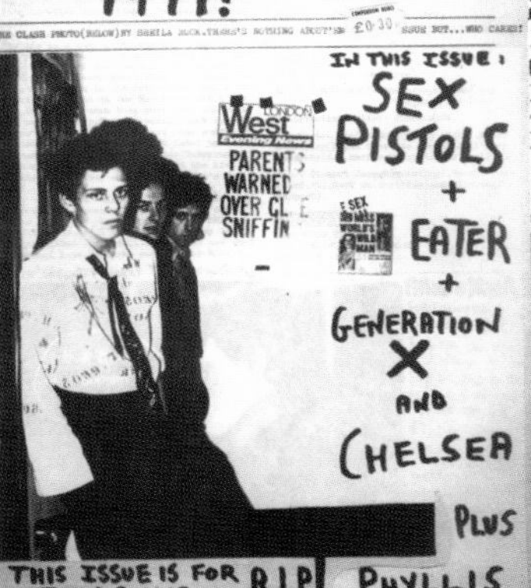
SNIFFIN' GLUE...
AND OTHER ROCK'N'ROLL HABITS, FOR
ANYBODY WHO CARES ABOUT 6 JAN '77
1977!
IN THIS ISSUE:
SEX PISTOLS
+
EATER
+
GENERATION X
AND
CHELSEA
PLUS
PHYLLIS
THIS ISSUE IS FOR JOHN COLLIS. R.I.P.

SNIFFIN' GLUE
30p
AND OTHER SELF-DEFENCE HABITS...
JULY '77
SO TELL US....
WHAT D'YA THINK
11

SNIFFIN' GLUE...
30p
AND OTHER ROCK 'N' ROLL HABITS
FOR PINHEADS AND SURFERS! 7 FEB '77
ADVERTS - DON LETTS - GORILLAS

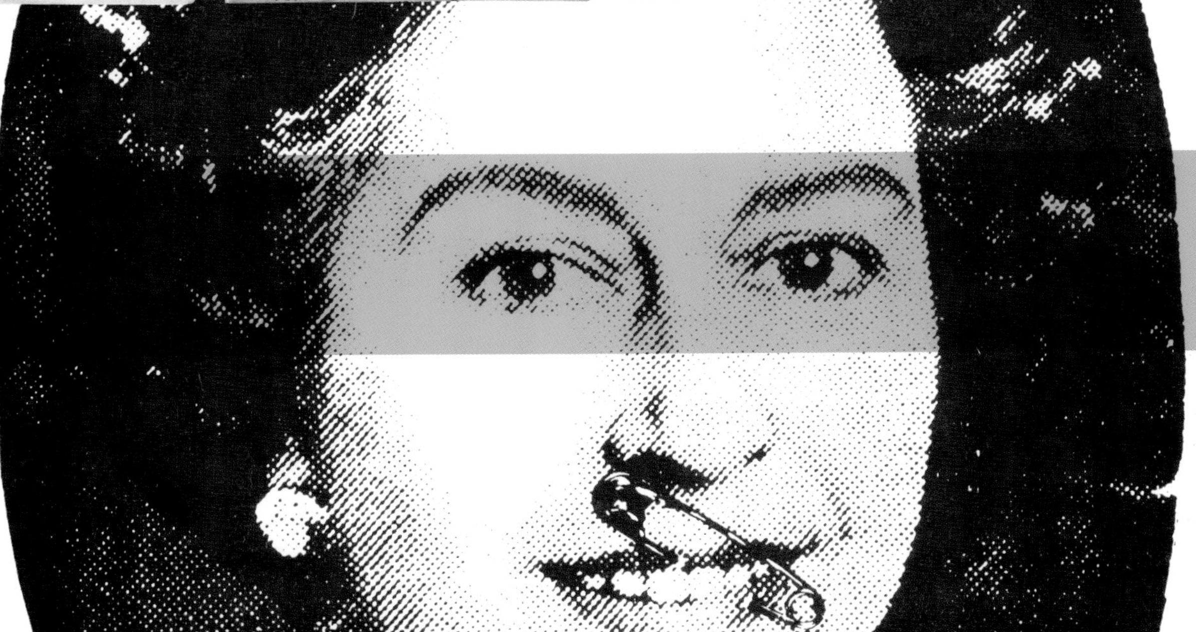

SNIFFIN' GLUE
ANNIVERSARY
AND OTHER ROCK 'N' ROLL HABITS.....
FOR AROUND AUG/SEPT '77
12
"HEY LITTLE RICH BOY TAKE A GOOD LOOK AT ME"

SNIFFIN' GLUE...
30p
AND OTHER ROCK 'N ROLL HABITS FOR PEOPLE
WHO THINK IT'S HIP TO READ THE "IN" MAG.
MARCH 1977.
8
NEW YORK INVASION!
HEARTBREAKERS, CHERRY VANILLA, WAYNE COUNTY.
BUZZCOCKS - THE JAM - THE CLASH.

SNIFFIN' GLUE...
AND OTHER ROCK'N'ROLL HABITS,
FOR PUNKS GIRLS! 3
WITH
THE DAMNED + SEX PISTOLS + IGGY POP +

SNIFFIN' GLUE...
AND OTHER ROCK'N'ROLL HABITS, FOR
A BUNCH OF BLEEDIN' IDIOTS! 5
EDDIE AND THE HOT RODS
LIVE AND ALBUM REVIEWS.
THE SUBWAY SECT + PLUS CHELSEA

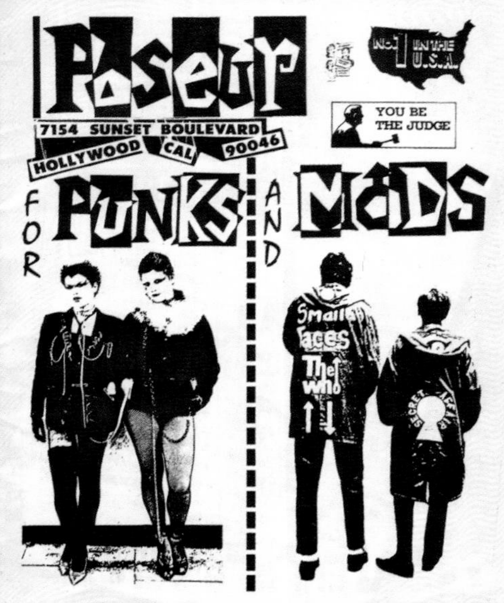

Poseur
No. 1 IN THE U.S.A.
YOU BE THE JUDGE
7154 SUNSET BOULEVARD
HOLLYWOOD CAL 90046
FOR PUNKS AND MODS
Small Faces
The Who

Subterranean Pop
80¢
U.S. UNDERGROUND
Kansas Cleveland Chicago Seattle S.F.
Life Elsewhere
epicycle
1980

SUB POP 1980

EGO MAGAZINE
ISSUE 3
$2
APPLIANCES
BOW WOW WOW
ESMERELDA
FASSBINDER
M.D.C.
MUTABARUKA
GARY PANTER
PERSONALITY CRISIS
JOHANNA WENT

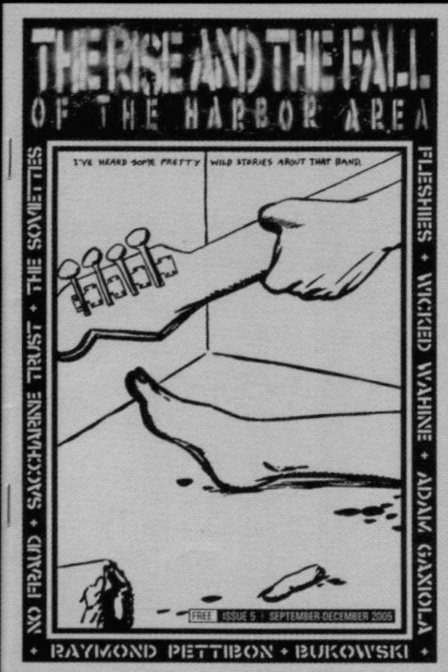

THE RISE AND THE FALL OF THE HARBOR AREA
I'VE HEARD SOME PRETTY WILD STORIES ABOUT THAT BAND.
NO FRAUD • SACCHARINE TRUST • THE SOVIETTES
FLESHIES • WICKED WAHINE • ADAM GAXIOLA
FREE | ISSUE 5 | SEPTEMBER-DECEMBER 2005
RAYMOND PETTIBON • BUKOWSKI

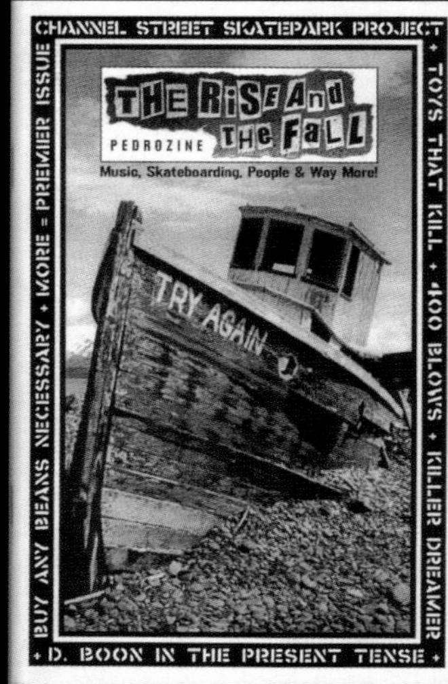

CHANNEL STREET SKATEPARK PROJECT
THE RISE and THE FALL
PEDROZINE
Music, Skateboarding, People & Way More!
TRY AGAIN
BUY ANY BEANS NECESSARY • MORE • PREMIER ISSUE
TOYS THAT KILL • 400 BLOWS • KILLER DREAMER
D. BOON IN THE PRESENT TENSE

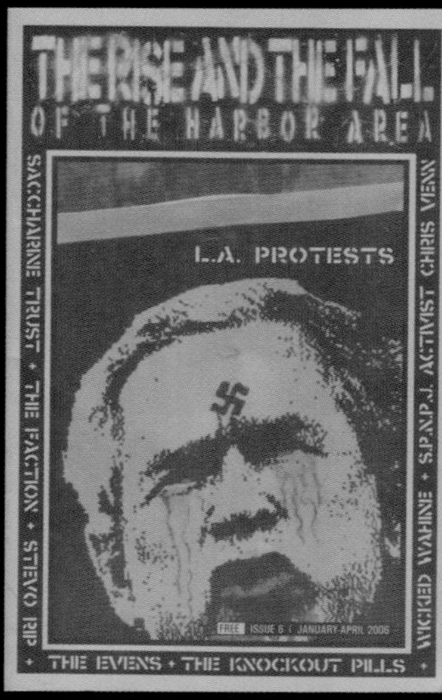

THE RISE AND THE FALL OF THE HARBOR AREA
L.A. PROTESTS
SACCHARINE TRUST • THE FACTION • OVERLORDS
CHRIS VIEW • ACTIVIST S.P.N.P.J. • WICKED WAHINE
FREE | ISSUE 6 | JANUARY-APRIL 2006
THE EVENS • THE KNOCKOUT PILLS

THE RISE AND THE FALL OF THE HARBOR AREA
KEITH MORRIS
SHAKEY BONES
SHAWN KERRI
BULLET TREATMENT
EPIC DEBAUCHERY
THE GRIMES
SLEEPOVER
ISSUE 9 | JANUARY-APRIL 2007

THE RISE AND THE FALL OF THE HARBOR AREA
FER YOUZ
ISSUE 8 | SEPTEMBER-DECEMBER 2006

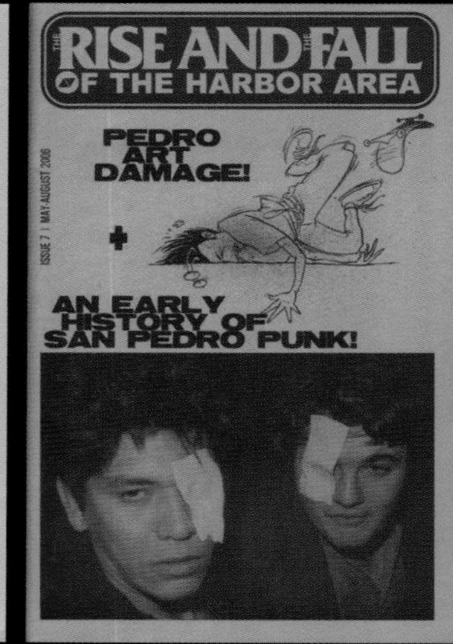

THE RISE AND THE FALL OF THE HARBOR AREA
PEDRO ART DAMAGE!
+
AN EARLY HISTORY OF SAN PEDRO PUNK!
ISSUE 7 | MAY-AUGUST 2006

SAN PEDRO!

the L.A. Beat
FIFTY CENTS
ONE FEB 78
MUMPS:
"WE ARE AMERICANA!"
THE FURYS
GENERATION X
THE STRANGLERS
MINK DeVILLE
SEX PISTOLS
THE ZIPPERS
DEVO

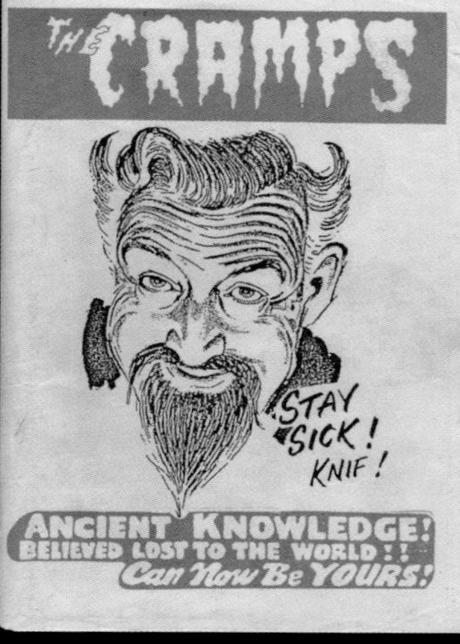

THE CRAMPS
STAY SICK! KNIF!
ANCIENT KNOWLEDGE!
BELIEVED LOST TO THE WORLD!!
Can Now Be YOURS!

BROWBEAT
NUMBER ZERO
BUY BUY
25¢
MC5
STRANGLERS
GRIP AMERICA
CONSUMERS:
RAT SCABIES!
A REAL PIN-UP, GIRLS! (and boys)
PLUS FREE! HIPPIE DETECTOR
reviews, fashions and more
ROTTEN: EXCLUSIVE INTERVIEW!

The NEW WAVE magazine
6
INSIDE : BUZZCOCKS INTERVIEW with Pete Shelley
HEARTBREAKERS INTERVIEW with Walter Lure
and Stranglers, Damned, X-Ray Spex...
30p

Super Rock
Special PUNK ROCK Issue!!
Dead Boys
John Cale
Iggy Pop
Starz
Talking Heads
Television
Ramones

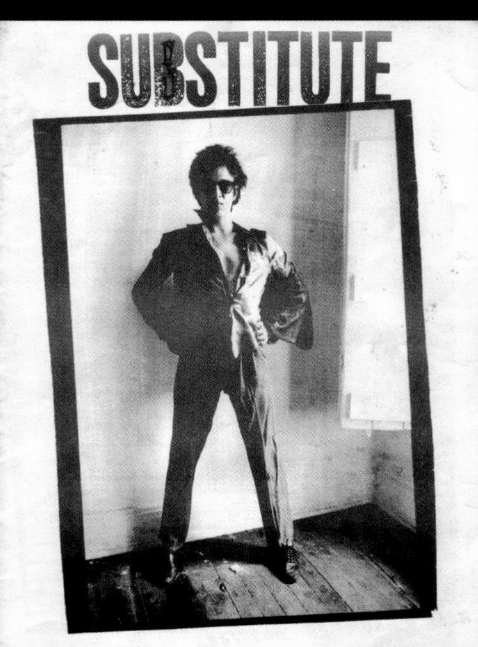
SUBSTITUTE
NUMBER ONE
FIFTY CENTS

PUNK GLOBE
DECEMBER
$1.00
FLIPPER

ROCK MARKET PRESENTS
PREMIER ISSUE $1.00
CATAZINE
THE MAIL ORDER RECORD STORE OF THE INDEPENDENT SCENE
INTERVIEWS WITH
BLACK FLAG
SWA & CHUCK DUKOWSKI
HARVEY KUBERNIK
RECORD REVIEWS
NETWORKING LISTS
INTERNATIONAL PLAYLISTS
FICTION
COMICS
AND MORE...
DO YOU REALLY WANT TO HAVE SEX WITH HENRY?

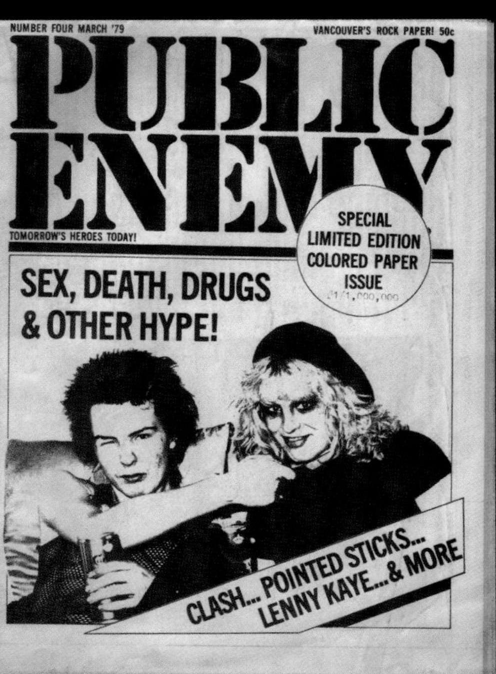
NUMBER FOUR MARCH '79
VANCOUVER'S ROCK PAPER! 50c
PUBLIC ENEMY
TOMORROW'S HEROES TODAY!
SPECIAL LIMITED EDITION COLORED PAPER ISSUE
SEX, DEATH, DRUGS & OTHER HYPE!
CLASH... POINTED STICKS... LENNY KAYE... & MORE

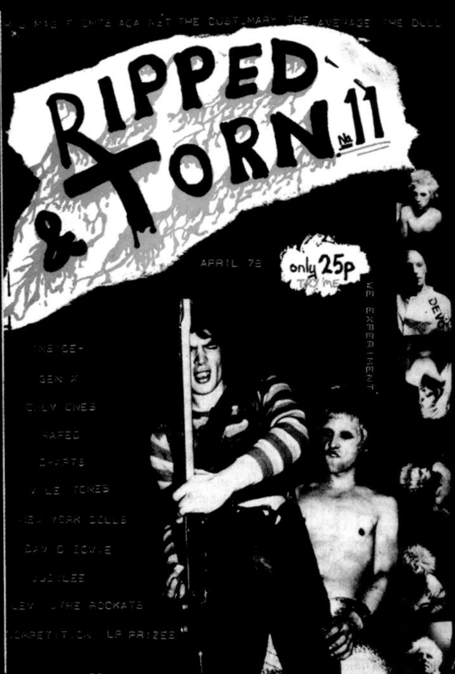
RIPPED & TORN No 11
APRIL 78
only 25p

TWISTED
60¢
ANOTHER ROCK 'N' ROLL MAGAZINE
NUMBER ONE
JULY 1977
IGGY
KNOBS
DANNY FIELDS
GROUPIES
MORE!
SCREAMERS
BLONDIE
DAMNED

NOMAG

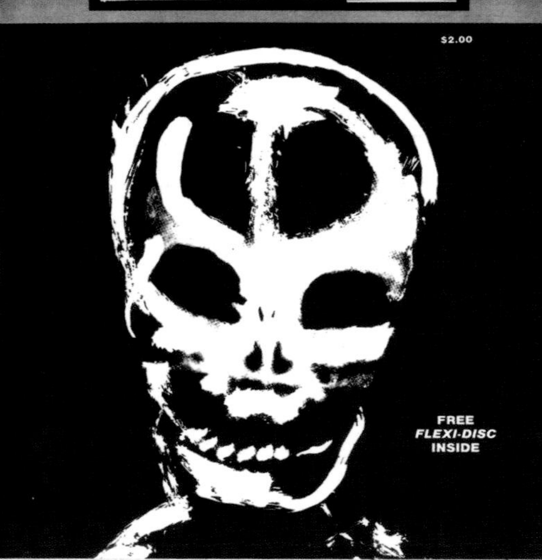
$2.00
FREE
FLEXI-DISC
INSIDE

LOS ANGELES 1984
$3.
NO MAG
THE JONESES

SCRAMBLED CULTURE

NOMAG
FREE RECORD
INSIDE
BY GEZA X
"MEAN MR. MOMMY MAN"
$2.00

NO MAG

NO MAGAZINE

ALL ZINES THIS PAGE: BRUCE KALBERG

NO
MAGAZINE
$1.25

NO MAG
$2
I'M SICK
OF SEX

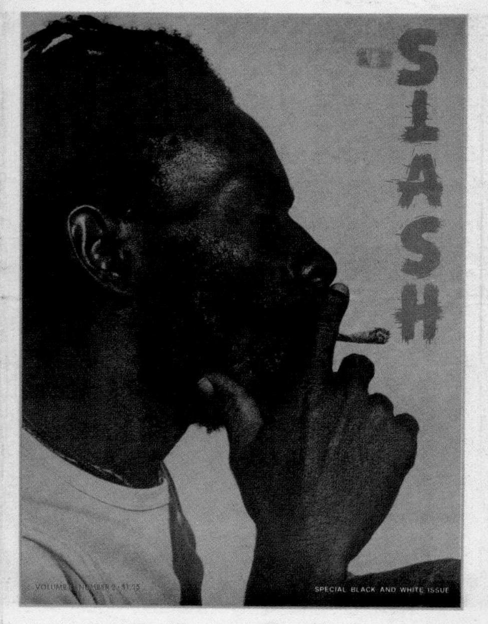
SLASH
SPECIAL BLACK AND WHITE ISSUE

SLASH
VOLUME 2 NUMBER 5 MAY 1979 ONE DOLLAR

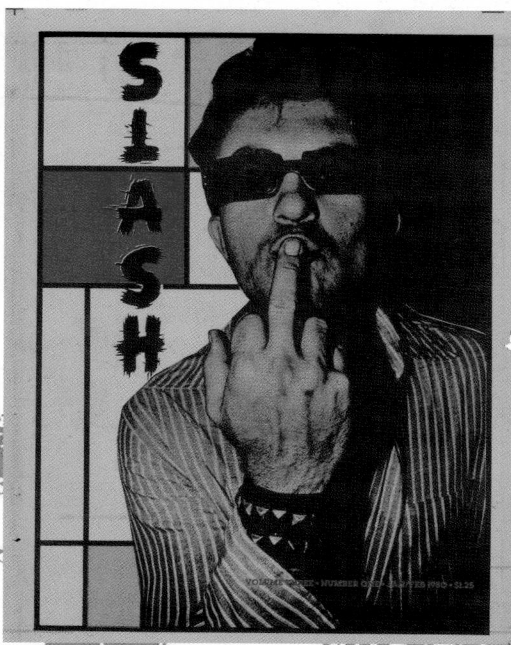
SLASH

Slash
RECORDS
Annual Xmas Party
PLACE: SLASH HQ - 7381 BEVERLY BLVD.
DATE: SATURDAY, FEBRUARY 4, 1984
TIME: 8:00PM - 'TIL THE COWS COME HOME
INFO: (213) 937-4660

ORIGINAL PHOTO USED TO CREATE RUBY RECORDS' FIST LOGO

Syd's PHARMACY
prescriptions
TOBACCO
OFFICIAL
Slash
REPRESENTATIVE
Winston

CLAUDE by JIM JOCOY

VOLUME 1 NUMBER 8
FEBRUARY 1978
FIFTY CENTS

FREE GIVEAWAY ISSUE! GO AHEAD, TAKE ONE! WHAT HAVE YOU GOT TO LOSE? PUNK ROCK! NEW WAVE! MANY ADS!
ONE YEAR ANNIVERSARY SPECIAL! ART, ANARCHY, ADVERTISING! MUSIC, MADNESS, MASTURBATORY MESSAGES! FREE, TAKE ONE!!!!

1 YEAR ANNIVERSARY GIVE AWAY - 'FREE' ISSUE

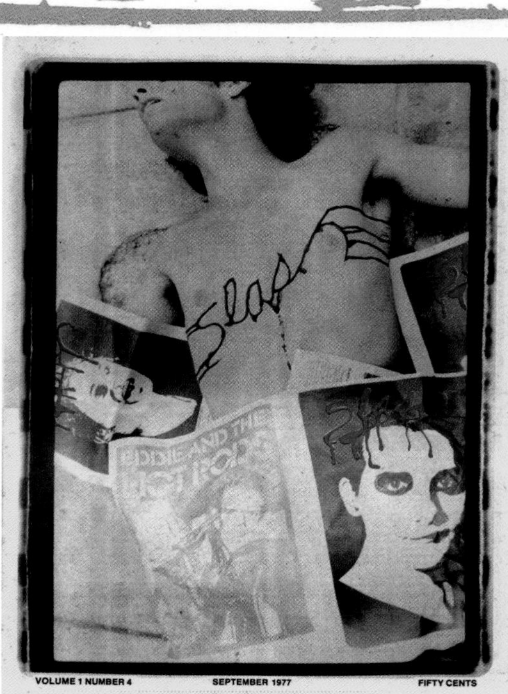
EDDIE AND THE HOT RODS
VOLUME 1 NUMBER 4
SEPTEMBER 1977
FIFTY CENTS

Trudie

TRUDIE

I had an urgent need to travel from Los Angeles to New York. It was probably the time that the Screamers were going on their first tour there and I had to go. I needed $75, the price of a Greyhound bus ticket. I was 18 and Hector of the Zeros had been selling "Trudie" buttons that he had made with my image on them. I decided to earn the $75 by selling a Trudie Magazine for $1. I had already been in the habit of taking photo-booth pictures of myself in different outfits and attitudes. Before the days of digital cameras kids would use photo-booths to play with their personas, something that seems to appeal to teenagers, not yet sure who they are. There were two photo-booths within blocks of the Canterbury apartments where I lived and The Masque, punk-rock's underground headquarters. The photo-booths were on Hollywood Blvd., both in front of stores, Woolworths, and JJ Newberry next to Frederick's of Hollywood. It was easy to sell all the Trudie Magazines at the Masque after completing xeroxing and stapling, and then I was off to New York. I never got around to the promised second issue. The cover photo of my face is actually cropped from an ad for a record single by Rodney Bingenheimer.

The infamous Plunger Pit before demolition.
"MEET THE REAL ME"
FOR
TRUDIE MAGAZINE #2
OR FOR MORE COPIES OF #1
(SPECIFY #1 OR #2)
SEE BACK PAGE.
MASS
FAN CLUB
the very first club that's all TRUDIE and the only official TRUDIE FAN CLUB!

$1.

IT'S WILD! IT'S NEW!!!
TRUDI MAGAZINE!
is hot off the presses!
just send me $1,
and i will personally
autograph one just for you!
be the first one on your block
to receive your own personalized
TRUDI MAGAZINE!
just send your name, address and $1. to:
TRUDI MAGAZINE!
c/o barrett
1746 north cherokee #202
hollywood, calif. 90028

A NEW FANZINE FOR "WILD" L.A PUNX
SLUSH
VOL 1 #1
(WILL IT LAST?)
FREE ONLY 35¢
¡¡ SCREAMER'S BALL !!
(DETAILS INSIDE)
SLUSH
SEPTEMBER/OCTOBER 1980 $1.50 #2
BRITISH ART STUDENTS / STRIPPER
SEXUALLY
JERRY #30
CASTRATION SQUAD
GANG OF FOUR'S
IRON LUNG DISCIPLES .
AGENT ORANGE RUINS .
ORANGE COUNTY . . NEXT
AMERICAN" BREED AND A CREDIT TO
ANOTHER "JOKE"
THE MOMMY MEN GO ????
"MADDOG" STILL IN CIRCLE JERK
BACK IN HOLLYWOOD JUST
THE INLAND BAND ROUND-UP
MEET THE JERRIES
THE FINAL CHAPTER OF
GREENSTEIN
THE SLUSH
A FINE
THE
MR.
THE
Beem Studios

FER YOUZ
VOL 1 NO 1
ALWAYS FREE 3-81
STARDUST BALLROOM 2-11-81
WHISKEY 2-5-81
STARWOOD 1-6-81
STARWOOD 1-20-81
BLACK FLAG STARWOOD 1-6-81
FEAR WHISKEY 2-5-81
WHISKEY 2-5-81
CRASS
I'm an UPSTART
STARWOOD 1-6-81
NEW YEARS HONG KONG CAFE
FEAR
HONG KONG
NEW YEARS HONG KONG CAFE
PUB.
ED.
PHOTOS
BY
NIKKI + BRIAN
STARDUST BALLROOM 2-11-81
WHISKEY 2-5-81
FER YOUZ

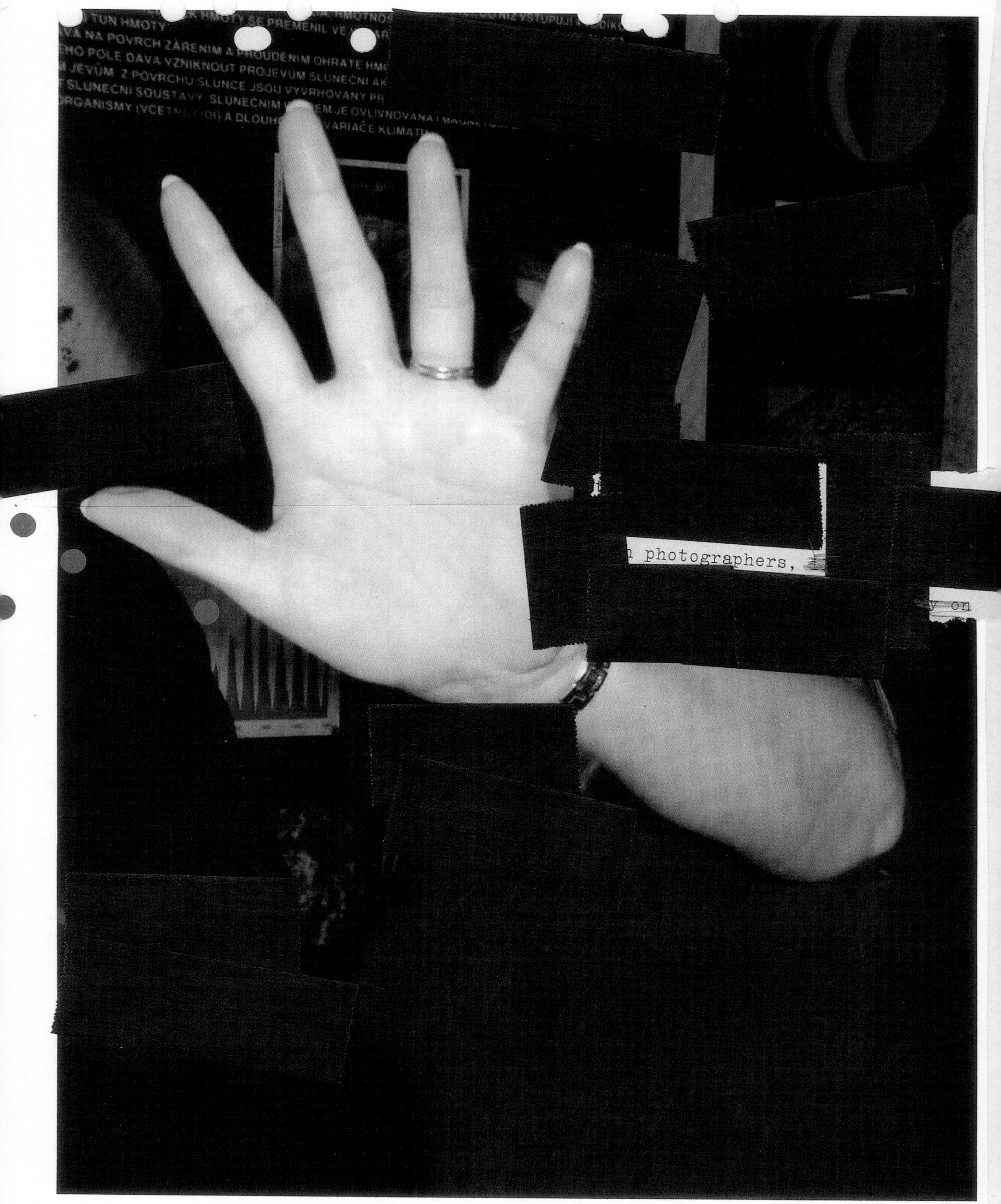

TUN HMOTY HMOTY SE PREMENIL VE
VA NA POVRCH ZARENIM A PROUDENIM OHRATE HM
EHO POLE DAVA VZNIKNOUT PROJEVUM SLUNECNI AK
JEVUM Z POVRCHU SLUNCE JSOU VYVRHOVANY PR
SLUNECNI SOUSTAVY SLUNECNIM EM JE OVLIVNOVANA
RGANISMY (VCETN A DLOUH VARIACE KLIMATU

photographers,

y on

ALL PHOTOS: MURRAY BOWLES

GINN

We put a song down on a TDK cassette and after rehearsal we rushed it up to KFJC in hopes they would play it leading up to the show this shot was taken at. (Foothill Community College Station- Truly Underground!). By Friday lunchtime, the day of our show, we'd heard it played three times over the air. That night we played with Ribzy in a garage off Winchester Blvd. overlooking the 280. By 8:30 the garage was packed, the party spilling out into the yard as well as the front and even the gas station across the street. Here was a reality event with true feeling!! Our set reflected no real saavy or any real musical development - it was all about intention. Did you really have to be good? Not really. I never thought we were, but still it had to be done - despite our too-few songs, despite all the defections, the shit talking, ad infinitum. For about twenty minutes we got to present something personal that came from within us; no one showed us how to do it. All my favorite people were there.

JASON HONEA

DECONTROL
HT THEM!

LARS FREDRICKSON SITTIN IN THE KICK DRUM. NECROS BACKYARD PARTY, SAN JOSE

ALL PHOTOS: JIM JOCOY

ALL PHOTOS: EILEEN POLK

RICHARD HELL, JOHNNY THUNDERS AND SID VICIOUS

DEAD BOYS (STIV WEARING SID'S SHIRT)

MISFITS AT MAX'S KANSAS CITY

GREEN PANTS!

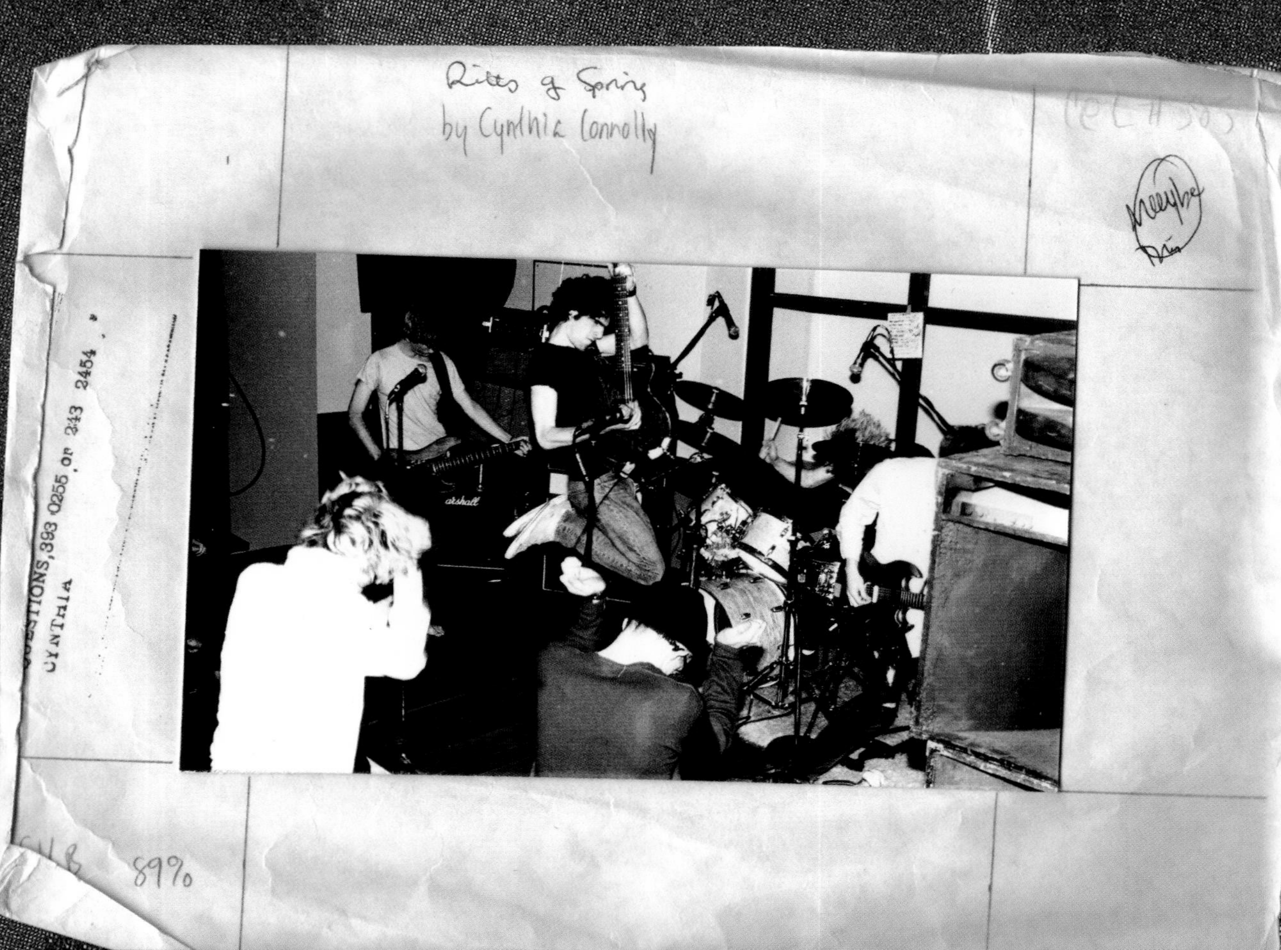
Rites of Spring
by Cynthia Connolly
QUESTIONS, 393 0255 or 243 2454
CYNTHIA
89%

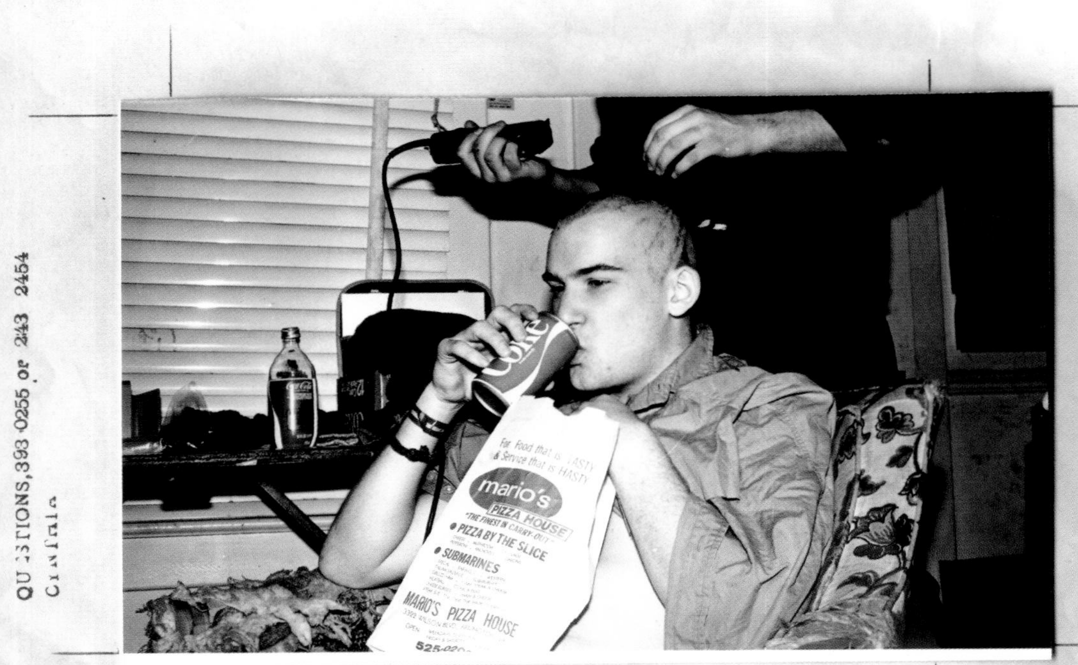
QUESTIONS, 393 0255 or 243 2454
CYNTHIA
mario's
PIZZA HOUSE
PIZZA BY THE SLICE
SUBMARINES
MARIO'S PIZZA HOUSE
PHOTO 98B
69%

QUESTIONS, 383 0255 or 243 2454
CYNTHIA

(106)
Cynthia

FEAR

FEAR PLAYING S.N.L.

Cynthia Connolly

PHOTO 41A 95%

Special!
ONLY
5¢
URP a 22oz

QUESTIONS, 383 0255 or 243 2454
CYNTHIA

PHOTO 98A
69%

HELMET LAWS

D.O.A.

CHAVO / BLACK FLAG

DEAD KENNEDYS

109

D.O.A.

22

X

JOHN DENNEY - WEIRDOS

CORP.
RIK L RIK

ALL PHOTOS: JILL ASH

JILL ASH

Being thoroughly indifferent to the popular music of the late 70's, I was searching for music with more substance and eventually found Punk Rock. I talked my high school friend into going to the Whisky in Hollywood one Saturday night to see an English band called The Jam. They had just come out with an album called 'In The City' and were touring the states. The Sex Pistols' 'Anarchy In The UK' played by Geza X between sets and The Jam's dynamic live sound just blew me away. This was the emotive, thinking, rebellious, raw force music should be. (I loved that the pretentious Johnny Cougar was jeered until he left the stage) That night I met many new people. Darby Crash, who had just recently changed him name from Bobby Pyn, leading a new LA band, The Germs, became an immediate friend. I was recruited to be the bands photographer when he learned that I was taking photography at my high school. The photographs I took were almost exclusively black and white because I had my own dark room and couldn't afford to use color. After losing Darby in 1980, all those photos and negatives I would only see the inside of the box I hid them away in. Little did I know that twenty-five years later I would be sharing those photographs of a band that is now recognized as one of the most influential Punk bands of our time with you.

DARBY CRASH

Circle Jerks

ROGER ROGERSON by ED COLVER

ROCKS
roller sports

RANDY 'BISCUIT' TURNER

Big Boys
GO-GO's
from Los Angeles
club foot
Big Boys
Sept. 10

RANDY TURNER

RANDY TURNER

BISCUIT, SAN FRANCISCO PARKING GARAGE, 1983

The future's a funny thing. One day you're a slug in a slow moving musical ballad and the next day punk rock turns you into a pogo-ing ant on a griddle! No seatbelts will bind thee to tunes of the past, you're careening bus to Beatsville has just left the station! The record world turned upside down in the late 1970's and Austin's music scene grabbed one of the front seats on that bus and it's been a long scenic carnival ride ever since. In 1978, Austin was a stench hole of cosmic cowboy has-beens and poofy hairdo metal reruns that were in dire need of purging. That movement called New Wave/Punk came along and dumped all prior bowel movements!

Yes! Something new and alive was electric in the air. The Ramones, Joan Jett, the Runaways, when "Put on your red dress" was hot, and Joe Jackson all playing at the Armadillo World Headquarters were a kaleidoscoptic peek at things to come. My friend Buck Davis played bass in the Violators with Kathy Valentine, later of the Go Go's, and he and I would go see the Skunks, the Skyscrapers, and the maniacally energetic Joe King Carrassco. The music was snotty rock-n-roll with that "do-it-my-way" mindset of lyrics and music. I knew I liked it! I caught the new wave battle of the bands on 6th street in 1978 and realized there was a lot of stuff going on across Texas with the unreal "Chatterbox" from San Antonio and the "Nervebreakers" from Dallas. I missed the Sex Pistols in S.A. in 1978 but friends in attendance said all the concert photos didn't lie, it was a mini-riot! We started out going to a weird little conjunto bar on the drag near U.T. on Monday nights called Raul's which some crazy Spanish outlaws ran. They started having new-wave Monday nights and since the burgeoning University of Texas populace was getting bit by the new music bug, lots of "alternatives" showed up and bought a lot of beers. Joseph Gonzales, Bobby Morales, and the elusive Raul himself said more nights should be dedicated to this punk – new wave thing because the money's good and the time is ripe for blossoming. That was what opened the floodgate for so many new bands, a great club with just the right improper décor and rat-like ambience located 50 feet from U.T. Every night for a while you could go see 3 and 4 band bills, granted, some were horrible but that was way overrid den by the camaraderie factor and the search for new adventures We are here, we are many, we play shitty and couldn't care less, so wake up, it's a signpost of things to come. Move ove cosmic cowturd! So much of this scene was ala "tongue in cheek attitude as three fourths of the crowds were pampered college kinds. A few truly lived the lifestyle and played straight razor games at night and picked at the scabs the next day during their shitty cook jobs. I appeared live on Raul's stage singing wit the Big Boys as the second show of our career in November of 1979 with 5 songs on our menu. We Big Boys were hideous musicians at first but grew to be mediocre so it did progress! The music at Raul's was the main reason to be there but many other interests of friendship and to gaze with astounded awe at what my beers were coming up with proved also a draw. The "guess my ," parties in the parking lot, lesbian stars being born, unbeliev- concerts" from people banging on the 75 foot tall lone star beer d adjacent poles, actual queers making out in

The fraternity/punk wars at Raul's seemed to be never ending he U.T. campus klan houses would delight in driving by and ng crap at everyone. One particular sultry evening when the e crowd was as huge as the inside crowd, some stupid frats/klan ers kept driving by in their hot new Firebird screaming ob

es and spraying beer and fire extinguisher juice on everyone. heir fourth "drive by", certain unnamed punkers lay in wait bushes a few yards south of Raul's with a huge cinder block. ou guessed it, their fifth and final pass saw the cinder block go gh the front windshield! The crowd roared approval as the frats screeched to a halt. Uh-oh, bad mistake as 100 punks made a e for the 'bird and the now wizened wise asses sped away just e to miss a good ass-whuppin! This crap happened as often as s related stories about how the frats beat them up, chased them, bally tortured them. It's real different today as some of the frats

he dorkiest punk rock hair do's. Store bought punky punk, from the mall! The last night of Raul's saw a lot of the graffitied

et rock come down and the toilet s taken home as souvenirs!

ch of the action was then picked y Duke's Royal Coach Inn at 4th

Congress ave, the site of the late)'s hip psychedelic art spot called Vulcan Gas Company. The state rickety and the dressing room he three foot wide hallway ng to the alley. You generally d the local bar flys off with loud d checks at 7:00 and then would

ve them out at 10:00 when the show began. I saw the "Cramps" ere and the Big Boys brought the "Butthole Surfers" there from an Antonio for their first Austin Show. Brad First, who had done a ot of the Duke's booking, started working with the people at Club Foot at 4th

and Brazos downtown so good shows were happening. This was one of the coolest clubs I have ever been to as five levels of seating and viewing spots from the basement to the second story rafters made for many great rock-n-roll nights. They even had a nice size cat-walk that went up and around the back of the band so you could get a total

overhead panorama of the club and stage. The Big Boys got to play

e a few times there and had the honor to get to open for bands like "X" from , "Flipper" from Frisco, "Go-Go's" from LA, (say it... Go Go's!), "The Plas- ics" from NY, and the futuristic "Grace Jones" from perhaps, Mars! 800 to 0 people shows for local acts were common as this was a scene hotspot. On corner of Lavaca and 4th Street a crazy bunker called Voltaire's Basement sted for a brief but insanely art filled period. Its

y escape hatch was one set of crowded stairs that made the element of danger nitely more concrete. Several razor edged art shows and music hearing doo rituals made this 125 degree sweat box sticky with rich with love. A nderful night there with Scratch Acid was made 11 times more strange en Gibby Butthole came from the crowd and started bitching at David Yow, atch's singer. Gibby broke a stage prop fake bottle over David's head and the wd went nuts. It was "gossip too much" for months afterwards as the singers ghed their heads off at the gullible sheep! One other small niche in the history

of hot spots around town was Sparkys out off Justin Lane that was around for 8-10 months during the 83-84 season. Hot as fresh lava and darker than the inside of a cow it was but revolution rose from the likes of Not For Sale,

the Reasons Why, and Last Rites. Several swinging shows were held at the odd Skyline Club on way North Lamar. This is where they say Elvis had performed before and it was a treat just to be inside to try to find

Elvis' stash or maybe a sweat stained hanky. We had a double twisted kung fu Hallow- een show there with the mighty Minor Threat from DC as they "kicked a toaster into the bathwater of normalcy" with their monstrous 2 guitar attack. A Kodak mo- ment! When you view old pictures of new wave punks from back then, please don't judge too harshly at what

you see. What we thought was totally gear in 1979 does look like cartoons today but the current brand of grunge filth-fashion will look like absolute wino horror to the silver suited platinum bewigged fringe rockers of 2013! Respect your roots for

you too will gather mold. Sid was vicious but Bobby Sox from Dallas could kick Sid's ass while sitting in a lawn chair!! Believe it. Love and donuts!

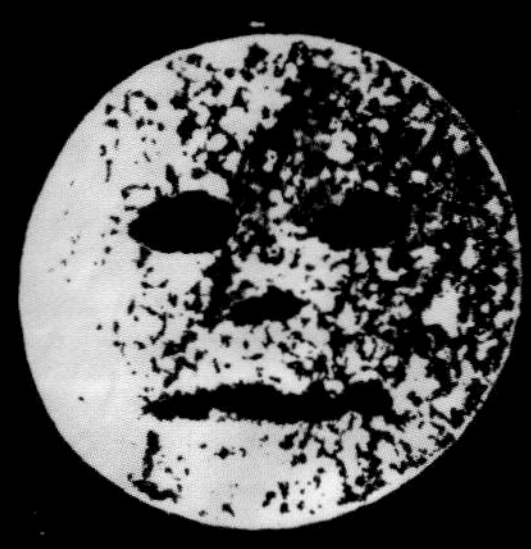
F? SYSTEMS
+
>ELECTROS
=
1·5·80
R·A·U·L·S
BIG BOYS

NEXT
STANDING WAVES
F-SYSTEMS
BIG BOYS
RAUL'S
NEW YEAR'S PARTY
1980-1981
big boys

Kids - Grown-ups
Party
Free
Cake
Beer
Thur.
June
5
BIG BOYS
EP
RELASE
Inner Sanctum Records
Punks
hippies

Thursday, 12th
RAUL'S
8 8's
ACES
KAMIKAZE
REFRIDGERATORS

'BISCUIT'

Oi
Big Boys
RANK AND FILE
AND
THE RIVALS
TONITE
4
DUKES
ROYAL COACH
4th & CONGRESS...

BAD BRAINS
(from New York)
&
big boys
(from Club Foot)
with guest bands
Esthers Pool
Tuesday 6

TIM KERR

TONY ALVA

If you had a punk rock band, you had to create punk rock flyers. Of course the only way to have 100% of the creative power was to do them your self. There was no Kinko's, so it wasn't easy to even make copies of the flyer once you attempted to even design one. There was a primitive barrage of artistic subversity that usually dominated our flyers. The Skoundrelz & my brothers band Ozie Hares were our shitty little attempts at being hardcore. It was kinda cool to be opening for other bands like the Circle Jerks, X, Black Flag, China White and Bad Religion. It added punk rock integrity to our little fucked up band. The sense of pissed off humor added even more interest for me. I'm glad I had a chance to be a part of the LA / SF punk scene. The flyers, all fucked up and photocopied, are definitely a jolt to my brain 25 years later.

T. Alva

Skoundrelz
Aug. 24th
Jak's
Team
Monskera
Skountrels
Skoundrelz Halloween Party at Music Machine Oct 31
Skoundrelz and Twisted Roots
Club Lingerie Oct 29

SKOUNDRELZ
PARTY
SEPT 22nd
HAPPY BIRTHDAY JOE!
Happy Birthday Bondage-Gram
Virgo bash
M.B.'s Warehouse
4253 Lincoln Blvd.
MDR at Maxella Ave.

RULE THE STREETS
WITH
the SKOUNDRELZ
BLACK ATHELETES
FRIGHTWIG
AND MORE!
THE Faction
$4
SATURDAY, DEC. 17TH - 9PM
TOOL AND DIE
974 VALENCIA S.F., CA.

SKOUNDRELZ
FRIGHTWIG
MORALLY BANKRUPT
absolute bankruptcy.
MAB
435 Broadway S.F.
10pm
1-18-Friday

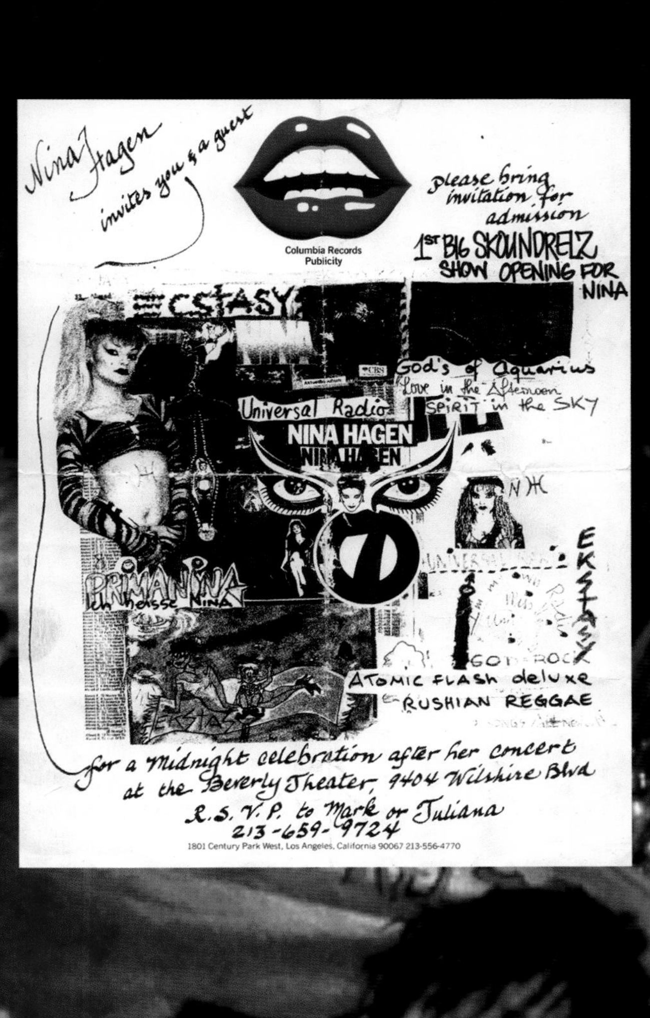
Nina Hagen invites you & a guest
Columbia Records Publicity
please bring invitation for admission
1ST BIG SKOUNDRELZ SHOW OPENING FOR NINA
ECSTASY
God's of Aquarius
Love in the Afternoon
SPIRIT in the SKY
Universal Radio
NINA HAGEN
EKSTASY
ATOMIC FLASH deluxe
RUSHIAN REGGAE
for a midnight celebration after her concert at the Beverly Theater, 9404 Wilshire Blvd
R.S.V.P. to Mark or Juliana
213-659-9724
1801 Century Park West, Los Angeles, California 90067 213-556-4770

SKATEBO
IS NOT A

NOT FOR F

THRASHER, NUMBER ONE

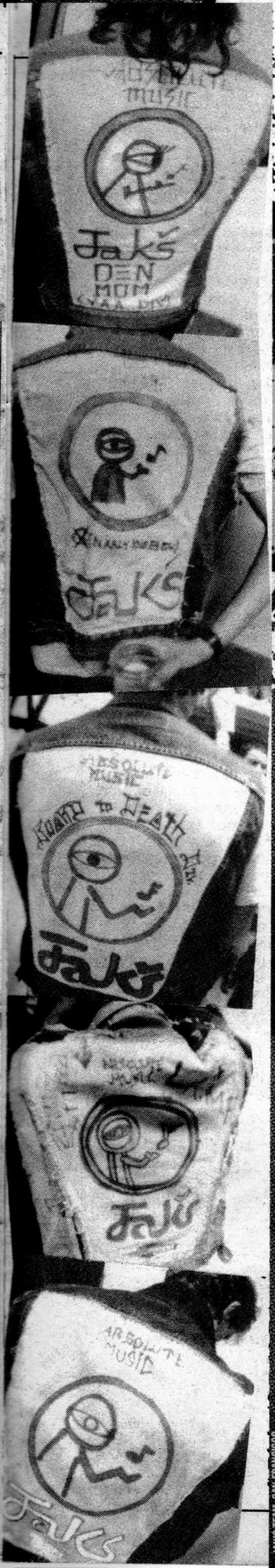

THIRSTY FOR THE BEST?
TRY
ZORLAC
10920 INDIAN TRAIL
SUITE 206
DALLAS TX 75229
214-243-1180
ZORLAC AM californias!
PHREAD CONRAD on mini-JG
oceanside, ca.
foto: swank

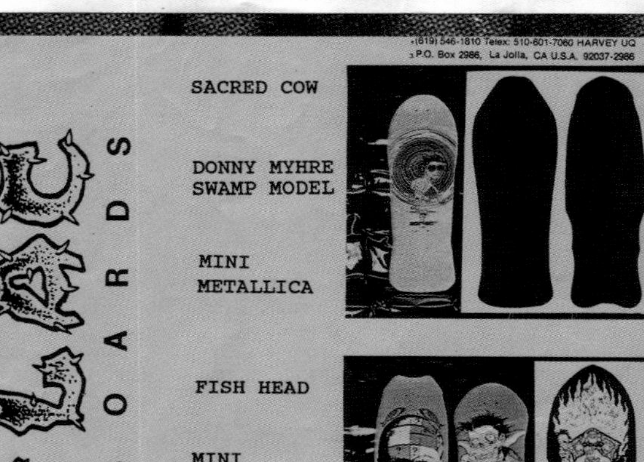

+(619) 546-1810 Telex: 510-601-7060 HARVEY UQ
P.O. Box 2986, La Jolla, CA U.S.A. 92037-2986
ZORLAC SKATEBOARDS
SACRED COW
DONNY MYHRE SWAMP MODEL
MINI METALLICA
FISH HEAD
MINI GARGOYLE
TODD PRINCE TOAD SIZE
TODD PRINCE FROG SIZE
METALLICA
GARGOYLE

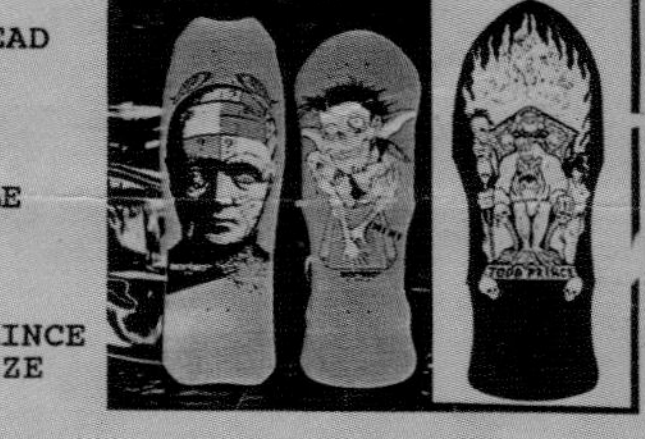

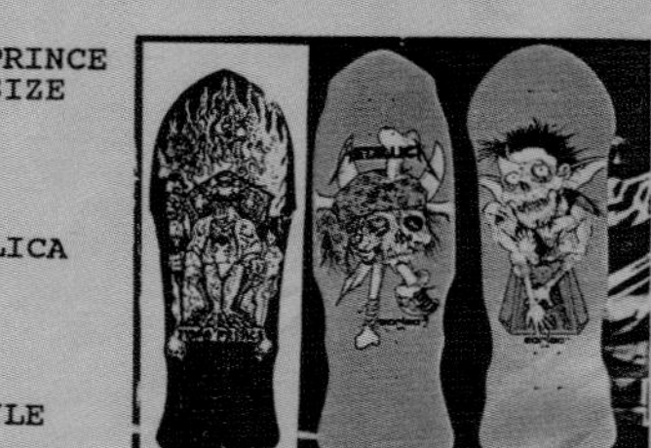

JAK'S TEAM, SAN FRANCISCO

ARDING
CRIME

TM

STALAG 13
'13
FOR INFO WRITE:
423 N. FIFTH ST., PORT HUENEME, CA 93041
JAIME 83

JAIME HERNANDEZ

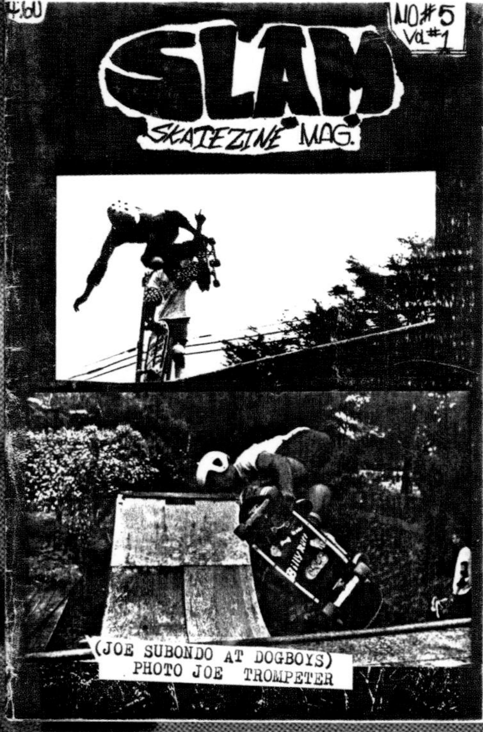
NO#5
Vol#1
SLAM
SKATEZINE MAG.
(JOE SUBONDO AT DOGBOYS)
PHOTO JOE TROMPETER

MIKE DELOSANTOS

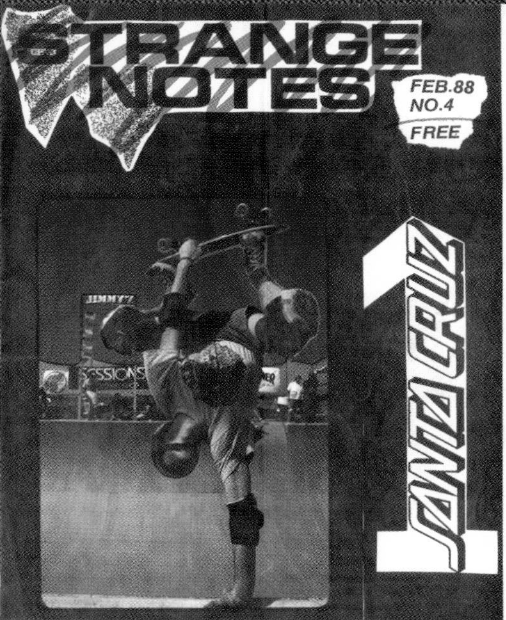
STRANGE NOTES
FEB.88
NO.4
FREE
SANTA CRUZ

(CRAIG STUART RAMSAI)
(RACE STREET RAMP)PHOTO,BY MIKE,D
(STUPID SKATE Mag)
1054 BROCKHAMPTON CT.
SAN,JOSE, CA 95136
LOOK FOR ISSUE
#3 OUT SOON
"NEXT SLAM MAG"
MORE ON THE SUMMIT
RAMP!!HOT PHOTO'S
OF THE CAMPBELL
GANG SKATING THERE
LOCAL POOL'S BY M,D
HOT PHOTO'S OF RACE
STREET.NEW MOVES BY
MIKE,ROMERO.ALL AND
MORE IN THE NEXT ISSUE
OF SLAM SKATE MAG.#6
STUPIL SKATE MAG.
© 1984

STRANGE NOTES
NO. 2
FREE
SEPT 87

San Jose's
no. 1
SKATE RIPPER
MAGAZINE
75¢
INTERVIEW: BOB DENIKE
Evolution of the Summit Ramp
SKATE FATE
Image Issue

and run lights. Half the time they'd get me, and other times, as long as I got to the BIG O parking lot, they'd be turned around by the dozen or so punks hanging out. The punks would yell and throw shit at them as I flew in. What's funny is we were all just kids and these bikers were like in their 30's.
DUANE PETERS
Everyday was war. We'd say "Open the door and go to war ". Even riding my scooter to the skate park meant a daily 'beat-down' from this biker gang called the 'Neopolitanos'. They hung at a house that I would pass by and when they'd see me coming they would
jump in front of me throwing rocks and then get on their bikes and chase me down yelling "DEVO SUCKS You Martian MOTHERFUCKER". I'd go up on the sidewalks, the wrong side of the road
INDEPENDENT
TRUCK COMPANY
DUANE PETERS
INDEPENDENT TRUCK COMPANY
P.O. BOX 2759, SANTA CRUZ, CA 95063 4084759434

INDEPENDENT
TRUCK COMPANY

INDEPENDENT
TRUCK COMPANY

Steve Olson

Free On The Streets

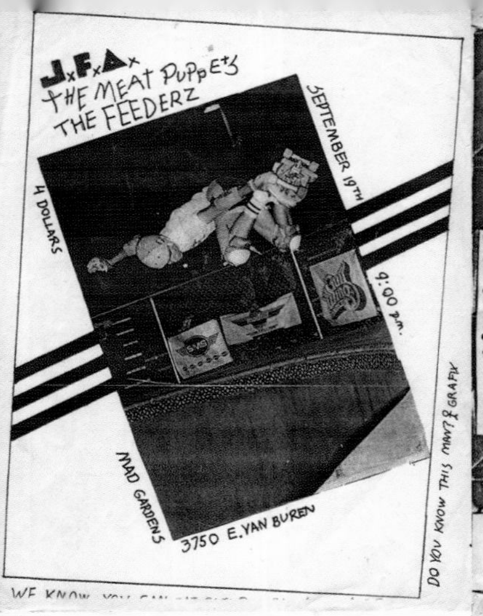
J.F.A.
THE MEAT PUPPETS
THE FEEDERZ
SEPTEMBER 19TH
4 DOLLARS
9:00 p.m.
MAD GARDENS
3750 E.VAN BUREN
DO YOU KNOW THIS MAN? GRAFIX

SOCIAL-DISTORTION
FROM O.C.
THE FACTION
LIVING ABORTIONS
DEC. 3
LOS OLVIDADOS
S.J.C.C.
$5.00
MINORS WELCOME
RIBSY &
THE UNAWARE

MILWAKEES
DIE KREUZEN
DON'T NO
NO FUSS NO MESS
JUST PURE UNLEASHED ATTITUDE; THE RULE
CHICAGOS
NAKED RAYGUN
RIP
SEPT 29TH SAT
CATHAY DE GRANDE
HOLLYWOOD
AND V x P x VIOLANT PHYCOSIS
AND SPECIAL GUEST POET LYNN GUNN
STARTS RIGHT AT 9:30
NO HOPE FOR THE WRETCHED

FRONTSIDE GRAFIX
MADISON SQUARE GARDEN
3750 EAST VAN BUREN
SAT AUG 15 9PM
ALLEY CATS
from l.a.
J.F.A
nova boys
HOOD

THE FINAL COUNTDOWN
W/ADAM BOMB
MONDAYS AT MIDNIGHT
ON 88.9 FM KXLU

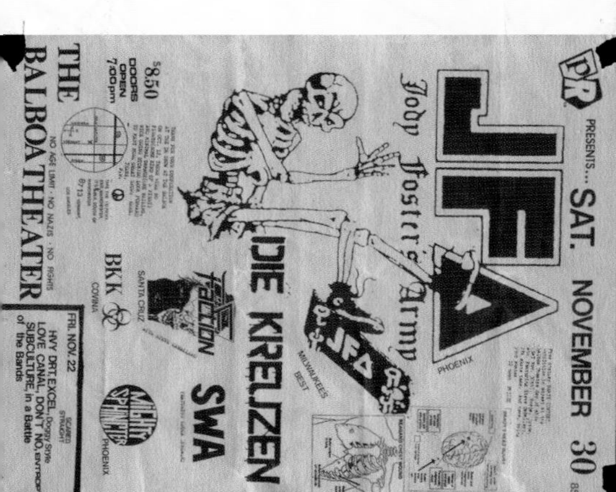
THE BALBOA THEATER
$8.50
DOORS OPEN 7:00pm
PR PRESENTS...
SAT. NOVEMBER 30
JFA
Jody Foster's Army
DIE KREUZEN
SWA
PHOENIX
FRI. NOV. 22

STRAIGHT RAZOR PRODUCTIONS PRESENTS:
the Faction
HOT STUFF
9:00 pm
Sunday Dec. 30th
at Club Culture
$5.00
WITH:
the KINGPINS
and DRAB
+ the LEGION of DOOM
ALL AGES ADMITTED!!
© JASON, TODD, BRYAN

UNDERGROUND-
SKATEBOARD CONTEST
10:PM (NO EARLIER) AT
TEUSDAY NIGHT 8/02/83
SAFWAY PARKING LOT ON
Pollard rd.-Los Gatos
Celebrating 2nd Anniversary
of WINCHESTER's DEATH.
SKATERS (ALL-NOVICE-PRO)
UNITE AT NIGHT! PARTY
AFTER!! NO ENTRY FEE,
NO BMX, NO HARRASSMENT!
SKATE or DIE
EVERY-SKATER

RIBZY
MISTAKEN IDENTITY
#1
INSURGENCY
FROM MORGAN HILL
SAN JOSE
QUEEN BEE
610 COLEMAN AVE
S.J.
6:00-10:00
Sunday April 21th

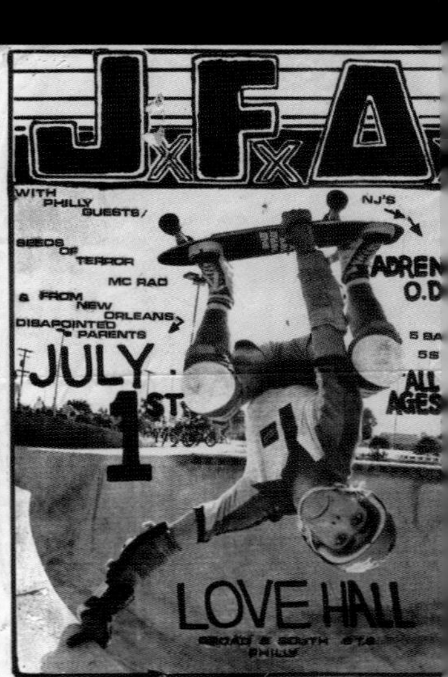
J x F x A
WITH PHILLY GUESTS/
SEEDS OF TERROR
MC RAD
& FROM NEW ORLEANS
DISAPOINTED PARENTS
NJ's
ADREN O.D.
JULY 1ST
ALL AGES
LOVE HALL

JFA
.22 cal. TOUR
mad garden phx
8/15 w/ alley cats
backstage tucson
8/21,22 w/ meat puppets, i.l.
cuckoo's nest
newport beach ca
8/27 w/ crowd
P.U.N.X. Presents...
DECRY
AND
CruciFix
Special Guests!
April 13th
cathay de Grande
AGRESSION
SIN 34
STALAG 13
DON'T KNOW
AND
RKL
WEDNESDAY OCT 19TH AT 7:00
PLUS SPECIAL GUESTS
HEROES of NOISE
AT
CASA TROPICAL
2425 WEST 5TH ST
NEXT TO THE AIRPORT
OXNARD
YES, THERE IS A COVER CHARGE!
BAR WITH I.D.
Rat Pack cancelled. To hell with Rat Pack
Heres...
RKL
ALSO FROM SAN FRANCISCO
NO FX
BAKERSFIELD'S OWN
FATAL VISION
AND
DEICIDE
THIS IS A PRIVATE PARTY. YOU MUST HAVE A COPY OF THIS INVITE TO GET IN
SAT. MAY 24TH 7PM
$7.00
BEER WITH I.D.
AT THE ENCORE THEATRE HALL
324 BERNARD
SKATE ROCK
SELFISH PRODUCTIONS PRESENT
L.A.s FIRST ALL SKATE GIG!
WITH:
THE BIG BOYS
J.F.A.
AGGRESSION
FACTION
(WITH STEVE CAVALLERO)
ILL REPUTE
TALES OF TERROR
DOOR PRIZES:
7:30 P.M.
FRIDAY, MAY 18th.
AT
STARDUST BALLROOM
5612 SUNSET BL.
464-2205
$6.50 ADV. $8 AT THE DOOR
NO AGE LIMIT!
AGRESSION
GOLDENVOICE productions
STALAG 13
OXNARD
THE VANDALS
J.F.A.
Only So.Cal Appearance
AT: LA CASA
SALSIPUEDES
601 E. MONTECITO
MILPAS OFFRAMP
101 NORTH
SATURDAY MAY 14
LA CASA
601 E. MONTECITO ST
SANTA BARBARA
SKATE TOUGH OR DIE!
TICKETS $6.50 ADVANCE
$7.00 AT THE DOOR
xxx ALL AGES xxx
For Info. Call (805) 964-2684
G.B.H
FRI MAR. 2
7:00 PM
YOUTH BRIGADE
AGRESSION
OXNARD
D.I.
HEART ATTACK
AND
ILL REPUTE
OXNARD
OLYMPIC AUDITORIUM
SURBURBAN PUNKS
PRESENTS...
A DAY OF BACKYARD CHAOS
WITH
SIMI VALLEY'S VERY OWN
SCARED STRAIGHT
PLUS
FATAL ERROR
AT 5887 AZTEC ST.
7:30
SATURDAY MAY 11 85
$2.00
DIRECTIONS
COCHRAN
AZTEC
SELFISH PRODUCTIONS PRESENTS A
SKATE BAND
EXTRAVAGANZA
FEATURING
THE BIG BOYS
JFA
AGRESSION
THE FACTION
ILL REPUTE
AND TALES OF TERROR
STARDUST BALLROOM
5612 SUNSET BLVD.
FRI. MAY 18TH
DOORS OPEN AT 7:30
$6.50 ADVANCE $8.00 AT THE DOOR
NO AGE LIMIT
MORE INFO: 464-2205
FILMED
SELFISH PRO. PREZENTS
BIG BOYS
AGRESSION
JFA
ILL REPUTE
FACTION
TALES OF TERROR
STARDUST BALLROOM
5612 SUNSET BL
FRI MAY 18
DOORS OPEN 7:30
TICKETS $6.50 ADVANCE $8 AT THE DOOR
NO AGE LIMIT
FOR MORE INFO: 464-2205

THE
Faction
THE FACTION

THE
FACTION
SAT.
MARCH 16TH
AT THE
NEW VARSITY THEATER
IN PALO ALTO
9PM
also:
AGRESSION
ILL REPUTE
and THE DRAB
BE THERE OR BE DEAD!
ALL AGES!

THE
FACTION

THE
AUG. 12TH FRESNO
13-17TH LOS ANGELES
18TH SAN FRANCISCO
19TH SACRAMENTO
20TH RENO (IN NEV.)
21ST CONCORD
22ND SAN FRANCISCO
FACTION
Calif. Summer Tour

THE FACTION
YESTERDAY IS GONE

FACTION
SUITE 109-222
15466 LOS GATOS BLVD
LOS GATOS, CA 95030

THANKS TO-Keith Renden, Chris Lentz, Chris Ide, Craig Bradford, THRASHER, TRANS-WORLD, etc.
HELLO, HOW ARE YOU'S, TO-FLIPSIDE, Alex Morgan, JFA, BIG BOYS, Fausto, GSD, K.T., Grant B., Mofo, & everyone we met on tour, M.I.D., The Drab, Social Unrest, Kraut, Ribsy, Drunk Injuns, Agression, & S.J. skaters.

OTHER FACTION RELEASES:

GROWING PAINS-San Jose Compilation Tape
ROOM 101-Demo Tape
YESTERDAY IS GONE-7 inch
THRASHER SKATE ROCK TAPE VOL. I
NO HIDDEN MESSAGES-12 inch
FROM THE VALLEY WITHIN-San Jose 7 inch Compilation
CORPSE IN DISGUISE-7 inch
THRASHER SKATE ROCK VOL. 2-12 inch Compilation
soon to be released-
DARK ROOM-12 inch

FACTION

CASSETTERARITIES

SIDE 1	SIDE 2
SPINELESS MAJORITY	INTRO
SPINELESS MAJORITY	LOST IN SPACE
BOREDOM AWAITS	100 YEARS WAR
IT MAKES ME SICK	PEGGED FOR LIFE
GAVIN BABBLING	GAVIN BABBLING AGAIN
LOUIE, LOUIE	TOUNGE LIKE A BATTERING RAM
ME	-ADAM BOMB: NO MORALS
BEING WATCHED	-GOSSIP COUNCIL: PUNK PARTY
FAST FOOD DIET	DEMONS
SKATE HARASSMENT	CORPSE IN DISGUISE
BULLETS ARE FASTER...	CALIFORNIA DREAMIN'
KFJC INTERVIEW	A.U.K.
BLACK BALLED	D.J.'ING ON KFJC
YESTERDAY IS GONE	
THE S.G.'S LAST STAND	

CINNAMON VANS!

the
Faction
SUMMER TOUR 84

FACTION

THE
Faction
"NO HIDDEN MESSAGES"
OUT NOW ON
IM RECORDS
$5.00 PLUS $1.00 POSTAGE
THE FACTION
2349 CARLTON AVE.
SAN JOSE, CA
95124
NEW ALBUM

NOT
JFA
All Ages

ROCK 'TILL YOU DROP WITH . . .

CELEBRATE

AN EVENING WITH

JFA

FRIDAY
JULY 1
7:30 P.M.

APPEARING LIVE AT:
THE BERNARD PUB
4063 Lafayette 771-3335

with
HIDDEN MOTIVES
DEAD PLANET

Doors Open
7:30 P.M.
ALL AGES WELCOME
FULL BAR AVAILABLE FOR ANYONE OVER 21

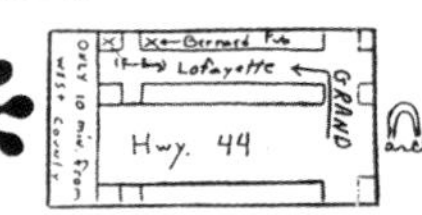
Bernard Pub
Lafayette
GRAND
Hwy. 44

TICKETS ARE $6.50 IN ADVANCE AND $ 7.75 AT THE DOOR AND ON SALE NOW AT EUCLID RECORDS, VINTAGE VINYL, WEST END WAX, MISSISSIPPI NIGHTS, SOUND REVOLUTIONS, ALL 4 RECORD CO. LOCATIONS DISC CONNECTION in Maplewood, Al ALTERED SKAT stores (Alton & S. County bands & 2ND STO COMIX in Kirkwood

SPREADING THE ROCK 'N' ROLL GOSPEL

7SECONDS

Dan Pozniak
Kevin Seconds
Steve Youth
Troy Mowat

Presented by POSITIVE DIRECTION and the ALL-AGES SHOW

ZERO MENTALITY also P.T.L KLUB HARDCORE

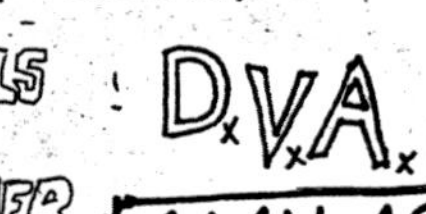
BALLS OF POWER

D.V.A.

AN ALL-AGES SHOW $4
September 8 1985 3pm
Granite State Room of Memorial Union Building, UNH, DURHAM, NH

KARI-VAN runs all day!!

sun jan 5th
8:00 Sharp
7 SECONDS
YOUTH OF TODAY
from CONNECTICUT
UPS
from Tucson
electric rhino
1013 N. 3rd ave

metal

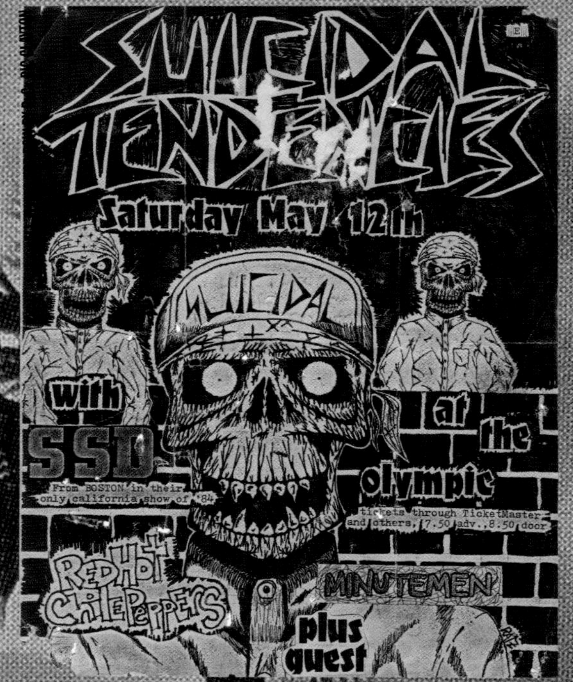
SUICIDAL TENDENCIES
Saturday May 12th
SUICIDAL
with
SSD
From BOSTON in their only california show of '84
at the olympic
tickets through TicketMaster and others. 7.50 adv.. 8.50 door
RED HOT CHILE PEPPERS
MINUTEMEN
plus guest

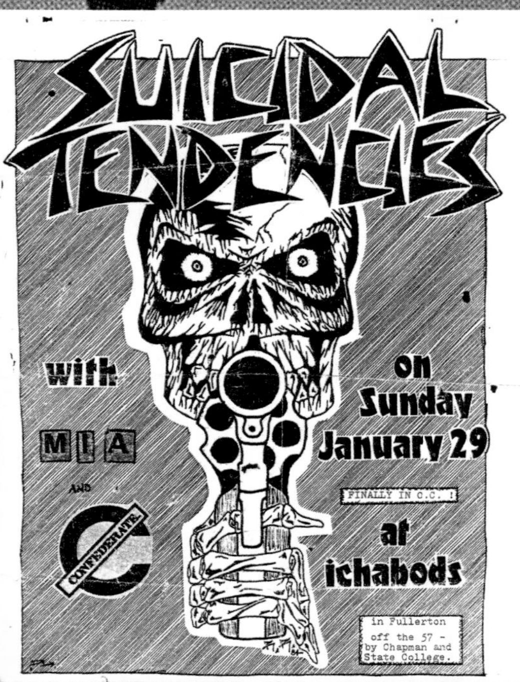
SUICIDAL TENDENCIES
with
M I A
AND
CONFEDERATE
on Sunday January 29
FINALLY IN O.C. !
at ichabods
in Fullerton off the 57 - by Chapman and State College.

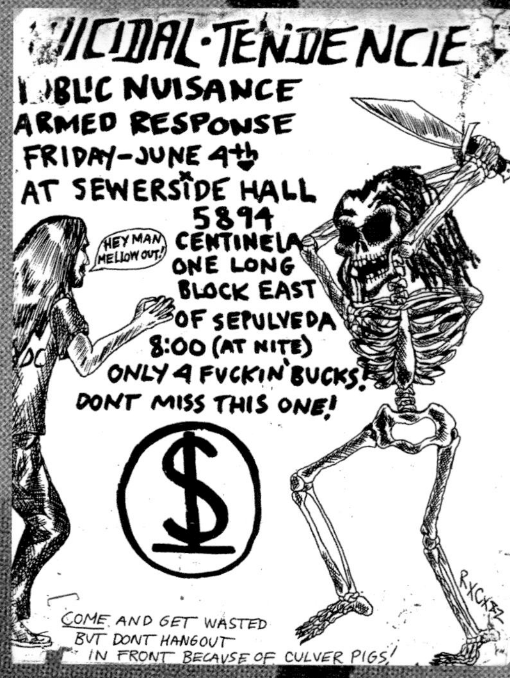
ICIDAL·TENDENCIE
BLIC NUISANCE
ARMED RESPONSE
FRIDAY-JUNE 4th
AT SEWERSIDE HALL
5894
CENTINELA
ONE LONG BLOCK EAST OF SEPULVEDA
8:00 (AT NITE)
ONLY 4 FUCKIN' BUCKS!
DONT MISS THIS ONE!
HEY MAN MELLOW OUT!
COME AND GET WASTED
BUT DONT HANGOUT IN FRONT BECAUSE OF CULVER PIGS!

Fri. March 21
SUICIDAL TENDENCIES
Beowülf
EXCEL
BLOODCUM
BALBOA THEATER
8713 Vermont, L.A.
info (818) 966-6581
SAVE AT THESE OUTLETS
MICHAEL SIEFF

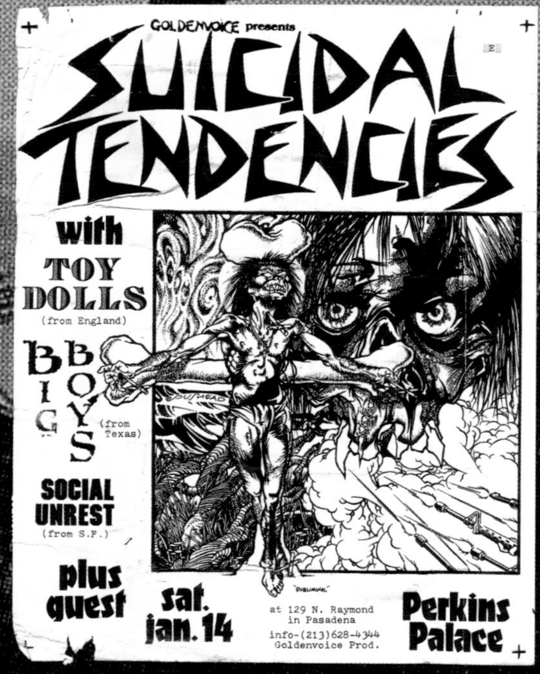
GOLDENVOICE presents
SUICIDAL TENDENCIES
with
TOY DOLLS
(from England)
BIG BOYS
(from Texas)
SOCIAL UNREST
(from S.F.)
plus guest
sat. jan. 14
at 129 N. Raymond in Pasadena
info-(213)628-4344
Goldenvoice Prod.
Perkins Palace

Watch
A very special interview with
SUICIDAL TENDENCIES
Sunday, July 29
on I.R.S.'s THE CUTTING EDGE on MTV
8:30 Pacific/11:30 Eastern
Sunday, July 29

Californi

TIME FOR ENJOYMENT!....
NEIGHBORHOOD WATCH PARTY
+ JUVENILE DELINQUENTS
FRIDAY, APRIL 29 '83
3607 CORNER OF BARRY AND CHARNOCK, MAR VISTA
INFO. DAVE 397-9667
FREE BEER! 4 BEDS!
FUCKIN LOP!
#8
NO BOULDERS!
RxCx85

NEIGHBORHOOD WATCH
BEOWÜLF
NO MERCY
STALAG 13
chaotic noise
THURS. SEPT. 6th 8:00
MUSIC MACHINE
12220 PICO
820-5151
HEY YOU! THIS

NEIGHBORHOOD WATCH
ONLY #1
NO MERCY
STARTS AT 8:00
SO GET THERE EARLY!!
FRI DEC 2
4448 HARDING AVE OFF OF CENTINELA SOUTH OF WASHINGTON IN CULVER CITY

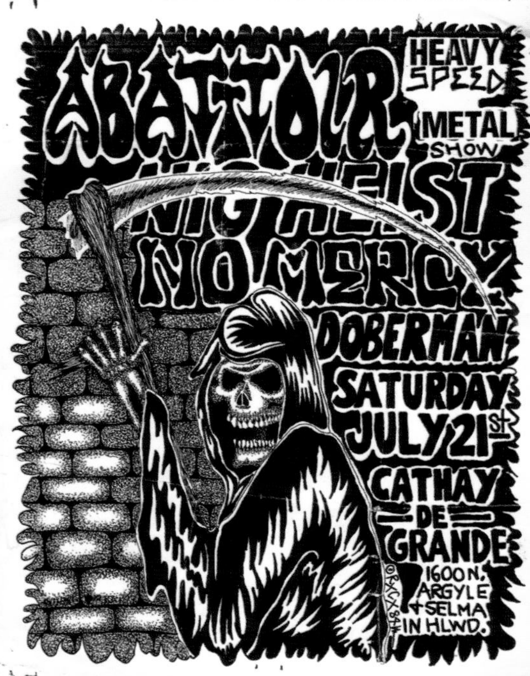
ABATTOIR
HEAVY SPEED METAL SHOW
NO MERCY
DOBERMAN
SATURDAY JULY 21st
CATHAY DE GRANDE
1600 N. ARGYLE + SELMA IN HLWD.

NO SCHOOL FRIDAY 31st
NO MERCY
Beowülf
AND SURPRISE GUESTS!
THIS THURSDAY!!! JANUARY 30th
NO AGE LIMIT
Chuck Landis' COUNTRY CLUB
18415 SHERMAN WAY · RESEDA
FREE PARKING · RESTAURANT
BOX OFFICE OPEN NOON – 6PM
RxCx84

TRIPLE M PRESENTS
WELCOME TO VENICE
THE ONLY COMPILATION ALBUM
FEATURING:
NO MERCY
BEOWÜLF
EXCEL
LOS CYCOS
AND SPECIAL GUESTS....
SUICIDAL TENDENCIES
T-SHIRTS $6.00 (STATE SIZE)
THE ALBUM $6.00
1ST CLASS DELIVERY ADD $1.00
SUICIDAL RECORDS P.O. BOX 5512 VENICE, CALIFORNIA 90296
WATCH FOR MORE VINYL TERRORIZING ON
SUICIDAL RECORDS

ALL FLYERS THIS PAGE BY RxCx RIC CLAYTON

mentors
AGRESSION
MIGHTY SPHINCTER
Saint Vitus
DEC 20
$8
ALL AGES WELCOME!
FULL BAR AVAILABLE WITH PROPER I.D.
5025 N. 7th AVE. 230-2568
(JUST NORTH OF CAMELBACK RD)
the metro

SANDI

METALBAR presents
BANNED BY THE PMRC
mentors
From L.A.
ONLY AREA APPEARANCE
plus
SST Recording Artists
Saint Vitus
DJ: STEVE BLUSH
Host: DAVID RATT
MON. JULY 13
$5
PYRAMID – 101 AVE. A

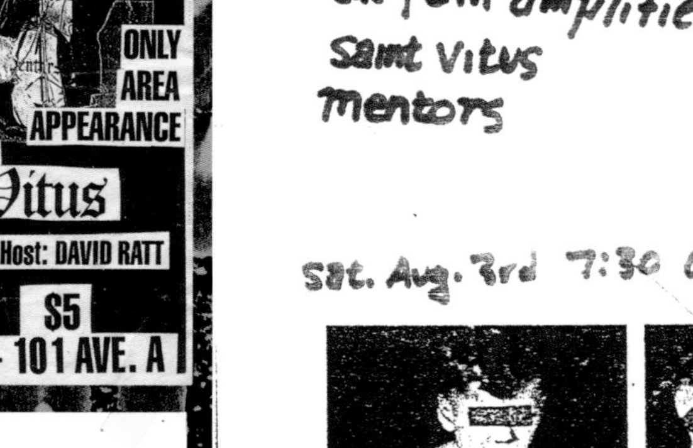
the pain amplifiers
saint vitus
mentors
sat. Aug. 3rd 7:30 O'CAYZ $8.00

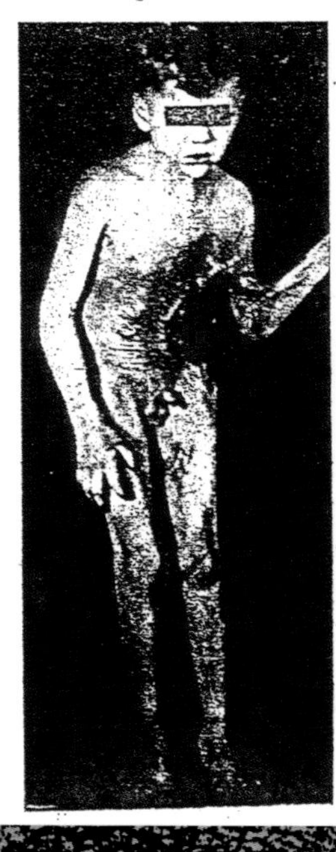

GIRLS GIRLS YOURE BAND IS HERE

THE MENTORS

AT BLACKIES ON LABREA & MELROSE

THURSDAY NIGHT with the Gears 13th March

AND REMEMBER NO CRY BABYS! SISSYS! Faggots!

NO TRENDIES

QUEER

MENTORS SUCK

Yank

New wave tie

BRENDON MULLEN

DARBY

My Life is

COME EARLY

NO CONCEPT

NEW WAVE PONYTAIL

POP

My Life is always the B...

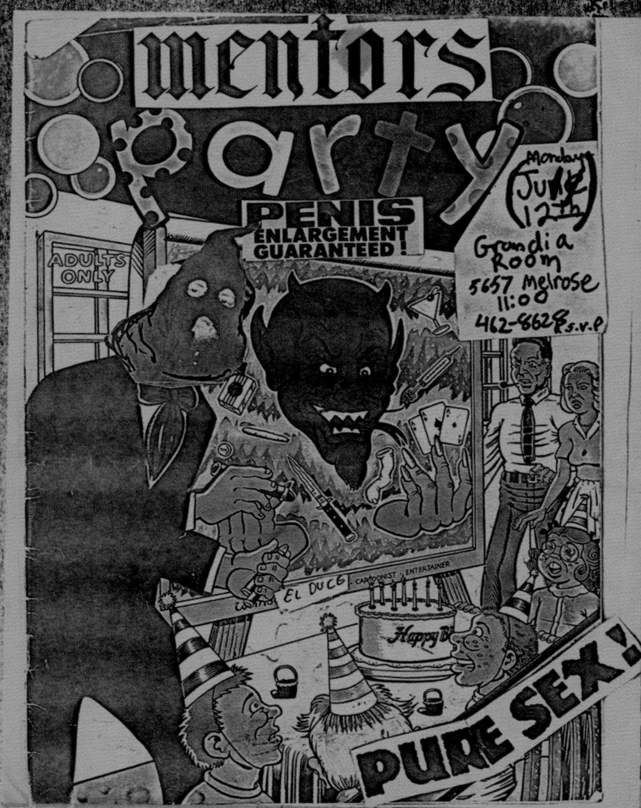
mentors
party
PENIS ENLARGEMENT GUARANTEED!
Monday June 12th
Grandia Room
5657 Melrose
11:00
462-8628 R.S.V.P.
ADULTS ONLY
EL DUCE
PURE SEX!

EL DUCE

mentors
SUPER HEROINES
UP SETTERS
CLUB 88
11784 W. Pico Blvd.
479-6923 WLA
TUESDAY
JUNE 14
8 PM
BRING I.D.

GG ALLIN

I BELIEVE THAT IT IS BEST TO DECIDE YOUR OWN FINAL END. I WILL NOT PUT MY LIFE IN THE HANDS OF FATE. WE ARE NOT ABLE TO HAVE ANY SAY IN OUR BIRTH, BUT WE CAN DECIDE WHEN WE WANT TO DIE, AND WE SHOULD. WHY HANG AROUND IF YOU'RE READY. I WILL PULL MY OWN TRIGGER. I'VE BEEN PLAYING RUSSIAN ROULET FOR A LONG TIME NOW, SO I'M READY TO BREAK ON THROUGH TO THE OTHER SIDE FOR GOOD. I'M ANNOUNCING MY DATE WITH DEATH FOR WEDNESDAY, OCTOBER 31st, 1990, MIDNIGHT. SOMEWHERE IN N.Y.C. THE STAGE HAS BEEN MY LIFE, SO I WILL TAKE MY LIFE ON STAGE. I WILL RECORD ONE MORE LP TO BE RELEASED THE FOLLOWING DAY. WELCOME TO MY DEATH.

SEE YOU IN HELL,

THE SACRIFICE

GOLDENVOICE presents
Motorhead
APRIL 24 full bar W/ID
All AGES FRIDAY 8pm.
Lizzie Borden
SAVAGE GRACE
PALLADIUM ✱ HOLLYWOOD
6215 W. Sunset BLvd
TICKETMASTER
AT MAY COMPANY, MUSIC PLUS AND SPORTMART. TICKETMASTER CHARGE (213) 480-3232 or (714) 740-2000

L.A. GUNS
with SPECIAL GUESTS
SAT. JULY 19
AT THE ROXY THEATRE 9009 SUNSET

MAD MARC RUDE

motörhead
Wednesday November 27, 1985
WENDY O. WILLIAMS
MEGADETH
MISS and DIE!

PRIVATE EYE

GOLDENVOICE presents IN ASSOCIATION WITH HIGH TIMES
motörhead
No sleep till FENDER'S BALLROOM
Cro-Mags
PLUS ITALY'S RAW POWER!
+ CANADA'S DAYGLO ABORTIONS
SAT. OCT. 18
FENDER'S BALLROOM

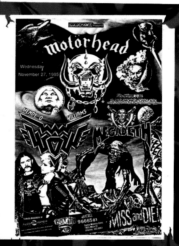

L.A. GUNS
L.A. GUNS
FRIDAY SEPTEMBER 6, 10:00PM
AT THE LIPSTICK FIX CLUB
6160 HOLLYWOOD BLVD.

B. OTIS

GOLDENVOICE
THE SECOND ANNUAL DAY OF INFAMY!! PEARL HARBOR DAY!
motörhead
Bombs away
D.O.A.
FROM CANADA BUB!!
NECROS
DieKreuzen
WHITE FLAG
THE COOLEST BAND IN THE WHOLE DANG WORLD......
Thelonious Monster
TICKETMASTER
AT MAY COMPANY, MUSIC PLUS AND SPORTMART. TICKETMASTER CHARGE
SAT Dec. 7th
OLYMPIC AUDITORIUM
starts AT 7:30

$4.00 ROCK N' SLEAZE
Rolling Stones

MEET MÖTLEY CRÜE

ON SUNDAY THE 18TH

2PM

AT UNIVERSAL RECORDS 2309 ½ TELEGRAPH

pR AND TRIPLE MMM PRESENTS... JANUARY 25

CORROSION
OF CONFORMITY

HIRAX
BEDWÜLF
PLUS SPECIAL GUEST
MAD 23 1974
17 1983

DOORS OPEN 8:00 pm
animosity tour '85/86
THE BALBOA THEATER
TAKE THE 110 FRWY EXIT MANCHESTER, IT'S 1 BLK SOUTH OF MANCHESTER 8713 VERMONT, LOS ANGELES

PUSHEAD

pR AND TRIPLE MMM PRESENTS... FRI. JANUARY 3rd
ONLY L.A. GIG!
EXODUS
D.R.I.
POSSESSED
DARK ANGEL
DEATH ANGEL
ON SALE MONDAY DEC. 2 10AM
TAKE THE 110 FRWY. EXIT MANCHESTER, IT'S 1 BLK SOUTH OF MANCHESTER 8713 VERMONT, LOS ANGELES
AT THE BALBOA THEATER
LIMITED TICKETS AVAILABLE
DONT BE LEFT OUT, BUY IN ADVANCE!
TICKETMASTER
AT MAY COMPANY, MUSIC PLUS AND SPORTMART

TOP CONCERTS
PROUDLY PRESENTS
MON. AUG. 15
SHOW STARTS
7:30 P.M.
ALL AGES
ALCOHOL SERVED WITH PROPER I.D.
LIMITED TICKETS!
SLAYER
AND
SOOTHSAYER
STUDIO WEST
33RD AVE. & INDIAN SCHOOL
TICKETS ARE STILL AVAILABLE IN ADVANCE AT DILLARDS ZIA RECORDS AND STUDIO WEST

PAUL STOTTLER

TOP CONCERTS PRESENTS
WED OCT. 5TH
ALL AGES 7:00 P.M.
King Diamond
AND SPECIAL GUESTS
FLOTSAM AND JETSAM
VFW HALL
TICKETS ARE AVAILABLE IN ADVANCE AT ZIA RECORDS -OR- TICKETMASTER INSIDE TOWER RECORDS
4853 E. THOMAS RD.

PAUL STOTTLER

pR PRESENTS... DEC. 14 85

SPEED METAL
BATTLE OF THE BANDS

BEOWÜLF
POWERTRIP
ABANDONED
SANCTUM
F.C.M.N. TORMENTOR
NO MERCY
BLOODCUM
TAKE THE 110 FRWY. EXIT MANCHESTER. IT'S 4 BLK. SOUTH OF MANCHESTER
8713 VERMONT, LOS ANGELES

Rockstar Richard Ramirez displays palm inked with star symbol sometimes associated with satanism.

NO AGE LIMIT · NO NAZIS · NO FIGHTS

DOORS OPEN 7:00pm $7.50

AT THE BALBOA THEATER

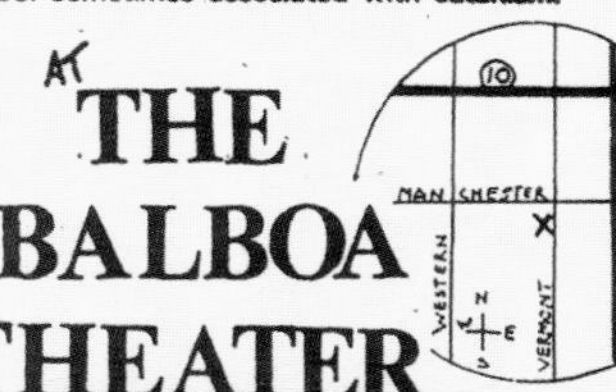
MANCHESTER
WESTERN
VERMONT
AVALON

TOP CONCERTS
PROUDLY PRESENTS
DEATH ANGEL
WITH:
RIGOR-MORTIS
Sacred Reich
KNIGHTS OF BLOODY STEEL
ALL AGES
Fri. SEPT. 9
7:30PM
TICKETS AVAILABLE IN ADVANCE AT TICKET MASTER or Z.I.A. RECORDS
VFW HALL 4853 E. THOMAS

METAL MAYHEM
CLUB 88 THUR MAY 16th
DOBERMAN
OVERLORD
TRI-FORCE
21 & OVER
$4.00 at Door $2.50 (with this flyer)
11784 PICO W. L.A. 479-6923

TROIT

GOLDENVOICE IN ASSOCIATION WITH AVALON
PRESENTS.......
MEGADETH
THE WORLDS STATE OF THE ART SPEEDMETAL BAND
NEW YORKS
OVERKILL
AND OHIOS
NECROS
JUNE 12TH 8PM
SANTA MONICA CIVIC

METAL WORTH DYING FOR

PRIVATE EYE

THIRD ANNIVERSARY SHOW with
ZOZOBRA
& from Fort Collins, The MASONS
Tuesday, Dec.15
Auction House and Art Gallery
1037 Walnut St., Boulder
8PM - $3

REMEMBER UNCLE STEVE SAYS 'I LUV YA

RATTUS

SAT. JULY 18
DRI
NEVADA CITY
SALT LAKE CITY
DENVER
MINNEAPOLIS
MILWAUKEE
CHICAGO
DETROIT
CINCINNATI
CLEVELAND
PITTSBURGH
BUFFALO
TORONTO
MONTREAL
BOSTON
PROVIDENCE
BROOKLYN
NEW YORK CITY
HARTFORD
TRENTON
BALTIMORE
WASHINGTON D.C.
RICHMOND
CHARLESTON
COLUMBIA
ATLANTA
BIRMINGHAM
NASHVILLE
MEMPHIS
NEW ORLEANS
HOUSTON
AUSTIN
SAN ANTONIO
EL PASO
TUCSON
PHOENIX
SAN DIEGO
LOS ANGELES
CROSSOVER WORLD TOUR '87
SF'S
PLUS!
TESTAMENT
HOLY TERROR
FENDERS BALLROOM
&
EXCEL
GOLDENVOICE Presentation

DRI

THRASH METAL
Sep. 19
détente
SHOW STARTS 8:00
DARK ANGEL AND MEGADETH
(DĀT.ÄNT')
DÉTENTE OPENS THE SHOW, COME EARLY!
MUSIC TO BRING BACK THE DEAD!!
James Huberty, McDonald's massacrer.
Charles Manson: Murder was all in the Family.
William Bonin, Freeway Killer.
Cousin Angelo Buono Hillside Strangler #2.
"It's me!" Richard Ramirez, accused Night Stalker.
"DENNIS" "ROSS" "DAWN" "CALEB" "STEVE"
EXPERIANCE REALITY AT IT'S HARSHEST,
WITH "DÉTENTE" THURSDAY SEPT. 19 8:00
HAVE ILLUSIONS SHATTERED AT
NO AGE LIMIT
Chuck Landis'
COUNTRY CLUB
ADVANCE DISCOUNT TICKETS
CALL 213•851-0859
Band Info: 5554 Romaine, Hollywood, CA 90038
BOX OFFICE OPEN NOON - 6PM

DIRTY ROTTEN IMBECILES
TUE. AUG 5
DRI
2 SHOWS: PSYCOTIC REACTION
LEGION OF DEATH
8:00 P.M.
10:30 P.M.
ALL AGES
NO ALCOHOL
$5 at the door

SUNDAY
MAY 25th
ALL AGES SHOW
DRI
SHELL SHOCK
ST MARKS-1130 RAMPART
8 P.M.
$6
THRASH Rock from CALIF.

DISCHARGE
discharge
8 P.M.
SATURDAY
SEPT. 6
1ST. SHOW
IN OVER
THREE YEARS
AT
FENDERS
521 E. 1st St. Long Beach
(213) 435-2838
TICKETS AT:
TICKETMASTER
MOBY DISC - Valley
RHINO - Westwood
LONDON EXCHANGE - COSTA MESA
ZED'S - Long Beach
VINYL FETISH - Hollyw
WITH SPECIAL GUESTS
DR. KNOW
Final Conflict
CRYPTIC SLAUGHTER
&
ATTITUDE ADJUSTMENT

jump on the new metalcore bandwagon. What was shocking was that they thought people were going to let them off the hook for it. People waited so long for their favorite British hardcore band to return to Los Angeles. This was a slap in the face. Fender's ballroom was a dangerous place. Its' low ceiling, poor ventilation and reputation as a place for gangs to clash made it tough to secure. I don't know what would have happened to Discharge if Big Frank, Scary Gary, Mr. Tiny and other brilliant security weren't there to coordinate a massive effort to protect and escort them out of the building.

They escaped throngs of angry punks through a back door in the kitchen, after only two and a half songs.

Never again indeed.

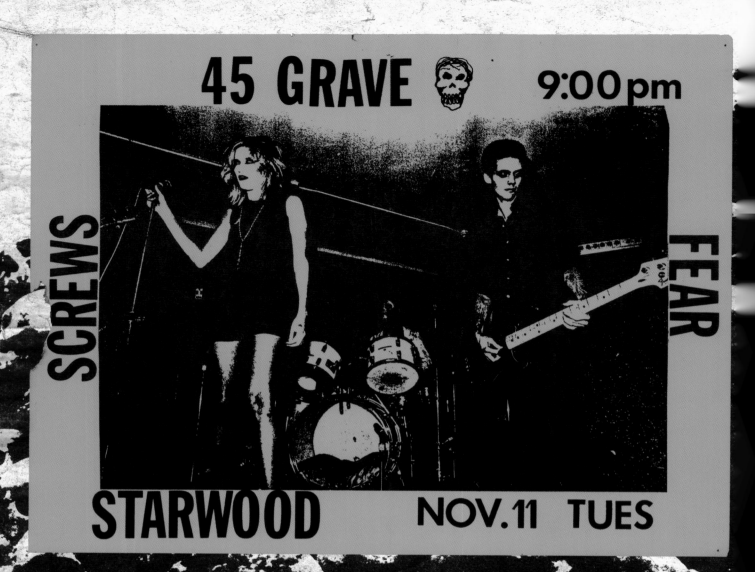

45 GRAVE 9:00 pm

SCREWS

FEAR

STARWOOD NOV. 11 TUES

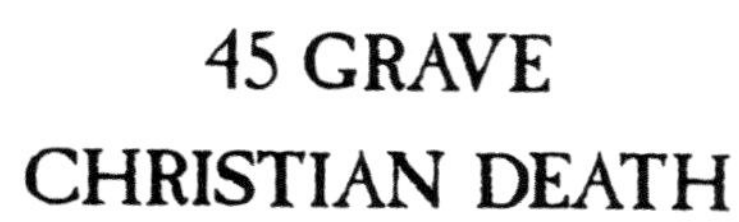
45 GRAVE
CHRISTIAN DEATH

AT AL'S BAR

FRI. OCT.30

GOLDENVOICE
presents
a
swinging
time
with
45 Grave
and
The Dickies
ALL HALLOWS
OCT 31
Fender's Ballroom
Open 8 P.M.
Adm. $7.50 Adv $8.50 Door
ADVANCE TICKET SALES AT:
Zed Records – Long Beach • White Slug – Long Beach
London Exchange – Newport •
Camel – Huntington Beach • Fenders Box Office
Middle Earth – Downey •
Info.: 435-6311
OLYMPIC AUDITORIUM
Oct 20 Suicidal Tendencies & One Way System
Nov 16 Public Image Limited & Butthole Surfers
OLYMPIC AUDITORIUM

WHAT IS 45 Grave ?
A TALE OF STRANGE PHENOMENA

45 GRAVE
Saturday, Dec. 18th
Galaxy
w/ Mau Maus
Shattered Faith
Scroungers
Monday, Dec. 20th
Rissmiller's
w/ 20/20
Paul Collins Beat
Lydia Lunch
NEW YORK ROCKER
BENIFIT

45 GRAVE
LYDIA LUNCH & 13.13
AL'S BAR
AUG 29

Joey Kill's
Bar
433 S. VICTORY
BURBANK
WED.
Oct. 8
45 GRAVE

DINAH CANCER

AAA PRESENTS
HALLOWEEN PARTY!!!
8:30 SAT. OCT. 30
45 GRAVE
AMERICAN INDIAN CENTER
229 VALENCIA ST.
SAN FRANCISCO
AND INTRODUCING
BEAST the UNDEAD
ADVANCE TICKETS AT BASS OUTLETS
SCREAM E.P AVAILABLE NOW
SCREAM

DON BOLLES

45 Grave was my dream team band: Paul Cutler -- my favorite guitarist, besides Pat Smear -- on guitar, Rob Graves -- my favorite bass player -- on bass, and me on

drums. Pat Smear -- my other favorite guitarist-- even played with us for a couple of shows and on our 1st 7 ". We also had my then girlfriend, the lovely and talented Dinah Cancer, as front person. With a name from a thrift store button Paul had given me for Christmas

that said "WE DIG 45 GRAVE", I assumed it was

the first fanclub item for our new "pop" band, which must therefore be called 45 Grave. Our sound was a hodgepodge of punk, metal, surf, prog, krautroc, and ghoul pop with a surreal horror-rock aesthetic. we soon found

ourselves playing shows at the Hong Kong Cafe, the Starwood, the Whiskey, and even Orange

County venues that usually didn't like the Hollywood bands because they weren't hard-core enough. Our music was totally evil sounding. Paul and I were

also way into outside experimental, Avant Garde and improvisational "free" music, and were doing that before we

did punk rock. Sometimes we would improvise half of our set or more at shows, with Dinah making up lyrics on the spot. It usually worked. Our 1st single, "Black Cros b/w "Wax" was the most requested thing on Rodney on the Roq for a month or two. Meanwhile, Somewhere in Pomona, former Darby Crash mascot Roz Williams was going for the jugular of what would soon be known as "Goth" with his new band, Christian Death, which featured Adolescent guitarist Rik Agnew as a Mick Ronson

to Roz's Bowie. Their first LP and the stuff on the "Hell Comes to Your House" comp are still dance floor fillers at modern Goth clubs, and rightfully so -- it was a sound that was unique and resonated pure ennui and despair. 45 Grave and Christian Death played shows together. Once at the Whiskey Roz and his performance art

partner Ron Athey crucified a dead cat on stage while wearing wedding gowns. That got people talking. Later, Christian Death was abandoned by Roz and taken over by other people and it wasn't ever really the same.

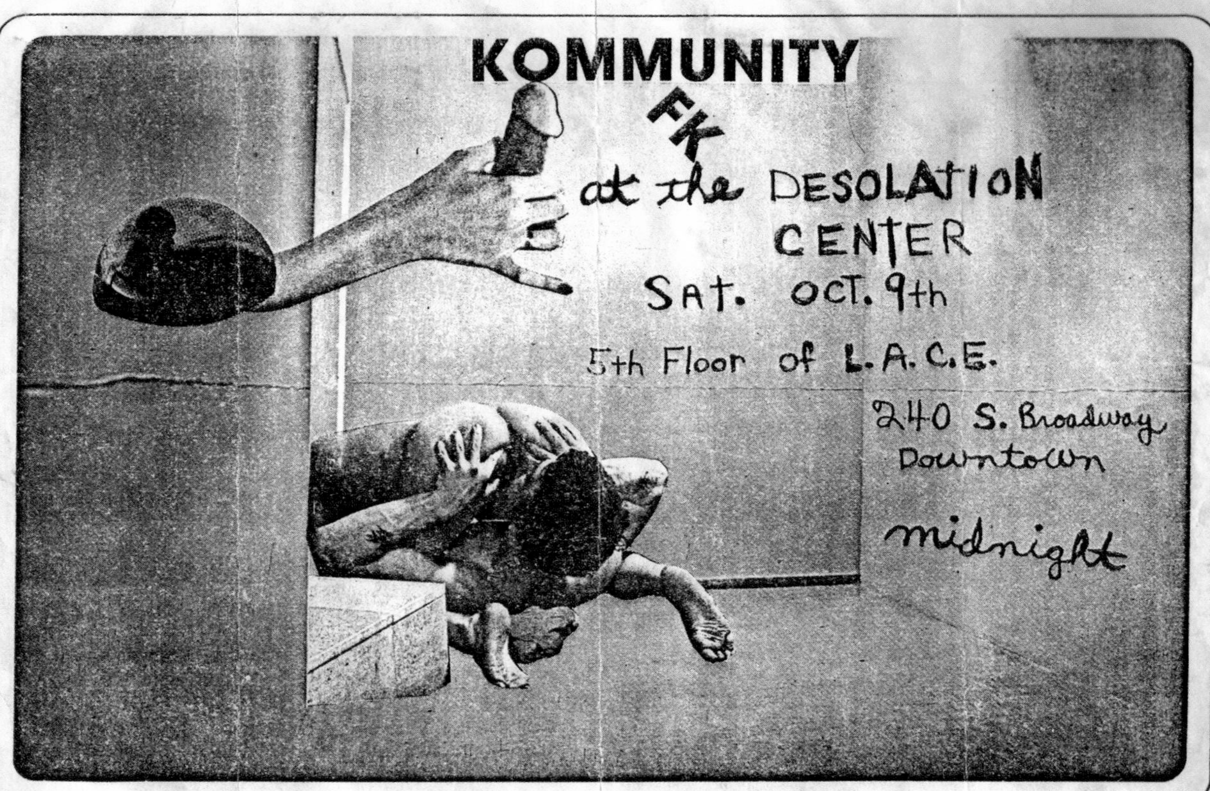
KOMMUNITY
FK
at the DESOLATION
CENTER
SAt. OCT. 9th
5th Floor of L.A.C.E.
240 S. Broadway
Downtown
midnight

KOMMUNITY FK
sept. 19 Brave Dog w/ Quiet Children
oct.
7 ON Klub w/ Videos
14 Cathay de Grande
w/ Jennifer Marot ex Nuns
& Rayonics
17 Beyond Baroque w/ Monitor
28 ON Klub w/ T.B.A.
* Just Added *
Sept. 24
C.A.S.H.
*

Kommunity F.K.
MAY 12 BLACKIES West
13 O.N. KLUB
JUNE 17 STARWOOD
306

KILLING JOKE
and
KOMMUNITY F.K.
FRI.
AUG. 28
at the
WHISKEY

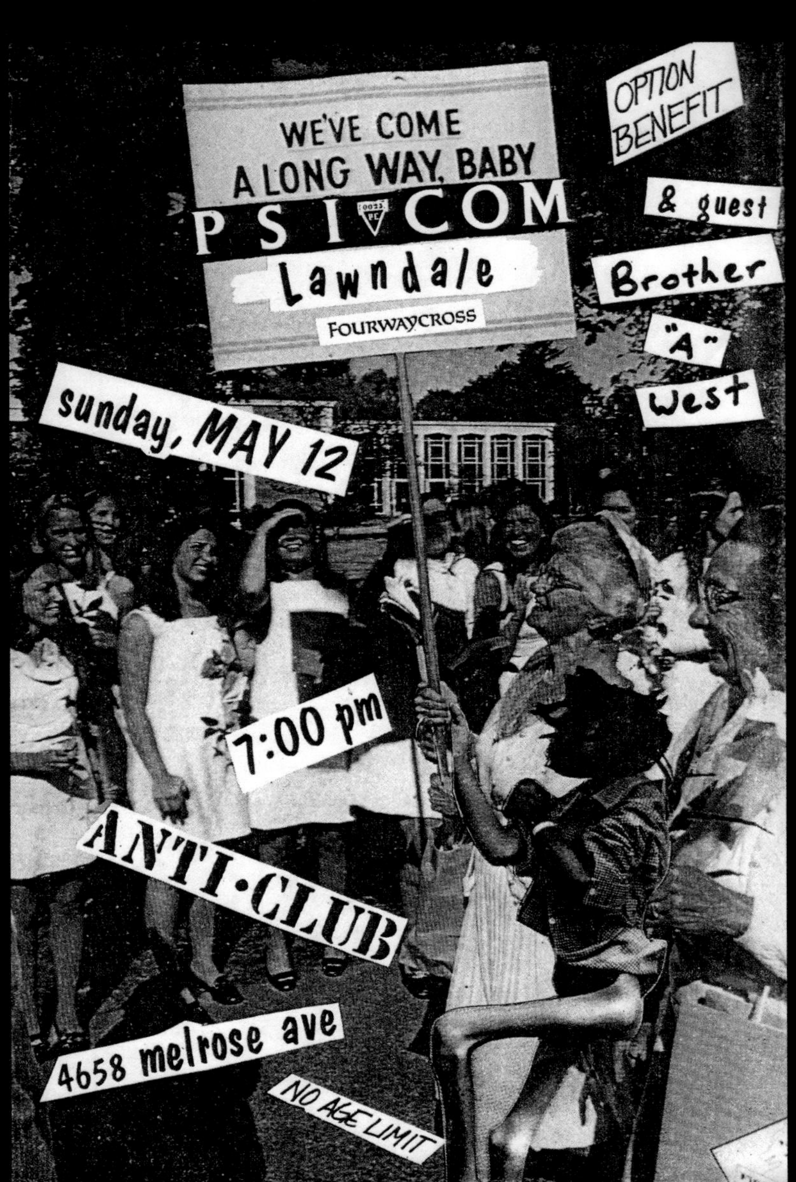
WE'VE COME
A LONG WAY, BABY
PSI COM
Lawndale
FOURWAYCROSS
OPTION BENEFIT
& guest
Brother
"A"
West
sunday, MAY 12
7:00 pm
ANTI·CLUB
4658 melrose ave
NO AGE LIMIT

PSI COM
RECORD
DEBUT
FUTURE DATES:
JUNE 1 O.N. KLUB
kommunity f.k.
JUNE 2 BEYOND BAROQUE
Nip Drivers
FIENDS
JUNE 13 CLUB LINGERIE
SAVAGE REPUBLIC
ABECEDARIANS
Mohini Records

PERRY FARRELL by BRUCE KALBERG

CHRISTIAN DEATH ARE A REAL GAS!

SEE THEM AT "CLUB 88" 11784 W. PICO BLVD.

Christian Death
YOUR HEAVEN AND HELL

45 GRAVE
AND
MODERN INDUSTRY
$3.50 ADVANCE
$4 Door
Sun. Jan. 4th
7:00 P.M.
NO BOTTLES!
AT ARTS BUILDING
565 POMONA MALL EAST
NEXT TO GOODWILL, ACROSS FROM BUFFUMS
ADVANCE TICKETS ONLY!
AVALIBLE AT TOXIC SHOCK
INFO
623-3050
R. WILLIAMS

Christian Death
AT THE GALLERY
126 E. C St.
ONTARIO
Ph.#986-0077
DEC 22
A CRY FROM HELL
R.WILLIAMS

BLACK MARKET FLOWERS
THURSDAY DEC. 10
DEATHTRAP AT OSKO'S
333 LA CIËNEGA

KRISTIAN HOFFMAN

Sex Gang Children:
THE LAST GANG IN TOWN
Dec 2 Friday
new T.S.O.L.
Minutemen
Butthole Surfers » Texas
GOLDENVOICE presents
Perkins Palace
129 N. Raymond $7.50 advance 8.50 day of
Pasadena
info-line 213-628-4344

WARNING
CONCERT 3
"ALASKA'S ONLY ALTERNATIVE"
featuring:
SPECIMENS
from MINNESOTA
ALSO:
Corrosion
AND
TEN-TEN
9pm till Midnite
BE THERE! (or DON'T)
Sept. 9TH
Live in Anchorage!
ADMISSION $4.50
NO ALCOHOL
ALL AGES ADMITTED
at: Carpenter's Hall
CORNER OF 4TH AVE. & Denali St.

·SEX-GANG·
·CHILDREN·
Dec 10 - 8pm - with Special Guest
LE CARGO 4177 ST. DENIS - TICKETS $8.50
AT UNDERGROUND (372 Sherbrooke W) info-288-0578
$9.00 DUTCHYS & DOOR presented by cinq-FM
produced by ZABO

SPECIMEN

GOLDENVOICE PRESENTS...

EAT'S NITE OUT SUMMER SOLSTICE...

COME HELP DIG 45s GRAVE

PLUS SPECIAL GUESTS. JUNE 22ND

FENDERS BALLROOM

521 E. 1st St. LONG BEACH

INFO LINE: 213-435-2838

TICKETS AVAILABLE AT:

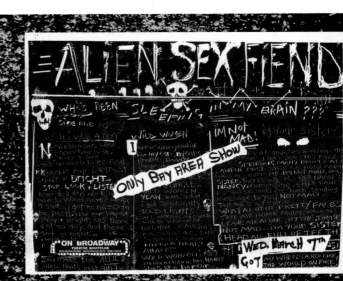

ALIEN SEX FIEND

WHO'S BEEN SLEEPING IN MY BRAIN???

WILD WOMEN

I'M NOT MAD!

ONLY BAY AREA SHOW

ON BROADWAY THEATRE NIGHTCLUB

WED. MARCH 7TH

GOT MY WHEELS A ROLLING THE WORLD ON FIRE

THROBBING GRISTLE
FRIDAY MAY 22
EIGHT O'CLOCK
VETERAN'S
AUDITORIUM
4117 OVERLAND AVE.
ONE MILE EAST OF CULVER BLVD EXIT 405 FREEWAY
$8 00 NOW
$9 00 THERE
CULVER CITY
AVAILABLE AT: MOBY DISC POO-BAH RHINO VINYL FETISH & ZED

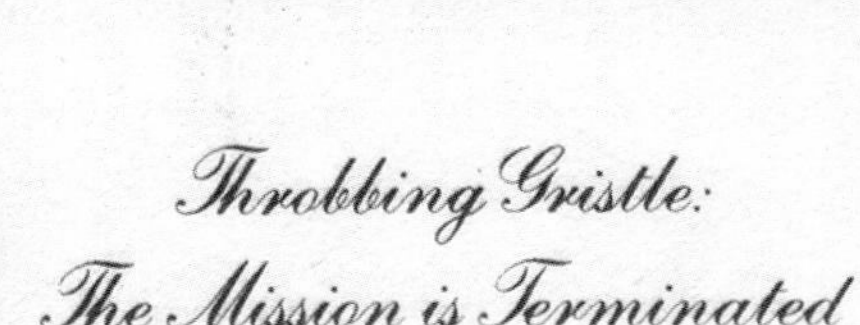
Throbbing Gristle:
The Mission is Terminated

THROBBING GRISTLE LIVE!
VOX POP
The centers of attention
Taken HOSTAGE Tonight!
Evenings with a difference
The pleasure
is back.
EVENT: THROBBING GRISTLE VOX POP NON & SWA LIVE IN CONCERT WITH FILMS
TIMEFIX: Friday MAY 22ND AT 8PM
LOCATION: VETERAN'S AUDITORIUM 4117 OVERLAND AVENUE
ONE MILE EAST OF CULVER BLVD EXIT 405 FREEWAY
CHANGE YOUR LIFE
TG
Unlock the secrets to the biggest mystery of all time!
TICKET PRICES: 8.00 IN ADVANCE 9.50 AT THE DOOR
AVAILABLE AT: MOBY DISC POO-BAH RHINO VINYL FETISH & ZED
ONLY TOTAL STARVATION WORKS FASTER!

Thee Temple ov Psychick Youth exists as a meeting place for those Individuals who find themselves, for one or another reasons, disaffected with Western culture as it is today. T.O.P.Y. advocates a return to thee TRIBE. Modern-HIGH TECH- Shamans. A return to a reverence for thee Earth and all entities/Life Spirits inhabiting it. Our totems, to name butter a few are thee Wolf, thee Coyote, thee Spider. We spin new webs, thee Network, stretching accross vast geographical distance to share information, idears-modern lore. Thee drum, once thee voice ov thee Tribe, gives way to thee coumputer and thee satelite. We look backwards in time, not out ov nostalgia, butter to seek out forgotten ways ov DO-ing Things, ways to help solve thee dilemna that WoMankind has created for HerSelf and Her Kind, Her Home. OUR PLANET.

These Issues are coumplex ones, and thee Temple claims no easy answers. We can offer only one tiny ray ov Hope. If We each can live our Lives as an Example, to show thee Rest ov our species how people COULD live, if they only dared to dream, to have and pursue a Vision, then perhaps others would be inspired to dream again.

We cannot change thee World, only OurSelves. Please join us in our Struggle!

TEMPLE OV PSYCHICK YOUTH
po box 18223 Denver, Co. 80218

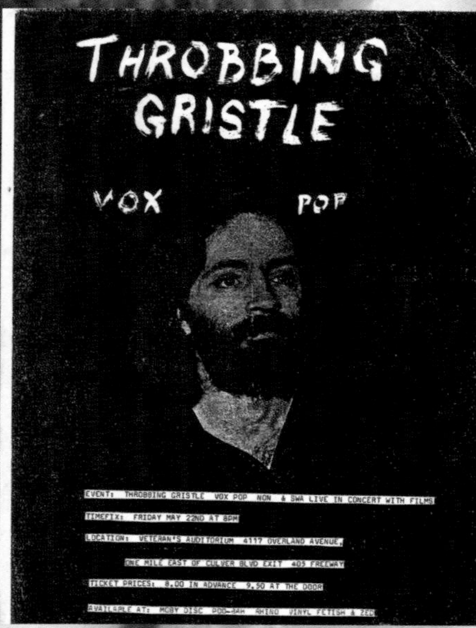
THROBBING GRISTLE
VOX POP
EVENT: THROBBING GRISTLE VOX POP NON & SWA LIVE IN CONCERT WITH FILMS
TIMEFIX: FRIDAY MAY 22ND AT 8PM
LOCATION: VETERAN'S AUDITORIUM 4117 OVERLAND AVENUE
ONE MILE EAST OF CULVER BLVD EXIT 405 FREEWAY
TICKET PRICES: 8.00 IN ADVANCE 9.50 AT THE DOOR

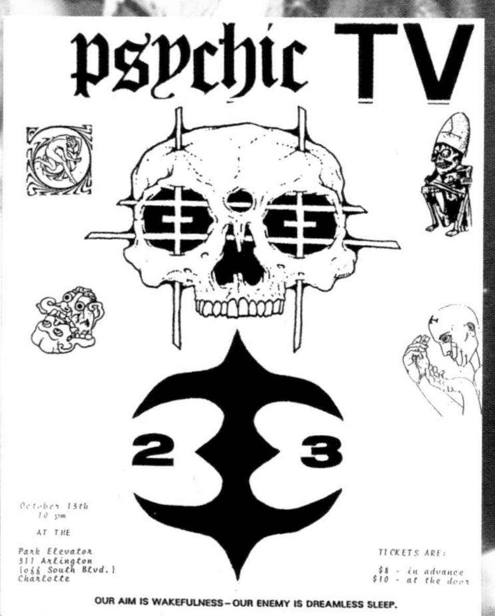
psychic TV
2 3
October 15th
10 pm
AT THE
Park Elevator
311 Arlington
(off South Blvd.)
Charlotte
TICKETS ARE:
$8 - in advance
$10 - at the door
OUR AIM IS WAKEFULNESS—OUR ENEMY IS DREAMLESS SLEEP.

October 19th-26th 1976

SEXUAL TRANSGRESSIONS NO. 5

PROSTITUTION

COUM Transmissions:- Founded 1969. Members (active) Oct 76 - P. Christopherson, Cosey Fanni Tutti, Genesis P-Orridge. Studio in London. Had a kind of manifesto in July/August Studio International 1976. Performed their works in Palais des Beaux Arts, Brussels; Musee d'Art Moderne, Paris; Galleria Borgogna, Milan; A.I.R. Gallery, London; and took part in Arte Inglese Oggi, Milan survey of British Art in 1976. November/December 1976 they perform in Los Angeles Institute of Contemporary Art; Deson Gallery, Chicago; N.A.M.E. Gallery, Chicago and in Canada. This exhibition was prompted as a comment on survival in Britain, and themselves.

2 years have passed since the above photo of Cosey in a magazine inspired this exhibition. Cosey has appeared in 40 magazines now as a deliberate policy. All of these framed form the core of this exhibition. Different ways of seeing and using Cosey with her consent, produced by people unaware of her reasons, as a woman and an artist, for participating. In that sense, pure views. In line with this all the photo documentation shown was taken, unbidden by COUM by people who decided on their own to photograph our actions. How other people saw and recorded us as information. Then there are xeroxes of our press cuttings, media write ups. COUM as raw material. All of them, who are they about and for? The only things here made by COUM are our objects. Things used in actions, intimate (previously private) assemblages made just for us. Everything in the show is for sale at a price, even the people. For us the party on the opening night is the key to our stance, the most important performance. We shall also do a few actions as counterpoint later in the week.

PERFORMANCES: Wed 20th 1pm - Fri 22nd 7pm
Sat 23rd 1pm - Sun 24th 7pm

INSTITUTE OF CONTEMPORARY ARTS LIMITED
NASH HOUSE THE MALL LONDON S.W.1. BOX OFFICE Telephone 01-930-6393

SWANS
DC 3
FRI APR.11
EAGLES
LODGE
$5
RECORDS ALBUM ON NEUTRAL RECORDS
SAT. OCT. 1
SIN CLUB
SAT. OCT. 1
10:00
I like the idea of standing in a room full of sledge hammers. Michael Gira

ALL FLYERS THIS PAGE: GIRA / JARBOE

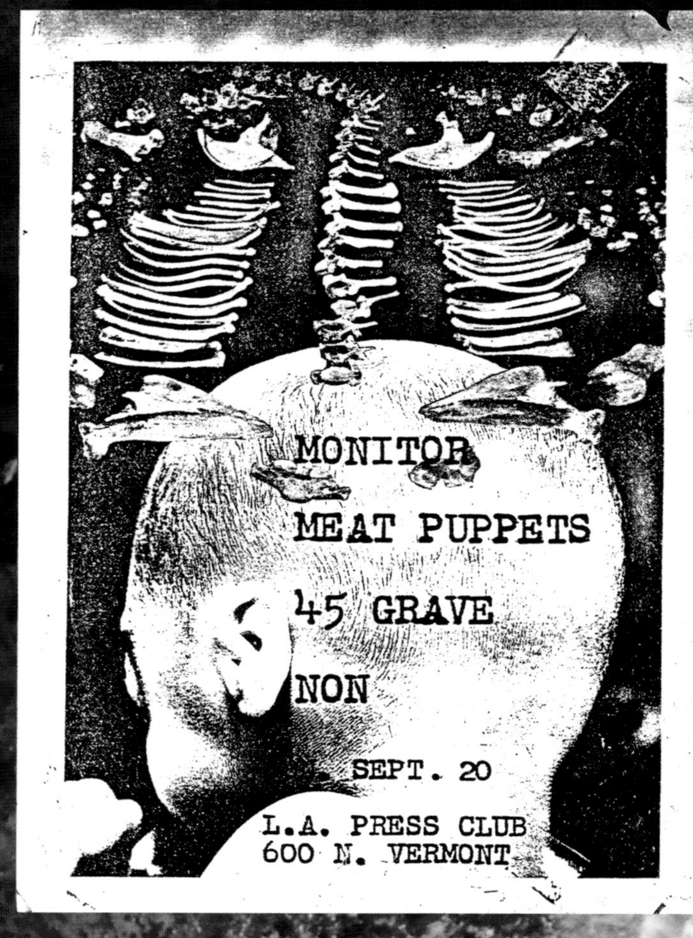
MONITOR
MEAT PUPPETS
45 GRAVE
NON
SEPT. 20
L.A. PRESS CLUB
600 N. VERMONT

DEATH SPEED
HARDCORE THRASH
PRIVATE EYE
112
E. COLLEGE
COVINA
CALL
818
9666581
BANDS
SEND
DEMOS

JEAN MICHEL BASQUIAT
IT'S GONE SOFT/NIL UNPAINT
EGG YOLK?/HARRAS
STINK BOMBS
gray

gray
JEAN MICHEL BASQUIAT

JEAN MICHEL BASQUIAT

XXX OOO

Glenn O'Brien
Suzanne Mallouk
Keith Haring
Arto Lindsay
Jennifer Goode
Nancy Brooks Brody
Fred Brathwaite
Gray: Wayne Clifford, Vincent Gallo,
Michael Holman, Nick Taylor
Roger Guenveur Smith
David Shapiro
Ingrid Sischy
John Lurie

Saturday, November 5, 1988
St. Peter's Church
New York, New York

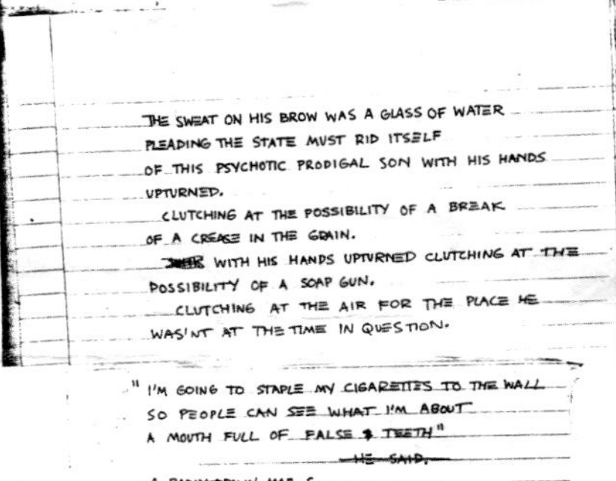

THE SWEAT ON HIS BROW WAS A GLASS OF WATER
PLEADING THE STATE MUST RID ITSELF
OF THIS PSYCHOTIC PRODIGAL SON WITH HIS HANDS
UPTURNED.
CLUTCHING AT THE POSSIBILITY OF A BREAK
OF A CREASE IN THE GRAIN.
~~HER~~ WITH HIS HANDS UPTURNED CLUTCHING AT THE
POSSIBILITY OF A SOAP GUN.
CLUTCHING AT THE AIR FOR THE PLACE HE
WAS'NT AT THE TIME IN QUESTION.

"I'M GOING TO STAPLE MY CIGARETTES TO THE WALL
SO PEOPLE CAN SEE WHAT I'M ABOUT
A MOUTH FULL OF FALSE $ TEETH"
—HE SAID.
A BADLY DRAWN MAP S

NOW THAT THE CIRCUS HAS LEFT TOWN
HE'S A PARKBENCH PHILOSOPHER
AT THE TOP OF HIS LUNGS.

3 AL JOLSONS IN SEPARATE HOTEL ROOMS/

art?
ists?

ART USED ON ORIGINAL 12" NOT CD RE-ISSUE
the Offspring
SCREAM
SCREAM
SCREAM
SCREAM
TIM MAZE AND MAD MARC RUDE PRESENTS
MISFITS
NECROS
SKULLBUSTERS
FRI OCT 8
N.P.L.C.
8PM 6$
SCREAM
SCREAM
SCREAM
SCREAM
MAD MARC RUDE
Something that pisses me off is that 100 or more punks woun't think twice about pushing, shoving, pogoing and kicking each others' ass for fun. But when four bouncers
go ape shit beating their heads in, everyone just looks at them and takes it, no retaliation.
This is war isn't it? We go to the hospital or jail anyway, so why not take a piece of the gorilla with you! -Friends of No One

IRIS BERRY

The first time we met was in June of 1984, it was seven in the morning and I was piled into a van with a bunch of punk rock extras. We were working for Janet Cunningham on a movie called

"Trancers," headed for Al's Bar. I remember Stevo and Mark Munsky were there, and not seeing Marc, but hearing this voice. It sounded way too early, especially before coffee, for this sandpaper New York accent of a voice. I turned to see who it was coming from and saw was a mass of

tattoo's and died black unkempt hair. He had more tattoo's than I'd ever seen on anyone before at that time. During the shoot I was

telling Nicky Beat how I didn't get much sleep because I'd just moved into the living room of Disgraceland and I was awakened at four AM to Tony Alva and Hank the cross-dresser, trying to take off my underwear. Marc butted into our conversation saying "well you should put someone in your bed

to keep that from happening." I just looked at him and said well it's an army cot and I don't think anyone else could fit. I walked away horrified though a little intrigued. A couple of weeks later I was home, it was about 2:30 in the morning and there was a knock at the door. I opened it to find Donny Popejoy screaming "cheers big ears" as he piled in

e house with what must have en all of the Cathay De Grande. ong with the group was Marc ude, and the beginning of a ven year, extremely turbulent ve affair. To know Marc

as amazing. He was funny and rilliant. He loved music and t, and we could talk about em for hours. He also loved to ght. Fighting was Marc's way of onding. His way of communi-cating was very physical and very motional. He was an amazing rtist and his view of the world

showed in his graphic, brutal, beautiful and tortured art. Despite our rocky and tumultuous relationship that ended in 1991, we stayed good friends and pretty much talked everyday. In the early 90's Marc moved back

New York to be with his sister endy. He'd gotten tired of LA d wanted to be with one of the ly remaining family members

e had. Unfortunately, not long fter, his sister was found in a otel room, murdered by a serial iller. Marc had to identify the ody.The last time I saw Marc as at a Greyhound bus station North Hollywood, it was for

alf an hour and we hadn't seen ach other in five years. He was iving in Las Vegas and talked

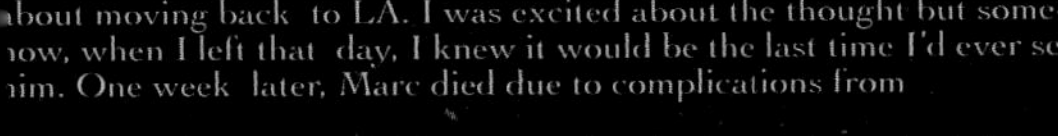

about moving back to LA. I was excited about the thought but somehow, when I left that day, I knew it would be the last time I'd ever see him. One week later, Marc died due to complications from

diabetes at the age of 47. Too young- but that's starting to look like the punk rock life expectancy.

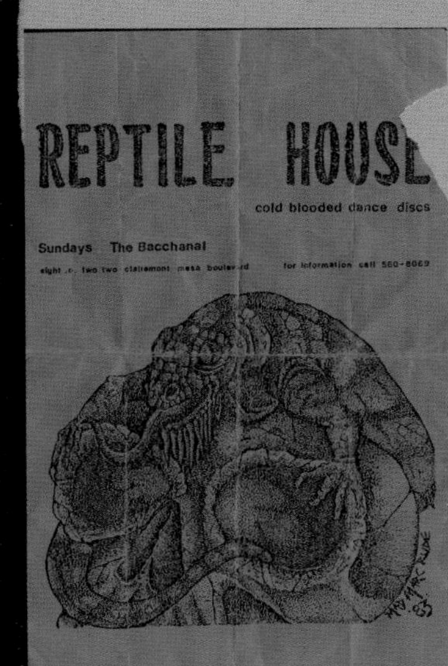
REPTILE HOUSE
cold blooded dance discs
Sundays The Bacchanal

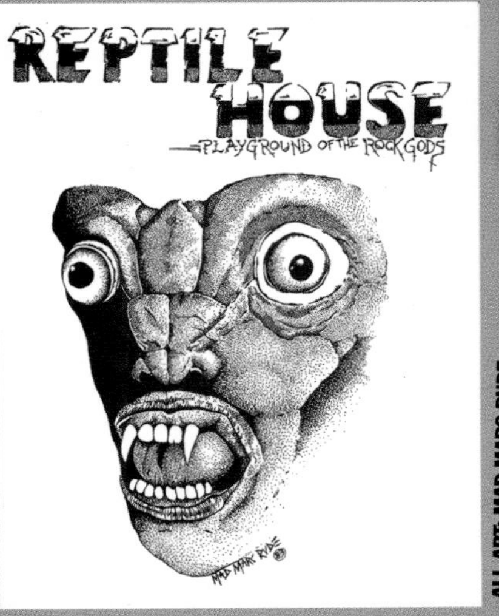
REPTILE HOUSE
PLAYGROUND OF THE ROCK GODS

ALL ART: MAD MARC RUDE

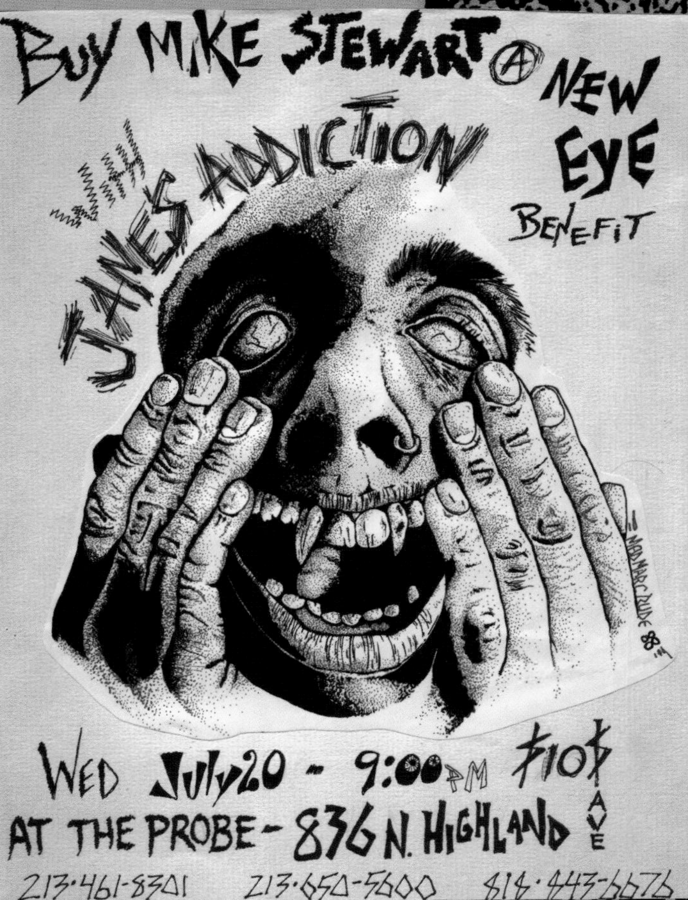
BUY MIKE STEWART A NEW EYE
BENEFIT
WITH JANE'S ADDICTION
WED July 20 - 9:00 PM $10
AT THE PROBE - 836 N. HIGHLAND AVE
213-461-8301 213-650-5600 818-843-6676

EARLY PIECE SIGNED MARC HOFFMAN

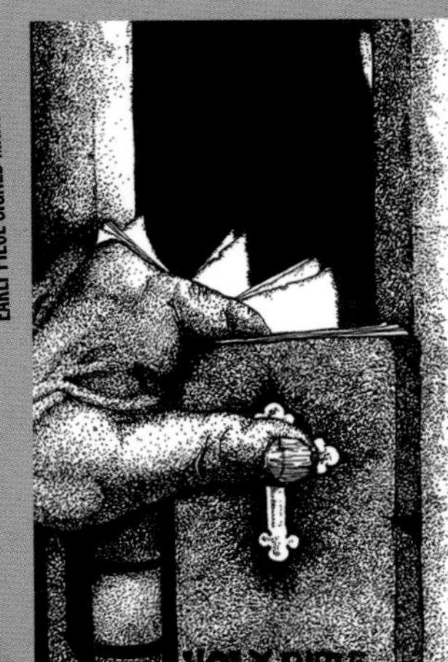
WHEN William HEIRENS WAS 11 YEARS OLD, HE ACCIDENTALLY CAME ACROSS A COUPLE FORNICATING. RELATING THIS TO HIS PURITANICAL MOTHER, THE BOY WAS TOLD "ALL SEX IS DIRTY. IF YOU TOUCH ANYONE YOU GET DISEASE."
SIX YEARS LATER HE TRIED TO OVERCOME HIS HATRED FOR WOMEN BY PETTING A GIRL. HE BROKE OUT IN TEARS IN HER PRESENCE AND VOMITED. HE THEN TOOK TO WEARING LADIES GARMENTS FOR SEXUAL RELEASE WHILE STARING AT PICTURES OF NAZI LEADERS HITLER, GOERING, AND HIMMLER. HEIRENS SEXUAL DESIRES STILL WENT UNFULFILLED.
HE IS NOW SERVING 3 CONSECUTIVE LIFE IMPRISONMENT TERMS FOR THE BRUTAL SLAYING OF 4 FEMALES, ONE OF WHICH WAS 6 YEARS OLD.
HOLY BIBLE

GARY PANTER by BRUCE KALBERG

INVASIÓN DE LOS ELVIS ZOMBIES

POR GARY PANTER

FACETASM

H SIMULATED AND REAL.

GARY PANTER

CHARLES BURNS

G. PANTER
SCREAMERS
WHISKY
JULY 20, 21, 22

RAW
NO. 3
$4.00
G.P.
THE GRAPHIX MAGAZINE THAT LOST ITS FAITH IN NIHILISM

ALL ART: GARY PANTER

SLASH
VOLUME 2 NUMBER 7 AUGUST 1979 ONE DOLLAR • U.K. 80p
SCREAMERS
SCREAMERS
JULY 5•6•7•8
WITH LOUNGE LIZARDS THURS. & SUN.
HURRAH
36 WEST 62ND ST., N.Y.C
THE WORLD DON'T Deserve this good of a MaGazine !!!
ALL ART: GARY PANTER
G.P.
L.A.
GARY PANTER

IF PUNX WOULD ONLY UNITE...
WE COULD DO ANY THING!
NW3

MY BOUT WITH DEPRESSION LASTED 5 CHAMBERS.

PETTIBON by BRUCE KALBERG

WE SURVIVED THE PIT!

P.D

drawing: Raymond Pettibone

RICHARD SANCHEZ

RICHARD SANCHEZ

My attention was captured by images from punk around 79. My brother Chris said punk rockers put razor blades on their jackets so when they danced they would slam into each other and cut each other up. I wanted to see this. I thought how could they dance , cut each other up and come back the next day or next week to do it again? Maybe late 79, 80 a TV show called Fridays had a band on called the Plasmatics that performed and a woman with a Mohawk and electrical tape covering her nipples blew everything I understood (like kiss) away. Wendy o Williams was her name; she smashed to pieces a huge TV set. She drove a school bus into a wall of televisions, drove her car off a bridge. Evil Kneivel had some serious competition.

The symbolism of smashing televisions changed my young mind and started turning the wheels with what she was try to convey. About the same time, my dad took my brothers and I to yum yum doughnuts on Broadway in San Francisco. Walking inside the donut shop, I noticed a commotion going on a couple of doors down. Curious, I wandered over to see what was going on. As I walked up, I noticed the people had bald head, Mohawks, wearing ripped up army fatigues, bandannas on their boots, spiked wristbands, overcoats and leather jackets. I felt I stepped into a comic book or a weird, cool movie. They had strange symbols drawn or painted on their jackets and armbands. I wanted what they had. I was nine years old. A couple of years later I learned that it was the Mabuhay Theater they were standing in front of, a place where some of my favorite punk rock bands played. Summer of 82, the first real punk moved into the neighborhood; he was a couple of years older than me. One day on the corner of my block where I lived I was practicing my ollies on my fairly new uncle wiggle skateboard (the argyle print). He skated up on his vision gator. He said his name was spike. His friends gave him the name 'cause of his jet black flattop hairdo that was spiked with pomade. He had just moved from Orange County. He skated and played drums; his style was that of Shawn Kerri's skank kid. I mean to the t: combat boots, ripped jeans, flannel shirt wrapped around his waist and his sleeves cut off his t-shirt. He said we should build a quarter pipe, I said "cool, let's do it". While building the ramp we listened to this band called Suicidal Tendencies. They were a bunch of cholos. It validated me, because I was Chicano and never heard of other Chicanos who were rockers. We finished building the ramp and spike drew a skull with a gun to his head and out the other side of the skulls head was a mushroom cloud (blowing his brains out). He wrote 'skate or die'. That's when I decided: I was punk.

4ft
CONCRETE
DISCIPLES
KEEP OUT
RICHARD SANCHEZ

VENCIMIENTO
O MUERTE
RICHARD SANCHEZ

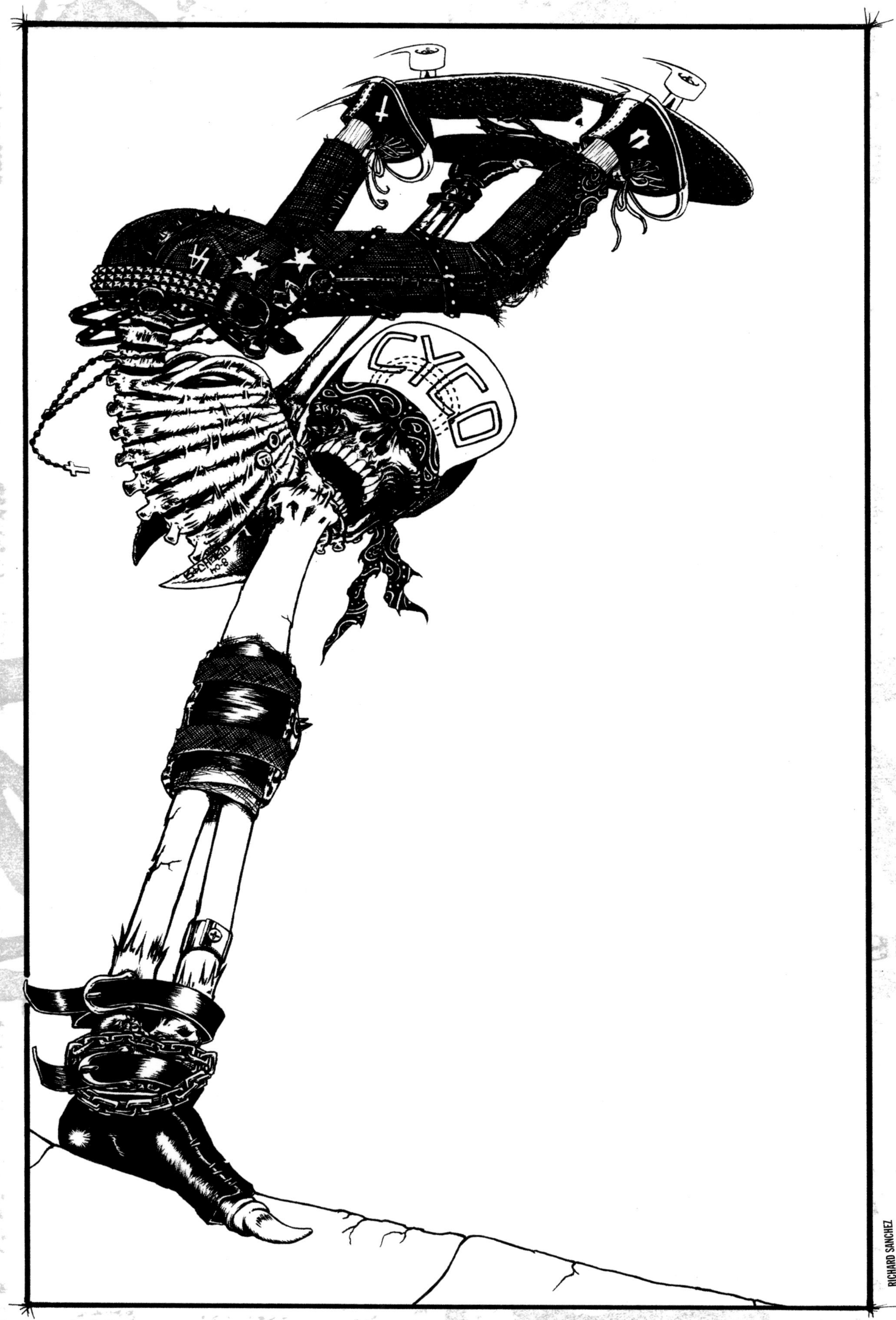
CYCO

RICHARD SANCHEZ

TOXIC SHOCK
for when you're on the rag
TOXIC SHOCK SYNDROME

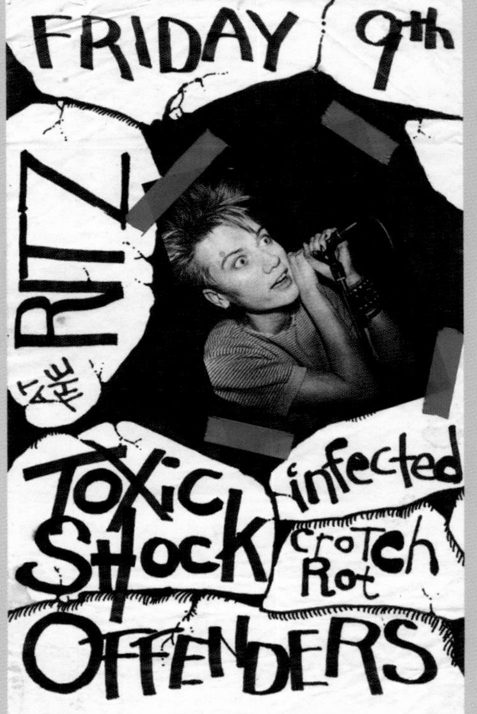
FRIDAY 9th
AT THE RITZ
TOXIC SHOCK
infected
crotch rot
OFFENDERS

DAVID YOW

The first punk show I ever saw was the Huns at Raul's in Austin on Halloween '79. That radically changed my idea of how music should be presented. I could hardly believe the tension, aggression, excitement, honesty, danger, etc., etc. Although I didn't play any instruments, I immediately wanted to be in a punk rock band. My best friend Steve Anderson and I were eating lunch when we saw the first mention of the newly discovered Toxic Shock Syndrome in the

SHARON TATES BABY
'80
YOW

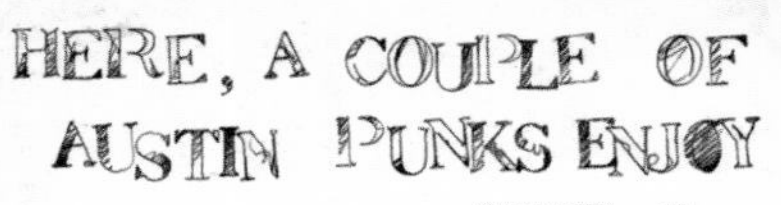
HERE, A COUPLE OF
AUSTIN PUNKS ENJOY
THE SUMMER
OF '68 -
NO doubt THEY recognize them-selves NOW !
THIS HOLIDAY gift to the short HAIRED Hippies - courtesy of
Toxic Shock

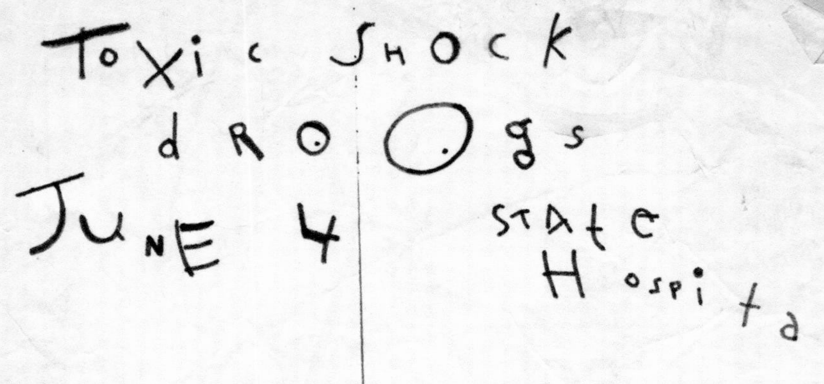
Toxic Shock
droOgs
June 4
State Hospital

WE gotta get outta here!
YOW

TOXIC SHOCK
DICKS
JERRYSKIDS
BUFFALO GALS
SUNDAY WORSHIP SERVICE
KANDS TARTAR IOT
GETID RUN
SAT. MAY 22 RITZ

The
DAMNED
FROM ENGLAND
Offenders
SUN
29
May 1983
SCRATCH ACID
CLUB
Foot

Scratch Acid
JEFFERSONS
HICKOIDS
MASTERS OF DISASTER
VOLTAIRES BASEMENT
FRIDAY THE 13th

ELEVENTH DREAM DAY
and
the JESUS LIZARD
EDGE of the
LOOKING GLASS
62 E.13th St. 939 4017
SATURDAY SEPTEMBER
SIXTEENTH

in THE Near FUTURE

Scratch Acid

THERE'S ONLY
sc ra t ch
ac i d
ONE THAT'S
RADICALLY
DIFFERENT.

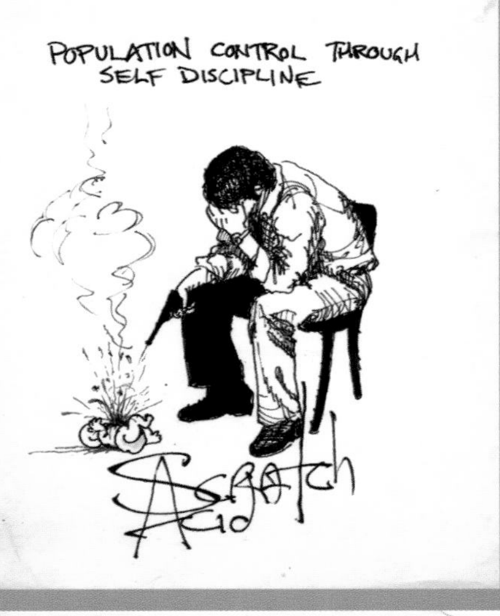

POPULATION CONTROL THROUGH
SELF DISCIPLINE
Scratch Acid

T.S.O.L.
(FROM CALIFORNIA)
Big boys
Butthole Surfers
SCRATCH ACID
THURS. MAR. 10th
AT THE
SKYLINE CLUB
(OLD SOAP CREEK)

I'm going to kill myself. Damn the whole world

SCRATCH ACID
RAGING WOODIES
BARBIES REVENGE
SAT. 15
Bone Club
S.A.

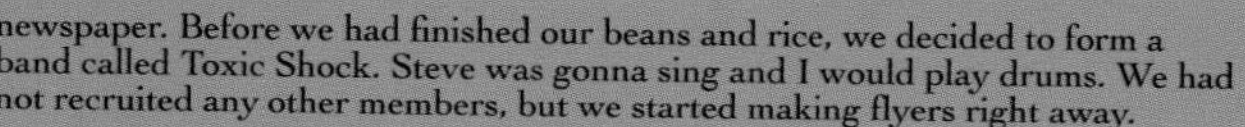

newspaper. Before we had finished our beans and rice, we decided to form a band called Toxic Shock. Steve was gonna sing and I would play drums. We had not recruited any other members, but we started making flyers right away.

Sometimes these flyers (or posters as I called 'em) were to announce the eventual existence of our band, sometimes to comment on social or political issues. They were always meant to offend someone. The telephone poles on the drag by the UT campus served as a gallery for all the punk rock posters that were continuously piling on top of each other. I ended up buying a shitty bass for $40 (that's a LOT of beer money) and we got Brian Flaherty to play drums (too difficult and expensive for me) and Fred Hawkins to play guitar. We had two singers, Steve and my girl friend Karla Eppler. Our first show, opening for the Dicks and the Stains (later MDC), was one of the most fun nights of my life. We even got paid $60! Payment hadn't entered our minds. Shortly after that show, Steve left the band for whatever reasons. Toxic Shock lasted for less than a year, but it seemed like a very long time. I'm not going to bother talking about Scratch Acid, that stuff is much better documented than the Toxic Shock stuff. As well as I can remember, The Jesus Lizard poster, heralding our first real show, is the only one I ever made. That's mostly because once we started playing we were always on tour.

ALL ART ON BOTH PAGES: DAVID YOW

BARKMARKET
At CBGB Thurs... 1/21/88
BARKMARKET
SPONGEHEAD
BLOWTOP
CBGB
THURSDAY
OCT 5
9:30
BARKMARKET
CBGB
THURSDAY
1/21

MARINA ZURKOW

presstype and rubber cement, rubbing at the disconnects between stress and kitsch ...we were making primitive, false theaters out of found materials. the subjects are

alone and cut out, cut off, and doing something violent with their hands. I remember feeling these fliers were kind of timid moves in typography and drawing, but big moves in terms of leaving empty (and in many ways those empty spaces became more anxious than the representations on

the page). and it's weird that even though my own materials have radically changed since then, the sentiment- the human theater of anxiety, pop crap, and isolation

haven't changed all that much although I'm much more cotton candy (and possibly hopeless) about it now.

ALL ART: MARINA ZURKOW

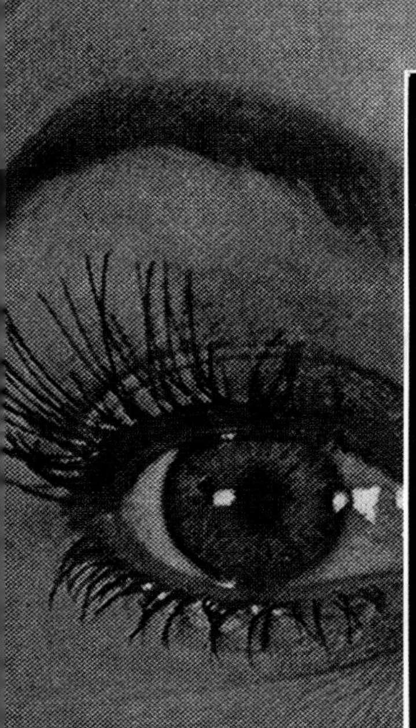

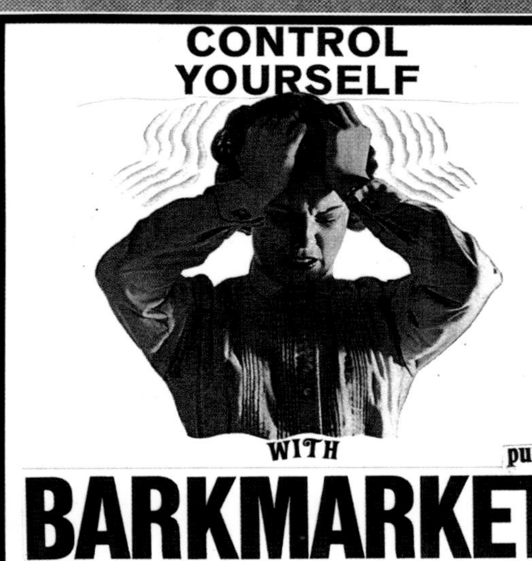

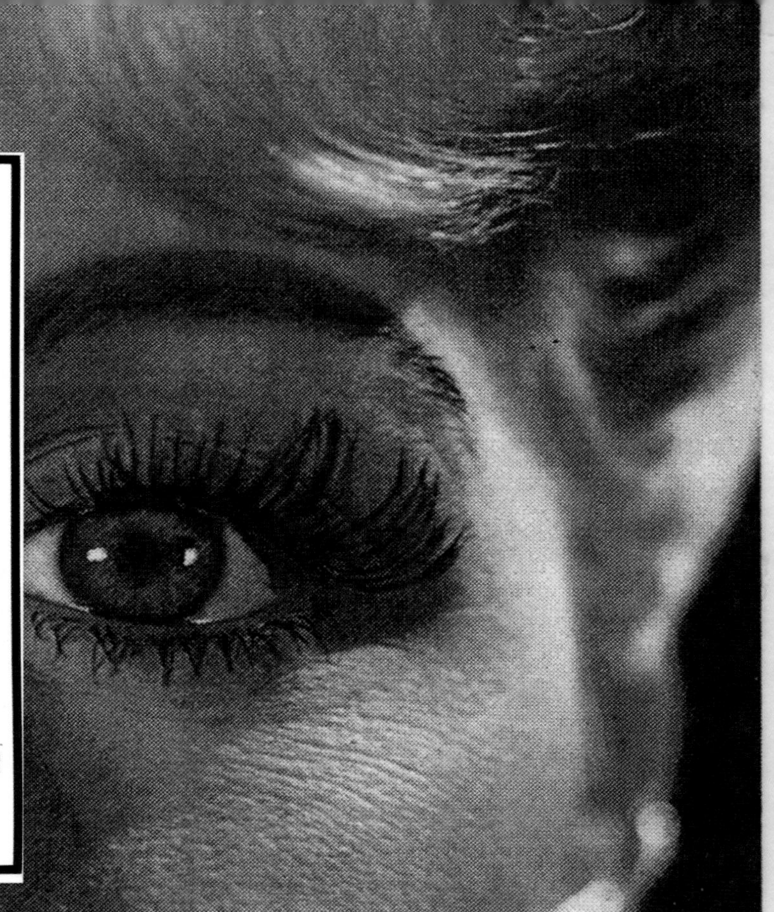

CONTROL YOURSELF

WITH

purge

BARKMARKET,

CAT BUTT, and L-7!

subpop

PYRAMID 101 AVE A

TUESDAY SEPT 19 9:30

BARKMARKET

BARKMARKET

CBGB's THURS. JAN. 21

INTAKE CONTROL
do it.

OPTIONS ON FUTURES
BARKMARKET
AT
CEMENT BEACH
P.S. 122
friday august 21, 9:30pm

Go see
KONTAKT 46
FREITAG_31_MAI
at ZWISCHENFALL
ALTE BAHNHOFSSTR 214
>> BOCHUM LANGENDREER
as special guest of
FLIEHENDE STÜRME
ALL ART ON BOTH PAGES: MATTHIAS GEPHART
Samstag
9.November
2004
Check WWW.KONTAKT46.COM
WWW.THEPHANTOMLIMBS.COM
PAGAN LOVE SONGS PRESENTS
THE PHANTOM LIMBS
AND
KONTAKT 46
WelcomeHOME

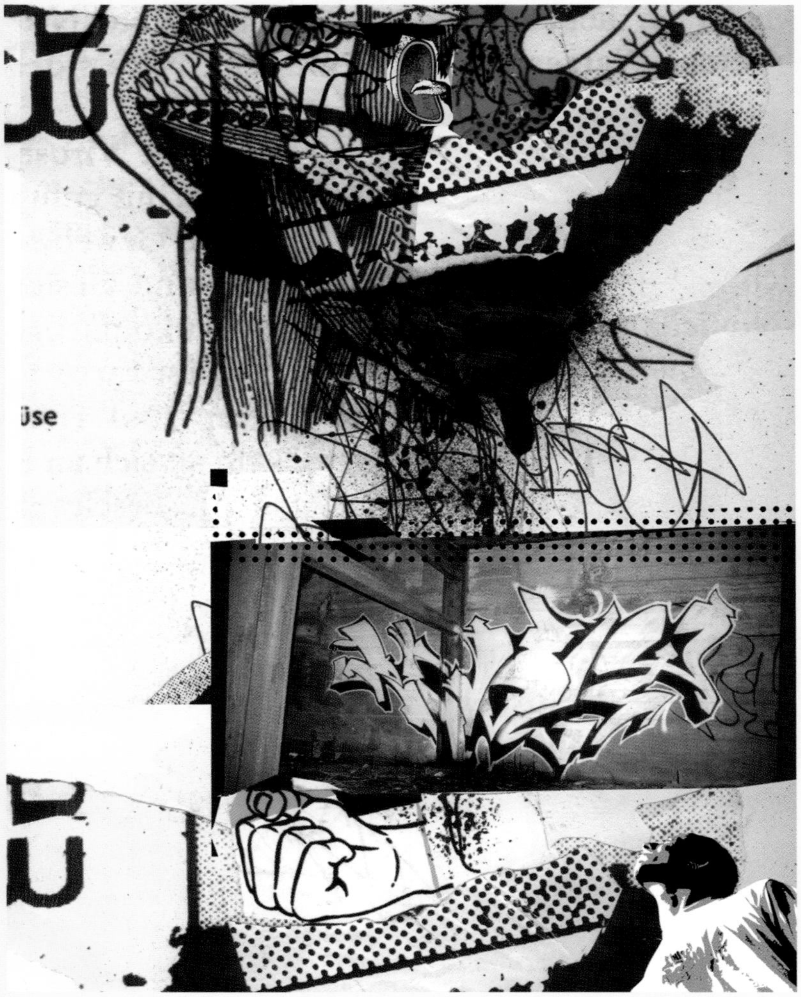

linker Vorhof

MAR K McCOY
was te land,usa

ALL ART: MARK McCOY

Punk is Dead!

The Ramones are dead. Stiv is dead. Darby Crash is Waaay Dead. Your old leather jacket sucks. And your Mohawk REALLY sucks. You might as well be an Old Hippy or a Teddy Boy, or a Goth Tweaker. You are a Dumb Monkey. Your identity is a silly pre packaged look that is now available in malls everywhere. This is true if you are 14 or 44. I don't care and I am not impressed that you are 'old school'. If anything that just means you've been a moron for a longer period of time. If you look at this book and think things were better 'Back In The Day' you never got it in the first place. All over the world there are new generations who want something different and something new. They are playing and creating in bedrooms and basements, identifying as nothing but them selves...moving FORWARD. There is no magic at a reunion show, and there is nothing beautiful about living in the past. Fuck your spinning wheels. I'm in love with today.

CALI DEWITT

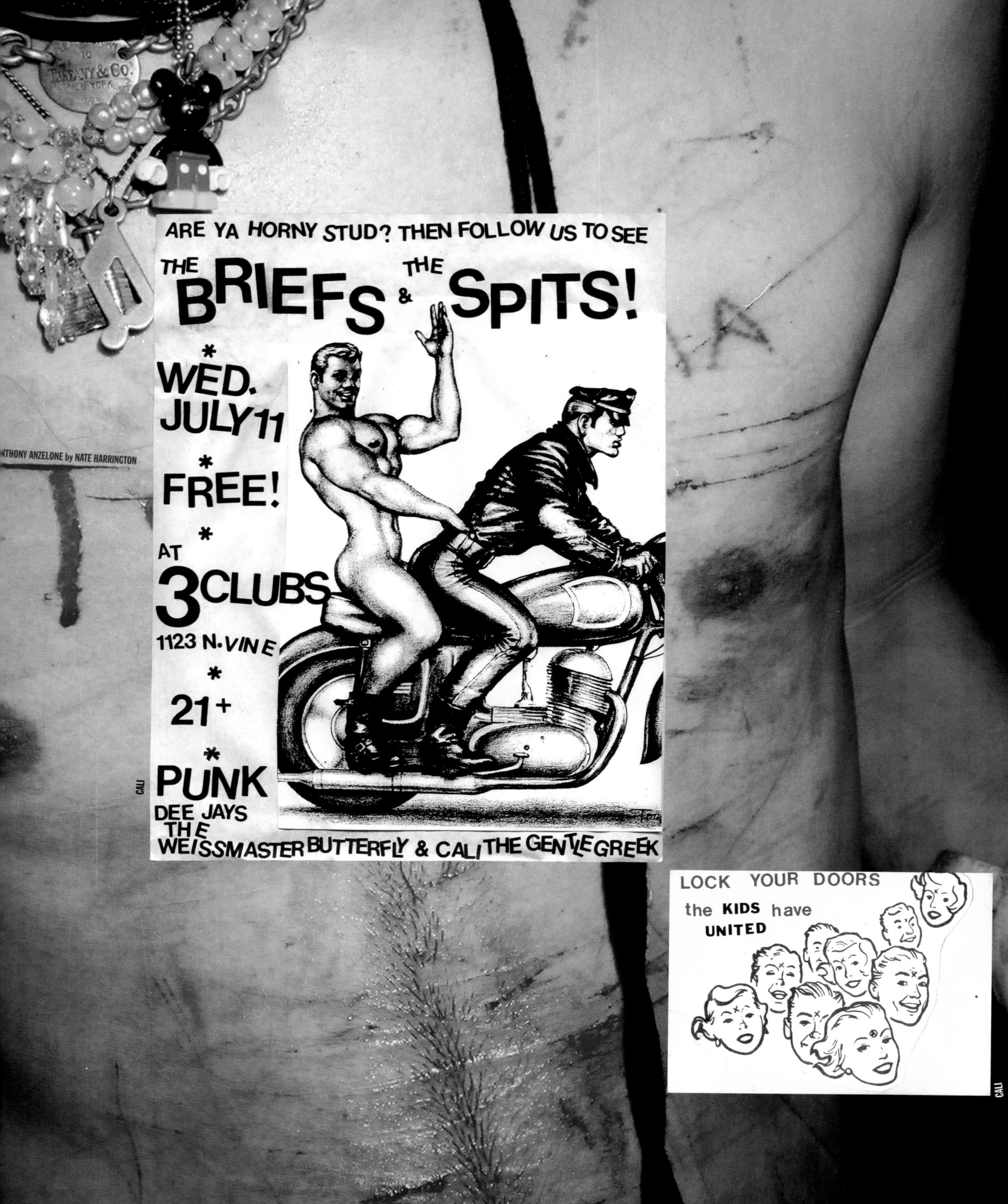

ARE YA HORNY STUD? THEN FOLLOW US TO SEE
THE BRIEFS & THE SPITS!
WED. JULY 11
FREE!
AT 3 CLUBS
1123 N. VINE
21+
PUNK
DEE JAYS THE WEISSMASTER BUTTERFLY & CALI THE GENTLE GREEK
LOCK YOUR DOORS
the KIDS have UNITED

NTHONY ANZELONE by NATE HARRINGTON

CALI

CALI

THE FUSE!
EVERY THURSDAY IN JUNE, SON!
DJ CIAO-WOW
3-CLUBS
LOS VERDADEROS PRESENTA
TRUE LOVE meets the ROCKERS UPTOWN
RROLLING BLACKOUTSSS
ROLLING BLACKOUTS
RROLLING BLACKOUTS
every thursday in may at the 3 clubs
1123vine
+dj baby-man
$free$$
BROADWAYJUNGLE PRESENTS:
I'M GONNA CREAM MY JEANS ...EVERY MONDAY AT 3 CLUBS
10 PM
1123N.VINE
323 462 1446
THE FUSE! 11TH NOV
18TH NOV FLASH EXPRESS
NIGHTHAWK 25TH NOV
2ND DEC THE STARVATIONS
ALSO FEATURING: SUBTITLE AND ADLIB
HOSTED BY: THE REAL CHEIF
NUMBNESS BY: BABY MAN AND THE FLORIDA ROAD DOG
AGGRO

CALI / LUIS FARFAN

CALI / DANIEL HOLDEN

America was not ready, as it seldom is, for these sorts of things.... 3 Hispanic gents, in fitted suits, criss-crossing the country; carrying instruments for musical and dangerous purposes (guitars, drums, throwing knives, wooden bats, an iron, and an ironing board etc.) ....We traveled, as our peers did, in a variety of US made passenger vans with a voluminous amount of illegal drugs hidden in various compartments. It was a beautiful living for four years. We fought our audiences fairly regularly, throwing bottles and bass drums at them, cursing and spitting on them, fighting with security guards, and lastly, with each other.

LUIS FARFAN

CALI / JAMES ROSS

DOWNTOWN LA

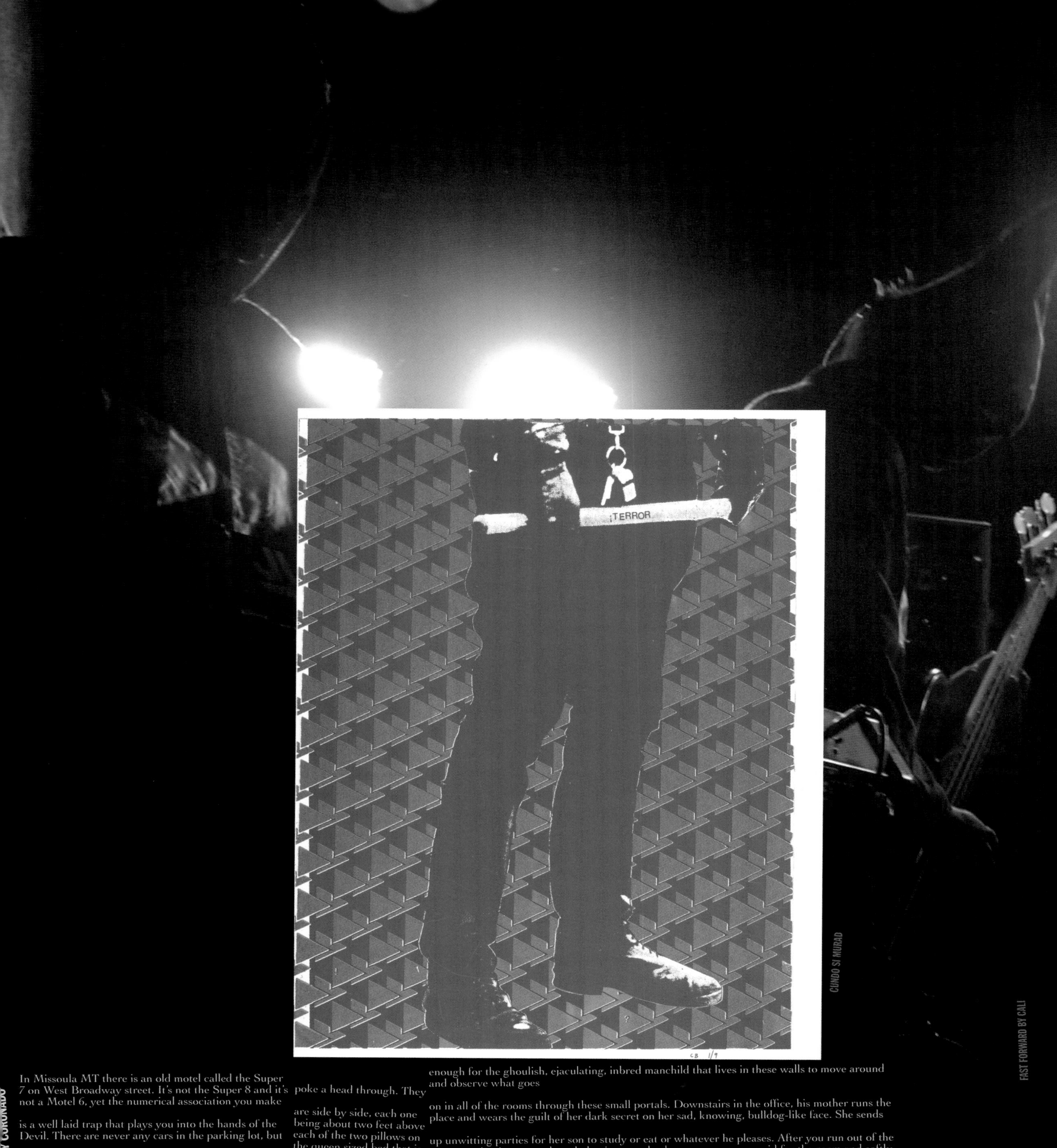
¡TERROR
CB 1/9

CUNDO SI MURAD

FAST FORWARD BY CALI

ANDY CORONADO

In Missoula MT there is an old motel called the Super 7 on West Broadway street. It's not the Super 8 and it's not a Motel 6, yet the numerical association you make

is a well laid trap that plays you into the hands of the Devil. There are never any cars in the parking lot, but

there's never a motel room available except for one.

It's on the 2nd floor, on the upper left hand side of the building, above where the office is. In this room there are many doors on the walls, each one leading to god knows where. Two of these doors are very small and are on one of the walls just above the bed, just big enough to poke a head through. They

are side by side, each one being about two feet above each of the two pillows on the queen sized bed that is

in the room. Behind these small doors is a crawlspace in the wall that is wide enough for the ghoulish, ejaculating, inbred manchild that lives in these walls to move around and observe what goes

on in all of the rooms through these small portals. Downstairs in the office, his mother runs the place and wears the guilt of her dark secret on her sad, knowing, bulldog-like face. She sends

up unwitting parties for her son to study or eat or whatever he pleases. After you run out of the room gasping in terror, she calmly gives you back your money you paid for the room and softly says to you, "I understand", as you try to cram your still-beating heart back into your body through your exploded ribcage. Never the less: it's a great bargain.

HOLY
MOLAR
DENTAL DAMNED TOUR 2002

WITH
L.A. COUNTY'S HIGHLY QUESTIONABLE
NAZTI
SKINZ
&
LOCAL VOKALS FROM BEYOND THE GRAVE
CREEPY CREEPS

POKEZ

10th & E

4
o'clock!
bucks!
the kids!

JANUARY 13th DON'T FLAKE OUT

MARK McCOY

HOLY
MOLAR
&
NAZTI
SKINZ
JAN 12TH
NEON
KING
KONG
3
DOLLARS
AT 8
HEADLINE
RECORDS

MARK McCOY

SATURDAY, JANUARY 2th (free)
holy molar
neon king
kong
the
naZti skinz
appearing
at: headline records
7708 Melrose
323.655-2125

SHAAN OBNEY

Go Naztic!
with
the
Nazti
Skinz
and
25 Suaves
&
Zeek Sheck
@ Nov. 24th
the Smell 247 S Main St Los Angeles

SHAAN OBNEY

BLACK DICE
VERMIN SCUM
WEST COAST TOUR
1999
CONVOCATION
VERMIN SCUM
EX U.O.A./G.U./B.C.D.
OF
AT
ON

SEW UP YOUR PUSSYS AND LOCK UP YOUR COCKS !
ON TOUR
ARAB ON RADAR
PROV.,RI
1999

SEASON'S BEATINGS
with:
RORSCHACH
Born Against
Fri. dec. 28 7pm.
AT: CASTILLO CULTURAL CENTER • 500 GREENWICH ST. 2ND FLR. BTWN SPRING AND CANAL 1 BLOCK W. OF HUDSON. FOR INFO: ANDREW-(212-233-8606) AFTER 12/17. ALSO-SUBZERO, EYE FOR AN EYE 3RD DEGREE, BAD TRIP. $6 DAMAGES
Born Against
HUASIPUNGO
•CRINGER
•CITIZEN FISH
ABC NO RIO APRIL 20, 1991. A.D.
Damages: $5 all ages always... buy stupid bullshit slit your wrists and jump off a bridge because joe hardcore does, don't come to our show.
Born Against
VOICE OF REASON
suiciety
SAY IT.
SUNDAY FEB. 2 8:00 COMMON GROUND ALL AGES (ALWAYS) $5
Born Against
ALSO RORSCHACH and BIG GULP ABC NO RIO april 14 3:30
Born Against
FEMALE MINK $2299
ABC NO RIO JUNE 9TH A.D. 1990. SATURDAY MATINEE
WOMEN ARE NOT PREY ANIMALS ARE NOT PREY WOMEN ARE NOT MEAT ANIMALS ARE NOT MEAT FUCK OFF.
be part of the scene, not just the scenery
friday, JULY 5 7:00 pm
INFEST
new york's Born Against
new jersey's RORSCHACH
HEROIN
CROSSED OUT
CHE CAFE

SAN MCPHEETERS

Flyers! What fun. An interesting thing about the 1990's; show flyers from this decade sucked less as a result of changing technology – cleaner copiers, laser printers, grey-scale scanners, scalable fonts – than from artistic precedent. The good punk flyers had been done by 1990. And it became harder to shock people. I find these Born Against flyers shocking, but not for the right reasons. The gay porn concept had been done much better, in Texas and San Francisco, ten years earlier. And why use someone else's art?

What, we couldn't have just drawn our own gay porn? How hard can it be? The 'Seasons Beatings' flyer really makes me cringe. I have a bad feeling I'm going to be meeting this guy in the afterlife, and he's not going to be pleased to see me. Who can blame him? You get beaten to death on a crowded street corner and some whiney college boys from New Jersey use a photo of your corpse to advertise their band? What the fuck is that? Oops. Sorry, guy. Sorry, world.

JUSTIN PEARSON

this was the best show i had ever been to. all the bands shreded beyond belief. the funny part was that i had just gotten chicken pocks and i was not about to miss this event. so alas, i went to the show and returned with chicken pocks.so did 2 friends of mine. oops.

PHOTO: RICH UNHOCH

WRANGLER
BRUTES

ANDY CORONADO

WRANGLER BRUTES by NATE HARRINGTON

WRANGLER BRUTES
SPRING IS IN THE AIR

ANDY CORONADO

WRANGLER
BRUTES
LOS ANGELES
APPEARING AT:

WRANGLER
BRUTES

ANDY CORONADO

On the ghetto streets of Coronado, San Diego, you gotta use your head to survive. You turn down the wrong alley

at night and you've got a sharpened tennis racket jammed into your gut. Take a chance stepping onto the wrong golf course and take a 110 MPH Titleist right in the skull. A lonely, pale,

dreadlocked warlord; my wits and my fists kept me alive, hardcore kept me going. I earned my fake last name the hard way, and I carry the scars to prove it. Listen and hear the brutal

agony and suffering, it is a portal into what I have seen.

ANDY CORONADO

WRANGLER BRUTES
OAKLAND CASTRATION
9/12/03

L.A.'s
WRANGLER BRUTES

ANDY CORONADO

WRANGLER BRUTES
--LIVE IN SAN DIEGO--
IT'S A MIRACLE!
w/ GODDAMN INSSEIN + MANN IKEN PIS
MUSE 7/13 2003

ANDY CORONADO

WLANGREL BLUTES
JUNE 8
VEGAN EXPLESS

ANDY CORONADO

WRANGLER BRUTES
AT Q-TOPIA JANUARY 20, 2004 $5

WRANGLER BRUTES by NATE HARRINGTON

At one point, years ago, Kinko's had used copy keys to keep track of how many copies one might make. Also at this point, people discovered that you could just take keys and make them your very own i.e. lift them. I was all over this, especially since everyone knows if your band is doing what, well bands have always done, you never made money. Also, so many half assed flyers would surface for shows that needed people to pay attention to. For a period of time I was booking a lot of shows at my house as well as the Che Café. So this method of promoting shows and events came routine for most of my comrades as well as myself. This all changed after a good buddy of mine. Kent McClard, was busted for this very thing. See, entering a Kinko's with one of their copy keys and scamming copies the way we did was legally viewed as robbery. So forget being charged with shoplifting, this was something a bit more serious for free flyers. For me, I have had my share of shoplifting escapades gone wrong. I sure the hell could not afford to get nabbed by some shit worker that was for some reason interested in becoming a hero for minimum wage pay. One specific time, I went in for the graveyard shift since things were way easier to get away with. So there I was copying and copying. I had at least 3,000 copies in my backpack at this one point. My personal copy key was registering some insane amount of copies made to where it was restarting and not making sense at all. The Kinko's key that I had used which would be what I would end up paying for said something like 4. It was beautiful until I noticed some people out front that I knew. One of them was this guy who I had a falling out with. Shortly after seeing them, his pal came in and was approaching me with this look as if he has a very specific agenda. I later found out from one of the dumb twins who had been dating this rival had paid the guy who was approaching me $20 to beat me up. Not sure if he could have done the job, but I was not about to go to jail for all the crap that I had in my bag. So I opted to go over to the desk where the employees were ? Working? I ended up waking one and tried to small talk With him about copying techniques, job opportunities, math, and whatever

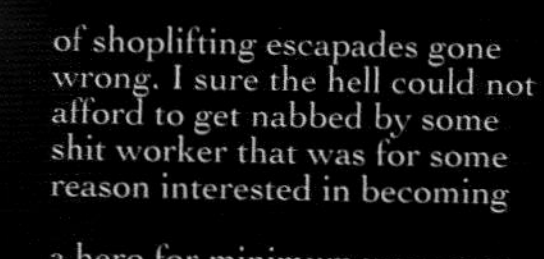

THE DILLINGER ESCAPE PLAN
THE LOCUST
YOUR ENEMIES FRIENDS
THE OATH
MONDAY JAN 26 2004
AT BABYLON
ALL AGES AND LICENSED
DOORS AT 6:30 PM
15 DOLLARS
TICKETS AT

THE LOCUST.
WAIFLE.
COMBAT WOUNDED VETERAN.
THE CHAIN LINK DISASTER.
THURSDAY.
JULY 12.
9pm-$6.
ALL AGES!!!
THE ORPHEUM

SUNDAY JULY 27
THE LOCUST
THE CHINESE STARS
RAH BRAHS
NEON HUNK
ALLAGES 5PM DOORS $10
THE TRIPLE ROCK
MINNEAPOLIS, MN
DWITT

DWITT

JULY 23RD
THE LOCUST
ARAB ON RADAR
LIGHTNING BOLT
QUINTRON
RAH BRAS
"OOPS" THE TOUR
ALL AGES
9PM
$10-12
at: the ORPHEUM
1902 REPUBLICA DE CUBA YBOR CITY

else to buy time to get this chump that had issues to split. At one point me and two employees went to the self-service copiers and I proceeded to show them how I was using different color inks to make 3D images with their copiers. I also showed them the way my copies were turning out on the paper that I had spray painted silver and gold. The best part about that was by running the spray painted paper through the copiers, eventually they broke. The employees not only noticed my excessive amount of copies in my possession, but they noticed this guy waiting for assistance, who was really just looking to sock me in the face. So insert a bit more confusion and the needed sleep that everyone involved needed, then the tough guy leaving for the fact that this was going on forever, I got out of the damn Kinko's without paying a cent and no sucker punch to the face.

8p.m.
A NIGHT OF mayhem
NOVEMBER 21st
THE LOCUST
VOLUME ELEVEN
RUN FOR YOUR FUCKING LIFE
TARANTULA HAWK
LABRADOR
ON THE CORNER OF UNION & BEACH IN SCENIC DOWNTOWN SAN DIEGO!

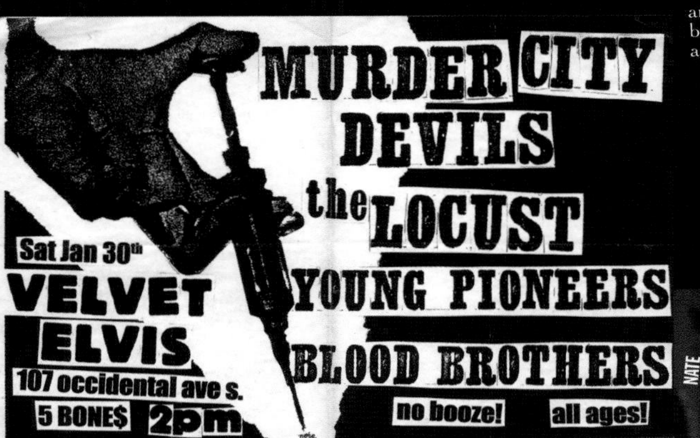
MURDER CITY DEVILS
the LOCUST
YOUNG PIONEERS
BLOOD BROTHERS
Sat Jan 30th
VELVET ELVIS
107 occidental ave s.
5 BONE$
2pm
no booze!
all ages!

NATE

JUNE 2
BRYCEHOUS

SPENCER EELLS MOODY

At age thirty I found myself moving back to Seattle...my tail between my legs...broke...defeated...a six year relationship ending. Living with my mom for the first time in 13 years... it was depressing...but not without hope. My mom had prepared for me...she decorated. You see, earlier in my life...when i was in

the Murder City Devils...we would tour around a lot...and people would often make big colorful silk-screened posters to advertise

our shows. At that time I had always wanted to be in a band with the 'big posters'...and by the end our band had about 100 pounds of them. Seriously I couldn't look at them... but I couldn't throw them out. When I left Seattle they ended up in two huge rolls in the basement at my moms...representing some

thing I hadn't figured out. I can sometimes look back on them with pleasure... but am

happy to leave that in the past. So anyway the point is...I came home and two of thes

fucking posters were framed and up in th house...one by the stairs leading to my roo in the basement and one in my room itself The one in the stairway stayed up...the on in my room came down in the middle of

the night. I turned it backwards and stuck it behind the bed. The next day I got up and went to Kinko's and made a shitty bu awesome flyer for my current band. I wa starting to feel better.

3 CHANCES TO GET BLOWN
LIMP WRIST
DEC. 7TH WATSONVILLE
W/ OUTRAGED, HOSTILE TAKEOVER, ROSENBOMBS
DEC. 8TH FUCKING S.F. EAGLE
W/ MODERN PROBLEMS, SCREAM CLUB
DEC. 9TH
BURNT RAMEN, RICHMOND, CA
STRUNG UP, DEADFALL, SUBURBAN DEATHCAMP

LIMP WRIST by NATE HARRINGTON

Murder City Devils
The SHOCK
Jan.10
the pch club
1832 pacific coast highway on the corner of alameda

LOS CRUDOS
Fields Lay Fallow
Fifth Hour Hero
MK-Ultra
My Lai
Wednesday, July 29th 7:00 PM
At The Living Room
6950 Los Carneros
$5
info:
(805) 964-6111

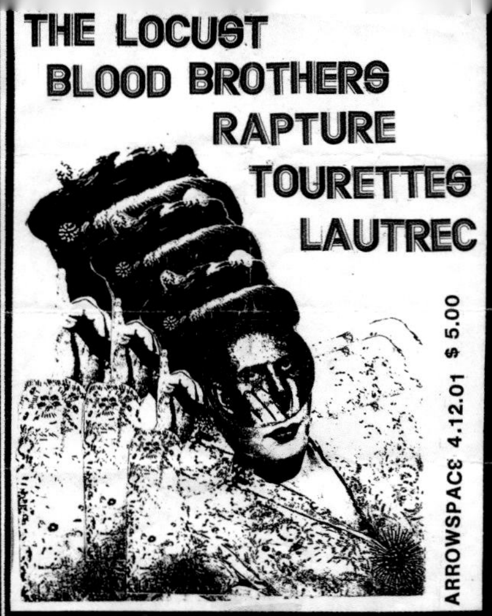

THE LOCUST
BLOOD BROTHERS
RAPTURE
TOURETTES
LAUTREC
ARROWSPACE 4.12.01 $ 5.00

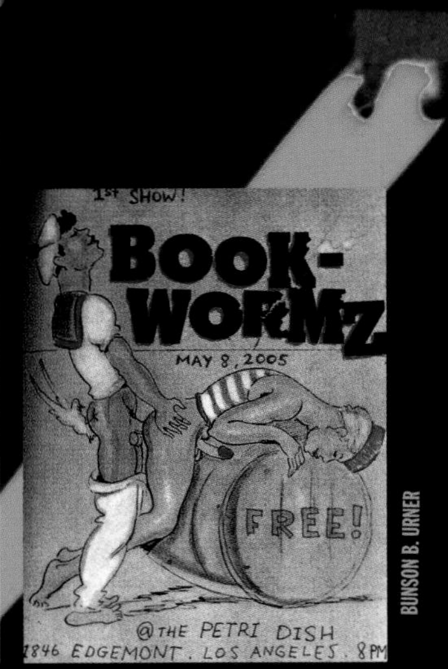

1st SHOW!
BOOK-WORMZ
MAY 8, 2005
FREE!
@THE PETRI DISH
1846 EDGEMONT, LOS ANGELES, 8PM

BUNSON B. URNER

JUSTIN PEARSON

THE VSS
SPANAKORZO
jenny piccolo
nuzzle
THE CRIMSON CURSE
SATURDAY NOVEMBER 30TH
AT THE CHE CAFE
UCSD CAMPUS
6195342311
FIVE DOLLARS
EIGHT P.M.

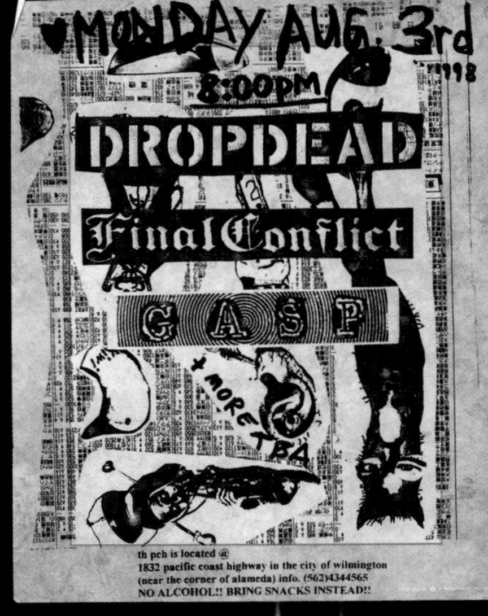

MONDAY AUG. 3rd 1998
8:00PM
DROPDEAD
Final Conflict
GASP
+ MORE TBA
th pch is located @
1832 pacific coast highway in the city of wilmington
(near the corner of alameda) info. (562)4344565
NO ALCOHOL!! BRING SNACKS INSTEAD!!

REFUSED
THE LOCUST
FRODUS
THE TRUTH MOVEMENT
THE DUSTERS

JUSTIN PEARSON

MIKE OTT

Kids started ripping décor off the walls, kicking tables and chairs over, stealing equipment and anything they could get their hands on, two kids at one point even teamed up and carried out some monitors that belonged to the club right out the back door. From there things just got worse, someone spit in the club owners face, someone else punched a fat kid in the nose, club merchandise was stolen and broken to pieces. It was complete and utter destruction. Hours later I stood looking at all the debris that littered the venue, someone at the club came up to me and said, "Sorry your show didn't work out."

August 8th and 9th 1997
Hopscotch Records Festival
HIS HERO IS GONE
THE YAHMOS
MAN IS THE BASTARD
APEFACE
BEHEAD THE PROPHET
GOB
GASP
FUCKFACE
HICKEY
DEAD BODIES EVERYWHERE
CATTLE DECAPITATION
SCALP LOCK
LOS DIABLETOS
SOUL SYSTEM BLACKOUT
aug 8th in san diego
aug 9th at THE HOUSE on 6th and Revolution in TIAJUANA
less than five minutes walking distance from the border
for more info and an update on who is playing
call (805) 255-2214

Saturday, November 16th
At The Impala Cafe, Los Angeles
418 E. 1st Street, downtown L.A.
(213) 621-2170
Show starts promptly at 7pm
$5 and All Ages
WEST COAST HARDCORE CARTEL IN FULL EFFECT
SPAZZ
INCREDIBLE KUNG-FU CRACK ATTACK
lack of interest
GASP
BAD ACID TRIP

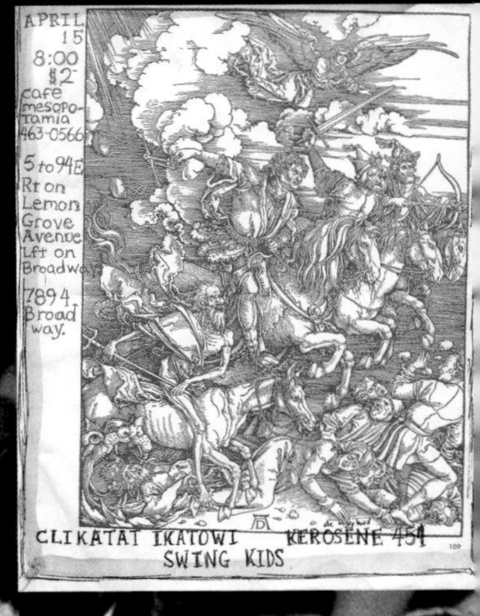

APRIL 15
8:00
$2
cafe mesopotamia
463-0566
5 to 94E
Rt on Lemon Grove Avenue
Lft on Broadway
7894 Broadway.
CLIKATAT IKATOWI
KEROSENE 454
SWING KIDS

CLIKATAT IKATOWI
MAN IS THE BASTARD
THE VSS
SATURDAY - MAY 18...
$5- 9pm - the Huntington Beach Library 7111 Talbert
information 714.509.0407

NATE HARRINGTON

When asked to write something for this book, the book you are holding in your hands right now, I first declined. But why would anyone turn down the chance to have their words forever cemented in such a prestigious book of punk history? I'll tell you why. I was born in 1985. I never saw Television at Max's Kansas City when Richard Hell was still in the band. I never saw Screamers and Crime at the Masque and I never ever saw Void play a Rec center to 50 kids in Washington, DC. I don't feel that I've accomplished or seen enough of anything that constitutes a space in this book reserved for the text you are readin Someone fairly recently told me in regards to me photographing the music and people around me "Keep documenting as much as you can because in 20 years yo never know, all of this could be really important." I don't much care to think about that kind of stuff right now. I'm 20 years old and as far as I'm concerned my life has just begun. You should have

JAN 13th 10PM
• THE SOULESS SOUNDS OF
DEATH DISCO.
FEATURING:
DJ MAX G
DJ HOWIE PYRO
SPECIAL GUESTS:
NEON KING KONG
AT 3 of CLUBS
1123 N. VINE ST
323 4626441
CHEAPER THAN YO MUTHA!
FREE
FLYER BY AGGRO

AGGRO / MAX GINNIS / SKULL BUDDY

THE MIGHTY HARRISON HAYNES

ERNESTO / LIFES HALT

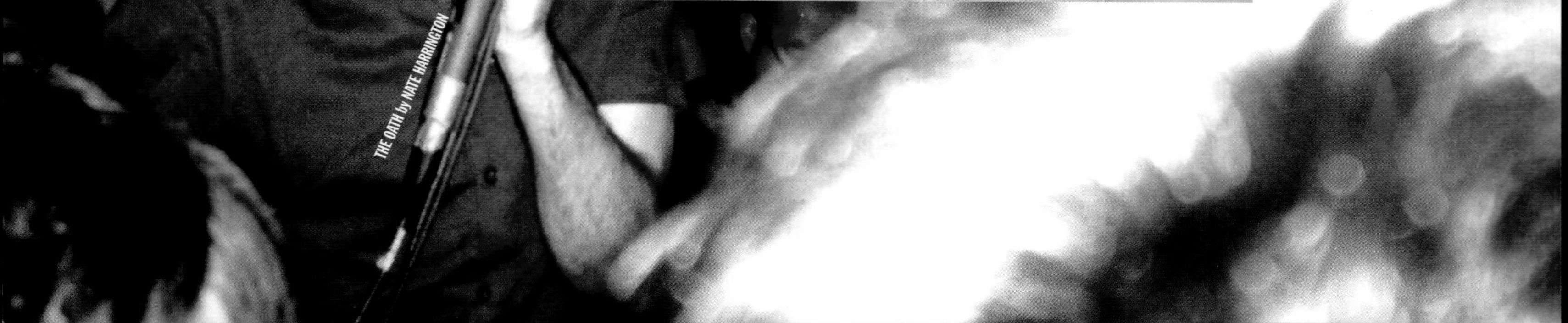

THE OATH by NATE HARRINGTON

...ed Brian Degraw to write
...ething instead of me, he
...d at the Embassy house
...n Nation of Ulysses.

CHRIS THOMSON

It doesn't make much sense. Most truly cool things never do. There is something about an 8 1/2 x 11 sheet of paper that makes it the perfect medium for announcing a live show. What is it about a Xeroxed piece of astro bright paper with uneven press type and ____________ < insert graphic iconography here (I always liked using Skulls) that legitimized a show. It didn't matter that it was taking place in an unfinished basement of a Punk Squat House or a Church Community Hall filled with fluorescent lights and folding chairs. Flyers made them real. The good ones always gave you a hint of what sub-genre of the under ground music you were in for based on the style of art used, be it Weird Art Damage, Speed Metal, Drunk Punk or Hardcore. Sometimes they all ended up on the same bill. I suppose it was foolish of me to think that a randomly placed flyer, positioned near a bus stop frequented by high school kids, was going to attract anyone. I could only hope that people saw them the way I do, like perfect 8 1/2 x 11 treasure maps hiding in plain sight. For those of us who know how to decipher them, they will always lead you some place worthwhile.

JUSTIN PEARSON

THE VSS
T TAURI
HEAT
THE FESTIVAL OF DEAD DEER
LIVE AT THE CHE CAFE
MONDAY MAY 5th
8 pm
5 DOLLARS

FREE SHOW
BLACK FORK
THE CRIMINALS
DEATH WISH KIDS
HALF EMPTY
PISS JAR
AT THE GENOA ST. HOUSE
SEP. 9th
OAKLAND
2 P.M.

skull control
at:

MEN'S RECOVERY PROJECT
ONE NIGHT ONLY
W/SPECIAL GUESTS
THE LOCUST
SLEESTAK
FAST FORWARD
JULY 13, 2000
@ GAUCHOS
8TH & VALENCIA, LA
213 989 0740
1417 W 8th st

MARCH 2ND
THESE FINE BANDS WILL PLAY:
BLACK FORK
THE CRIMINALS
DEATH WISH KIDS
FROM SEATTLE
HALF EMPTY
IN BERKELEY AT THE
CHATEAU
ALL AGES ALL FUN
STARTS AT 8 o'clock
3 BUX
OFF OF TELEGRAPH ON HILLEGRASS

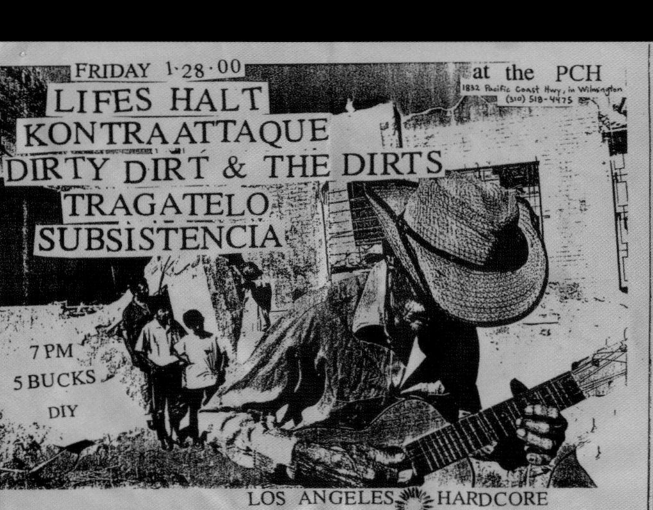

FRIDAY 1·28·00
at the PCH
1832 Pacific Coast Hwy, in Wilmington
(310) 518-4475
LIFES HALT
KONTRA ATTAQUE
DIRTY DIRT & THE DIRTS
TRAGATELO
SUBSISTENCIA
7 PM
5 BUCKS
DIY
LOS ANGELES HARDCORE

THE CATHETERS
IM GONNA STAB YOU
THE YOYOS
JULY 9 · 8PM
PCH. WILMINGTON
310 518-4475

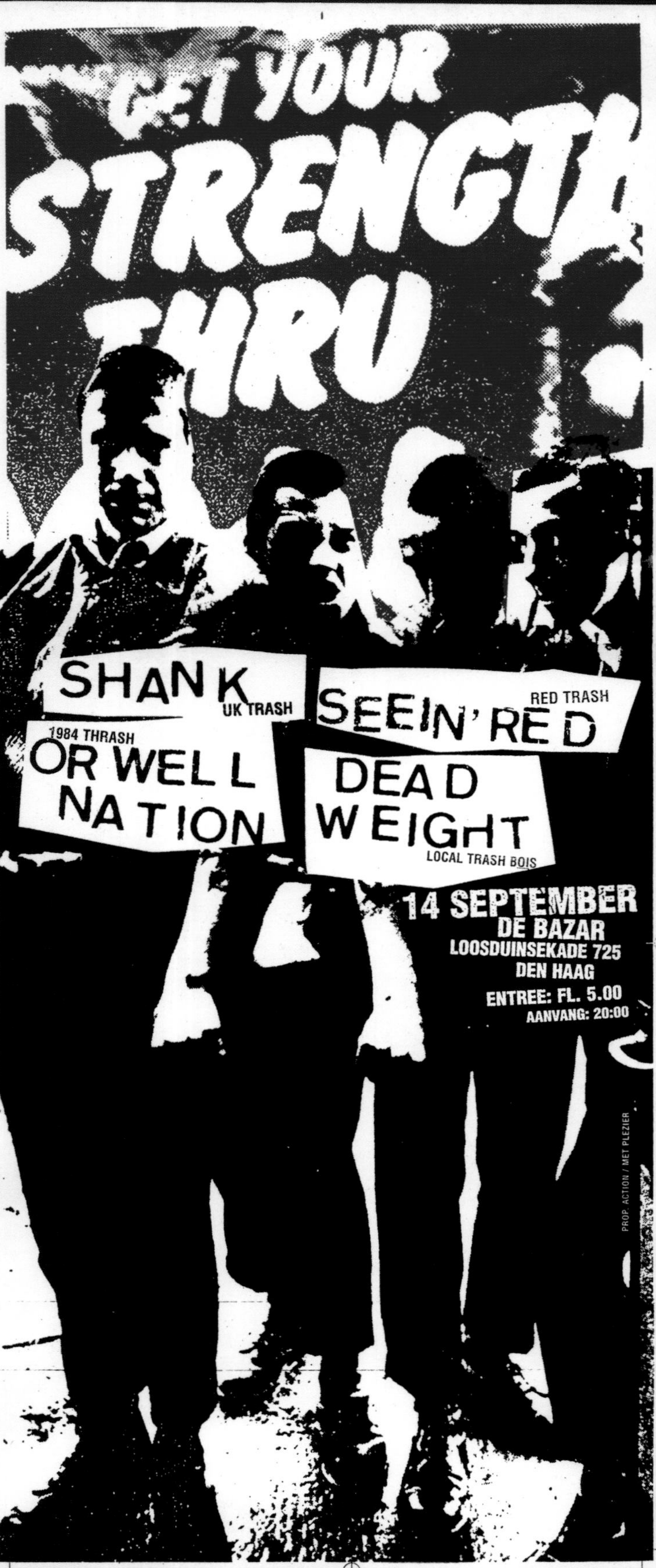

GET YOUR STRENGTH THRU

SHANK
UK TRASH

SEEIN' RED
RED TRASH

1984 THRASH
ORWELL NATION

DEAD WEIGHT
LOCAL TRASH BOIS

14 SEPTEMBER
DE BAZAR
LOOSDUINSEKADE 725
DEN HAAG
ENTREE: FL. 5.00
AANVANG: 20:00

PROP. ACTION / MET PLEZIER

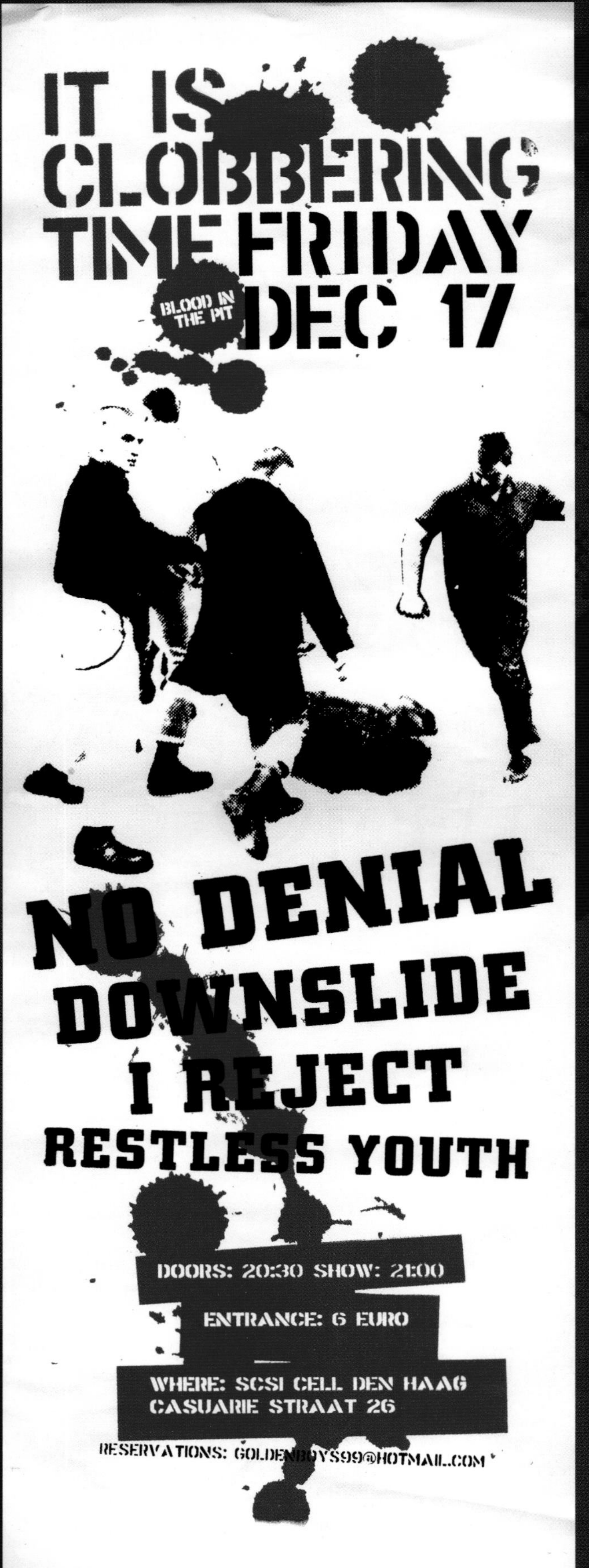

IT IS CLOBBERING TIME FRIDAY DEC 17

BLOOD IN THE PIT

NO DENIAL
DOWNSLIDE
I REJECT
RESTLESS YOUTH

DOORS: 20:30 SHOW: 21:00

ENTRANCE: 6 EURO

WHERE: SCSI CELL DEN HAAG
CASUARIE STRAAT 26

RESERVATIONS: GOLDENBOYS99@HOTMAIL.COM

JEROEN VRIJHOEF A.K.A. PAPA BEAR

September 2001, Das Oath once again went on a sewer safari (a.k.a. tour) through Europe. This time our partners in crime were our friends in The Locust. The setting of this story was a small punk rock venue in Gothenborg, Sweden. About 200 punks, weirdos and retards gathered in small club in the city centre. Some of the kids at the show were wearing helmets, which I initially thought was odd. Later that night it proved not to be such a bad idea at all. During our set it turned out that some of these kids descended straight from a bunch of barbaric Vikings. I lost three tuning picks from my guitar when I hit a kid who was attacking me. Later that night after The Locust left the battlefield as well everyone in our entourage decided to go hang out in the backstage. Someone scored some weed somewhere and obviously the lewd had to be consumed right away. While everyone was hanging out and this stash sash was going on some blonde Aryan Rasta dude with smelly dreadlocks appeared on the scene. He looked at everyone and added the following words to the relaxed atmosphere: "weed is for niggers... beer is for white men!". Everyone was completely speechless and in total doubt about if they actually heard the words this guy just said. At that moment another Swede walks into the room. The Rasta warrior unzips his pants and without saying a word he starts pissing in his friends mouth. Twenty seconds later the sexually twisted Swede finishes, zips up again and leaves the room with the legendary words: "see you in hell.... Or a gay bar!". The rest of that night could be summarized best as: !&YH!°!()°[(&#@Y°!&(?")(&??!@#&??????!!!!

NEW JERSEY'S FINEST
IN ACTION
TEAR IT UP
EUROPE IN 2003
(THE WORLD LATER!)
INVADING YOUR COUNTRY SOON:

Fl-Tragedy/Films 12-11-2001 13:40 Pagina 2
SMELLS LIKE
TEEN SPIRIT
HIS HERO IS GONE
ex-TRAGEDY
LÄRM
ex-SEEIN'RED
HARUM SCARUM
ex-VRIENDINNEN
30 NOVEMBER
SCSI CELL
FL 10,-
KIPPENHOK III
SCSI CELL CASUARIESTRAAT 16 DEN HAAG
info/reservations: goldenboys99@hotmail.com

BROOKS HEADLEY

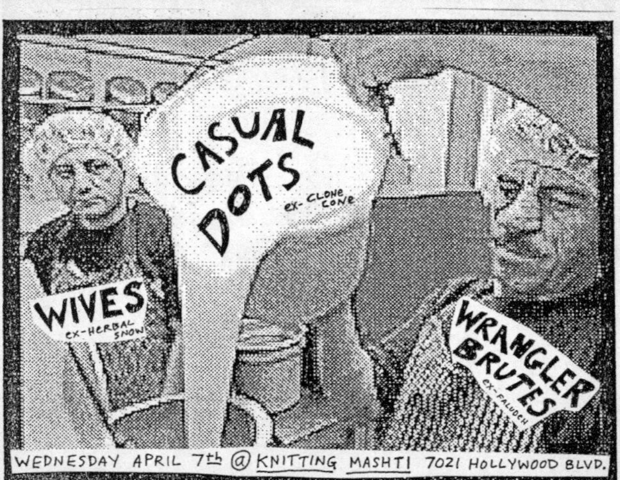

CASUAL DOTS
ex-CLONE CONE
WIVES
ex-HERBAL SNOW
WRANGLER BRUTES
WEDNESDAY APRIL 7th @ KNITTING MASHT! 7021 HOLLYWOOD BLVD.

DEAN SPUNT

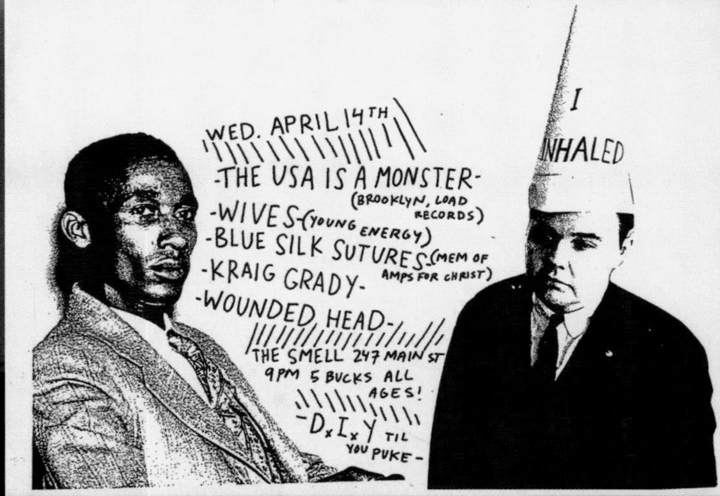

WED. APRIL 14TH
-THE USA IS A MONSTER-
(BROOKLYN, LOAD RECORDS)
-WIVES-(YOUNG ENERGY)
-BLUE SILK SUTURES-(MEM OF AMPS FOR CHRIST)
-KRAIG GRADY-
-WOUNDED HEAD-
THE SMELL 247 MAIN ST
9PM 5 BUCKS ALL AGES!
-DxIxY TIL YOU PUKE-
I INHALED

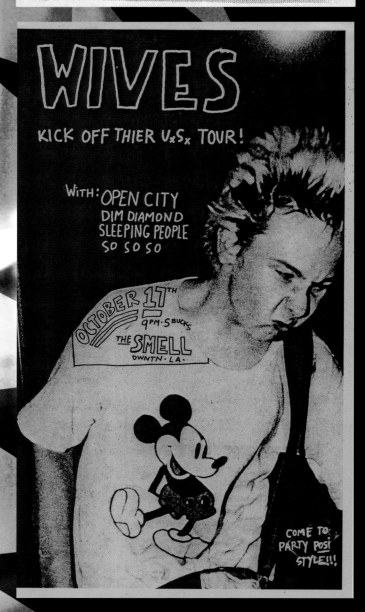

WIVES
KICK OFF THIER UxSx TOUR!
WITH: OPEN CITY
DIM DIAMOND
SLEEPING PEOPLE
SO SO SO
OCTOBER 17TH
9PM. 5 BUCKS
THE SMELL
DWNTN. LA.
COME TO PARTY POSI STYLE!!!

NO AGE

$250 is the amount the City of Los Angeles fined owners of the building where The Smell is locat This is how much it costs to print your own post and staple them on every telephone pole, freewa

onramp and off ramp in the LA area. A week or

after the show Jim showed us the letter he recei from the landlord. We were so bummed, we mad sure to leave the address and contact info off the poster. What the hell kinda poster is this? it doe give you any way of knowing where the show is

NO AGE
SOILED MATTRESS and the SPRINGS
BURRITO PILLOW
CORPSE-KISSER
at FOODHOLE 20 NW 3rd
Thurs August 10 $5 all ages

nn Inssein
nuhips 1-5-04
Smell
glorgus America!

SAM MCPHEETERS

NO AGE

"I'm about... To... Have a... Nervous... Breakdown... My... Head... Really... hurts."
-Martin Luther King jr.

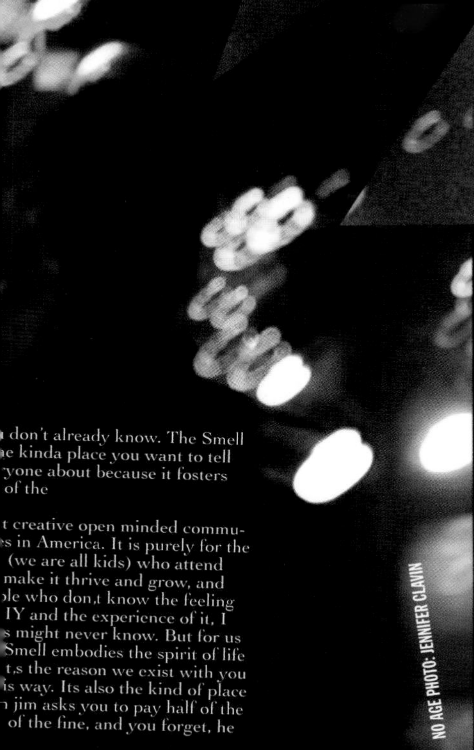

NO
AGE
BARR
MIKA MIKO

NO AGE

"We used to walk up and down the rows and think we knew everything there was to know about our palates. Further exploring led us to the zone of "the upper crust" and it is a nice zone, a very forgiving zone which we are proud to call home."
-Borgman Torst

Reshapela@yahoo.com
there is probably a problem.

NO AGE

"We are the type of person that can encourage A real sort of thing. It is like the begining of the end but reversed, and to someone like us that can mean a world of difference."
-Borgman Torst

Reshapela@yahoo.com
There is no age, so lets get hurt.

n don't already know. The Smell
he kinda place you want to tell
yone about because it fosters
of the

t creative open minded commu-
es in America. It is purely for the
(we are all kids) who attend
make it thrive and grow, and
ple who don,t know the feeling
IY and the experience of it, I
s might never know. But for us
Smell embodies the spirit of life
t,s the reason we exist with you
is way. Its also the kind of place
n jim asks you to pay half of the
of the fine, and you forget, he

n just forgets about it too then
n you offer to pay him he won't
he money.

NO AGE PHOTO: JENNIFER CLAVIN

NO
AGE

"There is nothing you can do that will make me forget the disgusting nature of this. To put it lightly, I am sort of "floating back and forth between this" and that, is putting it lightly."
-Borgman Torst

Reshapela@yahoo.com
There is no age, so lets get hurt.

NO
AGE

"Many of you don't have the time to read through a 650-page book on "possibilities under our control" or "things that look better when they are tucked away" but we do."

Reshapela@yahoo.com
There is no age, so lets get hurt.

5 NO AGE FLYERS: DEAN SPUNT

FAMILY
GRAND OPENING PARTY
FREE
SUNDAY, FEB 25. 7P
LAVENDER DIAMOND
and NO AGE
and also THEM JEANS
and artwork & installation by
SAELEE OH MATTHEW THURBER
436 N. FAIRFAX, 90036

WITH THEIR GLORY DAYS LONG BEHIND THEM, IT'S TIME TO SAY
FAREWELL
LAST PERFORMANCES EVER BY:
DAS OATH
PISSED JEANS
THE BOXES
+ One More T.B.A.
8pm NOVEMBER 30 $8
KNITTING FACTORY NYC
74 LEONARD ST.
www.das-oath.com

HARD CORE WILL NEVER FUCKIN DIE.
YO! THIS SATURDAY JUNE 22:
THE BRUTAL BLITZ ATTACK ONSLAUGHT FROM VIRGINIA
SUPPRESSION
SHOULDER TO SHOULDER WITH
Eucharist
CHARLES BRONSON
AUTONOMOUS ZONE

ROCK-OUT-WITH-YOUR-COCK-OUT
PRODUCTIONS PROUDLY PRESENTS
HARDCORE
FOR THOSE WHO BATHE REGULARLY
five bucks!
DEVOID OF FAITH
HAIL MARY
MK-ULTRA
SAETIA
SATURDAY NOVEMBER 14
FOOD FOR COCKROACHES: ONE DOLLAR OFF AT DOOR
NO DRUNK FREAKS, NO NEW JERSEY xJOCKSx
* ABC NO RIO * 156 RIVINGTON, NEW YUCK CITY

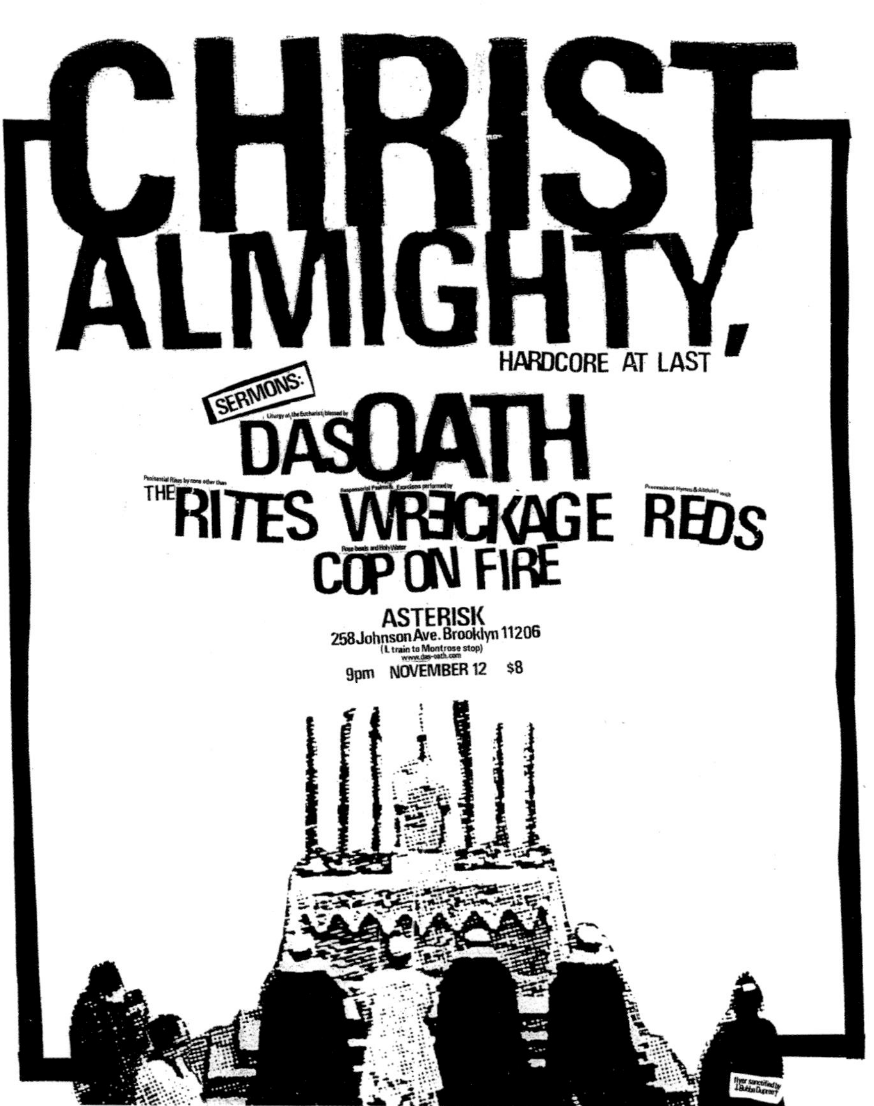
CHRIST ALMIGHTY,
HARDCORE AT LAST
SERMONS:
DAS OATH
THE RITES
WRECKAGE
REDS
COP ON FIRE
ASTERISK
258 Johnson Ave. Brooklyn 11206
(L train to Montrose stop)
9pm NOVEMBER 12 $8

CHARLES BRONSON
DEKALB WOLFPACK
HARD 1997 CORE

CHARLES BRONSON
DEKALB YOUTH CREW 1996

FLYERS ON BOTH PAGES: MARK McCOY

THE DESTRUCTION RETURNS TO D TOWN

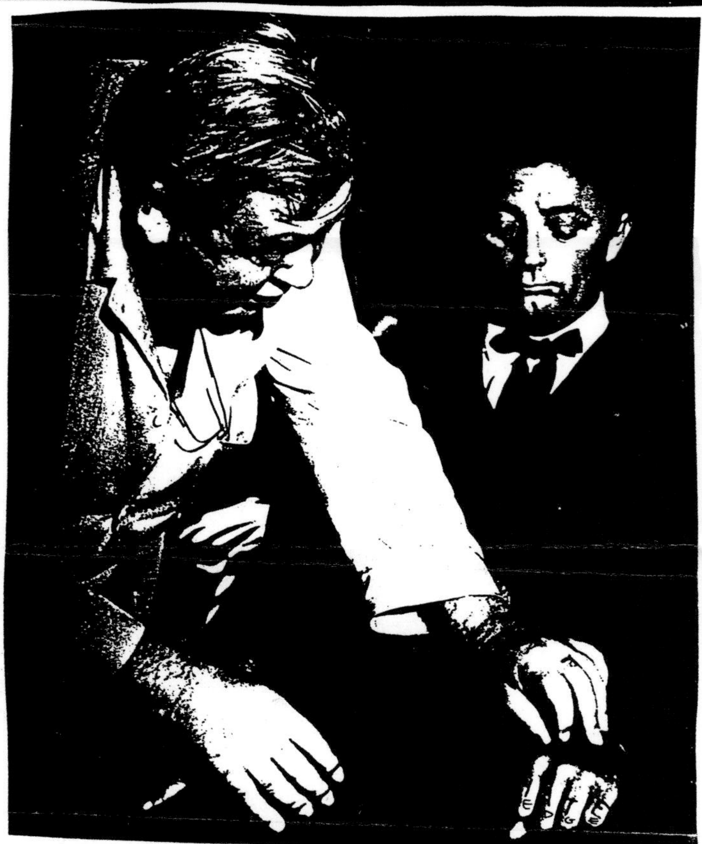

CHARLES BRONSON
ASSHOLE PARADE
xPALATKAx
DANGER MÖUSE

FRIDAY JANUARY 3RD.TWO BUCKS AT8 O'CLOK
LOCATED AT FOUR FIFTY COLLEGE AVE. IN
DEKALB,IL FOR INFO CALL MARK AT 815758DICK

FULL CIRCLE
thrash tour
fucking killer
RE EVALUATING YOUR MUNDANE ASS RECORD COLLECTION FROM
NOV 23 - DEC 3 2000
THE OATH
TRANS-ATLANTIC THUNDER BOMBASTICS,
ex-members of who fucking gives a shit
TOTAL FURY
ALL THE FUCKIN WAY FROM
SENDAI, JAPAN!!!
Appearing in This ShitTown on:

MARK MCCOY

The year before they gave me a used Schwinn BMX bike for my birthday, but by the time age seven rolled around the bike was stolen and all I wanted was a subscription to The National Geographic. Naturally being one to hound my parents until their breaking point, it seems I got what I'd begged months for only as a gesture to silence me. When the magazines first arrived I was elated. They were small and beautiful and the paper smelled of wisdom and worldly consciousness. Often i would witness my parents bragging to other adults that I was developing into quite the precocious child by having such a subscription. They had me pinned for a paleontologist, a brain surgeon, an astronomer. Occasionally I'd hang up the fold out maps in my room or play the flexi discs of the giant blue whales groaning. Before going to bed I'd briefly flip through the pages of an issue and neatly place it on the others stacked on the headboard over my bed. They were unreadable, written in a language that might as well have been Owambo. When my January 1983 issue arrived there was an article inside questioning the future of the Wayana Indians. The first picture displayed two filthy kids in ragged tunics dumbfounded over a Rubik's Cube. Idiots. Then page after page all I saw were naked bodies! Naked sweaty glistening Savages with their crazy hair and their breasts and their red slimy skin carousing around in the dirt. It was electrifying. I was pulsating with energy, throbbing from some unknown place within. I new this was dangerous stuff. But it wasn't long until my dad saw what I'd been getting in the mail, and without word he immediately canceled my subscription.

THANK YOUZ
IAN MACKAYE
DAVID LOPES
CHRISTOPHER T. MILLER
DAYNA MICHELLE TURCOTTE
STACEY MARIE MENDEZ
FORD AND RALSTON
MICHELLE MARINI
CLINT WOODSIDE
MAX GOLDSMITH
DOUG WOODS
RON FLEMING
JOHN SUSOEFF
SCUMKING
MATT NETH
CRAIG ROOSE
RYAN RICHARDSON
HELLIN KILLER
JESSICA HOPPER
CALI DEWITT
KK BARRETT
HOWIE PYRO
RIC CLAYTON
SHAWN KERRI
MARC RUDE
DAVID KING
MATT BORRUSO
WINSTON SMITH
ED COLVER
YVONNE HYATT
JOE SIB
BRENT CALLAHAN
BILL VITALE
JOE TROMPETER
SEAN GREGONIS
JAMES IGOE
COREY AND GAVIN O'BRIEN
CHRIS LUAN
CHARLES GAIENNIE
PAUL CRUIKSHANK
FAT MIKE
FLETCHER DRAGGE
GLEN E. FRIEDMAN
RAYMOND PETTIBON

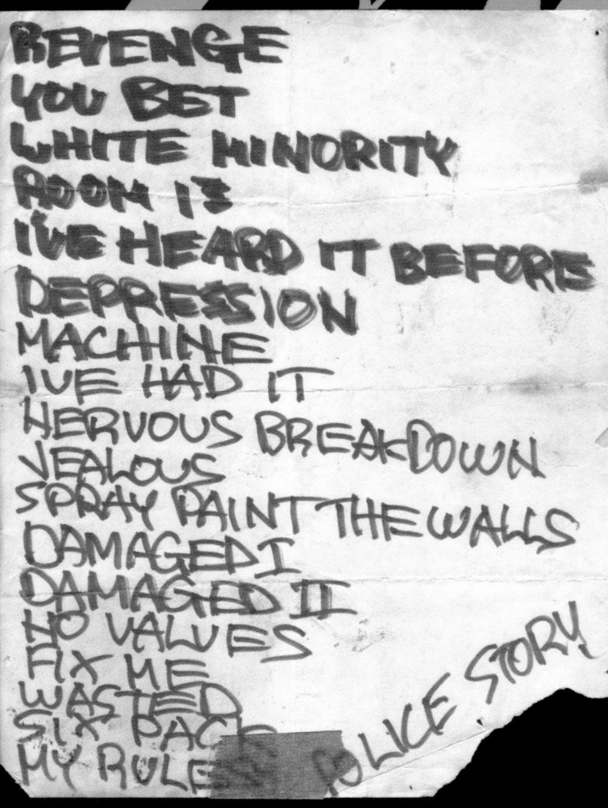
REVENGE
YOU BET
WHITE MINORITY
ROOM 13
I'VE HEARD IT BEFORE
DEPRESSION
MACHINE
I'VE HAD IT
NERVOUS BREAKDOWN
JEALOUS
SPRAY PAINT THE WALLS
DAMAGED I
DAMAGED II
NO VALUES
FIX ME
WASTED
SIX PACK
MY RULES
POLICE STORY

BUSINESS ON PARADE
DEAD COPS 1-11
AMERICA'S SO STRAIT
BORN TO DIE
CORPORATE DEATH BURGERS
VIOLENT REDNECKS
I REMEMBER
JOHN WAYNE
PICK FOR BRAINS
I HATE WORK
MY FAMILY
GREEDY & PATHETIC
CHURCH & STATE
KILL THE LIGHT
AMERICAN ACHIEVEMENTS
REVOLUTION'S IN ROCK
PECKING ORDER
RADIOACTIVE CHOCOLATE
DAY TO COME ALONG
SELFISH SHIT
NO PLACE TO PISS
CLEPTOMANIAC
MULTI-DEATH CORPORATIONS

VIOLENT WORLD
MEDIA OGRE
DIMENSION
MOTIVE
CAB DRIVER
STRANGLED GIRL
MY TYPE
CONCERNED CITIZEN
HUMAN SACRIFICE
ANGLE AGE
SICK DOG
PUNK CHURCH

BATTLE
CONQUEST
AMBASSADOR
SACRIFICE
LEFT FOR DEAD
NIGHTMARE
WALL OF STEEL
FREE TO KILL
CHASE IS ON
ORDEAL
ABSOLUTION
BRAINSTORM
FIVE DAYS
—
KILLING REIN
PSYCHO
SURVIVAL

INTRO
Attitude
I
BIG TAKE OVER
ROCK FOR LIGHT
I & I SURVIVE
DAY TRIPPER
F.V.K.
RIGHT BRIGADE
BANNED IN D.C.
RE-IGNITION
SECRET 77
COPTIC TIMES
HOUSE OF SUFFERING
HIRED GUN
SHE'S CALLING YOU
DESTROY BABYLON
I AGAINST I
LET ME HELP
AT THE MOVIES
RETURN TO HEAVEN

Bad Brains
NOV 22-23
FENDERS
*
ROXY

1. On Target
2. T.V. Life (segue)
3. Inc. Suicide
4. Babies
5. Victims
6. Held agnst.
7. Kill me
8. Rod Serling

1 MAKING TIME
2 SLOW DOWN
3 YOU DON'T GO AWAY.
4 PANTS & JACKETS
5 BAD TIME
6 IT'S ALRIGHT
7 TRAINS & BOATS & P.
8 JUMPIN IN THE NIGHT
9 TERMINAL TOWN
10 TWIST AND SHOUT
11 PRETTIEST GIRL
12 NIGHTS ARE SO LONG
13 MILLION MILES AWAY
14 WAR ZONE
15 REPTILE HOUSE
16 FRIDAY ON MY MIND
17 SON OF SAM

DURANGO 95
LOBOTOMY
PSYCHOTHERAPY
BLITZKRIEG BOP
ROCK-N-ROLL RADIO
MIRACLES
SHOCK TREATMENT
ROCK-N-ROLL HIGH SC
SEDATED
SPIDERMAN
KKK
I DON'T WANT TO GRO
~~COMMANDO~~ HAVA
SHEENA
ROCKAWAY BEACH
PET SEMATARY
STRENGTH TO ENDURE
CRETIN FAMILY
~~TAKE IT AS IT COMES~~
SOMETHING IN MY DRI
~~SEVEN AND SEVEN IS~~
WARTHOG
CRETIN HOP
RAMONES
TODAY YOUR LOVE
PINHEAD

MORSE CODE
HELLO THERE
NOTHING SACRED
HELL HOUNDS
FACES IN THE NIGHT
WARLORDS
BREAKDOWN
DEAD END ZONE
CALL TO GLORY
REST SONG
TWO MILES
RESSURECTION
SONIC REDUCER

WHITE GIRL
LYING ROAD
JESUS WASH
BAD THOUGHTS
BECAUSE I DO
SEE HOW WE ARE
VIGILANTE MAN
STAGE
NEW WORLD
CRITTER
TRUE LOVE
HOUSE I CALL HIM
I'M COMING OVER
I SEE RED
WHAT'S WRONG
BURN HOUSE
SKIN DEEP

Violent World
Wax
Dream Hits
Bad Love
Anti Anti Anti
Sleep in Safety
Concerned Citizen
Phantoms
Eye
45 Grave
My Type
The Plan
Black Cross
Evil
Akira

GERMS
DEC.3 80
STARWOOD

MANIMAL
CAUGHT IN MY EYE
LIONS SHARE
NO GOD
OUR WAY
STRANGE NOTES
SECRET
RICHIE DAGGERS
LAND OF TREASON
MY TUNNEL
MEDIA BLITZ
COMMUNIST EYES
OTHER NEWEST 1
LET'S PRETEND
FORMING
LEXICON DEVIL
SHUT DOWN

SACCHARINE
WATCH YOURSELF
MY FUTURE
TURN AWAY
GOIN AWAY
PREACHER MAN
HALL OF MIRRORS
BETTER THAN SEX
MADHOUSE
YOU!
MOUSETRAP
STATIC CLING
COP A PLEA
TOMMOROW

NOTHING FOR YOU
EVERBODY'S A COP
IN TIME
RED SHADOW'S
BLK MAJIC
JOHN
YOUR EYES
SILENT SCREAM
COLORS
JUST LIKE ME
NO TIME
SILENT MAJ
AMERICAN ZONE
CHANGE TODAY
FLOWERS
IT'S GREEN
BEST FRIENDS
SUPER FREAK A LOVE
T.S.O.L.

Circle One
LORNA D.
Strange Notes
Forming
Dragon Lady
No God
Our Way
What we Do is Secret
Richie Dagger's
Manimal
Slave
Shut Down
Lexicon Devil

SONIC
ALL THIS
MEAT
CALLING
WON'T LOOK
HIGH TENSION
AIN'T IT FUN
WHAT LOVE IS
LUNCH
AIN'T NOTHIN
DOWN FLAMES
SON OF SAM
TELL ME
DET. HOME
FLAME THROW
3 GEN
SEARCH +

DOOMSDAY
DEAD OR ALIVE
SEX AND THE SINGLE SNIPER
LAUGHTRACK
NEVER TALK TO STRANGERS
SEX GIRLS
GREENLIGHT
FAKER

SECRET
COMMIE EYES
FORMING
RICHIE D.
LAND O TREASON
CAUGHT IN MY EYE
LET'S PRETEND
NO GOD
LEXICON DEVIL
MEDIA BLITZ
~~OUR WAY~~
~~OTHER NEWEST ONE~~
MANIMAL
Shut Down

GERMS SET LIST

Hell Hole
L-Times
Cop
Time Bomb
Money
Black Spiders
Bad Brains

1. Died on a Monday
2. Nightlums
3. Drop on your Head
4. Take you Toker
5. On the other side
6. I.R. John
7. Next to you
8. Siren
9. Nothing But the Truth
10. Walked in the Rain
11. Kids
12. Dump

for
soldiers
prosti-
tutes
dykes +
punks